The Right to the Truth in International Law

The United Nations has established a right to the truth to be enjoyed by victims of gross violations of human rights. The origins of the right stem from the need to provide victims and relatives of the missing with a right to know what happened. It encompasses the verification and full public disclosure of the facts associated with the crimes from which they or their relatives suffered. The importance of the right to the truth is based on the belief that, by disclosing the truth, the suffering of victims is alleviated.

This book analyses the emergence of this right, as a response to an understanding of the needs of victims, through to its development and application in two particular legal contexts: international human rights law and international criminal justice. The book examines in detail the application of the right through the case law and jurisprudence of international tribunals in the human rights and also the criminal justice contexts, as well as looking at its place in transitional justice. The theoretical foundations of the right to the truth are considered as well as the various objectives appropriate for different truth-seeking mechanisms. The book then goes on to discuss to what extent it can be understood, constructed and applied as a hard, legally enforceable right with correlating duties on various people and institutions including state agencies, prosecutors and judges.

Melanie Klinkner is a Principal Academic in International Law at Bournemouth University, UK.

Howard Davis is Reader in Public Law at Bournemouth University, UK.

Human Rights and International Law

Series Editor: Professor Surya P. Subedi, OBE, QC (Hon)

About the Series Editor

Professor Surya P. Subedi, OBE, QC (Hon) is Professor of International Law, University of Leeds, member of the Institut de Droit International and former UN Special Rapporteur for human rights in Cambodia.

This series will explore human rights law's place within the international legal order, offering much-needed interdisciplinary and global perspectives on human rights' increasingly central role in the development and implementation of international law and policy.

Human Rights and International Law is committed to providing critical and contextual accounts of human rights' relationship with international law theory and practice. To achieve this, volumes in the series will take a thematic approach that focuses on major debates in the field, looking at how human rights impacts on areas as diverse and divisive as security, terrorism, climate change, refugee law, migration, bioethics, natural resources and international trade.

Exploring the interaction, interrelationship and potential conflicts between human rights and other branches of international law, books in the series will address both historical development and contemporary contexts, before outlining the most urgent questions facing scholars and policy makers today

Available titles:

Tax Havens and International Human Rights
Paul Beckett

The Effectiveness of the UN Human Rights System
Reform and the Judicialisation of Human Rights
Surya P. Subedi

Socio-economic Human Rights in Essential Public Services Provision
Marlies Hesselman, Antenor Hallo de Wolf and Brigit Toebes

The Right to the Truth in International Law
Victims' Rights in Human Rights and International Criminal Law
Melanie Klinkner and Howard Davis

www.routledge.com/Human-Rights-and-International-Law/book-series/HRIL

The Right to the Truth in International Law

Victims' Rights in Human Rights and International Criminal Law

Melanie Klinkner and Howard Davis

Routledge
Taylor & Francis Group
LONDON AND NEW YORK

First published 2020 by Routledge

2 Park Square, Milton Park, Abingdon, Oxon, OX14 4RN
605 Third Avenue, New York, NY 10017

Routledge is an imprint of the Taylor & Francis Group, an informa business

First issued in paperback 2020

British Library Cataloguing-in-Publication Data
A catalogue record for this book is available from the British Library

Library of Congress Cataloging-in-Publication Data
A catalog record for this book has been requested

ISBN: 978-1-138-96144-9 (hbk)
ISBN: 978-0-367-72686-7 (pbk)

Typeset in Galliard
by Apex CoVantage, LLC

Für die Unseren – wo immer sie sein mögen.

Contents

Detailed contents

Table of legislation and official materials

Regional instruments

Official materials: UN resolutions, documents and reports

UNGA, Assistance and co-operation in accounting for persons who are missing or dead in armed conflicts (6 November 1974) UN Doc A/RES/3220. 34

UNGA, Right to the truth (21 January 2014) Un Doc A/RES/68/165. 38, 51, 53

UNGA, Right to the truth (10 October 2012) UN Doc A/HRC/RES/21/7. 38

UNGA, Right to the Truth (12 October 2009) UN Doc A/HRC/REW12/12. 38

UNGA, Question of enforced or involuntary disappearances (18 December 1990) UN Doc A/RES/45/165. 38

UNGA, Question of enforced or involuntary disappearances (18 December 1992) UN Doc A/RES/47/132. 38

UNGA, Disappeared persons (20 December 1978) UN Doc A/RES/33/173. 38

UNGA, Resolution adopted by the General Assembly on 21 December 2010 (3 March 2011) UN Doc A/RES/65/196. 38

UNGA, Responsibility of States for internationally wrongful acts: Resolution adopted by the General Assembly (28 January 2002) UN Doc A/RES/56/83. 226

UNGA, Declaration on the Protection of All Persons from Enforced Disappearances (12 February 1993) UN Doc A/RES/47/133. 163, 168.

UNGA, Report of the Working Group on Enforced or Involuntary Disappearances, General Comment on the Right to the Truth in Relation to Enforced Disappearances (26 January 2011) UN Doc A/HRC/16/48 (in General Comments section) also available (www.ohchr.org/Documents/Issues/Disappearances/GeneralCommentsDisappearances_en.pdf). 163

UN Commission on Human Rights, Report of the independent expert to update the Set of Principles to combat impunity (18 February 2005) UN Doc E/CN.4/2005/102/Add.1. 11, 21, 36, 67, 72, 161, 173.

UN Commission on Human Rights, 'Promotion and Protection of Human Rights. Study on the Right to the Truth' (8 February 2006) UN Doc E/CN.4/2006/91. 1, 20, 21, 29, 33, 35, 38, 46, 51, 54, 67, 73, 163, 168, 169, 180.

UN Commission on Human Rights, Declaration on the Protection of All Persons from Enforced Disappearance (28 February 1992) UN Doc E/CN.4/RES/1992/29.

UN Commission on Human Rights, Question of the impunity of perpetrators of human rights violations (civil and political) (26 June 1997) UN Doc E/CN.4/Sub.2/1997. 67, 72.

UN Human Rights Council, Right to the truth: Report of the Office of the High Commissioner for Human Rights (21 August 2009) UN Doc A/HRC/12/19. 38, 53

UN Human Rights Council, Analytical study on human rights and transitional justice (6 August 2009) UN Doc A/HRC/12/18/Add.1. 38

UN Human Rights Council, Resolution 9/11 Right to the Truth (18 September 2008) UN Doc A/HRC/RES/9/11. 12.

UN Human Rights Council, Report of the UN Working Group on Enforced or Involuntary Disappearances, (26 January 1981) UN Doc E/CN.4/1435. 23, 35.

UN Human Rights Council, Report of the UN Working Group on Enforced and Involuntary Disappearances, (10 August 2015) UN Doc A/HRC/30/38. 38

UN Human Rights Council, Report of the Special Rapporteur on the Promotion of Truth, Justice, Reparation and Guarantees of Non-Recurrence (9 August 2012) UN Doc A/HRC/21/46. 58

UN Human Rights Council, The Right to the Truth. Report of the High Commission for Human Rights (7 June 2007) UN Doc A/HRC/5/7. 67

UN Human Rights Committee, CCPR General Comment No. 31: Nature of the General Legal Obligation on States Parties to the Covenant (26 May 2004), UN Doc CPR/C/21/Rev.1/Add.13. 123, 125

UN Human Rights Committee, CCPR General Comment No. 29: Article 4: Derogations during a State of Emergency (31 August 2001) CCPR/C/21/Rev.1/Add.11. 22

UN Human Rights Committee, CCPR General Comment No. 6: Article 6 (Right to Life) (30 April 1982). 27, 123

UN Human Rights Committee, CCPR General Comment No. 20: Article 7 (Prohibition of Torture, or other cruel, inhuman or degrading treatment or punishment) (10 March 1992). 123

UN High Commissioner for Refugees (UNHCR), Guiding Principles on Internal Displacement (22 July 1998) ADM 1.1, PRL 12.1, PR00/98/109. 36

UN Security Council, The rule of law and transitional justice in conflict and post-conflict societies (23 August 2004) UN Doc S/2004/616.

UN Security Council, Report of the UN Truth Commission on El Salvador. Annex: From Madness to Hope: The 12-Year War in El Salvador (1 April 1993) UN Doc S/25500. 91, 167

UN Security Council, Security Council resolution 1894 (2009) [on the protection of civilians in armed conflict] (11 November 2009) UN Doc S/RES/1894. 38

UN Security Council, Security Council resolution 1606 (2005) [On the Situation in Burundi] (20 June 2005) UN Doc S/RES/1606. 38

UN Secretary General, The Rule of Law and Transitional Justice in Conflict and Post-Conflict Societies. Report of the Secretary-General, (23 August 2004), UN Doc S/2004/616. 33, 157.

UN Secretary General, Guidance note of the United Nations Secretary General, United Nations approach to Transitional Justice (March 2010). 157.

UN Sub-Commission on the Promotion and Protection of Human Rights, Question of the impunity of perpetrators of human rights violations (civil and political) (26 June 1997) UN Doc E/CN.4/Sub.2/1997/20.

UN Department for Political Affairs, United Nations Manual on the Effective Prevention and Investigation of Extra-Legal, Arbitrary and Summary Executions, (24 May 1989) UN Doc E/ST/CSDHA/.12. 36

Office of the United Nations High Commissioner for Human Rights, Enforced or Involuntary Disappearance, (Factsheet 6/Rev.3, without year) www.ohchr.org/Documents/Publications/FactSheet6Rev3.pdf accessed 14 February 2019.

Office of the United Nations High Commissioner for Human Rights, The Minnesota Protocol on the Investigation of Potentially Unlawful Death (New York, Geneva 2017). 27

Office of the United Nations High Commissioner for Human Rights, Rule-of-Law Tools for Post-Conflict States: Truth Commissions' Report (New York, Geneva 2006) www.ohchr.org/Documents/Publications/RuleoflawTruth-Commissionsen.pdf accessed 14 February 2019. 170

WGEID, General comment on children and enforced disappearances adopted by the Working Group on Enforced or Involuntary Disappearances at its ninety-eighth session (31 October–9 November 2012), UN Doc A/HRC/WGEID/98/1 (14 February 2013). 24.

Regional official materials

European Parliament, Resolution on mass graves of the missing person of Ashia in Ornithi village in the occupied part of Cyprus (12 February 2015) 2015/2551 (RSP). 39

Organization of American States, 'The Right to Truth in the Americas' (13 August 2014) OEA/Ser.L/V/II.152 Doc 2. 1, 33, 40, 52, 105

Organisation of American States, Right to the truth (4 June 2009) AG/RES. 2509 (XXXIX-O/09). 39

Organization of American States, Inter-American Commission on Human Rights Annual Report of 1985–1986, Chapter V (26 September 1986) OEA/Ser.L/V/II.68 Doc. 8 rev. 1. 68

Parliamentary Assembly of the Council of Europe, Recommendation 1056 (5 May 1987). 23, 39

Parliamentary Assembly of the Council of Europe, Resolution 1414 (23 November 2004). 23, 39

Parliamentary Assembly of the Council of Europe, Resolution 1463 (3 October 2005). 23, 39

Parliamentary Assembly of the Council of Europe, Resolution 1868 (9 March 2012). 39

Parliamentary Assembly of the Council of Europe, Resolution 2067 (25 June 2015). 39

International Court materials

Assembly of State Parties, RC/11, Annex V(a) Stocktaking of international criminal justice, The impact of the Rome Statute system on victims and affected communities, Final report by the focal points (Chile and Finland). 227

International Criminal Court, Rules of Procedure and Evidence (9 September 2002). 96, 204, 211, 221

International Criminal Court, Regulations of the Court ICC-BD/01–01 (26 May 2004). 221

International Criminal Tribunal for the Former Yugoslavia, Rules of Procedure and Evidence UN Doc IT/32/Rev.40 (11 February 1994). 186

International Criminal Tribunal for Rwanda, Rules of Procedure and Evidence UN Doc. ITR/3/REV.1 (29 June 1995). none

Statute of the Court of Justice (adopted 26 June 2945) 33 UNTS 933. 47

Domestic legislation and official materials

Other

Table of cases

Permanent Court of International Justice and International Court of Justice

European Court of Human Rights

Inter-American Court of Human Rights cases

Inter-American Commission

African Commission

UN Human Rights Committee

International Criminal cases

International Criminal Tribunal for the Former Yugoslavia

International Criminal Tribunal for Rwanda

International Criminal Court

Extraordinary Chambers in the Courts of Cambodia

European Court of Justice

Domestic cases

Colombia

Peru

UK

Introduction

Across the world, and especially in conflict zones, legal norms aimed at protecting civilians and their fundamental human rights are often disregarded. At the same time, forms of post-truth politics have surged and pervade the discourses of both justification and experience with blatant contempt for the actual facts. Moreover, there are examples of policies constructing and maintaining silence after conflict.[1] Yet, there also exists a morally powerful and persuasive need for knowing the truth. For many thinkers and activists, truth is always a construct relevant to a political, moral or social context. There are critical arguments and valid concerns about the way truth is constructed. We cannot, and will not attempt to, fully diffuse these arguments, for their discussions belong elsewhere.

Our starting point, however, assumes that the right to the truth for victims of gross human rights violations derives from an intense interest victims have in knowing about the events relating to their suffering, and in knowing what happened to their family members that have gone missing. Furthermore, and based on the concept of a well-ordered society in which all are treated as political equals, there is a strong interest in knowing what happened in the past. On such a basis, the right to the truth cannot be brushed aside as a metaphor, culturally relativistic and without value. A universal claim for the need for truth has been made and is advocated by various actors, such as the UN, non-governmental organisations (NGOs), human rights lawyers, international criminal lawyers, jurists and lawyers operating in domestic legal systems, politicians and civil society. Through their initiatives, the right to the truth has been articulated with the state having the ultimate duty correlating to the right. It has been articulated in general terms and given some degree of recognition in various legal contexts, but as we will discuss, usually as an aspect of other expressed rights. Despite comprehensive attempts to systematise the existing jurisprudence and legal positions on the subject,[2] the

1 E.g. Iosif Kovras, *Truth Recovery and Transitional Justice. Deferring Human Rights Issues* (Routledge 2016) and Cyanne Loyle and Christian Davenport, 'Transitional Injustice: Subverting Justice in Transition and Postconflict Societies' (2016) 15 Journal of Human Rights 126.

2 Promotion and Protection of Human Rights. Study on the Right to the Truth (8 February 2006); The Right to Truth in the Americas (13 August 2014) and International Commission of Jurists, 'Enforced Disappearance and Extrajudicial Execution: The Right of Family Members' (Practitioners' Guide No. 10, July 2016).

question is less clear whether there is room for a stand-alone right to the truth which has significant normative force capable of taking it beyond mere statement, rhetoric or aspiration. What is also far from clear is what mechanisms, other than through the state, can address, enforce and satisfy the right to the truth requirements. Indeed, is there agreement on what the right to the truth encompasses? In other words, our inquiry begins with a moral imperative to discern what normative legal force, if any, it has, should and can have.

The purpose of this book is therefore fivefold: First, to ground the right in an interest based approach asking *why* is the right to the truth needed, to determine the foundational needs that have led to an expression as a right. Second, to fully explore and analyse *what* the right to the truth entails when considered as (1) an individual right, (2) a public right and (3) distinct from other rights. Based on this separation argument, that the right to the truth is distinct in its elements and aspects, we third propose a working definition of what the right would be if independent. Fourth, the book analyses *how* and in what ways (or not) the right to the truth, in our conceptualisation, is given effect within the context of transitional justice mechanisms (human rights courts, truth commissions and international criminal institutions). Finally, the book considers in what way a distinctly expressed and categorised autonomous right that finds consideration and reference in various transitional justice institutions offers victims anything more concrete than the right to an effective remedy in the form of an investigation.

Chapter 1 focuses on *why* a right to the truth is needed: victims of atrocity suffer from not knowing the truth about certain types of gross human rights abuse. But society too has a stake in the truth, since knowing the truth is instrumental for the purposes of justice, retributive and restorative, the rule of law and conditions for social recovery and advance under conditions of equality. Although the truth is a universal value, there are a number of important considerations which are discussed: the importance of truth may be culturally variable; social stability in a transitioning society may suggest limits on truth-seeking; and considerations of method, selection and scope impact upon truth-seeking.

Chapter 2 traces the origins of the right to the truth in the context of transitional justice from international humanitarian law to expression and references in international human rights law. It positions the right in the quartet of principles comprising the right to know, the right to reparations, the right to justice and the right to guarantees of non-repetition.

Chapter 3 examines the legal status and content of the right to the truth. It discusses what it entails and requires but also how the right differs from other rights and is related to a number of other rights, in particular the legal protection of rights and the right to reparation. We formulate a working definition based on the merits for an independent right to the truth.

Chapter 4 focuses on the public aspect of the right to the truth. Here we explore the relationship between the public (collective or social) aspects and the individual aspects. Can the two be separated and satisfied without the other? Alternatively, what common ground do they share?

We then, in Chapter 5, analyse the various mechanisms through which the right to the truth, in our definition, may be realised, that is through truth commissions, human rights courts and international criminal trials. We start in with a comparative overview of its application, generally, within a transitional justice context to get a sense of the ways in which human rights courts, truth commissions and international criminal trials may seek to fulfil aspects of the right to the truth.

Chapters 6 and 7 focus on the presence of the right in the context of human rights courts, specially the practice of the Inter-American Court of Human Rights (IACtHR) and the European Court of Human Rights (ECtHR). Chapter 6 in its analysis of IACtHR jurisprudence examines the relationship between the right to the truth as inherent in the right to justice and in opposition to impunity. But also, particularly from a public or collective perspective, it analyses its connection with freedom of thought and expression, since there is a clear interest in society to receive the truth, with individuals playing their part in seeking and imparting information. Chapter 7 on the ECtHR places emphasis on enforcing a state's duty to investigate and examines investigations as implicit in substantive rights and the rights to a remedy, and includes a brief section on reception of information.

Chapter 8 on truth commissions is an intermezzo in our examination of court and convention oriented mechanisms. Yet, truth commissions are seen as a vital instrument in post-conflict societies as they are typically mandated to investigate and shed light on past atrocities. Here we appraise their contribution to the right to the truth and how they may constitute a stepping stone toward prosecutions, reparations and reform.

Chapters 9 and 10 are concerned with international criminal trials. In Chapter 9 we introduce the various definitions of historical truth, forensic truth, narrative truth and legal truth that have been discussed in connection with international criminal trials. We examine features such as plea agreements, apologies, forensic expertise, witness testimonies and so on to analyse how they feed into judicial decisions and potential realisation of the right to the truth throughout the legal proceedings and outcome. Chapter 10 then takes a closer look at the International Criminal Court (ICC), particularly in light of it being a permanent institution, through its victim participation and reparation mechanism. We examine the references that have been made to the right to the truth before the ICC and how victims' interests may be in conflict with fair-trial requirements but also not congruent with the prosecutor's role. The chapter brings the role of the judges at the ICC to the fore, particularly in relation to Art 69(3), which states that "[t]he Court shall have the authority to request the submission of all evidence that it considers necessary for the determination of the truth". To what extent could this provision unlock a more victim-oriented truth-finding, and how does this chime with the wider point and purpose of the ICC?

Finally, the conclusion re-examines what can be reasonably expected from a fact and truth-finding effort, which is given legal force as a right, at the international level. This is significant, since the conceptualisation of the right to the truth is concerned with the processes of effectively investigating and communicating the truth. Therefore, the analysis returns to our separation argument and working definition and asks what does the right to the truth add to already existing legal obligations.

There are some pervading themes with various inherent challenges that resurface at different times in the book and which we would like to emphasise from the outset.

A firm basis for a right – but whose right?

Whether the right to the truth is a legal right or a moral right requires the consideration of the need base for such a right, to ensure it is not "rights inflation"[3] but rather that it tries to guarantee it is a condition in which the unbearable is born and a future made possible. From previous work on missing persons and the horrors of mass graves comes this need to examine the necessary precondition for a right. But what exactly is the relationship between the individual's right to know the truth and that of society? How does it find expression and judicial interpretation? And it poses questions whether those wishing to invoke the right to the truth (victims, victim representatives, NGOs, society, etc.) have standing to do so.

The right to the truth as independent?

The book traces the origins and nature of the right to the truth from different sources outlining the plurality of its meaning within transitional justice. This includes a discussion of what content and force the right currently has in international law and how it might relate to other rights (especially the right to justice and the right to reparation). In taking recourse to victims' interests of "needing to know to alleviate suffering", we deduce a separation argument in an attempt explore the point and consequences of uncoupling the right to the truth from the right to justice and the right to reparation, respectively. We formulate this separation argument on the basis that there are rights-justifying interests in knowing what happened independently of the interests served by prosecution, punishment or reparations.

Philosophical considerations: the arrogance of enlightenment versus relativism

When attempting to write on the right to the truth, there is the temptation, danger even, to engage in philosophical debates affiliated with the notion of truth, which is a task best left to experts in the field.[4] In a quest not to suc-

3 Michael Ignatieff, 'Human Rights as Idolatry', The Tanner Lecture on Human Values (Princeton University 4–7 April 2000) 346.

4 E.g. Simon Blackburn, *Truth. A Guide for the Perplexed* (Penguin 2006).

cumb to superficial and incomplete discussions on "truth" and what it means (as the "object" of the right to the truth), our thinking nonetheless risks vacillating between cognitive realism on the one hand and cognitive relativism on the other; or between correspondence theory and pragmatism when discussing the ways in which the right to the truth can be realised. This is because "what-if" questions have a bearing on truth-seeking scope. Whilst the questions "What if Germany had won the war? or "What truth narrative would have emerged on Nazi actions and defeated Allied forces?" may belong in the philosophy, politics and sociology classrooms, other variation of "what-if" questions are pertinent to our subject of human rights investigations, truth commissions or criminal investigations. What if the mandate of the investigation included a wider array of human rights violations? What if human rights conventions contained an express right to the truth? What if the truth commission had a broader mandate? What if criminal tribunals had a wider temporal or geographical jurisdiction? Not only have these issues considerable impact on the truth-outcome, but they also determine who – what victims – are a primary constituent for the truth-inquiry and the extent to which the right to the truth is satisfied. This is dependent on who is governing or in power. To this degree (whilst still relying on correspondence theory), we point to the "relativity" of truth within a particular political-power, but also temporal, constellation.

But we firmly steer clear from metaphysical disputes on what might or might not be truth, concentrating instead on factuality. However, as a starting point, we assume that legal systems are predicated on the belief that truth is discernible. They are epistemologically informed systems that may operate with variation but nonetheless with tried and tested fact-finding rules and processes. The outcome may be a particular type of truth, and within the systems different notions of truth can appear. In our discussion on international criminal justice mechanisms, for example, we discuss four frameworks of truth – historical truth, forensic truth, narrative truth and legal truth – in the context of international criminal justice. But the outcome for each of the mechanism we examine supposes independent fact-finders with the ability to render reasonable decisions and judgments that are independent and justified.

Right conceptualisation: duties independent of a right

The "right" in the right to the truth appears, when taking an interest theory approach, as a right which reflects an interest (reducing the suffering) which is capable of justifying a duty. This, broadly, is the interest theory of human rights. Thus, disclosure to the victim of an atrocity of what happened serves a basic human interest and is of sufficient importance to justify the imposition of feasible (capable of being carried out) duties on others.[5] A central point is, indeed,

5 John Tasioulas, 'On the Foundations of Human Rights' in Rowan Cruft, S. Matthew Liao, and Massimo Renzo (eds) *Philosophical Foundations of Human Rights* (Oxford University Press 2015) Chapter 1, 1772.

that victims have a right that their cases be properly investigated and reported. As a right, this should give them standing before domestic and (failing that) international human rights courts to achieve this outcome and may give them a significant role in other procedures including national and international criminal procedures.

But the idea of the right to the truth encompasses a range of rights, duties and expectations which cannot be reduced to the logical structure that S (the victim) controls the actions of D (the duty-bearing state) in relation to O (the disclosure and discovery of the truth) on a particular ground, G.[6] Significantly, the state's duty is independent of the victim's will. The state must investigate whether or not the victim so wishes; it must investigate in a way, to an extent and to a standard which victims may influence but do not ultimately determine (and which could even be against the victim's interests or wishes). The state must investigate not only to disclose to the victims but also to serve other purposes such as the identification and prosecution of alleged perpetrators; and it must investigate in order to assist a divided society to come to terms with its past and establish political equality between its members.

These points give reasons for justifying the duty to investigate independently of claims about victims' rights (though not to contradict those rights). That is to say: the right correlates with duties which are independently justified and therefore the subject of the right becomes problematic. The focus of discussion is then on the duty on the state (which is presumed to advance the interests of victims and society). We explore whether the right to the truth can be independently arrived at and not solely based on a duty correlating to the victim's right, which in turn would strengthen and justify the public element of the right to the truth.

We acknowledge that when examining the subject matter, its inherent nature invites an oscillating between the desirability of a morally convincing point with the balancing and operationalisation of principles in a legal sphere. To put it differently, one inherently sympathises particularly with individual victims who suffered such gross human rights violations wishing for them to have ways to secure their interests, but one is confronted with the (international) institutional frameworks that may (for good reason) be ill-designed to fully realise such interests since the ultimate responsibility to realise the right to the truth rests with the state. Like other universal human rights who require the state as guarantor and protector, the right to the truth, if universal human rights through torture, extrajudicial killings or enforced disappearances have been violated, requires the state to realise a right that follows from its own failure. The immediate impulse for seeking to balance and redress potential abuse of state power is great. As we will discuss throughout the book, the limited means to compel states to act is, on the other hand, rather sobering.

6 E.g. Alan Gerwith, 'Are There Any Absolute Rights?' in Jeremy Waldron (ed) *Theories of Rights* (Oxford University Press 1984) 93.

References

Blackburn S, *Truth. A Guide for the Perplexed* (Penguin 2006).

Gerwith A, 'Are there any Absolute Rights?' in Waldron J (ed) *Theories of Rights* (Oxford University Press 1984).

Ignatieff M, 'Human Rights as Idolatry', The Tanner Lecture on Human Values (Princeton University 4–7 April 2000).

International Commission of Jurists, 'Enforced Disappearance and Extrajudicial Execution: The Right of Family Members' (Practitioners' Guide No. 10, July 2016).

Kovras I, *Truth Recovery and Transitional Justice. Deferring human rights issues* (Routledge 2014).

Loyle C and Davenport C, 'Transitional Injustice: Subverting Justice in Transition and Postconflict Societies' (2016) 15 Journal of Human Rights 126.

Tasioulas J, 'On the Foundations of Human Rights' in Cruft R, Liao S M and Renzo M (eds) *Philosophical Foundations of Human Rights* (Oxford University Press 2015).

1 The need for truth

Introduction

Human suffering provides the starting point for understanding, analytically and morally, the idea of a legal right to the truth in respect of atrocity. Human rights reflect those human interests which are sufficiently strong to compel the performance of duties in others. Ameliorating the suffering of relatives in not knowing the fate of loved ones or of living victims in not knowing the circumstances and explanation for why they were attacked, is a ground of such an interest. In the first part of this chapter the nature of suffering from not knowing is explored in various historical contexts and psychological forms. But the value of knowing the truth behind atrocities is not confined to victims and this chapter continues by identifying and discussing other contexts in which knowing the truth behind atrocity is vital. As we will examine, important questions can arise in relation to the way, extent and interpretation of the right and its corresponding duties, dependent on the stakeholders. The categories of abuses that are linked with the right to the truth are introduced to conduct a comprehensive needs analysis on behalf of individuals and society following such gross human rights abuses.

Victims' need for truth

There are numerous powerful stories told, and many more untold, evidencing the need for survivors to know the truth following gross human rights violations. Whether the woman in Nepal who seeks to know the fate of her husband; the daughters of fathers who disappeared in the 1990 Yugoslav war; grieving mothers and grandmothers in Latin America; or Lebanese activists lobbying for families of the missing to know their fate, the desire to find out the truth is well documented.[1]

1 E.g. International Centre for Transitional Justice, 'Truth and Memory' (2017) www.ictj.org/our-work/transitional-justice-issues/truth-and-memory accessed 14 February 2019. The Inter-American Court of Human Rights expressly acknowledges that children and siblings of disappeared persons who were not yet born when the actual disappearance occurred may still be considered victims of enforced disappearance (*Gudiel Álvarez et al. ("Diario Militar") v Guatemala* (20 November 2012)).

The exact reasons as to why seeking the truth is so important may vary:

- The return of human remains is necessary to provide opportunities for commemoration practices, funerals and – it is hoped – some sense of healing or closure;
- A death certificate may be required for insurance purposes to safeguard the livelihood of the family;
- Information as to the events that led up to the disappearance may explain the absence of a father as well as restoring basic human dignity to the disappeared and the family that is left (though the truth may also have undesired effects in evidencing previously not known family ties, for example);
- Understanding and investigating the fate of lost children may work towards answers, accountability and criminal justice efforts; documenting the patterns of violence and disappearance not only serves as a record of the human rights abuse but may lead to finding forcibly disappeared people who may still be alive.

The key reason behind a "right to the truth" at an individual level is that it seeks to answer existential questions. Existential not in an intellectual, philosophical understanding of existentialism as such (though typical existentialist questions such as "who am I" may arise), but rather as necessary for the continued existence of the survivors. They have and continue to suffer as a consequence of the human rights abuses and a lack of understanding as to what happened to their loved ones. There is a reason why so many human rights activists, NGOs and civil society initiatives have dedicated their efforts to urging governments to investigate and provide the truth by recording the stories of past human rights abuses such as genocide, crimes against humanity and war crimes: "we want to tell this story for a reason: it matters".[2] One way of insisting on the right to the truth is to demonstrate the need for truth by giving victims an opportunity to tell their story and document human rights abuses in that way. This form of activism can be seen as giving victims a role in lobbying for the right to the truth to be realised by the state. Having an opportunity to tell one's story, as we will discuss in the following chapter, can form part of the right to the truth realisation itself.

Evidence from the field indicates that the need of families to know the truth is vital and sometimes has primacy over wanting justice; the desire for justice may be a secondary consequence of the primary desire to know the truth.[3] In addition to knowing the truth, livelihood issues and ensuring economic security may be

2 Louis Bickford and Others, 'Documenting Truth' (International Centre for Transitional Justice Report 2009), 5 www.ictj.org/sites/default/files/ICTJ-DAG-Global-Documenting-Truth-2009-English.pdf accessed 14 February 2019.

3 Simon Robins, 'Towards Victim-Centred Transitional Justice: Understanding the Needs of Families of the Disappeared in Postconflict Nepal' (2011), 5 International Journal of Transitional Justice 75. Truth is therefore of the utmost significance. In line with our separation argument, it facilitates important secondary consequences, including reparation and justice.

equally important and take precedence over seeking judicial processes.[4] Therefore, where possible, survivors wish to receive their human remains as an absolute proof of death and to facilitate burial and commemoration rituals.

Years after the events, the children of the disappeared, who were infants at the time of the events, continue to be affected by what happened decades ago.[5] Many of them go through life searching for answers about the circumstances of their parents' disappearance. This points to the longevity and legacy of gross human rights abuses and the long-term effects truth-telling or shielding from the truth can have.

Futile searches and frustration with the official channels have also created networks and associations designed to search for the disappeared and to document and denounce those responsible for human rights abuses. Argentina's *Madres de Plaza de Mayo* and the *Abuelas de Plaza de Mayo* (Mothers and Grandmothers of Buenos Aires' main public square, the Plaza de Mayo) are perhaps the best known examples of such activism where, mainly housewives, searched for their husbands and children despite intimidations from the authorities.[6] Searching, finding and documenting the truth can serve to gain a full and complete account of the repression mechanism and individuals involved. Such documentation efforts are not only vital elements of human rights advocacy but are also seen as precursors of transitional justice mechanisms.[7]

As the right to the truth has evolved over the past decades, activists take recourse to it. Lebanese activists, for example, have expressed that they "will not give up this fight as long as we are armed with the right to truth and with our hope".[8] Many years after the civil war ended in 1990, there is still hope that some of those that disappeared may still be alive.[9] For them, the right to the truth has developed from a need into a right that they are trying to invoke.

From this level of need, a moral background right can be deduced to the effect that individual victims ought to be informed about the fate of their family members, pointing to the importance of an effective investigation of events and the communication of results. The political aim of such activists, not just in Lebanon but around the world, is to develop the moral right into an enforceable legal entitlement.

4 Simon Robins, *Families of the Missing. A Test for Contemporary Approaches to Transitional Justice* (Routledge 2013).

5 Azra Hodzic 'Remember Me' (2014 documentary), www.ictj.org/news/documentary-film-remember-me accessed 14 February 2019.

6 E.g. Jo Fisher, *Mothers of the Disappeared* (Zed Books 1989); Adam Rosenblatt, *Digging for the Disappeared. Forensic Science After Atrocity* (Stanford Studies in Human Rights, Stanford University Press 2015) at 88–89.

7 Bickford and others *supra* note 2 at 4.

8 International Centre for Transitional Justice, 'Armed With the Right to Truth, Families of the Missing Lobby to Learn Their Fate' (*Interview With Wadad Halwani and Ghazi Aad*, 3 May 2012) www.ictj.org/news/armed-right-truth-families-missing-lobby-learn-their-fate accessed 14 February 2019.

9 Ibid.

Society's need for truth

International human rights law has long recognised that persons may be victims of human rights violation as individuals and collectively.[10]

The right to the truth has therefore also been raised in relation to society.[11] In fact, there are a number of truth-stakeholders involved, some that may be bearers of rights and other stakeholders that have a corresponding duty. Arguments can be made to safeguard the rights of the surviving population by extending the right to know to society more generally. Victims experience crimes and their effects in varying and concomitant capacities: as an individual, direct victim; indirectly, as a family member of a direct victim; and also as a member of a victimised group. In addition, victims may feel an allegiance to a community or societal affiliation as a facet of their social and cultural identity, and if that group or community is a target of crimes, the sense of group identity and allegiance may produce a strong collective solidarity, identity and mutual support.

Conversely, a corresponding duty may be placed upon the state to investigate the circumstances resulting in the abuse and gross human rights violations. Furthermore, the international community may become a stakeholder with its appropriate institutions that are mandated to investigate, prosecute and punish grave breaches of human rights or international humanitarian law. Particularly if the international community is part of an intervention and transitional justice effort, it too becomes part of the truth narrative whilst working towards the realisation of the right to the truth.

Transitional justice literature points to the societal need to know the truth in the aftermath of gross human rights violations.[12] Fulfilling individuals' need for truth is not only of benefit for victims but also, it is thought, for society more generally. However, and this is an experience the South African Truth and Reconciliation Commission pointed out in its report, learning and knowing the truth can have complex and unpredictable effects on the individual and may exacerbate strains between the individual, the past and society.[13] Competing narratives may prevail, dividing societies along ethnic, political or religious lines. This cautions us about the potential for truth to serve purposes other than the realisation of

10 Principle 1 of the Declaration of Basic Principles of Justice for Victims of Crime and Abuse of Power (29 November 1985) and Article 8 of the Basic Principles and Guidelines on the Right to a Remedy and Reparation for Victims of Gross Violations of International Human Rights Law and Serious Violations of International Humanitarian Law (21 March 2006) (hereinafter Basic Principles).

11 Report of the Independent Expert to Update the Set of Principles to Combat Impunity (18 February 2005), Principle 2 (hereinafter Updated Principles on Impunity).

12 E.g. Eduardo González and Howard Varney (eds) 'Truth Seeking: Elements of Creating and Effective Truth Commission' (Amnesty Commission of the Ministry of Justice of Brazil/ International Center for Transitional Justice 2013) www.ictj.org/sites/default/files/ICTJ-Book-Truth-Seeking-2013-English.pdf accessed 14 February 2019.

13 Truth and Reconciliation Commission, 'Truth and Reconciliation Commission of South Africa Final Report (Volume 1)' (29 October 1998) at 106.

the right for direct or indirect victims, and points to the power web surrounding "truth" narratives.[14]

At a public level, the right to truth exists as a means of ensuring transparency, ending impunity and protecting human rights.[15] If impunity reigns, this may correspond to the truth remaining hidden. This in turn will not only have adverse effects on the victims but also, it is suggested, erode peace and undermine the rule of law.[16] This sentiment has found expression in a decision of the European Court of Human Rights (ECtHR), where the court acknowledges the public relevance of the right to truth, noting its significance in strengthening public confidence in the workings of state institutions and the rule of law more generally. It is part of such efforts to break down "the wall of silence and the cloak of secrecy"[17] that prevented victims from understanding what had happened to them and hindered their recovery.[18] When events remain uninvestigated, the fear is that they may become sites of conflict and continuing reminders or sources of political instability.

In the following chapters, we will therefore examine the international judicial approaches taken to the right to the truth.

This is not to minimise the importance of state-level domestic legislation, for example on state transparency, freedom of information, government obligations to hold inquiries, search and identification efforts may exist to respond to the individual and public needs towards the truth. Non-judicial inquiries too may be important, such as state organised truth commissions. Or, separate from state functions, unofficial efforts by civil society, including the creation of documentation centres, can offer a response to this need.[19]

14 Michel Foucault, *Power/Knowledge – Selected Interviews and Other Writings 1972–1977* (Prentice Hall 1980).

15 Resolution 9/11 Right to the Truth (18 September 2008) para 1; Updated Principles on Impunity *supra* note 11 at Principle 2. The Constitutional Court of Colombia suggests that the rights to the truth and justice may "acquire a collective character. This collective character has different dimensions, reaching the level of society as a whole when the foundations of civilized society and the basic elements of the legal order – peace, human rights, and restriction and rational use of military force – are threatened and compliance with the State's basic function is jeopardized." Constitutional Court of Colombia, Decision No T-249/03 (21 May 2003) para 18; Translation from Eduardo Ferrer Mac-Gregor, 'The Right to the Truth as an autonomous right under the Inter-American Human Rights System' (2016) IX(1) Mexican Law Review 121 at footnote 47.

16 E.g. Eduardo González Cueva, 'Seeking Options for the Right to the Truth in Nepal', (International Centre for Transitional Justice Report 2012) www.ictj.org/sites/default/files/ICTJ-Briefing-Paper-Nepal-Ordinance-Dec-2012-ENG.pdf accessed 14 February 2019 at 1.

17 *El-Masri v The former Yugoslav Republic of Macedonia* (12 December 2012), Joint concurring opinion para 6. Although it should be noted that there was disagreement on this point as some judges felt there was an implied (as opposed to a freestanding) right. This will be discussed in Chapter 7.

18 Ibid.

19 Louis Bickford and others *supra* note 2. See also Chapter 8 on Truth Commissions.

Truth as a precondition?

A great many transitional justice efforts seem to hinge on the notion of truth, and crucially on learning and knowing the truth, as advocated by transitional justice scholars who claim:

> The right to truth is not subject to conditions or trade-offs. Victims cannot be forced to waive their right to pursue justice and reparations or to accept an apology in order to obtain the truth. On the contrary, the right to truth is complementary to all other aspects of an effective transitional justice strategy, such as judicial action and reparation.[20]

Ascertaining the truth about the events that led to the gross human rights abuses and the details of the abuse itself, are seen as an important precondition for transitional justice goals.

But truth scepticism has also been voiced, drawing attention to the complexities – political, societal and legal – in which the right to the truth realisation may be situated and that may have an effect on the perception and impact of truth.[21] Furthermore, the question about whether truth-telling leads to peace-building has been asked.[22] A distinction can therefore be made between the truth-finding (i.e. investigative efforts) and truth-telling efforts (i.e. testimonies by witnesses, victims and offenders). The latter may form part of the former. For the purposes of the right to the truth, as we will outline in the following chapters, truth-telling is insufficient because it requires a thorough investigation into past abuses.

It appears that further and longitudinal studies are needed to ascertain the importance of truth within transitional justice settings, since for every anecdote suggesting benefits, an anecdote outlining the drawbacks can be told. Mendeloff, for example, notes eight speculative peace-building consequences of truth-seeking and truth-telling contending that they:

> (1) encourage social healing and reconciliation, (2) promote justice, (3) allow for the establishment of an official historical record, (4) serve as public education function, (5) aid institutional reform, (6) help promote democracy, (7) pre-empt as well as (8) deter future atrocities.[23]

20 Gonzalez *supra* note 16 at 2.

21 Bronwyn Anne Leebaw, 'The Irreconcilable Goals of Transitional Justice' (2008) 30 Human Rights Quarterly 95.

22 Tristan Anne Borer, 'Truth Telling as a Peace-Building Activity. A Theoretical Overview' in Tristan Anne Borer (ed), *Telling the Truth: Truth Telling and Peace-Building in Post-Conflict Societies* (University of Notre Dame Press 2006).

23 David Mendeloff, 'Truth-Seeking, Truth-Telling, and Postconflict Peacebuilding: Curb the Enthusiasm?' (2004) 6 International Studies Review 355 at 358.

He refutes them with (equally empirically unsubstantiated) counterarguments: social healing and reconciliation, for example, extrapolate from the assumption that "hearing the truth" is beneficial to the individual and transposes this benefit to a nation. Truth, however, can also retraumatise and aggravate suffering. Whilst truth-seeking and truth-telling may have value, he suggests it is limited and dependent on circumstances and the conflict itself. He argues truth efforts are unlikely to be successful in conflicts "marked by predatory motivations or hegemonic ambition".[24] Instead they require sustained institutional and educational efforts; may take a very long time, possibly generations, to effect change; are likely to be most effective in peaceful and stable states that already are a democracy; and require society to have a desire to engage in and debate the past. Finally he suggests effectiveness of truth-telling may be enhanced when accompanied by reparations and an apology.[25] Leebaw identifies a less expansive justification for truth-finding in the form of truth commissions and trials aimed at (1) countering denial and promoting accountability, (2) expanding debate and creating a political space for marginalised or silenced sections of society (3) alleviating "volatile emotions associated with trauma and the desire for revenge".[26] She notes that since truth-telling engages with and delves into a divisive and violent past, it has been seen as an obstacle as opposed to a promoter of reconciliation, creating instability instead.[27] In fact, she concludes:

> [i]t is possible for transitional justice institutions to establish accountability, promote remembrance, and challenge denial, yet at the same time advance political myths that obfuscate responsibility, distort the legacy of political violence, and encourage people to forget potentially volatile issues. In other contexts transitional justice institutions may function primarily as tools for legitimization of state power, yet also open avenues for widening accountability, dialogue and ongoing political reform over the long term.[28]

And finally, it is perhaps worth pointing to Ignatieff's remark that, for all the truth-searching, truth-telling and truth-finding, at a public, national level there is a need for forgetting, "forging myths of unity, an identity that allows a society to forget its hidden crimes, its hidden injuries and divisions, its unhealed wounds".[29]

Regardless, the notion of truth plays an important role in judicial and extrajudicial proceedings, since their procedures are premised on the possibility of ascertaining the truth. Bearing in mind such reservations, the presumed relationship between truth and transitional justice goals is perhaps most obvious in the title

24 Ibid at 376.
25 Ibid.
26 Leebaw *supra* note 21 at 97.
27 Ibid at 96.
28 Ibid at 118.
29 Michael Ignatieff, *The Warrior's Honor: Ethnic War and the Modern Conscience* (Holt Paperbacks 1998) at 170.

of "Truth and Reconciliation Commissions". No-one speaks of "Reconciliation and Truth Commissions". Instead, it seems that reconciliation can only follow once an authoritative version of the truth has been arrived at. Though reconciliation, or rather conflict resolution, can never be imposed or be demanded, it does require knowledge of the facts. Furthermore, those perceiving themselves as victims may feel that without the other side accepting and facing the truth, reconciliation is not an option.[30] In addition, Méndez suggests that, for reconciliation purposes, the recognition of wrongdoing and the making of amends is needed.[31] Hayner stresses that a distinction has to be drawn between the individual and the national or political reconciliation that can follow from truth commissions.[32] To what extent reconciliation in the aftermath of atrocity is an achievable objective is another question entirely, and not one pursued within the parameters of this book, but in Chapter 8 we will examine the relationship between the right to the truth and truth commissions more closely.

Similarly, truth is needed to achieve justice that is perceived to be fair. Without knowing what happened, those responsible are unlikely to be held to account. When a justice approach to prosecution and punishment of those responsible for the crimes committed is taken, then an affirmative, open-minded institutional effort, conducted in good faith, must be placed in the service of truth-seeking; a mere pro-forma compliance will not suffice. Accountability that would neglect or even undermine the truth is not acceptable,[33] especially as through the testing process of evidence, the narrative emerging from trials ought to be persuasive.

Furthermore, a heartfelt apology – if offered – only makes sense in the context of acknowledging the truth of what happened. An apology – and they have been offered by a number of defendants standing trial before international criminal institutions or by state officials for what was done in the state's name (often many years after the events) – cannot be associated with denial but rather with a sentiment of responsibility for the wrong done. And it needs to be clear and acknowledged what that wrongdoing entailed.[34]

30 This was a response given in Bosnia and Herzegovina: "there can be no reconciliation until Bosnian Serbs face and accept the truth" (Janine Natalya Clark, *International Trials and Reconciliation: Assessing the Impact of the International Criminal Tribunal for the Former Yugoslavia* (Routledge 2014) at 96).

31 Juan Méndez, 'Accountability for Past Abuses' (1997) 19 *Human Rights Quarterly* 255 at 274. He distinguishes three elements: first, reconciliation efforts must be a process "to be built in the hearts and minds of all members of society through a process that recognizes every human being's worth and dignity". Second, knowledge of the facts is essential followed, third, by the requirement of atonement (ibid).

32 Priscilla Hayner, *Unspeakable Truths. Transitional Justice and the Challenge of Truth Commissions* (2nd edn, Routledge 2011) at 183.

33 Though plea bargaining has been criticised as potentially undermining the truth-seeking efforts of trials (see William Schabas, *Unimaginable Atrocities* (Oxford University Press 2012)). This will be examined in greater detail in Chapter 10 on international criminal trials.

34 However, a study on apologies and remorse within international criminal proceedings reveals that many such apologies were not sincere or connected to remorse but rather a way of luring trial chambers into considering apologies as mitigating factors. (Oliver Diggelmann,

Whilst reparation can, in theory, be offered without the acknowledgment of the truth, many victims may not be prepared to trade their "silence" for reparations and, under international law, this may not qualify as reparation at all. According to the Permanent Court of Justice, "reparation must, as far as possible, wipe out all the consequences of the illegal act and re-establish the situation which would, in all probability, have existed if that act had not been committed".[35] Through the Basic Principles,[36] the UN General Assembly has recognised the interests of victims for violations of human rights and international humanitarian law[37] and includes access to justice, reparation for harm suffered and access to information concerning the violations, thus acknowledging possible existing rights to reparations.[38] Without an understanding of the events and the consequences of wrongful acts, it is hard to imagine how an appropriate reparations policy is arrived at. Instead reparations are most likely to follow on from an establishment of the facts.

A universal right

In the aftermath of violence and atrocities, for many, it is too late for human rights. Those who survive may seek the truth not only to gain an understanding of what happened, but also in an effort to seek acknowledgment of the violations and express their protest against the violation and infringement on human security. It seems relatively uncontroversial that the extra-legal rationale for a right to the truth is strong, as evidenced earlier, precisely because time and time again, specifically in post-conflict situations, the demand for truth has been voiced. Its universality is thus predicated on ordinary victims' need to know – whether they live in Nepal, Argentina, Lebanon, Bosnia and Herzegovina, or Cambodia. In other words, whilst the need for truth emerges from culturally and politically very diverse situations, it transcends this diversity and stands out as a universal feature of post-conflict societies. The right to the truth reflects a universal norm because it is anchored in a universal need and emerges as part of "existing norms of universal applicability".[39]

Universal but not homogeneous

Whilst the need for truth may be universal, the religious, ethnic, cultural, economic, social or political context is not homogenous. Furthermore, the voices of those victims wishing for the truth have been heard, but there may be a silent

---

'International Criminal Tribunals and Reconciliation. Reflections on the Role of Remorse and Apology' (2016) 14(5) *Journal of International Criminal Justice* 1073).

35 *Factory at Chorzów, Germany v Poland* (13 September 1928) at 47.

36 Basic Principles *supra* note 10.

37 E.g. Liesbeth Zegveld, 'Victims' Reparations Claims under International Criminal Courts: Incompatible Values?' (2010) 8(1) *Journal of International Criminal Justice* 79.

38 Basic Principles *supra* note 10.

39 Méndez *supra* note 31 at 261.

other view: those not wishing to find out the truth. This possibility has to be contemplated, at least in theory, if not verified in practice by virtue of the silence. That said, those wishing to be forgotten in order to protect their individual, private and public life in a world shaped by mass media, big data and social networks have made some noise arguing for a "right to be forgotten".[40]

The moral universalism for pursuing and ascertaining the truth may thus run into counterclaims based on the right-bearers' (both as an individual and a society) political, religious and cultural grounds for not pursuing the truth (or curtailing the pursuit). They may still be exercising their right: the right not to make use of the right to know the truth. However, such non-invocation of the right has implications for others. And the matter becomes more complicated for both the invoker and non-invoker of the right, since it may have different consequences for oneself than for others or for a group of people. Such tensions are explored throughout the chapters of this book.

Some indication of the variance in the extent that the truth is pursued can be discerned in the literature on the missing and disappeared, not least because efforts to investigate the remains of those deceased has differed from context to context. For example, in the former Yugoslavia identification efforts are still ongoing decades after the event,[41] whereas in Rwanda little effort towards DNA identification of the 500,000–1,000,000 estimated victims has been made.[42] Ad hoc tribunals were established for both countries following the collapse of the former Yugoslavia and the "100-day genocide" in Rwanda. Whilst there may be scientific, political and cultural reasons for the discrepancy, Rosenblatt suspects that

> [o]ne of the features that distinguished Rwanda from the former Yugoslavia, however, is that the families of victims of the Rwandan genocide appear, at least in most accounts not to have clamoured as loudly for individual identifications.[43]

The truth – but not at all cost

There may be cultural, political or religious reasons for rejecting elements of truth-finding. Similarly, sometimes the scale of truth-finding and investigations necessary to satisfy identification and repatriation may not always be feasible, as in the case of Cambodia or perhaps in Rwanda, where the sheer number of

40 E.g. Alessandro Mantelero, 'The EU Proposal for a General Data Protection Regulation and the roots of the "right to be forgotten"' (2013) 29 *Computer Law & Security Review* 229 and *Google Spain SL and Google Inc. v Agencia Española de Protección de Datos (AEPD) and Mario Costeja González* (13 May 2014).

41 For the latest statistics see International Commission on Missing Persons, 'Western Balkans' (2018) www.icmp.int/where-we-work/europe/western-balkans/ accessed 14 February 2019.

42 Rosenblatt *supra* note 6 at 29.

43 Ibid.

the atrocities and the extent to which evidence has been destroyed or degraded over time make such efforts exceedingly difficult, even if the political will were forthcoming.

And not all aspects of ascertaining the truth, however, are equally acceptable to survivors. Mass grave excavations may be such an area: when done, finding the disappeared, identifying and repatriating them are crucial aspects of realising the right to the truth. Some "Mothers" perceived the exhumation started in Argentina under the new Alfonsin regime to form part of the government's efforts to put an end to the Madre de Plaza de Mayo's human rights activism. They thought the exhumations would first ensure that through exposing the horrors of the regime at a public level, the appetite for receiving such horror stories would be saturated, thus curtailing activism and, second, silence individuals who received the human remains of their children. Through receiving the human remains, their individual need for continued activism seemingly evaporated: they had found and received their loved ones and had no further need to fight. But this was rejected by some mothers:

> To receive the bodies before knowing who is responsible is a form of *punto final* (full stop, a policy by the Alfonsin government) all the more unjust when you consider how many mothers will never receive the bodies – all those who were thrown into the sea by the navy and air force, dynamited, incinerated, who are never going to be found. Exhumations have nothing to do with justice.[44]

Evidence and certified truth about the fate of their loved ones through grave excavations would not be sufficient. Instead a full accounting of all mechanisms of repression of all the people involved then followed by prosecutions was important. Individual excavation and identification efforts, in fact, were seen as undermining the cause of the mother's key demand of "*apparicion de vida*" – that the disappeared had to come back alive. As Rosenblatt explains:

> [a]chieving certainty about a loved one's fate and mourning over a body are, in this formulation [of apparicion de vida], not merely apolitical but actually *depoliticising*: they turn *Madres*, members of an activist organization, back into merely *madres*, mothers in the conventional sense.[45]

An example of objections to identifying the disappeared for religious reasons comes from the efforts to understand the events surrounding the Jedwabne massacre of 1941. In June 1941 Jedwabne, a small town in north-eastern Poland, was occupied by Nazi Germany, replacing Soviet occupation. On 10 July 1941, an estimated 1,600 Jewish inhabitants were rounded up and burned alive in a

44 Interview with Beatriz de Rubinstein, in Fisher *supra* note 6 at 129.

45 Rosenblatt *supra* note 6 at 99, though Rosenblatt hastens to add that he was not aware of anyone who left activism once receiving human remains of their loved ones.

barn. The killings were attributed to the Nazis, though in 2000 a book by Polish-born political scientist Jan Tomasz Gross suggested Poles had killed their 1,600 Jewish neighbours in Jedwabne, thus sparking political debates on Polish-Jewish relations during World War II.[46] Interesting for the discourse here was the reaction of Orthodox Jews to the proposed scientific excavation of the massacres' burial site to ascertain information on the number of victims, their identity and way in which they were killed. Work was brought to a halt by claims that the disturbance of the bodies would be contrary to Jewish law.[47] Similarly, in Cambodia, investigations, excavations and autopsies may not be easily acceptable to those Cambodians who feel culturally and religiously sensitive about the treatment of the dead, believing that the spirits of those who die unnatural deaths cannot rest and therefore may cause misfortune among the living.[48] Whilst religious and cultural sensitivities may be very genuine reasons for limits to truth-seeking mechanism, they can also be used as smokescreens to detract from political motives not to investigate.[49]

In the universal need for truth, there may thus be some limits to the extent that truth-seeking is desired, since digging up the past can have destabilising, disruptive and even dangerous effects. Though one also has to bear in mind that continued truth denial may operate concurrently as a rational defence mechanism of those seeking an alternate account of events. Thus, in a sense, within the universalism of the need, a right with sufficient flexibility ought to follow, so that a truth may emerge, not at all costs, but sensible enough to reflect what is appropriate in the given circumstances.

A question of method, selection and scope

The method by which truth about events and information is arrived at can be subject to dispute, with not all attempts at investigating the truth being acceptable, whether for cultural, religious or political motives.[50] In fact, a particular choice of method may be deliberately made to arrive at and advance a particular narrative of events. This would be against the idea of a good faith, impartial investigation. Whilst the subject of choosing a (or the most appropriate) method to ascertain the truth is not the topic of this book, we nonetheless encounter related issues later in the book when we discuss the scope (or narrowness) of truth that can be pursued within the international human rights

46 Ewa Wolentarska-Ochman, 'Collective Remembrance in Jedwabne' (2006) 18(1) *History & Memory: Studies in Representation of the Past* 152.

47 Rosenblatt *supra* note 6 at 126.

48 Wynne Cougill, 'Buddhist Cremation Traditions for the Dead and the Need to Preserve Forensic Evidence in Cambodia' (Documentation Centre Cambodia, without date) www.d.dccam.org/Projects/Maps/Buddhist_Cremation_Traditions.htm accessed 14 February 2019.

49 Suspicions have been voiced that this may have happened prior to the commencement of a Physicians for Human Rights Planned excavation in Congo (Rosenblatt, *supra* note 6 at 132–133).

50 Rosenblatt *supra* note 6.

and international criminal frameworks, respectively, due to their differing mandates.[51] Methods also carry with them error rates; this too has to be taken into account and is reflected in the authority with which an institution declares the truth: whether the sciences through testing, truth commissions through questioning witnesses, documentation centres through methods of corroboration, cross-tabulation and cross-referencing, or judicial fora through their methods of fact-finding. False identifications in Argentina as in Bosnia and Herzegovina have been reminders of the need for sound methods at all times.[52]

Similarly to methods, selectivity is inherent in justice systems since "[n]o system of justice in the world even pretends that it punishes each and every case that arises".[53] Within the search for truth, therefore, the parameters of the truth-finding inquiry, mission or mandate will be a limiting factor. Questions surrounding the feasibility and depth of investigating truth too will play a role in achieving knowledge. Many choices need to be considered: is truth best portrayed through facts and figures or through a rich, representative story of a select few individuals? These tensions exist within transitional justice mechanisms including truth-seeking organisation and memorialisation efforts but also tribunals, as we will come to see.

All this has a bearing on the reliability of the truth sought. The veracity of it will be established through a degree of probability as opposed to certainty. In short, a potential for falsehood to emerge remains.

Categories of abuse as grounds for the right

Whilst the anecdotes, examples and challenges from across the world described earlier are canvassing some of the main issues in broad brush, the following section outlines the types of human rights abuses that have become associated with the right to the truth and what specific needs arise from them. Understandably, any victims who incurred injustice may feel that an explanation is owed to them though the right to the truth had initially been associated with enforced disappearances. Enforced disappearances practiced by several Latin American governments in the 1960s, '70s and '80s as a form of state terrorism can be seen as the trigger for the emergence of the right to the truth. The right has now been extended to also refer to extrajudicial killings and torture.[54]

Today, the right to the truth presumes that massive or systematic human rights violations which also form part of international criminal offences such as

51 NGOs and truth commission can find themselves in a similar position through the boundaries of their mandate and the choice of methods used within their working framework to document and record the truth (Bickford and others *supra* note 2).

52 False identifications are doubly problematic: not only has a body been misidentified but also a person's name has erroneously been attached to the wrong body. Thus, someone that may still be missing has been misidentified as dead.

53 Méndez *supra* note 31 at 274.

54 Promotion and Protection of Human Rights. Study on the Right to the Truth (8 February 2006) para 8 (hereinafter 2006 Study on the Right to the Truth).

genocide, war crimes or crimes against humanity have been perpetrated.[55] The Updated Principles on Impunity define serious crimes under international law as grave breaches of the Geneva Conventions/Additional Protocols and other violations of international humanitarian law that are crimes under international law, genocide, crimes against humanity, and other violations such as torture, enforced disappearance, extrajudicial execution, and slavery.[56] In other words, the condemnation of all three (enforced disappearance, torture and extrajudicial killings) has found expression in international human rights, international humanitarian law, international criminal law and often in domestic law as well. Like gross human rights violations, serious violations of international humanitarian law, the *lex specialis* applicable during armed conflict, also forms part of the material scope of the right to the truth.[57]

Enforced disappearances and the missing

Enforced disappearances have been used to spread terror and fear among a population as the effect of the *Nacht und Nebel* directive by Adolf Hitler amply demonstrated in Nazi-occupied territories. It results in the abduction, arrest or detention of an individual, often for political motives, typically at the hands of a member of a military group accompanied by the denial by the authorities as to the disappearance and whereabouts of the individual.[58] Through this vanishing or disappearing act, the individual finds herself outside the protection of the law and subject to arbitrary measures including torture or extrajudicial killings whilst the family is left without information or official avenues to understand what happened. In that sense, enforced disappearances have been described as having a

> doubly paralysing impact: on the victims, frequently tortured and in constant fear for their lives, and on their families, ignorant of the fate of their loved ones, their emotions alternating between hope and despair, wondering and waiting, sometimes for years, for news that may never come.[59]

55 Juan Méndez and Francisco Bariffi, 'Truth, Right to, International Protection' (2011) Max Planck Encyclopedia of Public International Law (online).

56 Updated Principles on Impunity *supra* note 11 at B. This definition is in turn informed by jurisprudence of international criminal tribunals, human rights treaty bodies, national courts, UN General Assembly resolutions and UN bodies.

57 2006 Study on the Right to the Truth *supra* note 54 para 33.

58 E.g. Kirsten Anderson, 'How Effective is the International Convention for the Protection of All Persons From Enforced Disappearance Likely to be in Holding Individuals Criminally Responsible for Acts of Enforced Disappearance?' (2006) 7 *Melbourne Journal of International Law* 245.

59 Office of the United Nations High Commissioner for Human Rights, Enforced or Involuntary Disappearance, (Factsheet 6/Rev.3, without year) www.ohchr.org/Documents/Publications/FactSheet6Rev3.pdf accessed 14 February 2019.

It is not only the disappeared who are facing injustice; the families too are deprived of rights and in turn suffer from injustice, resulting in this dual victimhood for essentially the same act of abuse. In Argentina, the existence of an estimated 15,000 disappeared who passed through some 340 illegal detention centres was denied during the first years of the military rule.[60] Because these people officially did not exist, they could seemingly be held without time limit and subjected to maltreatment often ending in death and execution. The UN Human Rights Committee stresses that "[t]he prohibitions against taking of hostages, abductions or unacknowledged detention are not subject to derogation. The absolute nature of these prohibitions, even in times of emergency, is justified by their status as norms of general international law".[61] The Office of United Nations High Commissioner for Human Rights lists the following catalogue of civil and political rights that may be infringed through enforced and involuntary disappearances:

- The right to recognition as a person before the law;
- The right to liberty and security of the person;
- The right not to be subjected to torture and other cruel, inhuman or degrading treatment or punishment;
- The right to life, when the disappeared person is killed;
- The right to an identity;
- The right to a fair trial and to judicial guarantees;
- The right to an effective remedy, including reparation and compensation;
- The right to know the truth regarding the circumstances of a disappearance.[62]

Through their adverse effect on the families, and often children, enforced disappearance can violate

- The right to protection and assistance to the family;
- The right to an adequate standard of living;
- The right to health;
- The right to education.[63]

The right to know the truth about the disappearances is listed as one such recognised right. Case-law of the IACtHR and the work of intergovernmental bodies[64] responded to the problem of enforced disappearances and the need of the families

60 Fisher *supra* note 6 at 62.

61 UNHRC, CCPR General Comment No. 29: Article 4: Derogations During a State of Emergency (31 August 2001) para 13(b).

62 Office of the United Nations High Commissioner for Human Rights *supra* note 59 at 3.

63 Ibid at 4.

64 Including the UN Working Group on Enforced or Involuntary Disappearances (WGEID) and the Ad Hoc Working Group on Human Rights in Chile. See also the Inter-American Convention on Forced Disappearance of Persons.

of the missing to know the fate or whereabouts of relatives or loved ones. The right to the truth relating to enforced disappearances has been recognised by regional and international bodies[65] and will be discussed in Chapters 6 and 7. In the early 1980s the right to know what happened to one's disappeared daughter was acknowledged in an individual complaint to the Human Rights Committee.[66] The UN Working Group on Enforced or Involuntary Disappearances[67] and the Parliamentary Assembly of the Council of Europe[68] refer to the right in relation to enforced disappearances. Furthermore, there is reference to the right of the victims in Article 24(2) of the 2006 International Convention for the Protection for All Persons from Enforced Disappearance.[69] The Rome Statute too reflects this element of the crime in its codification of "Enforced disappearance" in Article 7(2)(i) of the Statute as encompassing

> the arrest, detention or abduction of persons by, or with the authorization, support or acquiescence of, a State or a political organization, followed by a refusal to acknowledge that deprivation of freedom *or to give information on the fate or whereabouts of those persons*, with the intention of removing them from the protection of the law for a prolonged period of time. [emphasis added]

The failure to provide information in this situation is an element of the crime itself and has been emphasised as cruel and inhuman treatment. In the *Kupreskić* case before the International Criminal Tribunal for the Former Yugoslavia (ICTY), enforced disappearance was categorised as a crime against humanity since it constituted an inhumane act, though the ICTY statute does not list enforced disappearances as such as a crime against humanity.[70]

For a poignant example where the need for truth has a prolonged effect and may go beyond the need to understand what happened to the individual disappeared, we return to Argentina, where many pregnant women were among the abducted in the Dirty War of 1976–1983. The grandmothers were keen to collect evidence not just to provide evidential material against those responsible for the abduction, torture, rape and killing, but also to find out whether an individual woman had given birth and whether a foetus was buried with the disappeared or

65 E.g. *Velásquez Rodriguez v Honduras* (29 July 1988) para 181. By 2016, the Inter-American Court had heard 42 cases concerning enforced disappearance (Ferrer Mac-Gregor *supra* note 15).

66 *Almeida de Quinteros et al. v Uruguay* (21 July 1983) para 14.

67 Report of the UN Working Group on Enforced or Involuntary Disappearances (26 January 1981) para 187.

68 Parliamentary Assembly of the Council of Europe, Recommendation 1056 (5 May 1987); Resolution 1414 (23 November 2004) para 3; and Resolution 1463 (3 October 2005) para 10(2).

69 International Convention for the Protection of All Persons From Enforced Disappearance (20 December 2006).

70 *Prosecutor v Kupreskić et al.* (14 January 2000).

whether that child was stolen and thus also a missing relative. This demonstrates the anguish and stress enforced disappearances can cause. Therefore, the International Commission of Jurists in their Practitioner Guide on Enforced Disappearances and Extrajudicial Execution suggest the right to the truth also in relation to the appropriation of children.[71] This is supported by the Working Group on Enforced and Involuntary Disappearance, who state that many disappeared children were subsequently registered under false information with adverse effects on the child and biological family:

> on the one hand, for the children whom were appropriated, it makes it impossible to find their family and learn their biological identity – and in some cases their own nationality – and, on the other, for the family of origin, whom are prevented from exercising the legal remedies to re-establish the child's biological identity and the family ties and end the deprivation of liberty. That situation only ceases when the truth about the identity is revealed and the child victims are guaranteed the legal and real possibility of re-establishing their true identity and, where appropriate, the family ties, with the pertinent legal consequences.[72]

Torture and inhuman treatment

While torture may seem less severe than killing and depriving someone of life, torture is an action that is never excusable under international law but often forms part of enforced disappearance and attempts to silence political opponents and dissidents. Under international law, torture is recognised as a peremptory norm and unacceptable, for example, under Article 5 of the Universal Declaration of Human Rights. Provisions under the Geneva Conventions and the Additional Protocols condemn the use of torture during armed conflict, with common Article 3 prohibiting "cruel treatment and torture" as well as "outrages upon personal dignity, in particular humiliating and degrading treatment".[73] Through the Convention against Torture and Other Cruel, Inhuman or Degrading Treatment or Punishment, the prevention of torture has found further universal expression and condemnation. The latter obliges signatories to make torture a punishable offence under domestic law, to arrest suspects, extradite the perpetrators to another jurisdiction or prosecute them and to fully cooperate in preserving and gathering the necessary evidence for prosecuting.[74] The prohibition can also be

71 International Commission of Jurists, 'Enforced Disappearance and Extrajudicial Execution: The Right of Family Members' (Practitioners' Guide No. 10, July 2016) at 132–134.

72 General Comment on Children and Enforced Disappearances Adopted by the Working Group on Enforced or Involuntary Disappearances at Its Ninety-Eighth Session (14 February 2013) para 16.

73 Common Article 3 to the Geneva Conventions.

74 Convention Against Torture and Other Cruel, Inhuman or Degrading Treatment or Punishment (10 December 1984).

found in general human rights treaties.[75] Whilst human rights law requires the instigation, consent or acquiescence of a public official or someone acting in an official capacity,[76] the Elements of Crimes for the International Criminal Court list no such requisite to a state actor. It defines torture as "severe physical or mental pain or suffering" as part of war crimes and crimes against humanity.[77] The International Criminal Tribunal for the Former Yugoslavia in the *Kunarac* case established that elements of torture for customary international humanitarian law are:

(i) The infliction, by act or omission, of severe pain or suffering, whether physical or mental.
(ii) The act or omission must be intentional.
(iii) The act or omission must aim at obtaining information or a confession, or at punishing, intimidating or coercing the victim or a third person, or at discriminating, on any ground, against the victim or a third person.[78]

Also noteworthy is that rape, according to the International Criminal Tribunal for the Former Yugoslavia and human rights bodies, can constitute torture.[79]

An aspect of the abhorrence of torture lies in the fact that it can have prolonged ill-effects, physical and psychological, on those who have endured torture. Examples of systematic ill-treatment that have been subject to international attention are the concentration camps in the municipality of Prijedor and in Čelebići, both in Bosnia Herzegovina, though operated by opposing parties in the conflict. In the Omarska camp, mistreatment inflicted on the non-Serb, Muslim and Bosnian Croat prisoners was described as particularly horrific, with the trial chamber noting "that interrogations were regularly conducted in Omarska in a cruel and inhumane manner and that these interrogations resulted in an atmosphere of terror and violence".[80] Interestingly, in her study into the impact of the International Criminal Tribunal of the Former Yugoslavia, Clark found

75 International Covenant on Civil and Political Rights (19 December 1966), Article 7; European Convention for the Protection of Human Rights and Fundamental Freedoms (4 November 1950), Article 3; American Convention on Human Rights 'Pact of San Jose, Costa Rica' (22 January 1969), Article 5(2); African Charter on Human and Peoples' Rights ('Banjul Charter') (27 June 1981), Article 5; Convention on the Rights of the Child (20 November 1989), Article 37.

76 Convention Against Torture and Other Cruel, Inhuman or Degrading Treatment or Punishment CAT, *supra* note 74, Article 1. Though this requirement is not universal and not found, for instance, in Article 3 of the European Convention on Human Rights.

77 International Criminal Court, *Elements of Crimes* (2011) ISBN No. 92-9227-232-2; definitions for torture as a crime against humanity and war crime are found in Articles 7(1)(f) and 8(2)(a)(ii) of the Rome Statute (17 July 1998).

78 *Prosecutor v Kunarac, Kovač and Vuković* (22 February 2001) para 497.

79 *Prosecutor v Delalić et al.* (16 November 1998), *Aydin v Turkey* (25 September 1997) and *de Mejía v Perú Case 10.970* (1 March 1996).

80 *Prosecutor v Kvočka et al.* (2 November 2001) para 73.

that Serb interviewees from the area of Prijedor "typically maintained that there were no camps in Prijedor municipality. Instead, there were only collective/ detention centres in which Bosnian Muslims (and some Bosnian Croats) were temporarily held".[81] In her assessment, in this region of Bosnia and Herzegovina, "competing truths" prevail as to what happened depending on what side of the ethnic divide one identifies with,[82] thus underscoring the fact that there may be more than one version of events. Some versions of the truth, by virtue of what they claim, exclude others and may actually constitute falsehood as opposed to "competing" or partial accounts of the truth. This in turn reinforces the need for a right to the truth established through an authoritative investigation and higher standard of proof than merely "telling one's story". In the case of Čelebići, similarly, extensive evidence regarding physical and psychological abuse against the Serb population was presented.[83] According to Stover, witnesses "saw the Čelebići trial as a vehicle for setting the record straight about Serb losses and suffering".[84] It may also be a vehicle for understanding incomprehensible atrocities.

Extrajudicial executions

Extrajudicial executions, like torture, may form part of an enforced disappearance. But, under international law it is not criminalised in the same manner as torture which, as a jus cogens, enjoys a blanket ban (at least in theory). States are permitted to intentionally kill individuals in a number of circumstances. Killings may occur following due judicial process or individuals may be incapacitated as part of law enforcement, subject to a proportionality test. International humanitarian law also allows for killing in armed conflict.[85] That said, killings on behalf of state officials in pursuit of supressing dissent, eliminating political opponents or instilling fear in the population are not permitted. According to the UN Principles on the Effective Prevention and Investigation of Extra-legal, Arbitrary and Summary Executions:

> [e]xceptional circumstances including a state of war or threat of war, internal political instability or any other public emergency may not be invoked as a justification of such executions. Such executions shall not be carried out under any circumstances including, but not limited to, situations of internal armed conflict, excessive or illegal use of force by a public official or other person acting in an official capacity or by a person acting at the instigation,

81 Clark *supra* note 30 at 94.
82 Ibid.
83 *Prosecutor v Zejnil Delalić et al.* (16 November 1998).
84 Eric Stover, *The Witnesses. War Crimes and the Promise of Justice in The Hague* (University of Pennsylvania Press 2005) at 69.
85 Erin Creegan, 'Criminalizing Extrajudicial Killings' (2013) 41(2) *Denver Journal of International Law and Policy* 185.

or with the consent or acquiescence of such person, and situations in which deaths occur in custody.[86]

The Principles specify that prompt, thorough and impartial investigations need to follow from all suspected incidents of extra-legal, arbitrary and summary executions with the aim to determine the cause, manner and time of death; those responsible, and the events and practice of pattern that led to the death. Equally, during internal conflicts, when armed forces are involved, it has been stressed by the judicial human rights institutions that the use of force must be limited to what is strictly necessary and for investigations to follow when suspicious deaths occur.[87]

A well-known example of extrajudicial killings in the literature and through case law of the ECtHR[88] but also in relation to the Nuremberg trials,[89] is the Katyn massacre. The massacre of thousands of Polish military leaders, professionals and intellectuals took place in March and April 1940, following the attacks on Poland by Nazi Germany in the west and its occupation in the eastern part by Soviet troops. The Polish nationals had been taken prisoner as they were believed to be enemies of Soviet power. The Polish prisoners' execution, which was approved by the Soviet Politburo under the leadership of Joseph Stalin, took place on Russian territory in the Katyn forest, which was three years later discovered by Nazi Germany. The results of a commission of international experts set up to investigate the massacre confirmed the Nazi-German version of events, that the Soviet Union was responsible for the atrocities; the Soviet Union denied such allegations, blaming Germany instead. Katyn is a stark example of how the "truth", or rather falsehood, about events can be instrumentalised for political purposes by attributing blame and further anti-Bolshevik or anti-Nazi sentiment. The alleged Soviet "truth" was, in fact, a falsehood. The question of "who is to blame?" was at the centre – not with a view to identifying the actual individual perpetrators, but rather in an attempt to attribute blame to a state or a system for political purposes. Consequently, the right to the truth must be different and work towards information for victims that will foster basic elements of trust in the rule of law[90]

86 Principles on the Effective Prevention and Investigation of Extra-legal, Arbitrary and Summary Executions (15 December 1989) para. 1. Revised and updated guidelines for the investigation have been introduced (Minnesota Protocol on the Investigation of Potentially Unlawful Death (2017)).

87 E.g. CCPR *General Comment No. 6: Article 6 (Right to Life)* (30 April 1982); *Chumbivilcas v Perú Case 10.559*, Inter-American Commission Report No. 1/96 (1 March 1996); *McCann and Other v UK* (27 September 1995); *Commission Nationale des Droits de l'Homme et des Libertes v Chad* (11 October 1995); *Neira Alegría et al. v Peru* (19 January 1995). See also International Committee of the Red Cross (ICRC), *Customary International Humanitarian Law* (2005) Volume I: Rules, Rule 89.

88 *Janowiec and Others v Russia* (21 October 2013), which was found inadmissible due to lack of temporal jurisdiction.

89 Schabas *supra* note 33 at 153–156.

90 International Center for Transitional Justice, 'Transitional Justice in the United Nations Human Rights Council' (Policy briefing June 2011) at 2.

and institutions in addition to offering the information they need to continue with their lives.

Categorising truth-seeking needs for an interest-based rights conceptualisation

Reflecting on the elements within the universal need for truth experienced by victims across the globe, and in an attempt to categorise truth needs which would form the basis for the right, the following categories can be identified.[91] At the *individual* level, and resulting from gross human rights violations such as enforced disappearances, torture and extrajudicial killings, we can summarise that a number of information needs arise:

1 Information about the events leading to the human rights abuse
2 In the case of death, return of the human remains for commemoration purpose but also to safeguard economic survival of family, including education and health needs
3 Identity of the victim and identity of survivors
4 Identity of perpetrators.

From this information, ancillary needs and legal claims can be met to:

1 Ascertain reparation, including official recognition, compensation, satisfaction (direct and indirect claims)
2 Make human rights claims
3 Lodge civil claims
4 Advance criminal prosecutions.

Crucially, the absence thereof may undermine the rule of law, which in turn also has also wider public implications. Needs therefore arise from a social or public perspective and include contribution truth-seeking makes to

1 Historical memory
2 National discourse on the past
3 Future policies
4 The rule of law
5 Basic condition of a just society.

Finally, one can also derive a need on behalf of *humanity and the international community*: such gross human rights violations require an awareness and expression of solidarity and concern that transcends cultural, national, ethnic and religious boundaries. This need for expression of outrage and condemnation may

91 Significantly expanded from Bickford and others *supra* note 2.

be felt at the individual, societal and global level, underscoring the common denominator of needs which also gives the right to the truth its universal moral appeal, quite like the cosmopolitan conceptualisation of people and rights Immanuel Kant offered:

> Since the narrower or wider community of the peoples of the earth has developed so far that a violation of rights in one place is felt throughout the world, the idea of a law of world citizenship is no high-flown or exaggerated notion. It is a supplement to the unwritten code of the civil and international law, indispensable for the maintenance of the public human rights and hence also of perpetual peace.[92]

From this "needs analysis" on behalf of individuals and society, the right to the truth as a moral background right takes compelling shape. Furthermore, the right to the truth and the need for state investigations has been expressly included in the formulation of abuses, notably enforced disappearance, torture and extrajudicial killings. On this basis, the need for investigations into human rights abuses for the benefit of survivors, individuals and society is evident and has been formulated as follows:

> The right to the truth implies knowing the full and complete truth as to the events that transpired, their specific circumstances, and who participated in them, including knowing the circumstances in which the violations took place, as well as the reasons for them. In cases of enforced disappearance, missing persons, children abducted or during the captivity of a mother subjected to enforced disappearance, secret executions and secret burial place, the right to the truth also has a special dimension: to know the fate and whereabouts of the victim.[93]

In this statement, the moral force behind the legal right to the truth is articulated.

Conclusion

This chapter has identified the importance of the right to the truth to individuals and how it might be extended to societies. The core value of "truth" as a moral good in itself rests undisputed, but the way in which truth is ascertained or woven into discourses can be highly contentious. On this basis of a universal human need for truth, the legal need for the right emerges. How this is recognised by international authorities, such as the United Nations, is the subject of the following chapter. It will examine the rationale behind a recommendation for the right

92 Immanuel Kant, *Zum Ewigen Frieden: ein philosophischer Entwurf* [Perpetual Peace: A Philosophical Sketch] (AA VIII 1795) 360.
93 2006 Study on the Right to the Truth *supra* note 54 para 59.

to the truth as a stand-alone right of individuals,[94] analysing the legal emergence, notion and content of the right to the truth in the context of transitional justice and international law.

References

Anderson K, 'How effective is the International Convention for the Protection of All Persons from Enforced Disappearance likely to be in holding individuals criminally responsible for acts of Enforced Disappearance?' (2006) 7 Melbourne Journal of International Law 245.

Bickford L and others, 'Documenting Truth', (International Centre for Transitional Justice Report 2009) www.ictj.org/sites/default/files/ICTJ-DAG-Global-Documenting-Truth-2009-English.pdf accessed 14 February 2019.

Borer T A, 'Truth Telling as a Peace-Building Activity. A Theoretical Overview' in Borer T A (ed), *Telling the Truth: Truth Telling and Peace-Building in Post-Conflict Societies* (University of Notre Dame Press 2006).

Clark J N, *International Trials and Reconciliation: assessing the impact of the international criminal tribunal for the former Yugoslavia* (Routledge 2014).

Cougill W, 'Buddhist Cremation Traditions for the Dead and the Need to Preserve Forensic Evidence in Cambodia' (Documentation Centre Cambodia, without date) www.d.dccam.org/Projects/Maps/Buddhist_Cremation_Traditions.htm accessed 14 February 2019.

Creegan E, 'Criminalizing Extrajudicial Killings' (2013) 41(2) Denver Journal of International Law and Policy 185.

Diggelmann O, 'International Criminal Tribunals and Reconciliation. Reflections on the Role of Remorse and Apology' (2016) 14(5) Journal of International Criminal Justice 1073.

Ferrer Mac-Gregor E, 'The Right to the Truth as an autonomous right under the Inter-American Human Rights System' (2016) IX(1) Mexican Law Review 121.

Fisher J, *Mothers of the Disappeared* (Zed Books 1989).

Foucault M, *Power/Knowledge – Selected Interviews and Other Writings 1972–1977* (Prentice Hall 1980).

González E and Varney H (eds) 'Truth Seeking: Elements of Creating and Effective Truth Commission. (Amnesty Commission of the Ministry of Justice of Brazil/International Center for Transitional Justice 2013) www.ictj.org/sites/default/files/ICTJ-Book-Truth-Seeking-2013-English.pdf accessed 14 February 2019.

González Cueva E, 'Seeking Options for the Right to the Truth in Nepal', (International Centre for Transitional Justice Report 2012) www.ictj.org/sites/default/files/ICTJ-Briefing-Paper-Nepal-Ordinance-Dec-2012-ENG.pdf accessed 14 February 2019.

Hayner P, *Unspeakable Truths. Transitional Justice and the Challenge of Truth Commissions* (2nd edn, Routledge 2011).

Hodzic A 'Remember Me' (2014 documentary) www.ictj.org/news/documentary-film-remember-me accessed 14 February 2019.

94 Ibid. para. 60.

Ignatieff M, *The Warrior's Honor: Ethnic War and the Modern Conscience* (Holt Paperbacks 1998).

International Center for Transitional Justice, 'Armed with the Right to Truth, Families of the Missing Lobby to Learn Their Fate (*Interview with Wadad Halwani and Ghazi Aad*, 3 May 2012) www.ictj.org/news/armed-right-truth-families-missing-lobby-learn-their-fate accessed 14 February 2019.

International Center for Transitional Justice, 'Transitional Justice in the United Nations Human Rights Council' (Policy briefing June 2011).

International Center for Transitional Justice, 'Truth and Memory' (2017) www.ictj.org/our-work/transitional-justice-issues/truth-and-memory accessed 14 February 2019.

International Commission of Jurists, 'Enforced Disappearance and Extrajudicial Execution: The Right of Family Members' (Practitioners' Guide No. 10, July 2016).

International Commission on Missing Persons, 'Western Balkans' (2018) www.icmp.int/where-we-work/europe/western-balkans/ accessed 14 February 2019.

International Committee of the Red Cross (ICRC), *Customary International Humanitarian Law* (2005) Volume I: Rules.

International Criminal Court, *Elements of Crimes* (2011) ISBN No. 92-9227-232-2.

Kant I, *Zum Ewigen Frieden: ein philosophischer Entwurf (Perpetual Peace: A philosophical Sketch)* (AA VIII 1795).

Leebaw B A, 'The Irreconcilable Goals of Transitional Justice', (2008) 30 Human Rights Quarterly 95.

Mantelero A, 'The EU Proposal for a General Data Protection Regulation and the roots of the "right to be forgotten"' (2013) 29 Computer Law & Security Review 229.

Mendeloff D, 'Truth-Seeking, Truth-Telling, and Postconflict Peacebuilding: Curb the Enthusiasm?' (2004) 6 International Studies Review 355.

Méndez J, 'Accountability for Past Abuses' (1997) 19 Human Rights Quarterly 255.

Méndez J and Bariffi F, 'Truth, Right to, International Protection' (2011) Max Planck Encyclopedia of Public International Law (online).

Office of the United Nations High Commissioner for Human Rights, Enforced or Involuntary Disappearance, (Factsheet 6/Rev.3, without year) www.ohchr.org/Documents/Publications/FactSheet6Rev3.pdf accessed 14 February 2019.

Robins S, *Families of the Missing. A test for contemporary approaches to Transitional Justice* (Routledge 2013).

Robins S, 'Towards Victim-Centred Transitional Justice: Understanding the Needs of Families of the Disappeared in Postconflict Nepal' (2011) 5 International Journal of Transitional Justice 75.

Rosenblatt A, *Digging for the Disappeared: Forensic Science after Atrocity* (Stanford University Press 2015).

Schabas W, *Unimaginable Atrocities* (Oxford University Press 2012).

Stover E, *The Witnesses. War Crimes and the Promise of Justice in The Hague* (University of Pennsylvania Press 2005).

Truth and Reconciliation Commission, 'Truth and Reconciliation Commission of South Africa Final Report (Volume 1)' (29 October 1998).

Wolentarska-Ochman E, 'Collective Remembrance in Jedwabne' (2006) 18(1) History & Memory: Studies in Representation of the Past 152.

Zegveld L, 'Victims' Reparations Claims under International Criminal Courts: Incompatible Values?' (2010) 8(1) Journal of International Criminal Justice 79.

2 The emergence of a right to the truth

Introduction

The needs of victims, societies and others for truth, and the underlying recognition of this by international authorities, has been charted in Chapter 1. Chapter 2 explores the way in which such authorities have developed and articulated the idea of a right to the truth as a general, background legal norm – a legal requirement that requires and ought to have specific institutional recognition and application. In this chapter we trace the way in which the idea of a moral right has become thus expressed as a right to the truth, first within the realm of transitional justice, and second within international law as a general, background legal norm.

Extra-legal emergence within transitional justice efforts

The emergence and development of the right to the truth came from the realisation that truth has a critical importance, especially for justice purposes, and is applicable to culturally diverse post-conflict contexts, much as Chapter 1 on the needs of victims seeks to outline. In that sense the right has emerged "in a diffuse manner in which non-legal academics and activists have served as essential contributors".[1] The right to the truth has the capacity to galvanise ethical and legal support, for example through expressing a moral imperative to search and account for those who disappeared, by a multitude of stakeholders bringing together such disparate fields as forensic sciences, human rights and transitional justice but also history and politics.[2] Practical issues with the implementation of the right to the truth and its exact meaning may remain with potentially conflicting interests. Regardless, a "global institutionalization of truth-seeking practice"[3] can be observed. This professionalisation of truth-finding, for example

1 Gloria Y. Park, 'Truth as Justice. Legal and Extralegal Development of the Right to Truth' (2010) February 1, *Harvard International Review* 24 at 24.
2 Claire Moon, 'Interpreters of the Dead: Forensic Knowledge, Human Remains and the Politics of the Past' (2013) 22(2) *Social and Legal Studies* 149.
3 Patricia Naftali 'Crafting a "Right to Truth" in International Law: Converging Mobilizations, Diverging Agendas?' (2016) XIII Champ penal/Penal field 1 at 7.

by NGOs such as the International Center for Transitional Justice, is not a surprise and its expansion can be seen in parallel with the developments in the field of transitional justice more generally. The latter includes the tasks of establishing the truth, developing reparation policies, remembrance, reconciliation and institutional reform as well as prosecution of perpetrators.[4] The UN Secretary-General defined transitional justice as encompassing "the full range of processes and mechanisms associated with a society's attempt to come to terms with a legacy of large-scale past abuses, in order to ensure accountability, serve justice and achieve reconciliation".[5] These mechanisms can be judicial or non-judicial[6] and are designed to offer practical strategies to address the complex legacies of gross human rights abuses whilst being responsive to victims. The term "transitional justice" itself originates from the 1990s and is perhaps better described as "justice during transition", with transition meaning a period of often complex political changes.[7] Transitional justice came into being through human rights activists, lawyers, legal and political scholars, policymakers and journalists' interaction facilitated by donors to advance human rights and also transitions to democracy.[8] A key premise was to compare experiences from across the world, noticing varying transitions and conflicts rather than identifying an ideal model for transition.[9]

Much like within the wider field of transitional justice, the extra-legal component to the origins of the right to the truth has been seen as a key strength due to its relevance for victims as individuals and society more generally. How the right is realised in practice, however, remains to be seen in the forthcoming chapters. In its core idea, however, it seeks to maintain the connection with the local contexts across the world, both individually and societally.

Legal genealogy

A number of efforts have sought to systematise the existing legal thinking.[10] Here we recapitulate key developments without seeking to replicate those systematising works that have come before us.

4 Louis Bickford, 'Transitional Justice' in Shelton D (ed), *The Encyclopaedia of Genocide and Crimes Against Humanity* (Macmillan Library Reference 2004).
5 The Rule of Law and Transitional Justice in Conflict and Post-Conflict Societies (23 August 2004) para 8.
6 Ibid.
7 Bickford, *supra* note 4. For a discussion on the appearance and content of the term "transitional justice", see Paige Arthur, 'How "Transitions" Reshaped Human Rights: A Conceptual History of Transitional Justice' (2009) 31 *Human Rights Quarterly* 321. On the genealogy of transitional Justice as a dynamic relationship with politics over time, see Ruti Teitel, who distinguishes three broad phases (1) postwar transitional justice, (2) post-cold war transitional justice and (3) steady-state transitional justice (Ruti Teitel, 'Transitional Justice Genealogy' (2003) 16 *Harvard Human Rights Journal* 69).
8 Ibid (Arthur) at 324.
9 Ibid 326.
10 Promotion and Protection of Human Rights. Study on the Right to the Truth (8 February 2006) (hereinafter 2006 Study on the Right to the Truth); The Right to Truth in the

Origin in international humanitarian law

The root of the expansion of the need for truth as a right can be traced to Articles 32 and 33 of the Additional Protocol I to the Geneva Conventions of 1949.[11] Whilst the Geneva Conventions provide for the recovery of the dead during armed conflict "[a]s far as military considerations allow",[12] and all four Geneva Conventions require the examination of the dead bodies,[13] Article 32 of the Additional Protocols speaks of "the right of families to know the fate of their relatives" as a general principle relating to the protection of victims of international armed conflict, placing an obligation on parties to the armed conflict to search for missing persons. Article 33 requires that

> each Party to the conflict shall search for the persons who have been reported missing by an adverse Party. Such adverse Party shall transmit all relevant information concerning such persons in order to facilitate such searches.[14]

The International Committee of the Red Cross (ICRC) Commentary to Article 32 further explains that the drafters had taken note of United Nations General Assembly Resolution 3220 (XXIX), which in its last preambular paragraph states "the desire to know the fate of loved ones in armed conflict is a basic human need which should be satisfied to the greatest extent possible".[15] Interestingly the Additional Protocol turns the "basic human need" into a right. But what the exact content of the obligation is, is perhaps less clear. Whilst the provision imposes a duty on those responsible for the adherence to international humanitarian law, it has been noted that there may not be an individual right for a family representative to insist that a government or organisation takes a particular action (especially as no obligations are placed on a state regarding its own nationals).[16] The ICRC study on customary international humanitarian law, reviewing the practice of states not (or not at the time) party to the Additional Protocol and

---

Americas (13 August 2014) and International Commission of Jurists, 'Enforced Disappearance and Extrajudicial Execution: The Right of Family Members' (Practitioners' Guide No. 10, July 2016).

11 Protocol Additional I to the Geneva Conventions of 12 August 1949 (8 June 1977).

12 Geneva Convention IV, Article 16(2).

13 Geneva Convention I, Article 17(1); Geneva Convention II, Article 20(1); Geneva Convention III Article 120(3); Geneva Convention IV Article 129(2).

14 Protocol I *supra* note 11, Article 33.

15 Assistance and co-operation in accounting for persons who are missing or dead in armed conflicts (6 November 1974), preamble, and Claude Pilloud and Others, Commentary on the Additional Protocols of 8 June 1977 to the Geneva Conventions of 12 August 1949 (Martinus Nijhoff 1987) (hereinafter ICRC Commentary).

16 Ibid ICRC Commentary at 346. Interestingly Germany, on ratifying the Additional Protocol, in an explanatory memorandum clarifies that it does not confer a subjective right on the relatives of a missing person to gain information (see Jean-Marie Henckaerts and Louise Doswald-Beck, *Customary International Humanitarian Law, Volume I: Rules* (Cambridge University Press 2006) at 424 hereinafter ICRC Study on Customary International Law).

due to wide support and no expressions of dissent at General Assembly[17] level, suggests the following rule as forming part of customary international humanitarian law for both international and internal armed conflict: "Each party to the conflict must take all feasible measures to account for persons missing as a result of armed conflict and must provide their family members with any information it has on their fate".[18] Support for this position can also be found in military manuals and national laws on the missing.[19] Under international humanitarian law, therefore, the duty exists to account for those who have gone missing and to inform the respective family member. Such duties have also found expression in international human rights law where the right-bearer (individuals and society) has also been positively identified.

International human rights law

Express codification of the right to the truth in convention law can be found in Article 24(4) of the International Convention for the Protection of All Persons from Enforced Disappearance, which grants each victim

> the right to know the truth regarding the circumstances of the enforced disappearance, the progress and results of the investigation and the fate of the disappeared person. Each State Party shall take appropriate measures in this regard.[20]

This convention entered into force in December 2010, binding its signatories. As outlined in the previous chapter, whilst initially linked to enforced disappearance,[21] the right to the truth has been broadened into other areas of gross human rights violations including torture and extrajudicial killings.[22] Before this codification, the right to families to know the fate of their loved ones has been echoed in multiple declarative human rights provisions and judicial decisions. But fundamentally, the right to the truth arises from a general international norm that places an obligation on the state to respect and safeguard human rights.[23]

17 Assistance and co-operation in accounting for persons who are missing or dead in armed conflicts (1974) *supra* note 15.

18 ICRC Study on Customary International Law *supra* note 16 at 421.

19 Both the 2006 Study on the Right to the Truth (*supra* note 10 footnote 8) and the ICRR Study on Customary International Law Rules (*supra* note 16 footnote 21) list, inter alia, Argentina, Australia, New Zealand, Spain, United Kingdom and the United States.

20 International Convention for the Protection of All Persons from Enforced Disappearance (12 January 2007) Article 24(2).

21 Report of the UN Working Group on Enforced or Involuntary Disappearances (26 January 1981) para 81; Inter-American Convention on Forced Disappearance of Persons (9 June 1994).

22 *Ellacuría et al. v El Salvador Case 10.488* (22 December 1999) para 221.

23 Juan Méndez and Francisco Bariffi, 'Truth, Right to, International Protection' (2011) Max Planck Encyclopedia of Public International Law (online) para 20.

Declarative human rights provisions

Acknowledgment of the right has been made in the context of refugees and displacement[24] and with regards to extra-legal, arbitrary and summary executions. Principle 9 of the Principles on the Effective Prevention and Investigation of Extra-legal, Arbitrary and Summary Executions adopted by the Economic and Social Council in Resolution 1989/65 provides a clear obligation on states, in that

> [t]here shall be thorough, prompt and impartial investigation of all suspected cases of extra-legal, arbitrary and summary executions, including cases where complaints by relatives or other reliable reports suggest unnatural death in the above circumstances. Governments shall maintain investigative offices and procedures to undertake such inquiries. The purpose of the investigation shall be to determine the cause, manner and time of death, the person responsible, and any pattern or practice which may have brought about that death. It shall include an adequate autopsy, collection and analysis of all physical and documentary evidence and statements from witnesses.[25]

The right to the truth forms a central element in efforts to combat impunity with Principle 4 of the Updated Set of Principles for the protection and promotion of human rights through action to combat impunity.[26] It identifies victims as having the right to the truth:

> Irrespective of any legal proceedings, victims and their families have the imprescriptible right to know the truth about circumstances in which violations took place and, in the event of death or disappearance, the victims' fate.[27]

In the document, the right to know is identified in Principles 2–18, outlining its foundational importance not for individuals but also for society:

> A people's knowledge of the history of its oppression is part of its heritage and, as such, must be ensured by appropriate measures in fulfilment of the State's duty to preserve archives and other evidence concerning violations of human rights and humanitarian law and to facilitate knowledge of those

24 Guiding Principles on Internal Displacement (22 July 1998) Principles 16(1) and 17(4).

25 Principles on the Effective Prevention and Investigation of Extra-legal, Arbitrary and Summary Executions (15 December 1989) Principle 9. The United Nations Manual on the Effective Prevention and Investigation of Extra-Legal, Arbitrary and Summary Executions refers to Principle 9's goal to discover the truth (United Nations Manual on the Effective Prevention and Investigation of Extra-Legal, Arbitrary and Summary Executions (24 May 1989)).

26 Report of the independent expert to update the Set of Principles to combat impunity (18 February 2005) (hereinafter Updated Principles on Impunity).

27 Ibid.

> violations. Such measures shall be aimed at preserving the collective memory from extinction and, in particular, at guarding against the development of revisionist and negationist arguments.[28]

The principles on the right to know are followed by other core Principles, namely the right to justice (Principles 19–30); the right to reparation (Principles 31–34) and guarantees of non-repetition (Principles 35–38).[29] Whilst not binding in themselves, the Principles "nonetheless reflect and comport with pertinent legal standards".[30] Furthermore they situate the right to the truth in a *quadriga* of human rights principles and the obligations they place on states which form the legal basis for transitional justice efforts. In this conceptualisation of key principles aimed at countering impunity, the right to the truth is part of a mix of obligations including the right to justice, the right to reparation and also the obligation to remove from office those that participated in the crimes.[31]

The right to the truth shares clear links with other rights and the corresponding transitional justice mechanisms to realise them. For example, it may be seen as a remedy for victims, survivors and their families and may serve as a vehicle towards the realisation of the right to justice. Transitional justice practices may not be able to address each set of principles concurrently, outlining the importance of conceptualising these aspects separately.

The right to the truth has also found explicit expression in the UN's Basic Principles,[32] which attempt to bring together, in a cohesive way, the legal positions on remedies for victim of gross violations in both fields of international humanitarian and human rights law given there is significant overlap. In particular, the authors had in mind gross violations that would constitute international crimes under the Rome Statute.[33] The Basic Principles are also important by way of offering a definition of "victims" as having suffered physical or mental harm, economic loss or substantial impairment of their fundamental rights; that there can be direct and indirect victims, including family members or dependents of the direct victim; and that persons can suffer harm both individually or collectively.[34] The definition is significant for the right to the truth, as it has both a public and

28 Ibid.

29 Ibid.

30 Ibid para 11.

31 Méndez and Bariffi *supra* note 23.

32 Basic Principles and Guidelines on the Right to a Remedy and Reparation for Victims of Gross Violations of International Human Rights Law and Serious Violations of International Humanitarian Law (21 March 2006) (hereinafter Basic Principles).

33 Theo van Bowen, 'The United Nations Basic Principles and Guidelines on the Right to a Remedy and Reparations for Victims of Gross Violations of International Human Rights Law and Serious Violations of International Law' (2010) (United Nations Audiovisual Library of International Law) http://legal.un.org/avl/pdf/ha/ga_60-147/ga_60-147_e.pdf accessed 14 February 2019.

34 Basic Principles *supra* note 32 Principle 8. See also The van Bowen (ibid.), who links the definition back to the 1985 Declaration of the Basic Principles of Justice for Victims of Crime and Abuse of Power (29 November 1985).

individual dimension and since the right is applicable to family members. Principle 24, in full, covers the following obligation:

> States should develop means of informing the general public and, in particular, victims of gross violations of international human rights law and serious violations of international humanitarian law of the rights and remedies addressed by these Basic Principles and Guidelines and of all available legal, medical, psychological, social, administrative and all other services to which victims may have a right of access. Moreover, victims and their representatives should be entitled to seek and obtain information on the causes leading to their victimization and on the causes and conditions pertaining to the gross violations of international human rights law and serious violations of international humanitarian law and to learn the truth in regard to these violations.[35]

Under this provision, the state is thus under an obligation to develop ways to fulfil the rights of individuals seeking information on the reasons and circumstances of the abuse suffered. The unanimous adoption of the Basic Principles by the General Assembly signifies authoritative backing.

The topic has also been subject to multiple resolutions adopted by international organisations, including at the United Nations Human Rights Council and General Assembly level.[36] The United Nations General Assembly proclaimed the 24th of March "the international Day for the Right to the Truth concerning Gross Human Rights Violations and for the Dignity of Victims";[37] the Office of the High Commissioner on Human Rights (OHCHR) has produced studies on the subject;[38] and the UN Working Group on Enforced or Involuntary Disappearances is inherently concerned with the right to the truth.[39] In 2009 the United Nations Security Council in Resolution 1894 makes reference to the need for truth-seeking as part of states' responsibility to comply with obligations "to thoroughly investigate and prosecute persons"[40] following serious violations of international humanitarian law and human rights law. The Security Council also

35 Basic Principles *supra* note 32 Principle 24.

36 These include at UNGA level: Right to the Truth (21 January 2014); Right to the Truth (10 October 2012) UN; Right to the Truth (12 October 2009); Question of Enforced or Involuntary Disappearances (18 December 1990); UNGA, Question of Enforced or Involuntary Disappearances (18 December 1992); UNGA, Disappeared Persons (20 December 1978); and at Human Rights Council level: Right to the Truth: Report of the Office of the High Commissioner for Human Rights (21 August 2009).

37 Resolution adopted by the General Assembly on 21 December 2010 (3 March 2011).

38 Analytical study on human rights and transitional justice (6 August 2009); 2006 Study on the Right to the Truth *supra* note 10 and the Right to the Truth: Report (2009) *supra* note 36.

39 Report on Enforced or Involuntary Disappearances (1981) *supra* note 21 para 187 and Report of the UN Working Group on Enforced and Involuntary Disappearances (10 August 2015).

40 Security Council Resolution 1894 (2009) [On the Protection of Civilians in Armed Conflict] (11 November 2009) para 10; and the call on Burundi to "establish the truth" (Security Council Resolution 1606 (2005) [on the situation in Burundi] (20 June 2005) at para 1).

affirms the need for the truth in the context of seeking sustainable peace, justice and reconciliation.[41]

Regional bodies too recognise the importance of the right to the truth. In response to the conflict in Ukraine and the resulting issue of missing persons, the Parliamentary Assembly of the Council of Europe urged states adopt legislation to safeguard

> the right of families to know what happened to their relatives who remain unaccounted for in connection with armed conflicts and internal violence, in compliance with the relevant provisions of international humanitarian law.[42]

Similarly in 2012 the Parliamentary Assembly welcomed the International Convention for the Protection of all Persons from Enforced Disappearance and in particular the "new rights" it enshrines, namely the right to the truth and asked its members to sign and ratify the treaty.[43] The European Parliament too is concerned with the fate of missing persons, recognising the right of the relatives to know the missing person's fate.[44] The General Assembly of the Organization of American States (OAS) has also endorsed the right to the truth, recognising "the importance of respecting and ensuring the right to the truth so as to contribute to ending impunity and to promoting and protecting human rights",[45] thus explicitly referring to the right as one applicable to gross violations of human rights. The resolution also welcomes judicial and non-judicial mechanisms that will contribute to the investigation of such abuses.[46]

Judgments of international, regional and domestic tribunals

On the basis of international human rights law, non-judicial mechanisms such as truth commissions have had significant impact on the development of the right to the truth. Likewise, in the work of the Human Rights Committee, and the jurisprudence of regional human rights courts, which will be discussed in the following chapters, can be seen the influence of the idea and adoption of its norms. Particularly the Inter-American Commission on Human Rights, as a response to the problem

41 Ibid (Resolution 1894).

42 Parliamentary Assembly of the Council of Europe, Resolution 2067 (25 June 2015) Missing Persons During the Conflict in Ukraine at 7.2.

43 Parliamentary Assembly of the Council of Europe, Resolution 1868 (9 March 2012) The International Convention for the Protection of All Persons From Enforced Disappearance at 6.1.4 and 9.2. See also Parliamentary Assembly of the Council of Europe, Recommendation 1056 (5 May 1987); Resolution 1414 (23 November 2004) para. 3; and Resolution 1463 (3 October 2005) para 10(2).

44 European Parliament, Resolution on Mass Graves of the Missing Person of Ashia in Ornithi Village in the Occupied Part of Cyprus (12 February 2015).

45 Organization of American States, Right to the Truth (4 June 2009) at 1.

46 Ibid.

of enforced disappearances, recognised and emphasised the need of the families of the missing to know the fate or whereabouts of relatives or loved ones in its case law.[47] Whilst the right to the truth does not have express recognition in the Inter-American human rights instruments, the Inter-American Commission on Human Rights (IACH) and the Inter-American Court of Human Rights (IACtHR) have established the substance of the right to the truth and the obligations it creates for states which, in turn, is based on the American Declaration on the Rights and Duties of Man and the American Convention on Human Rights.[48] The Inter-American Commission on Human Rights also recommends that its member states ratify the International Convention for the Protection of All Persons from Enforced Disappearance as well as the Inter-American Convention on Forced Disappearance.[49]

Despite the international legal duties placed on the state, in the case of *Heliodoro Portugal* the IACtHR also recognised that such obligations can derive from domestic laws:

> It is worth noting that the obligation to investigate arises not only from provisions of the international legal conventions that are binding for the States Parties, but also from the domestic laws that refer to the obligation to investigate ex officio certain unlawful conducts and the provisions that allow the victims or their next of kin to denounce or file complaints, in order to participate procedurally in the criminal investigations undertaken to establish the truth about the facts.[50]

Particularly Latin American courts have made reference to the right to the truth[51] and linked the right to constitutional principles such as "human dignity, democratic and social rule of law and the republican way of government",[52] indicating the right's importance in safeguarding as well as constituting governmental activities. When approving the International Convention for the Protection of All Persons from Enforced Disappearance, the Colombian Constitutional Court went so far to suggest that the right to the truth formed part of *jus cogens* norms.[53]

47 *Velásquez Rodriguez v Honduras* (29 July 1988) para 181.
48 The Right to Truth in the Americas *supra* note 10.
49 Ibid para 39(2).
50 *Heliodoro Portugal v Panama* (12 August 2008) para 143.
51 Examples of such domestic legal interpretation of the right to the truth can be found in Colombia, Peru, Argentina, Mexico and El Salvador. See Eduardo Ferrer Mac-Gregor, "The Right to the Truth as an Autonomous Right Under the Inter-American Human Rights System" (2016) IX(1) *Mexican Law Review* 121 footnote 46; International Commission of Jurists (2016) *supra* note 10 at 117–118, and *Genaro Villegas Namuche* (18 March 2004) para 13 (Fundamentos). Translation courtesy of the International Commission of Jurists (2016) *supra* note 10 at 113.
52 Ibid para 15 (Fundamentos).
53 Constitutional Court of Colombia, Review of Constitutionality of Law 1418 of 1 December 2010 (18 August 2011).

Conclusion

From the various needs discussed in the previous chapter, in this chapter we traced the origins of the right to the truth in international law, first with a focus on the transitional justice movements and then from an international humanitarian law and international human rights perspective. Given an interest theory of human rights, we can say there is a background moral right to the truth which has been given institutional recognition through the agency of the UN and other bodies. From these codifications, declarations and statements of the underlying norm, in the following chapter we offer an analysis of the content of the right to the truth.

References

Arthur P, 'How "Transitions" Reshaped Human Rights: A Conceptual History of Transitional Justice' (2009) 31 Human Rights Quarterly 321.

Bickford L, 'Transitional Justice' in Shelton D (ed), *The Encyclopaedia of Genocide and Crimes Against Humanity* (Macmillan Library Reference 2004).

Ferrer Mac-Gregor E, 'The Right to the Truth as an autonomous right under the Inter-American Human Rights System' (2016) IX(1) Mexican Law Review 121.

Henckaerts J-M and Doswald-Beck L, *Customary International Humanitarian Law, Volume I: Rules* (Cambridge University Press 2006).

International Commission of Jurists, 'Enforced Disappearance and Extrajudicial Execution: The Right of Family Members' (Practitioners' Guide No. 10 July 2016).

Méndez J and Bariffi F, 'Truth, Right to, International Protection' (2011) Max Planck Encyclopedia of Public International Law (online).

Moon C, 'Interpreters of the dead: forensic knowledge, human remains and the politics of the past' (2013) 22(2) *Social and Legal Studies* 149.

Naftali P, 'Crafting a "Right to truth" in International Law: Converging Mobilizations, Diverging Agendas?' (2016) XIII Champ penal/Penal field 1.

Park G Y, 'Truth as Justice. Legal and Extralegal Development of the Right to Truth' (2010) February 1, Harvard International Review 24.

Pilloud C and others, *Commentary on the additional protocols of 8 June 1977 to the Geneva Conventions of 12 August 1949* (Martinus Nijhoff 1987).

Teitel R, 'Transitional Justice Genealogy' (2013) 16 Harvard Human Rights Journal 69.

van Bowen T, 'The United Nations Basic Principles and Guidelines on the Right to a Remedy and Reparations for Victims of Gross Violations of International Human Rights Law and Serious Violations of International Law' (2010) (United Nations Audiovisual Library of International Law) http://legal.un.org/avl/pdf/ha/ga_60-147/ga_60-147_e.pdf accessed 14 February 2019.

3 Content of the right to the truth

Introduction

The previous chapters have suggested that the needs of victims of gross violations of human rights include needs involving knowledge of what happened and why and who was responsible. Based on an interest theory of human rights, the right to the truth has received some institutional recognition. In this chapter we move on to the discussion of the structure and content of the right, followed by an appraisal of "other rights" that may be associated with or bear resemblance to the right to the truth, and we discuss the case for understanding the right to the truth as being freestanding and of value, which is independent of the value of other rights.

In its persuasive institutional form, the background right presupposes the existence of gross/massive or systematic human rights abuses.[1] In that context victims should be able to seek and obtain information relating to the consequences, reasons for and circumstances of his or her victimisation. Likewise, as discussed in the next chapter, there is also an inchoate claim vested in society – an entitlement of society to know of and come to terms with its history. At the core of the claimed right is a correlating duty requiring positive (i.e. not needing to be initiated by a victim) actions leading to continued and systematic efforts to investigate the abuses by gathering the evidence in an attempt to answer questions about what happened, why it happened, identifying those responsible, directly and indirectly[2] and exposing any patterns of abuse. In the words of the Inter-American Court of Human Rights (IACtHR):

> [t]his right to the truth requires a procedural determination of the most complete historical truth possible, including the determination of patterns of collective action and of all those who, in different ways, took part in the said violations, as well as their corresponding responsibilities.[3]

1 The commentary on the principle to combat impunity suggests that "massive or systematic violations" reflects current international law (Report of the Independent Expert to Update the Set of Principles to Combat Impunity (18 February 2005) (hereinafter Updated Principles on Impunity), para 20).

2 Juan Méndez and Francisco Bariffi, 'Truth, Right to, International Protection' (2011) Max Planck Encyclopedia of Public International Law (online).

3 *Valle Jaramillo et al. v Colombia* (27 November 2008) para 102.

The grounding of the right to the truth

The (usually silent) assumption that this is a right of victims in relation to which others have duties can be justified by standard jurisprudential arguments about rights (which cannot be pursued in this book) which are likely to provide good grounds for a victim's right to know what happened. As indicated in Chapters 1 and 2, empirical evidence and self-reflection both explain the idea that victims and their close relatives have a strong desire (or "need") to know the truth of what happened and who was directly and indirectly responsible. This applies at least to the specific detail of the direct events and, also, to the wider explanatory context. Given the seriousness of the events, it is convincing to conceptualise this desire as a human right. In the light of the principal general theories of human rights, it seems clear that victims can be said to have a strong interest in this knowledge,[4] that its possession is likely to be necessary for their autonomy and dignity[5] and is a condition necessary for their capacity to flourish and lead a fruitful life;[6] and any of these reasons can be the ground of a right as an "individuated political aim".[7]

The necessary stage in an argument seeking to justify a human right – that someone, or all of us, have a correlating duty to secure the right – can be made out in respect of the state. The obvious reasons are, first, that it is fair to put the duty on the state. Ideally, liberal and cosmopolitan theories of the state give sovereign states the overriding duty of indifferent protection of the population, and the kinds of outrages to which the right to the truth relates clearly involve significant state failure which should be remedied by the responsible regime but also by successors. Second, the state, enjoying the monopoly of legitimate coercive power, has the powers and resources available to it, and in some respects it alone, to undertake the necessary investigations; it is also subject to doctrines of care and responsibility (e.g. care with evidence or protection of witnesses) that are not applicable as enforceable obligations to others. Others, NGOs in particular, may be, like all of us, morally obliged in this matter. Investigations and reports by organisations such as Human Rights Watch may be vital and well conducted; importantly NGOs are conforming to the duty but they are not legally obliged by it.

Given the foregoing, we can say that the right to the truth is a morally grounded individual right. But its grounding may also have a more "political" basis. For instance, in most cases refusing to disclose the truth to suffering victims and relatives is likely to be contrary to moral values that can be claimed to be universal,

4 For the interest theory of human rights, see Rowan Cruft, Matthew Liao and Massimo Renzo (eds), *Philosophical Foundations of Human Rights* (Oxford University Press 2015).

5 Human rights grounded on "dignity" as a reflection of practical autonomy are explored, for example, in James Griffin, *On Human Rights* (Oxford University Press 2008).

6 Rights derived from the conditions of human flourishing are explored, for instance, in John Finnis, *Natural Law and Natural Rights* (Clarendon Press 1980).

7 Ronald Dworkin, *Taking Rights Seriously* (Duckworth 1977) at 91.

not culturally or socially specific.[8] This second "political" basis of the right to the truth lies in political theory in the sense of the theoretical exploration of the conditions for legitimate government. On this view a right to the truth, found in positive law, would follow from the requirements of a just and democratic (a "well-ordered") society. This is the idea of a society based upon fair terms of cooperation on which all can agree, even though they hold very different social, religious or other beliefs or political opinions. The idea is that in such a society all persons are to be treated as equals. It would not be eccentric to suggest that people who live under the burden of not knowing what has happened to their relatives and who experience the inactivity of the state and its institutions are socially paralysed, subordinated and not treated as equals.[9] As we shall see, particularly in direct relation to the public aspect of the right to the truth, some background idea of the nature and duties of a democratic society informs the legal judgments which, expressly or by implication, give effect to the norms of the right to the truth.

The suggestion is, therefore, that the right to the truth can be shown[10] to have a strong basis in the theory of individual rights. It can also be justified by broader arguments building on universal moral values and also on political theory and the idea of the grounds of political legitimacy. Both of these broader arguments can be made on grounds of their own. The latter argument is particularly relevant in relation to the public aspect of the right to the truth, discussed in the next chapter. But it also necessarily underlies, usually unarticulated, the justification for laying on states the primary duty of satisfying the right to the truth.

Legal status – *lex ferenda* or *lex lata?*

Chapter 2 and the previous section suggest that there is a set of norms relating to "knowing what happened" which has been given non-judicial institutional recognition by, in particular, various institutions of the UN. The aim and authority of these articulations of the right is to lay down legal standards and to make a case to persuade and assist nation states and other bodies, including courts, in responding to atrocities and, consequently, it also has a judicial-institutional

8 Though, see section 'The Truth – But Not at All Cost' in Chapter 1 for morally grounded exceptions.

9 Under a liberal theory such as Rawls's, at the constitutional stage the possibility of being a victim of crime and atrocity might penetrate the veil of ignorance and thereby justify a duty to investigate and prosecute. See also Pablo De Greiff, 'Truth Telling and the Rule of Law' in Borer T A (ed) *Telling the Truth: Truth-Telling and Peace Building in Post-Conflict Societies* (Notre Dame University Press 2006), who links telling and accepting the truth on past abuses to the notion of civic trust and the values of a well-ordered (Rawlsian) society.

10 The preceding paragraph has merely indicated the arguments rather than made them in depth and substance. If anything, given the nature of the suffering, the burden of proof should be on those who would deny what others might think is obvious.

presence.[11] These norms have also been given some degree of judicial recognition in (to give the primary instance) the case reports of the Inter-American Commission on Human Rights, form part of the content of the cases presented to the Inter-American Court of Human Rights (IACtHR) and emerge as part of the reasoning of the Court in particular cases. Judicially, these articulations of the norms of the right to the truth are at least of persuasive authority in the sense that they are taken into account and followed by a court in its authoritative adjudications; indeed, not to take them into account would be a failure of judicial reasoning. These norms may also influence other judicial bodies, such as the prosecutor of the International Criminal Court in the way she exercises her discretion or the judges of the Court in the way they exercise their power to seek the truth.[12] But such statements remain of persuasive authority only – they must be considered, the point must be answered, but they are not rules of law that must be applied by a court in deciding cases.

The question is whether the foregoing, which is "at least" true, understates the properly understood status of the right to the truth in international law. Has it developed from soft, merely persuasive law to become a formal source of international law binding on relevant institutions and more than just persuasive authority?[13] There are only two instances of treaty provisions which express norms inherent in the right,[14] and these, of course, are limited to their own spheres of effect. In formal terms, therefore, the question is whether the right to the truth has now become a rule of customary international law or a general principle of international law?

The right to the truth clearly has a heritage in universal human needs and, consequently, the idea of a right is normatively convincing. Yet it may still lack legal clarity in content, contour and pathway to realisation. In her 2006 study, Yasmin Naqvi called it "on the threshold of a legal norm and a narrative device".[15] By 2015, Szoke-Burke felt able to state that, through building on jurisprudence and commentary from the last decade, "the right to truth, often viewed as soft (*lex ferenda*) obligation, has now crystallized into a legally binding (*lex lata*) norm".[16] This view was echoed a year later by Judge Ferrer Mac-Gregor, who,

11 This is a broad-brush distinction that does not depend on a hard distinction between judicial and non-judicial institutions. But any decision which directly affects a person's rights or legitimate expectations of her state would count as judicial in this context.

12 Discussed in Chapters 9 and 10.

13 Alice Panepinto, 'The right to the truth in international law: The significance of Strasbourg's contributions' (2017) 37 *Legal Studies* 739, who sees the right to the truth as in an "upward trajectory in international law" (at 739).

14 Article 24(2) of the International Convention for the Protection for All Persons from Enforced Disappearance (12 January 2007) and Article 7(2)(i) of the Rome Statute in defining the crime of enforced disappearance, i.e. the non-provision of information forms part of the crime (Rome Statute of the International Criminal Court (17 July 1998)).

15 Yasmin Naqvi, 'The right to the truth in international law: fact or fiction?' (2006) 88(862) International Review of the Red Cross 245.

16 Sam Szoke-Burke, 'Searching for the Right to Truth: The Impact of International Human Rights Law on National Transitional Justice Policies' (2015) 33(2) Berkeley Journal of International Law 526 at 528.

at least in the Inter-American Human Rights system, believes the right to the truth to be "recognized as an autonomous and independent right".[17] His view finds backing by the International Commission of Jurists in their analysis of jurisprudence regionally and domestically.[18] In its 2006 "Study on the Right to the Truth", the Office of the UN High Commissioner for Human Rights concluded that

> [t]he right to the truth about gross human rights violations and serious violations of humanitarian law is an inalienable right, recognized in several international treaties and instruments as well as by national, regional and international jurisprudence and numerous resolutions of intergovernmental bodies at the universal and regional levels.[19]

The study does not make a finding on the customary international status of the right, nonetheless it offers much evidence that would qualify as material sources for the right to the truth to have this status.

The implication of these views is that the right to the truth is of more than persuasive force and could be the ground of a direct right of action in international courts and domestic courts insofar as they are bound by treaty or customary international law. The absence of express treaty provisions then becomes merely a matter of form. Human rights treaties provide (by implication from substantive rights or through the right to a legal remedy) for the legal protection of human rights and consequently, if the right to the truth is *lex lata*, reading and applying treaty provisions in ways which give effect to the right to the truth is a judicial duty.

In one instance it is probable that an application of the right to the truth has crystallised into a rule of customary international law. The International Committee of the Red Cross (ICRC) study on international humanitarian law, in Rule 177, imposes, as a core minimum, a duty on state and non-state actors alike to "take all feasible measures to account for persons missing as a result of armed conflict and must provide their family members with any information it has on their fate". This core idea, albeit limited to missing persons resulting from armed conflict, has been traced back to the 1974 Additional Protocol to the Geneva Conventions and, according to the ICRC study, has since crystallised into customary international humanitarian law.[20]

17 Eduardo Ferrer Mac-Gregor, 'The Right to the Truth as an autonomous right under the Inter-American Human Rights System' (2016) IX(1) Mexican Law Review 121 at 121.

18 Commission of Jurists, 'Enforced Disappearance and Extrajudicial Execution: The Right of Family Members' (Practitioners' Guide No. 10, July 2016) at 113–134.

19 Promotion and Protection of Human Rights. Study on the Right to the Truth (8 February 2006) at 14 (hereinafter 2006 Study on the Right to the Truth).

20 Jean-Marie Henckaerts and Louise Doswald-Beck, *Customary International Humanitarian Law, Volume I: Rules* (Cambridge University Press 2006) at 421.

This is not the place to explore the general grounds for determining that a norm is a rule of customary international law. In summary, there needs to be "evidence of a general practice accepted in law".[21]

Evidence of "practice" can include

> international and national judicial decisions, recitals in treaties and other international instruments (especially when in "all states" form), and extensive pattern of treaties in the same terms, the practice of international organs, and resolutions relating to legal questions in UN organs, notably the General Assembly.[22]

These sources are then tested against three criteria: the duration and consistency of practice, the generality of practice and whether it is accepted as law (*opinio juris sive necessitates*).[23]

It is clear that it is possible to point to a relatively wide-ranging practice with elements of duration and consistency. Navqi (for whom the right to the truth is "approaching"[24] being a rule of customary international law) and Szoke-Burke[25] both point to the range of human rights jurisprudence, truth commissions, UN General Assembly and Security Council decisions and so on – the kinds of matter outlined in Chapter 2 – as evidence of the legal status of the right to the truth. They are also both aware of national divergences from a strict duty to disclose, such as in terms of policy towards amnesties or the weight given to national security arguments against disclosure; but the test for customary international law does not require absolute unanimity of state practice and, in any case, the tendency is to reduce the scope of legitimate amnesty and increase scepticism concerning the credibility of the national security argument. Though there is this evidence of state practice, the prevailing difficulty on allocating the right to the truth clearly to customary international law is the degree to which this practice is accepted as "law". Panepinto,[26] citing the same kinds of material as Navqi and Szoke-Burke and in Chapter 2, but focusing on some recent jurisprudence of the European Court of Human Rights (discussed in Chapter 7), suggests that the human rights jurisprudence is "undertheorised" in terms of its contribution to customary international law, to practice and acceptance as law. As such, "qualifying the right to the truth as customary international law would be imprecise". Panepinto is similarly, and for the same reason, cautious about a claim that the right to the truth has the formal character of a general principle

21 Article 38(1)(b) of the International Court of Justice's Statute (Statute of the Court of Justice (26 June 1945)).
22 See James Crawford, *Brownlie's Principles of Public International Law* (8th edn Oxford University Press 2012) at 24 for a more extensive list.
23 Ibid.
24 Naqvi *supra* note 15 at 267.
25 Szoke-Burke *supra* note 16 at 539–545.
26 Panepinto *supra* note 13 at 757–761.

of law.[27] Panepinto's conclusion, however, is that the reiterations of the right to the truth in many different contexts, whilst not meeting the formal criteria of customary international law or of a general principle, nevertheless indicate its importance in practice: that it is used in various contexts (in particular human rights courts) to deliver practical ends – victims' and a society's knowledge of "what happened" in the context of the suffering attendant on gross violations of human rights.[28]

If we assume that the right to the truth, as an idea with a specific content (see below), has not yet fulfilled the formal criteria of either a rule of customary international law or of a general principle of international law, its reiterations in various contexts and fora are not without significance. In practical terms, the idea is clearly of persuasive value. By this is meant that, in the absence of clear words to the contrary (in a treaty, for example) and as limited, directed, or refined by context (the needs of criminal prosecutions which must be fair and may have to be selective, for example), judicial bodies have recognised the importance of giving effect to all or some of the norms encapsulated in the idea of the right to the truth in the way they interpret their powers and duties. They read and apply treaty provisions in ways which give effect to the main incidents of the right.

The question this gives rise to, and which is pursued in the chapters that follow, is whether anything is lost by not enforcing the core of the right to the truth directly, as a right in itself (an independent right as we discuss later in our separation argument) or whether the full benefit of the right, for victims and for society, is sufficiently achieved through the way treaty provisions are interpreted and applied.

The content of the right

Institutional expression of the right to the truth includes legal contexts and the right now has sufficient normative force that, if not a binding rule of customary international law, it does seem to be accepted in some contexts (especially the IACtHR) as a "general principle of law", meaning by this that it is a source of law which has, at least, persuasive authority and may complement the way a treaty provision is given effect by guiding a court's interpretation thereof and affect the way in which a treaty rule is applied.[29] The next question, therefore, is to consider what the content of the right is to be, and from this the effectiveness of any legal provision can be considered.

27 Navqi suggested that the status of the right to the truth as a general principle of law is, based on national and international practice, "arguable" (Naqvi *supra* note 15 at 268).

28 Panepinto *supra* note 13 uses the concept of "performativity" (derived from J L Austin) to indicate a concept that is neither true nor false but which, through its various utterances, has practical impact.

29 Giorgio Gaja 'General Principles of Law' (2013) Max Planck Encyclopedia of Public International Law (online) section E.

Méndez in 1998,[30] reiterated by Méndez and Bariffi,[31] has suggested that a three-tiered approach captures the content of the right (at least as understood in 2011).[32] This entails the need of both victims' and society for (1) structural truth, (2) individualised truth and (3) victim involvement. The essence of the right to the truth can be grasped by expanding on each of these, and this again provides a basis for critical examination of the implementation of the norms of the right to the truth in various fora.

Structural truth

Structural truth obliges the state to ascertain the political and administrative structure that allowed for the abuse to take place. This includes establishing the chain of command, what orders were given by whom, what infrastructure was used to operationalise the widespread and systematic abuse and the mechanisms that were consciously and deliberately employed to guarantee secrecy of the operations and impunity for the operators. Therefore, in a first step, structural clarity on the system of the repressive regime is needed.

This focus on political and administrative structures needs adaptation to take into account the role of non-state actors. In the past, transitional justice efforts have been concerned with repressive regimes, and, following a regime change, investigations into the former regimes' abuses. Today's conflicts, however, are increasingly shaped by non-state actors with states either unable to prevent non-state actors from committing gross human rights abuses or allowing them to engage in such human rights violations. The United Nations, in the Basic Principles on remedies and reparations, allocates some responsibility with the non-state abusers. The last sentence of Principle 15 states that "where a person, a legal person, or other entity is found liable for reparation for a victim, such party should provide reparation to the victim or compensate the State if the State has already provided reparation to the victim".[33] According to Principle 3(c), equal and effective access to justice must be given "irrespective of who may ultimately be the bearer of responsibility for the violation". Whether that includes, *sensu stricto*, the right to access information is not expressly made clear in the Basic Principles, but as outlined in Principle 15, it seems to apply to reparations (which can include a duty to investigate). Van Boven's commentary on the Basic Principles explains that

> [i]t was generally felt that non-State actors are to be held responsible for their policies and practices, allowing victims to seek redress and reparation

30 Juan Méndez 'The Right to Truth' in Joyner C C (ed), *Reining in Impunity for International Crimes and Serious Violations of Fundamental Human Rights: Proceedings of the Siracusa Conference* (Erès Toulouse 1998) 255.

31 Méndez and Bariffi *supra* note 2 para 6 which adopts Méndez's text.

32 Méndez and Bariffi was last updated in 2011.

33 Basic Principles and Guidelines on the Right to a Remedy and Reparation for Victims of Gross Violations of International Human Rights Law and Serious Violations of International Humanitarian Law (21 March 2006) (hereinafter Basic Principles).

> on the basis of legal liability and human solidarity, and not on the basis of State responsibility.[34]

This is interesting, since for non-state actors to be involved in mass atrocities still presupposes state failure,[35] but the point to note here is that non-state actors could be required to compensate the state for any compensation paid by the state to victims. In that sense, not only the state but also non-state actors are bound by the moral obligation to work towards truth insofar as it is a precondition to justice and reparations.

Other sources too point to non-state actor liability. The Rome Statute, in its definition of enforced disappearances, identifies a "political organization" as distinct from the state and a potential perpetrator of the crime:

> the arrest, detention or abduction of persons by, or with the authorization, support or acquiescence of, a State or a political organization, followed by a refusal to acknowledge that deprivation of freedom or to give information on the fate or whereabouts of those persons, with the intention of removing them from the protection of the law for a prolonged period of time.[36]

On the other hand, however, the Convention on Enforced Disappearances only defines enforced disappearances in relation to states (through agents of the state or persons acting with the support of acquiescence of the state).[37] Therefore the Convention, and with it the right to the truth contained therein, is seemingly not applicable to non-state actors pointing to a discrepancy in codification with potential ramifications in terms of who is bound by the right to the truth.

Furthermore, the collapse of a regime (which may be caused by non-state actors) may mean that the state is unable effectively to implement this first structure-orientated step of inquiry. In that circumstance, the task of structural scrutiny can also be taken up by the international community through interventions, fact-finding missions and post-conflict stabilisation[38] efforts, and in conjunction with the successor regime to ensure this first level of structural truth-seeking is ensured.[39] The Human Rights Council's establishment of Special Procedures or

34 Theo van Bowen, 'The United Nations Basic Principles and Guidelines on the Right to a Remedy and Reparations for Victims of Gross Violations of International Human Rights Law and Serious Violations of International Law' (2010) (United Nations Audiovisual Library of International Law) http://legal.un.org/avl/pdf/ha/ga_60-147/ga_60-147_e.pdf accessed 14 February 2019.

35 The "positive duties" doctrine in the human rights context does require proper state protection against non-state actors.

36 Rome Statute *supra* note 14 Article 7(2)(i) (emphasis added).

37 Convention on Enforced Disappearance *supra* note 14 Article 2.

38 Outside its Human rights focused activities, the United Nation works in peace-keeping and peace-making which are relevant to transitional justice in general and the right to the truth implicitly.

39 This can include fact-finding missions established by international organisations.

commissions of inquiry, as have been established for Libya, Côte d'Ivoire or Syria in recent years, exemplifies these possibilities of a first step towards accountability. A difficulty, as pointed out in an NGO report, is that there may be little political will to implement recommendations for further transitional justice efforts, and many examples of inaction on behalf of the Council can also be cited.[40]

Uncovering and understanding the structural elements that led to the commission of systematic or mass human rights violations is likely to be a precondition for the other truth-seeking elements. The structural level of truth-seeking also responds to some of the truth-seeking needs identified in the previous chapter. Not only does it implicitly acknowledge that there may have been human rights violations, but it also recognises the need for transparency as to the structures permitting the abuse to take place. The right to the truth, therefore, emphasises that individuals and the public are entitled to access to information, to the fullest extent practicable, concerning the decision-making and structural processes of a government.[41] This information in turn can be useful to generate social awareness, information for historical purposes and understanding to shape future policy, and it can form the basis for condemnation and/or apology by the successor regime. Public benefit can be achieved through access to this information, which may be crucial to the development of democratic systems.[42] However, this structural approach, which may reveal controversial or politically sensitive information and with it spark controversy or division, should not detract from the need for investigations into the individual abuses.

Individual truth

The second-level approach can be described as the need for individual truth, or as Méndez and Bariffi suggest, "individualized truth".[43] This obligation is owed by the state (and society) to the victims of the human rights violations. It consists in investigating the fate of each known victim including information concerning the particular circumstances in which the violation took place, the facts of the violations themselves and, in the event of death or enforced disappearance, the fate and whereabouts of the victim. The right, as codified in the Convention for Enforced Disappearances, also encompasses knowledge as to the progress and results of the state investigation into the matter, together with the identity of the perpetrators.[44] Knowing the identity of the perpetrators is also identified by the Study on the Right to the Truth as an element of the content of the right.[45] This,

40 International Centre for Transitional Justice, 'Transitional Justice in the United Nations Human Rights Council' (Policy briefing June 2011) at 5, lamenting inaction in relation to Sri Lanka, Afghanistan, Zimbabwe, China, Chechnya, Bahrain and Yemen.

41 Resolution 68/165 Right to the truth (21 January 2014).

42 *Parada Ce, et al. v El Salvador Case 10.480* (27 January 1999) para 151.

43 Méndez and Bariffi, *supra* note 2 para 6.

44 See investigative obligations arising from the Convention on Enforced Disappearance *supra* note 14 Articles 9–14.

45 2006 Study on the Right to the Truth *supra* note 19 para 60.

of course, raises issues for criminal justice. First, the level of perpetrator differs. There are those bearing the greatest responsibility for the structures and policies leading to the abuse and those executing policies by targeting specific individuals and committing the actual abuse. Second, the presumption of innocence and due process, fair trial and guarantees may be harder to protect if potential perpetrators are named in extrajudicial fora such as a truth commission.[46]

So long as uncertainty about the fate and whereabouts of the victim persists, the obligations remain valid. In fact, the obligation is to investigate, at the state's own initiative, gross human rights violations.[47] In addition to the state, this individual truth can be sought via judicial and non-judicial mechanisms, including criminal or civil proceedings before domestic and international adjudicatory bodies and human rights cases but also via truth and reconciliation commissions.

Narrative truth

By the third level of investigation, victims are given the opportunity by the state or representative body to be heard – to tell their own stories. Within the repressive regime, victims and their families most likely were not able to receive information from the authorities, instead suffering intimidation or threats. After the event, the inclusion of an opportunity to be heard within the ambit of the right to the truth positions survivors in a contributing role in the achievement of both structural and individualised truth. It also provides society (itself a beneficiary of the right to the truth), which may have diminished trust in the ability of the state to provide accurate and reliable information about the abuses, with an alternative source of information. The South African Truth and Reconciliation Commission operated with the label "narrative truth", which was believed to have benefits to the individual, as opposed to society as a receiver of truth.[48] Information from Truth Commission reports have been used as a source of evidence within the Inter-American Commission and Court.[49]

Survivor truth-telling, as we will discuss in the chapters on criminal prosecutions, may not always live up to the expectation of judicial fact-finding and can be adversely affected by (continuing) psychological trauma, which in turn can negatively impact the ability of the individual to recall their experiences and to construct and articulate a clear, coherent account of events.[50]

46 We return to this issue in the chapter on Truth Commissions.

47 Organization of American States, The Right to Truth in the Americas (13 August 2014).

48 E.g. Stephen Ellis, 'Truth and Reconciliation Commission of South Africa Report, Volumes 1–5. Pretoria: Government Printer, October 1998' (2000) 42 Transformation 61.

49 The Right to truth in the Americas *supra* note 47.

50 Nancy Armour Combs, *Fact-finding Without Facts. The Uncertain Evidentiary Foundations of International Criminal Convictions* (Cambridge University Press 2010) 14–20.

Archives

As a means to structural and individualised truth and to conserve narrative truth, the scope of the right to the truth extends to an obligation on states to establish archives. States

> should preserve archives and other evidence concerning gross human rights and serious violations of international humanitarian law to facilitate knowledge of such violations, the investigation of allegations and the provision for victims of access to an effective remedy in accordance with international law.[51]

Truth-seeking and with it the truth-telling process themselves create important records, as acknowledged in the Report of the Office of the High Commissioner for Human Rights, stating that "[t]he records of a transitional justice institution are a concentrated, rich source of information for the history of the country and its people and must be preserved and made available to future users".[52] Revealing the truth by those who have suffered can therefore be identified as a constitutive element of realising the right to truth as part of judicial and non-judicial processes.

Whilst the first two aspects, repressive structures and the individualised truth, already address the significant needs outlined in the first chapter of this book, truth-telling reveals the potential to go beyond the immediately identified needs and acknowledges the importance of bearing witness. To the extent that such truth-telling, or narrative truth, falls within the remit of the right to the truth, the state may be required to find avenues other than through truth commissions or judicial fora to facilitate this truth-telling. The establishment of a specific victims' forum or an oral histories public documentation and archiving mechanism might achieve this too.

Obligation of means or ends?

Legal recognition of the right to the truth is, by implication and sometimes expressly, an obligation of means rather than results.[53] From the Geneva Convention onwards, the obligation on states is expressed as being to search, to investigate, to report rather than supply. This is made expressly and consistently clear by judicial reiterations of the duty to investigate by the IACtHR and the ECtHR.[54] The same is not always true of non-judicial statements of the right: the UN

51 Right to the truth (21 January 2014). See also Dermot Groome, 'The Right to Truth in the Fight Against Impunity' (2011) 29(1) Berkeley Journal of International Law 181.

52 Right to the truth: Report of the Office of the High Commissioner for Human Rights (21 August 2009) para 7. The same report also discusses the need to protect witnesses providing evidence during trials (ibid).

53 Méndez and Bariffi *supra* note 2 para 7.

54 Discussed in detail in chapters 6 and 7.

Commission on Human Rights "Study on the Right to the Truth",[55] in summarising the content of the right, refers to an entitlement to "seek and obtain" information. Being an obligation of means is not understood as detracting from the states' obligations to investigate in good faith, but is best understood as recognising the natural, practical and logical limits to an investigation and that, for instance, "it is not inconceivable that certain aspects of the truth may be lost forever".[56]

It is not clear that much turns on this. The state remains under a duty to ensure that an investigation is effective and undertaken in good faith motivated by a desire to get at the truth. This duty, as discussed in later chapters on human rights, truth commissions and international criminal law, arises in fulfilment of various treaty rights, such as the right to life or the right to a judicial remedy for human rights violations. It is possible that the burden of the right to the truth, as having its own significance as, at least, a general principle of law guiding the understanding and application of treaty rights, may have a strengthening effect on judicial resistance to claims that an investigation seeking structural or individualised truth should be limited by resources, national security, political consequences and so on. This raises the question of what, if anything, the right to the truth brings over and above the investigative and other duties derived from treaty rights. Even where a trajectory towards the right to the truth becoming an obligation of results is claimed, the point remains one of emphasis and seriousness – that an investigation must be exhaustive, motivated by discovering the truth and requiring the full cooperation of state institutions.[57]

Indeed, the extent of the state's obligation remains unclear. The Inter-American Court refers to "the means at its disposal",[58] although the European Court simply lays down the duty to secure the evidence with all steps available to them; the "Study on the Right to the Truth" focuses on the right rather than the duty. The extent to which there is or ought to be a reasonableness test, related to the political and social context and to the resources available, is not a prominent issue in terms of the articulation of the right to the truth. Any such concern is displaced by, as mentioned earlier, the need to resist state excuses. Perhaps the best that can be said is that "must" implies "can", and the duty of an effective investigation is to do what the state can be properly expected to do with the focus on the reasons the state has for failures in achieving the anticipated result.

The duty over time

A state's duty to investigate in the context of gross violations appears as a continuing duty binding not just on the state responsible at the time but also on

55 2006 Study on the Right to the Truth *supra* note 19 para 38.

56 Méndez and Bariffi, *supra* note 2 para 7.

57 *Cifuentes Elgueta v Chile* (28th July 2009), dissenting opinion of H Keller and F Salvioli paras 26–27.

58 *Velásquez Rodriguez v Honduras* (29 July 1988) para 181 (repeating *Ellacuría et al v El Salvador Case 10.488* (22 December 1999)).

successor regimes. This matter raises what can be complex legal issues of identifying not only how and therefore when the duty has been discharged as a matter of law, but also of the moment when a state accepts legal responsibility for past events, and how far back that responsibility may stretch. The latter issue, in particular, can create tension between the positive legal rules governing the assumption of responsibility, the moral imperative to find the truth and the extent to which that moral imperative should drive the development of the law.[59] The issue mainly arises in the context of human rights law and is discussed further in those chapters.

Authority

The obligation is to disclose the truth of what happened but, of course, the truth and its desirability can be controversial.

We have seen[60] that statements of structural truth may be controversial and vary according to the standpoint and ideology of different sides in a war or socio-political crisis, and it follows that participants from either side may believe themselves to have reasons to reject accounts which do not confirm their prejudgments. Reactions to the Radovan Karadžić judgment issued by the International Criminal Tribunal for the Former Yugoslavia amply portrayed the ethnic divisions, with Bosniaks having their perceptions of Karadžić as the guilty genocidal mastermind confirmed, whilst some Bosnian Serbs continue to celebrate him as a national hero.[61] We have also seen that there is a range of political, personal, cultural and religious reasons why disclosures of the truth, structural or individual, may be undesired.

The right to the truth, in contrast, presupposes the real possibility of a disclosure of the truth which is authoritative even if controversial in some eyes, and even if produced despite the desires of some involved. A disclosure can be said to be authoritative, it is suggested, not necessarily because it is accepted but because it results from a process that is fair, impartial, done in good faith and aiming at the truth. To stand for the right to the truth is to presume and to accept that there can be, in Hannah Arendt's words, "public institutions, established and supported by the powers that be, in which, contrary to all political rules, truth and truthfulness have always constituted the highest criterion of speech and endeavour".[62] Arendt's examples include the judiciary and the academy. In terms of the right to the truth, it is clear that the various national and international

59 See the grounds of dissent by Keller et al in *Cifuentes Elgueta supra* note *57*.
60 E.g. in Chapter 1 in the context of concentration camps and above in the section on structural truth.
61 For example, Refik 'Post-Karadzic Bosnia and Herzegovina: The End of the Criminal Justice Era' (4 November 2016) www.ictj.org/news/karadzic-bosnia-herzegovina-criminal-justice#.VwvL_wtXbgc.twitter, (accessed 14 February 2019).
62 Hannah Arendt, 'Truth and politics' *The New Yorker*, 25 February 1967, https://idanlandau.files.wordpress.com/2014/12/arendt-truth-and-politics.pdf, (accessed 14 February 2019) at 310.

commissions and investigative bodies which, along with courts, discover and disclose the structural and individual truths must also meet, mutatis mutandis, the judicial standard as being outside the political perversions of truth that it is Arendt's main purpose to describe. The point is that acceptance of the idea and possibility of such impartiality and of its practical (no doubt imperfect) expression in various human institutions is a necessary feature of the right to the truth. The right to the truth "takes seriously" ideas of impartiality, neutrality, fairness as having procedural aspects and requirements through which the truth emerges. Proper judicial process, inherent in the rule of law, is also adversarial, open and public (features which, as discussed in the next chapter, also indicate the public aspect of the right to the truth).

The truth is that which emerges through those procedures, conducted in good faith; open in some ultimate sense to the possibility of error with procedures to correct.

In what sense a right?

The suffering of individuals, we suggest, provides the grounding for a right on the basis of conventional theories of human rights; in particular, suffering creates an interest of sufficient weight to justify imposing a duty on others, particularly the state.

But, having said this, there are conceptual grounds for distinguishing the right to the truth from what might be called a right in *sensu stricto* by which S, the subject of the right (here a victim) can control the actions of D, the duty holder (here the state) in respect of some matter or ground G (here the response to atrocity).[63] The right is justified as an expression of S's autonomy and it is S's ability to control D's actions, D's loss of freedom in respect of G, being subject to S's will, that is essential to the characterising of a right. But this concept of a right fails to grasp the extent and nature of what is involved with the right to the truth. Significantly, the state's duty is independent of the victim's will. The state must investigate whether or not the victim so wishes; it must investigate in a way, to an extent, and to a standard, which victims may influence but do not ultimately determine (and which could even be against the victim's interests or wishes and something they might wish to stop). In criminal cases it is essential that, notwithstanding victims' influence, decisions on investigation and resulting prosecution are taken independently by the prosecutor's office.[64] The state must investigate not only to disclose to the victims but also to serve other purposes, such as the identification and prosecution of alleged perpetrators.

Furthermore there is, as discussed in the next chapter, a public aspect to the right to the truth by which the state, as a condition of its legitimacy, must investigate atrocities and promulgate the results in order to assist a divided society to

63 E.g. Alan Gerwith, 'Are there any Absolute Rights' in Waldron J (ed) *Theories of Rights* (Oxford University Press 1984) at 93.

64 This will be discussed in relation to the International Criminal Court. See also *supra* Chapter 1 for some reasons why victims may not want an investigation.

come to terms with its past and establish political equality between its members. The public aspect of the right to the truth is difficult to conceive of in conventional rights terms. Who is the subject of the right; who can represent the public, the society, in order to enforce the duty? The public aspect, at least, is perhaps best described in terms of duties required of legitimate states which are enforced by the courts as manifestations of the idea of a legitimate, just (usually called "democratic") state taken to be inherent in the principles of law underlying the positive treaty law they are enforcing.

These points give reasons for justifying the duty to investigate independently of claims about victims' rights (though not to contradict those rights). That is to say, the right correlates with duties on states which are independently justified and therefore may not fully fit the classic conceptualisation of a right in terms of "subject, duty and ground". We therefore explore whether the right to the truth can be independently derived and not solely based on a duty correlating to the victim's right, which in turn would strengthen and justify the public element of the right to truth.

The status of the right to the truth as a "right" in *sensu stricto* also raises the question whether victims should have the option and opportunity to stop or prevent such an investigation. Disclosure of the truth may be controversial, may be thought to serve one political interest rather than another, may be emotionally painful or may show a victim to be compromised in some way. It is possible to imagine that individual contributions made to a wider inquiry by virtue of truth-telling or providing information could be redacted from an official public account of events, though perhaps not from statistics pertaining to the systematic nature of the abuse. Privacy rights[65] may conflict with the public aspect of the right to the truth and are, perhaps, it is uncertain, grounds on which an individual victim could stop an investigation into specific events relating solely to his or her victimisation. By way of an example, Szoke-Burke draws attention to this in relation to child soldiers who are at the same time perpetrators and victims,[66] adding rights of children into the mix of rights that may need balancing in cases of conflicting interests and conflicting rights.

Separation argument for an independent right

A significant question is whether this right to the truth should be conceived as having a value (for victims and, as we shall see in the next chapter, for society), which is independent of the achievement of other rights and duties that are associated with the proper response of a legitimate state to widespread atrocity. This would mean that the right to the truth should be fulfilled even if other rights and duties required as part of the proper response to atrocity are not or cannot be fulfilled.

65 For example under the International Covenant on Civil and Political Rights (19 December 1966) Article 17(1).

66 Szoke-Burke *supra* note 16 at 542–3.

Formulations of the right to the truth frequently link it to other rights.[67] A right to seek and receive information held by the state or public body is recognised in international and regional human rights instruments[68] and also in domestic laws. The extent to which this right can achieve the aims of the right to the truth is discussed in later chapters. A particular issue is that freedom of information rights are rights in *sensu stricto*; meaning, as mentioned earlier, that it is the right holder, alone, who controls the actions of the person under a duty. The right to the truth, on the other hand, is conceived in terms of obligations on the state, is applicable in the absence of any official investigation or judicial process and does not depend upon the making of any formal request for information.[69]

Likewise, knowing the structural and individualised truth is instrumental (necessary) for the effective enforcement of various rights. The UNCHR Study on the Right to Truth identifies the following rights as closely linked to the right to truth:

> the right to an effective remedy; the right to judicial and legal protection; the right to the family life; the right to an effective investigation; the right to a hearing by a competent, independent, and impartial tribunal; and the right to obtain reparation.[70]

They are linked instrumentally since rights to an effective investigation and to a judicial remedy for a violation arise from the positive obligation of the state to guarantee and protect individuals within its territory from human rights abuses.[71] One of the aims of such investigations is the clarification of facts,[72] and any comprehensive investigation will entail thorough evidence-gathering and factual analysis, which is key to the establishment of the truth about past violations. In this sense, the right to the truth can also be seen as a reparative measure: through the acknowledgment of facts, recognition of individuals as victims and right-bearers finds implicit if not explicit recognition,[73] and may constitute an important step towards further reparation.

Furthermore, as shown in the later chapters on human rights and international criminal law, the absence of treaty-based rights to the truth *expressis verbis* leaves the background right to be formulated for juristic purposes in terms of aspects of other rights, powers and duties. Examples are the right to life (under

67 2006 Study on the Right to Truth *supra* note 19, para 42; see also chapters 6 and 7.

68 E.g. Article 13 of the American Convention on Human Rights (22 January 1969) and Inter-American Declaration of Principles on Freedom of Expression (19 October 2000) para 4.

69 E.g. Principle 4 of the Report of the independent expert to update the Set of Principles to combat impunity (18 February 2005) (hereinafter Updates Set of Principles).

70 2006 Study on the Right to Truth *supra* note 19.

71 E.g. in relation to the right to legal and judicial protection, *Ellacuría*, *supra* note 58 or *Gómez Paquiyauri Brothers v Peru* (8 July 2004) and *Tibi v Ecuador* (7th September 2004).

72 *Gomes Lund et al. ("Guerrilha do Araguaia) v Brazil* (24 November 2010) para 197.

73 Report of the Special Rapporteur on the Promotion of Truth, Justice, Reparation and Guarantees of Non-Recurrence (9 August 2012).

the European Convention),[74] the right to judicial protection of rights (in the American Convention) and the powers of judges, under the Rome Statute, to pursue the truth. It follows, perhaps as a consequence, that the right to the truth is often given juristic expression as being a necessary part of the general move in international law against impunity and to the rights to justice and reparation that are inherent in that task.

It is also the case that, as discussed in Chapter 1, the right to the truth can be conceived as a vehicle to realise other needs. Particularly the pursuit of justice can take centre stage, since an understanding of what occurred and who might have been involved are preconditions for the bringing of prosecutions. In this regard the right to the truth can be conceived part of the opposition to impunity.[75]

Some commentators have argued that, despite these considerations, there is a point to conceiving the right to the truth in a more freestanding fashion, in which its specific point and purpose should be given effect independently of other rights. Méndez and Bariffi suggest that it remains unclear whether the right might develop into an independent right or whether it may remain as part of a right to reparations, the right to remedies, or the right not to be subjected to inhuman, cruel and degrading treatment.[76] In their view there is, indeed, a point to conceiving the right as independent: subsuming the right under other rights, such as the right to reparation, risks undermining the political and moral gravitas that truth-seeking and truth-telling can bring to individuals and society. One of the pillars of transitional justice, that of ascertaining the truth through a multitude of possible judicial, non-judicial, government, individual or civil-society-driven efforts, may be undermined.

Conceptual clarity and resulting normative force is also at the heart of Judge Mac-Gregor's argument,[77] mentioned earlier in this chapter. This is that recognising the right to the truth as an "autonomous and independent right" is justified because it prevents distortion and so preserves the independent purpose and point of each right in issue; this is endangered by subsuming the right to the truth into the right to judicial protection and so forth. Each right, including truth, has a separate point and focus which should not be endangered.[78]

Other arguments, which may be thought to be pointing towards the independent importance of truth, emphasise the near to absolute importance of truth by which some degree of contrast can be made with other rights and which may justify, given the politics of particular transitional situations, compromises with other rights and obligations. Zalaquett, for example, asserts that obtaining and

74 Although, as we shall see, in the context of the ECHR the right to have a use of lethal force investigated is an independent duty of a contracting state which is not dependent on an alleged breach by that state of its substantive duty to protect life.

75 E.g. Groome *supra* note 51.

76 Méndez and Bariffi *supra* note 2 paras 28–29.

77 Ferrer Mac-Gregor *supra* note 17.

78 Subsumption of the right to the truth into other rights "encourages the distortion of the essence and intrinsic content of each right" (ibid at 137).

disclosing the truth is fundamental if a state's response to atrocity is to be legitimate.[79] The complete truth must be known, officially sanctioned and publicly disclosed. In the context of the politics of a society in transition, pursing the truth can have negative consequences. It can therefore be appropriate to allow certain compromises, such as limited amnesty, which may provide an incentive to disclose, allowing "creative plea bargains" where a degree of punishment may be traded for information, and so on. There are, of course, limits to this. But what is not allowed are trade off against disclosure of truth – more compensation but less truth. Limited amnesty may be possible, but again, not if the consequence is to forestall the disclosure of the truth. This position, therefore, is one which broadly speaking permits compromise in relation to some rights, but not in respect of the right to the truth, which has something like an overriding importance.

Truth and justice

In support of the idea that the right to the truth should be conceived independently of other rights is doubting whether the same arguments which apply to explain and justify a right to know "what happened" and who was responsible also apply, with equal force, to explain and justify a victim's right that the direct and indirect perpetrators be prosecuted and, if convicted, punished (the doing of justice). First, these two things (knowing what happened and doing justice) are different. It may be plausible that victims view prosecution, conviction and punishment as less important to their interests and well-being, or had different significance, than knowing the truth. Second, whilst the disclosure of the truth harms no one directly,[80] the application of the criminal law to a perpetrator will be seriously detrimental to him or her, and so significant obligations and limits (such as the right to a fair trial) are required. Third, the state, taking into account the interests of the population as a whole, can reasonably and properly balance the possibly adverse political and social consequences of prosecution with other interests, such as long-term peace. To put it bluntly, the moral arguments against impunity and amnesty are, for consequential reasons, not so self-evidently beneficial as the argument for disclosure and truth.[81] The failures to investigate and to disclose the truth to victims and their relatives has been held (in respect of "disappeared" persons) to be, in itself, a form of torture or inhuman treatment (and thus an independent ground for a breach of Article 5 ACHR or Article 3

79 Jose Zalaquett, 'Confronting Human Rights Violations Committed by Former Governments: Applicable Principles and Political Constraints'(1990) 13 Hamline Law Review 623 at 623–632.

80 Indirect or consequential harm is different. The human right to life may impose on state institutions a duty to protect, perhaps even the most vicious perpetrator, from life threatening attacks by others; this can involve keeping information out of the public domain.

81 For discussion of grounds for reasonable deference to amnesties (in the context of the interests of justice and the International Criminal Court) see Darryl Robinson, 'Serving the interests of justice: amnesties, truth commissions and the International Criminal Court' (2003) 14(3) European Journal of International Law 481.

ECHR).[82] The same intensity of suffering has not been said to follow from a failure to prosecute and punish. Furthermore, prosecution is a public duty and, at most, an inchoate private right.[83] It follows that prosecution is less a right of victims and more a duty predicated on the responsibilities of the judicial authorities in a well-ordered society. Victims may play a significant role in these decisions but not, in the full sense of the word, as right holders (i.e. decisively controlling the actions of the correlating duty-bearer). This is not an argument for amnesty and impunity; just that there are grounds for maintaining the distinction between a victim's right to the truth and the doing of justice by the state. Perhaps the former is absolute, or at least based on a presumption that is almost unassailable, whilst the latter is nuanced and open to reasonable qualification. They are distinguishable on those grounds.

Truth and reparations

Through the acknowledgment of facts, recognition of individuals as victims and right-bearers finds implicit if not explicit recognition[84] and may constitute an important step towards further reparation, since the provision of information is itself a remedy, and not a necessary step toward some other remedy.

This link of truth to remedies is not instrumental as the claimed link to the right to justice. Being offered the truth through an investigation is a remedial act by the state and an enforcement of the right. Conceived in this way, the right to the truth, seamlessly, encompasses the right (to know what happened) and the remedy (consequentially, knowing what has happened).

But ascertaining the structural and individualised truth can, of course, also be an important and necessary step in seeking other reparations. Claims for reparation need to be based on accurate facts. The establishment of what happened is logically prior to the lodging and assessment of such claims. This "knowing what happened" will also serve as evidence about the harm suffered by victims and family members. From this understanding of harm, the needs of survivors for appropriate reparations becomes clear. But (as with the pursuit of justice) the making of reparations resulting from an investigation is different from the investigation itself as a reparative measure of providing the truth. This is because the specific correlating duty to a right to the truth is the investigative obligation of the state. The right to reparation, distinctively, seeks to address a violation by "making good" that violation in some way. The right to the truth is different as it seeks to understand the violation that has occurred in its detail, ramification and (il)logicality. The two issues are not congruent with each other.

82 As discussed in chapters 6 and 7.

83 The UN Human Rights Committee makes it clear that, at least under the ICCPR, there is no victim's right that a person should be prosecuted (see Chapter 6).

84 Report on the Promotion of Truth, Justice, Reparation and Guarantees of Non-Recurrence *supra* note 73.

Under international law, the crime of enforced disappearance may serve to illustrate the complexity of the relationship between the right to the truth and the right to reparation. The "not knowing what happened to family members" constitutes inhumane and degrading treatment. Being kept in the dark forms part of the crime of enforced disappearance.[85] The "not knowing on behalf of relatives" is integral to the overarching violation, the disappearance itself. The right to truth will offer information on this primary violation and with it stop the corollary effect of the crime element that extends to the families and relatives. In other words, and with regards to the crime of enforced disappearance, the right to the truth will help bring to an end the level of suffering associated with not knowing and with it that part of the crime. Until such a point, technically, the crime is still ongoing. However, knowing what happened and therefore "ending" the crime in relation to the families is not the same as offering a reparative measure to compensate for the suffering and enduring of the crime. Other reparative measures may still arise depending on circumstances, such as whether the individual victims actively seek those reparations. They may, for various reasons, not want to lodge reparation claims, or those may not be available to them. The realisation of the right to the truth terminates the offence but is then a precondition for further reparations, such as rehabilitation or monetary awards.

This distinction between the right to the truth and the right to reparation can also be seen in the public conceptualisation of the right to the truth, which is discussed in the next chapter. This is the view that society, too, has a right to know the truth. From this point of view, structural and individualised knowledge of the violations is necessarily linked to a duty to communicate and disseminate widely the information and make the truth known. For the realisation of the right to the truth documentation efforts, archives and other such mechanisms to preserve and communicate the information are required. They are vehicles for the realisation of the right to the truth. However, such communication activities are different from reparative collective or symbolic mechanisms, such as memorials, public apologies and commemoration efforts that go beyond the mere investigation and communication duty of the state that is enshrined in the right to the truth.

In summary, the separation argument suggests that there are grounds for accepting that the right to the truth has a profound freestanding function which is purposively, logically and conceptually independent of other rights to which it is, no doubt, related; in particular from the right to information, to justice (retribution) and to reparations. Truth may be instrumentally linked to other rights; but there are also gains from seeking and expressing the truth, whether or not those other rights are enforced.

85 See Article 7(2)(i) of the Rome Statute (*supra* note 14) with regards to enforced disappearance.

Conceiving the right to the truth as separate emphasises the independent worth (morally and experientially) of knowing the truth. From knowing the truth, decisions then can be made at public and individual level as to what to "do" with that truth, giving a sense of autonomy. This can include forgetting and not pursuing reparations.

It is, of course, more complex than this. The right to the truth has its place within a framework of international law which cannot be simply reduced to a structure within which individuals and societies are, in their "autonomy", free to respond to gross violations of human rights as they see fit. The law is more demanding than that. In general terms, the purpose of this area of international law involves removing or limiting impunity, issuing of reparations, avoiding repetition and, in the case of enforced disappearances, ending the intolerable suffering caused through not knowing. Although it has been suggested here that the right to the truth has independent merit, it is nevertheless an important instrumental aspect in respect of these overall purposes.

A working definition

The separation argument suggests that the right to the truth encapsulates human interests and gives rise to a group of norms which, though capable of furthering other rights and interests, nevertheless have sufficient importance in themselves to justify legal enforcement in their own terms, independently of the enforcement of those other rights and interests. The separation argument, therefore, provides a standard against which a range of practices relating to transitional justice and the position of victims and exemplified in truth and reconciliation commissions, international criminal law trials and international human rights courts can be examined and analysed.

On this basis, and following the preceding discussion in this chapter, an abstract working definition of the right to the truth suggests that individual victims have an imperfect right to the benefit of and a polity has an independent, incongruent, duty to accept the burden of (a)(i) an authoritative structural investigation of both the events and politico-social structures that led to atrocity and (ii) to the individualised, particular circumstances of an individual's suffering; (b) an authoritative reporting or communication of the results of these investigations. The right to the truth also implies (c) an opportunity for victims to narrate their stories. Importantly, (a) and (b) connote a conventional correspondence theory involving the truth of events which is synthetic/a posteriori and historical. In other words, the duty to tell the truth is satisfied through applying the familiar procedures of justification of judicial or quasi-judicial enquiry in which, for example, the reasonableness of the perspective of the fair-minded impartial observer is accepted.

With regards to (c), this element of truth-telling might be less concerned with the truth in the sense of correspondence theory and more with the psychological satisfaction of the victim and attempts at restoring faith in the rule of law and state institutions.

Conclusion

This chapter examined the content of the right in terms of its grounding, it legal status, its general content, its continuing nature, and the need for authoritative statements of truth. We suggest that, although in its institutional realisation, it is often conceived as being closely associated with other rights (particularly justice, reparation and guarantees for non-repetition), there are reasons for upholding the idea that a freestanding right to the truth has crystallised into, at least, a general principle of international law capable of guiding the interpretation and application of positive treaty provisions.

In the principal expressions of the right to the truth, an important public or social aspect to the right is identified. This is the idea that the expression of the truth about atrocities benefits societies generally, not just individuals. In the following chapter we examine this public aspect of the right to the truth before proceeding to consider the ways in which the right to the truth impacts on the workings of transitional justice mechanisms.

References

Arendt, 'Truth and politics' *The New Yorker*, 25 February 1967, https://idanlandau.files.wordpress.com/2014/12/arendt-truth-and-politics.pdf, (accessed 14 February 2019).

Combs N, *Fact-finding Without Facts. The Uncertain Evidentiary Foundations of International Criminal Convictions* (Cambridge University Press 2010).

Cruft R, Liao M and Renzo M (eds), *Philosophical Foundations of Human Rights* (Oxford 2105).

Crownford J, *Brownlie's Principles of Public International Law* (8th edn Oxford University Press 2012).

De Greiff P, 'Truth Telling and the Rule of Law' in Borer T A (ed) *Telling the Truth: truth telling and peace building in post-conflict societies* (Notre Dame University Press 2006).

Dworkin R, *Taking Rights Seriously* (Duckworth 1977).

Ellis S, 'Truth and Reconciliation Commission of South Africa Report, Volumes 1–5. Pretoria: Government Printer, October 1998' (2000) 42 Transformation 61.

Ferrer Mac-Gregor E, 'The Right to the Truth as an autonomous right under the Inter-American Human Rights System' (2016) IX(1) Mexican Law Review 121.

Finnis J, *Natural Law and Natural Rights* (Clarendon Press 1980).

Gaja G, 'General Principles of Law' (2013) Max Planck Encyclopedia of Public International Law (online).

Gerwith A, 'Are there any Absolute Rights?' in Waldron J (ed) *Theories of Rights* (Oxford University Press 1984).

Griffin J, *On Human Rights* (Oxford University Press 2008).

Groome D, 'The Right to Truth in the Fight Against Impunity' (2011) 29(1) Berkeley Journal of International Law 181.

Henckaerts J-M and Doswald-Beck L, *Customary International Humanitarian Law, Volume I: Rules* (Cambridge University Press 2006).

Hodzic R, 'Post-Karadzic Bosnia and Herzegovina: The End of the Criminal Justice Era' (4 November 2016) www.ictj.org/news/karadzic-bosnia-herzegovina-criminal-justice#.VwvL_wtXbgc.twitter, (accessed 14 February 2019).

International Center for Transitional Justice, 'Transitional Justice in the United Nations Human Rights Council' (Policy briefing June 2011).

International Commission of Jurists, 'Enforced Disappearance and Extrajudicial Execution: The Right of Family Members' (Practitioners' Guide No. 10, July 2016).

Méndez J and Bariffi F, 'Truth, Right to, International Protection' (2011) Max Planck Encyclopedia of Public International Law (online).

Méndez J, 'The Right to Truth' in Joyner C C (ed), *Reining in Impunity for International Crimes and Serious Violations of Fundamental Human Rights: Proceedings of the Siracusa Conference* (Erès Toulouse 1998) 255.

Naqvi Y, 'The right to the truth in international law: fact or fiction?' (2006) 88(862) International Review of the Red Cross 245.

Panepinto A, 'The right to the truth in international law: The significance of Strasbourg's contributions' (2017) 37 Legal Studies 739.

Robinson D, 'Serving the interests of justice: amnesties, truth commissions and the International Criminal Court' (2003) 14(3) European Journal of International Law 481.

Szoke-Burke S, 'Searching for the Right to Truth: The Impact of International Human Rights Law on National Transitional Justice Policies' (2015) 33(2) Berkeley Journal of International Law 526.

van Bowen T, 'The United Nations Basic Principles and Guidelines on the Right to a Remedy and Reparations for Victims of Gross Violations of International Human Rights Law and Serious Violations of International Law' (2010) (United Nations Audiovisual Library of International Law) http://legal.un.org/avl/pdf/ha/ga_60-147/ga_60-147_e.pdf accessed 14 February 2019.

Zalaquett J, 'Confronting Human Rights Violations Committed by Former Governments: Applicable Principles and Political Constraints'(1990) 13 Hamline Law Review 623.

4 The public aspect of the right to the truth

Introduction

In the previous chapter, the right to the truth was defined predominantly by reference to the individual interests of victims which grounds a right to knowledge and a correlating duty on states to investigate and promulgate authoritatively. It was suggested that this is a right/duty to both structural and individual truth about atrocities that has now reached the status of a general principle of law. As a victim's right, it is "imperfect" in the sense that the state's duty includes obligations which are independent of the will of the victim. Partly this is because, as well as correlating to a victim's rights, the "right to the truth" correlates with a duty inherent in the idea of a democratic or just state, an idea which also informs judicial reasoning. This idea of the duty on well-ordered states indicates the public aspect of the right to the truth.

All elements of our working definition on the right to the truth are relevant to this public aspect of the right to the truth, since fulfilling the right in individual terms is a necessary condition for fulfilment in the social sense, though the public aspect, given its purpose, may be broader in scope. For individuals, the main support for a right to the truth comes from the moral need to know, so as to not cause continued psychological and physical suffering that comes with uncertainty. The public rationale results from an inherent moral value associated with the truth but for the purpose of upholding the rule of law and the idea of a just polity.

In the following, we predominantly refer to this aspect as public rather than social. Public is more satisfactory since it denotes "the people" as part of a community, nation or state, and second, points to the political relationship between people and the government and the sense that seeking the truth is a proper concern of the polis, of the state and its institutions.

The authority for the public aspect of the right to the truth

The institutional but non-judicial expressions of the right to the truth (such as by organs of the UN, discussed in Chapter 2) include the idea that the right to the truth has a public, social or collective subject – it is expressed as a right of society or of peoples and not confined to a right of victims. As well as an affair of victims it is also an affair of the polis and it imposes correlating duties on the state. State duties in the context of the right to the truth have this additional justification that is independent of victims' rights. The justification embodies the requirements of the well-ordered society, which is democratic and pluralist, committed to the rule of law, concerned for the well-being of all its citizens and willing to treat them all as equals, which is the normally unarticulated idea of the proper attributes of the state inherent in human rights adjudication which aim to remedy state failures.

Some declarative statements in this regard work with a distinction between the "right to the truth" and the "right to know" (though, confusingly, there is no settled agreement as to which is which). A good example is the 1997 report for the UN Commission of Human Rights, which identifies a general "right to know" as having two aspects: the first, described as the "the right to the truth", which is the right of the individual to know what happened to his or her nearest and dearest; and the other, by which the right to know is "also a collective right" which has social purposes.[1] Similarly, the 2005 Updated Principles on Impunity (or Orentlicher Principles), produced under the auspices of the Commission on Human Rights by independent expert Orentlicher,[2] intended to assist states in combating impunity, make a principled distinction between the "inalienable right to the truth" (Principle 2) which, as expressed, is exclusively public with the right being predicated upon "peoples" and including a state duty to preserve archives (Principle 3); and the victim's "right to know" (Principle 4), with a duty on states to give effect to this right (Principle 5). In the 2006 Study on the Right to the Truth, the report discusses the "collective dimension" of the right to the truth as it has developed – with references to the UN, regional and national authorities.[3] The UN General Assembly's Resolution on the Right to the Truth, passed in 2013, is focused on the right of individual victims, but it does "emphasise" the public's qualified right of access to information and stresses the role of "civil society" in the concept of the right to the truth. It is based upon a range of UN documents which also give credit to the public aspect of the right. The Principles of 2005,[4] referenced in the Resolution, refer in relation to restitution to the duty of "full public disclosure" insofar as this is consistent with victim safety

1 Question of the impunity of perpetrators of human rights violations (civil and political) (26 June 1997) (Joinet Report).

2 Report of the independent expert to update the Set of Principles to combat impunity (18 February 2005) (Updated Principles on Impunity).

3 The Right to the Truth. Report of the High Commission for Human Rights (7 June 2007) para 83, referring to the right having a "collective and a societal dimension". See also Promotion and Protection of Human Rights. Study on the Right to Truth (8 February 2006) para 36 (2006 Study on the Right to the Truth).

4 Basic Principles and Guidelines on the Right to a Remedy and Reparation for Victims of Gross Violations of International Human Rights Law and Serious Violations of International Humanitarian Law (21 March 2006). These have no express reference to the right to the truth but do refer, in the context of reparations, to "full public disclosure" so long as this

(Principle 22), and Principle 24 imposes a duty on states to develop means of informing the public as well as victims of gross violations.

The public aspect of the right to the truth has also been recognised in a judicial or quasi-judicial context. As illustrated and discussed in Chapter 6, it is found in the perspective of the Inter-American Commission on Human Rights; in the Annual Report 1985–1986, written in the context of determining the proper role of transitional democratic national authorities in the South and Central American environment of the time, for example.[5] The point can also be found focused on the facts of individual cases presented to the Inter-American Court by the Commission. A good example is *Ellacuría v El Salvador*, involving the assassination of liberation theologians and others allegedly by state agents. The right to the truth (knowledge of what happened) is not driven exclusively by the victim's rights and interests. Knowledge of the truth is also a necessary consequence of a democratic society and the rule of law.

> The right to know the truth is a collective right that ensures society access to information that is essential for the workings of democratic systems, and it is also a private right for relatives of the victims, which affords a form of compensation, in particular, in cases where amnesty laws are adopted. Article 13 of the American Convention protects the right of access to information.[6]

The reference to Article 13 is significant. The right to seek and obtain information is an express part of the right to freedom of expression in the American Convention. It is a political right which applies not only to victims and those with a direct interest in the information but also to politicians, NGOs and others seeking information of public matters in order to promote, through protected expressive acts, a public cause. Such NGO activity and campaigning is one of the ways in which the public aspect of the right to the truth can be furthered. Such people and groups have standing (at least in regional and international law),[7] and their international success means they should also have standing to seek information in domestic law. Grounding this on the right to freedom of expression means that the information can be circulated, it is for public consumption and it is in the public interest that it be disclosed, discussed and allowed to contribute to the national political discourse.

The Inter-American Court, which determines individual cases on the basis of the text of the American Convention of Human Rights, has also moved towards

---

is compatible with the safety of victims. Principle 24 refers to the duty on states to develop means of informing the public.

5 Inter-American Commission on Human Rights Annual Report of 1985–1986, Chapter V (26 September 1986).

6 *Ellacuría et al. v El Salvador Case 10.488* (22 December 1999) para 224.

7 E.g. *Claude Reyes et al. v Chile* (19 September 2006) and, regarding the ECHR, *Magyar Helsinki Bizottság v Hungary* (8 November 2016). Both cases were brought by pressure groups under the admissibility provisions of the Inter-American system (to the Commission) and the ECHR (right of individual petition).

recognising a public aspect to the right to the truth. In early cases it did not accept – it implicitly rejected – the idea of a public aspect to the right to the truth as having juristic standing and being capable of enforcement through Article 13. In *Bámaca-Velásquez v Guatemala* 2000 (maltreatment of prisoners from a revolutionary organisation), it did not adopt the Commission's conception of the right to the truth as having both a "particular nature", focused on victims, and a "collective nature, which includes the right of society to 'have access to essential information for the development of democratic systems' ". The right to the truth was sufficiently satisfied by ("subsumed in") the rights of individual victims to an effective investigation by which they would know what happened to them and by the correlating duties on the state to satisfy those rights.[8] Judge Ramirez's concurring judgment points out this focus on individual rights. He goes on to accept that the demand for society to know about its past is legitimate and that, in any case, this public knowledge will be a consequence of publication and subsequent prosecution. Judge Ramirez is clear that the collective aspect of the right would strengthen anti-impunity.[9]

In later cases, a public aspect to the right to the truth has been expressly accepted by the Court as part of the justification for the implicit duty to conduct an effective investigation. Investigations which (as will be discussed in Chapter 6) are the form in which the norms of the right to the truth have been given effect by the Inter-American Court. Investigation should result in public promulgation of the truth. This is justified as being a "fair expectation" of a state in a "democratic society".[10] The same broad point, in other cases, is made just in relation to "society".[11] A clear example of this approach is in *The Massacres of El Mozote and Other Places v El Salvador* 2012[12] (a series of massacres of hundreds of civilians by El Salvadorian military units in 1981). The Court found a breach of the duty to investigate alleged violations of substantive rights. As discussed in Chapter 6, these derive as necessary implications from the individual victim's right to judicial protection of her Convention rights. But referring to the Commission's argument basing the right to the truth in the right to receive information, the Court also accepted that the right to the truth had a significance in the case, and this included its public aspect. The public aspect was particularly significant by

8 *Bámaca-Velásquez v Guatemala* (25 November 2000) paras 199–202; Dermot Groome, 'The Right to Truth in the Fight Against Impunity' (2011) 29(1) Berkeley Journal of International Law 181 at 184.

9 Ibid.

10 E.g. "*Las Dos Erres*" *Massacre v Guatemala* (24 November 2009) para 149 (massacres of at least 251 persons in 1982 by a special group in the armed forces); *Contreras et al. v El Salvador* (31 August 2011) para 170 (systemic abductions of children as part of counter-terrorism policy); and Groome (ibid.) at 184–5.

11 E.g. *Anzualdo Castro v Peru* (22 September 2009) para 116 *passim* – in the express context of "The Right to Know the Truth", albeit that this right is still seen as given effect through the judicial guarantees provisions of the Convention (forced disappearances, in 1993, involving the Army intelligence services).

12 *The Massacres of El Mozote and other Places v El Salvador* (25 October 2012).

reference to Article 13. It was recognised that Article 13 ("any person" has a right to know the truth) had persuasive authority, but was not directly in issue and was not breached.[13] More recently, however, the position has developed and in *Gomez Lund v Brazil* 2010 (detention, torture and disappearance, between 1972 and 1975, of 70 members of the Brazilian Communist Party by the Brazilian army) the Court, inter alia, explains the violation of the duty of an effective investigation as a breach of Article 13 "in relation" to breaches of the rights to judicial protection.[14] The point, to repeat, is that Article 13 is a political right and its use in this context provides a justification for the right to the truth which engages its public aspect. This justification through Article 13 relates to the necessary conditions of a properly functioning democratic society – the jurisprudential idea of the just and democratic state, outlined earlier. Though not the focus in *Gomez Lund*, the right enhances the power of civil society institutions to influence the public (and the government), it ensures transparency in government and, consequently, the more effective scrutiny of government actions, and it facilitates greater participation in public affairs.

The public aspect of the norms of the right to the truth is also disclosed through the public aspect of judicial remedies. This is particularly true of the IACtHR. As we shall see in Chapter 6, the Court has been highly innovative in its remedies flowing from findings of state failure in relation to the general right to judicial protection of human rights and the inherent duty of an effective investigation. The remedies ordered can be extensive, going far beyond the particular needs and losses of victims and endorsing the social goals of the right to the truth. The Court frequently orders a range of significant publicity measures by which the atrocity is introduced and maintained in the public memory, such as by public acknowledgment and apology and by audiovisual documentary for wide public distribution.[15]

Public promulgation of investigations is nothing new and is, indeed, a presumption of an effective state investigation – there would need to be special reasons sufficient to outweigh this presumption for its results to be kept private between the investigation and the victims. But their growing extensiveness, in cases which deal with large-scale atrocity subject to long-standing impunity, may indicate how the background right to the truth, with its public aspect, has influenced the application of the legal rights to fair hearings and judicial protection in

13 Ibid paras 297–298 but see para 301 for no breach of article 13. See also *Barrios Altos v Peru* (14 March 2001) paras 45–49 (shootings by Peruvian security forces in 1991) where the Commission had argued that the right to the truth has its "roots" in the right to seek and receive information. Again, the Court rejected this as an independent ground for satisfying the right to the truth.

14 *Gomes Lund et al. ("Guerrilha do Araguaia) v Brazil* (24 November 2010) operative paragraph 6 and paras 196–202. See also fuller discussion in Chapter 6.

15 As in *The Massacres of El Mozote and other Places* (*supra* note 12).

respect of alleged violations of the substantive rights in the American Convention at least.[16]

The European Court of Human Rights, as will be discussed in Chapter 7, has been more reticent than the Inter-American Court in going beyond upholding individual rights to an effective investigation of atrocities in its case law. It has begun to make reference to the right to the truth, such as in the illegal rendition case *El Masri v Macedonia* 2013.[17] Though not central to the case, the Court's reference to the right to the truth recognises the importance of a proper investigation not only for the victim but also for other victims and for the "general public". For four judges, in their concurring opinion, it is the public aspect – the public effects – of the right to the truth which provide its particular, distinctive normative standard to which, in their view, the investigative duty under Articles 2 and 3 must comply.[18] This argument, no doubt, reflects the widespread political importance of the case, including its importance for the general public. The presumption is that atrocities, gross, systematic and widespread violations of human rights have a general and social importance. The right to the truth, taken as a principle influencing the application of Convention rights, justifies the investigation and promulgation of what happened as much in terms of its public aspect as in relation to victims' needs. Truth in this context is necessarily and conceptually a public matter and prosecutions in the public interest.

Finally, it is worth recalling that at the heart of not just the right to the truth but more generally is the idea that human rights need to be protected by law and judicial action. This principle finds expression in domestic courts, human rights courts and international criminal courts and tribunals. Violations and criminal offences must be established through proper judicial process. Though usually the meaning of this is just assumed, it presumably means a process that is, as well as being adversarial in the general sense, open and public. The public nature of doing justice is an essential feature of the rule of law which has nothing directly to do with the interests of victims and, indeed, may be done even against their wishes.[19] The public aspect of the right to the truth, therefore, is inherent in the judicial process that it invokes.

16 Ibid.

17 *El-Masri v The former Yugoslav Republic of Macedonia* (12 December 2012).

18 Concurring opinion of Judges Tulkens, Spielmann, Sicilianos and Keller: "For society in general, the desire to ascertain the truth plays a part in strengthening confidence in public institutions and hence the rule of law. For those concerned – the victims' families and close friends – establishing the true facts and securing an acknowledgment of serious breaches of human rights and humanitarian law constitute forms of redress that are just as important as compensation, and sometimes even more so" (ibid at 83, para 6). Confer with the more orthodox concurring opinion of Judge Casadevall and Judge López Guerra "Therefore, as far as the right to the truth is concerned, it is the victim, and not the general public, who is entitled to this right as resulting from Article 3 of the Convention in the light of the Court's case law" (ibid at 85).

19 This is a general principle about the rule of law. Of course, there are normally in both domestic and international systems reasons for holding trials outside the public gaze – such as national security, children's interests, and perhaps overwhelming privacy rights; furthermore victims of human rights abuses may need adequate protection.

Furthermore, as discussed in the next chapter, the right to the truth can be given effect through the non-judicial processes of truth and reconciliation commissions. These bodies have acting in the public sphere as their *raison d'être*.

Justification

The preceding suggests that the institutional authorities on the right to the truth, the authorities that promulgate it as a principle with legal effects, all, to some degree, accept there is a social reason for knowing the truth about gross and systematic violations of human rights.

There is a danger of over-categorising. Some formulations of the right to the truth (some of the UN declarations and the minority approach of the European Court) give it a distinctive purpose: the public promulgation of the truth where "the right to know" or the duty to investigate is predicated on victims. Alternatively the public aspect may be conceived in terms of a single right to know with two pillars: one victim predicated, the other social and public. A third view, which is not clearly articulated, is to see it as a seamless relationship. An effective investigation for the victims will necessarily be public given the requirement for a proper judicial process. However conceived, there are clearly areas of overlap between the public aspect and the victims' rights in terms of the content. More importantly, it remains the case that it is the victims and their relatives, the facts of dreadful atrocities whose victims are individuals and with the continued presence of alleged perpetrators, that is the context and reason for both the individual and the public "aspects".

With that caveat, however, different purposes are pursued by the two aspects; they have a different justification. Victims' rights are there to meet the needs of victims which may be psychological, economic and based on their reasonable expectation of justice in their cause. The justification for the public or collective right is different. There are what might be called "social" purposes (relating in a general way to the requirements of social change) and "political" purposes (relating to the nature of the polity). "Social" purposes include the belief that public disclosure is necessary to prevent future violations.[20] There is also a duty to remember and perhaps prevent future atrocities or historical perversions which deny the full depth of the oppression. The national heritage, which by implication sets the context of future politics, includes the history of oppression.[21]

The "political" purpose of the right to the truth is to link investigation and publicity to the duties of a state in a reasonable and well-functioning democracy.

20 "Full and effective exercise of the right to the truth provides a vital safeguard against the recurrence of violations." (Updated Principles on Impunity, *supra* note 2 Principle 2.

21 Joinet Report *supra* note 1 para 17. "The right to know is also a collective right, drawing upon history to prevent violations from recurring in the future. Its corollary is a "duty to remember" on the part of the State: to be forearmed against the perversions of history that go under the names of revisionism or negationism, for the history of its oppression is part of a people's national heritage and as such must be preserved."

This is partly, as said earlier, an indication of the necessarily public nature of the right to justice: fair trials and judicial guarantees are conducted in public; justice must be seen to be done. But there is also a broader sense which links investigation and publicity to an implicit ideal of a just and democratic state. The point is made explicitly by the 2006 "Study on the Right to the Truth":

> While the right to the truth is an individual right of victims and their families, it also has a collective and a societal dimension. At that level, the right to the truth is closely linked to the rule of law and the principles of transparency, accountability and good governance in a democratic society.[22]

As mentioned in Chapter 3, the right to the truth has a political basis found in the idea, referenced in judicial and non-judicial institutional expressions, of a well-ordered society in which all are treated as equals, an equality which is denied by lack of knowledge and by the inactivity of the state. The public aspect of the right to the truth is, it is suggested, best understood as integrated with the idea of a just and democratic society that is presupposed, as an unarticulated premise, in both non-judicial analysis of the right to the truth but also in judicial reasoning. And included in that general idea of good governance in a democratic society is the notion of true information being available to political actors, such as parties, pressure groups and NGOs – and this is one of the core purposes of the right to receive information.

Domestic courts in South America have also recognised the political and public aspect of the right to the truth.[23] One of the fullest judicial justifications for the public aspect is given by the Supreme Court of Colombia in *J.G. Moreno v Attorney General of Colombia* 2003. The Court held that, in the context of forced disappearances, the eradication of impunity is in the general interest of society. By implication, the public aspect is independent of a victim's rights. Public knowledge can create an awareness of the magnitude of the harm caused. Knowing the truth, therefore, has different dimensions to victims' rights and its object is not just individual redress but also political: the protection of the very foundations of civilized society and of social peace (in which all have an interest). Truth promotes peace and is properly conceived as a legal right with a social subject. To focus the legal right solely and sufficiently on victims' interests and leave the public aspect, the pursuit of peace, to the legislature and executive free of legal obligation, is to interfere with a major aspect of the right to the truth and inhibit its ability to advance peace. Whatever else it is, it is a political right: a right of the population to know not only that their rights are protected but also to participate in political action by which state power is controlled (by implication, in line with the conditions of reasonable cooperation in a well-ordered society).[24]

22 2006 Study on the Right to the Truth *supra* note 3 para 83.
23 Ibid para 36.
24 Constitutional Court of Colombia No T-249/03 (21 May 2003) also cited by Eduardo Ferrer Mac-Gregor 'The Right to the Truth as an autonomous right under the Inter-American

Issues for a legal right

The argument summarised earlier is a statement of the right to the truth in its public aspect. But as a legal right, there are clear issues about how this public aspect is to be given effect. It may be simply a consequence of victims exercising their rights or criminal courts convicting particular defendants. On this "seamless", consequential approach, the public aspect has no independent force but is a reason that judges, in their discretion, accept as persuading them towards giving remedies a social scope beyond what might be necessary for victims alone, or going beyond the immediately relevant facts in relation to the extent of the truth that is told in the judgment.

A stronger assertion of a legal right of a society to the truth is problematic. There is no wilful, acting subject of the right, and this is particularly so if the right is predicated on a "people". If we are talking about persons owing allegiance to a state, then a state official, such as an attorney general, can commence actions to vindicate the right. Alternatively, the collective nature of the right may manifest itself through a rule of standing by which NGOs, for example, can bring actions alleging gross human rights abuses. But in both these instances it can be objected that the agent may not speak for society as a whole.[25] This is clearly true as regards the NGO; but even the attorney general figure who may represent an elected government lacks independence in making a judgment about the wishes of society, since she is part of the state apparatus whose activities are being questioned by invoking the right to the truth. A more convincing case can be made concerning an independent, international office, such as that of the prosecutor at the International Criminal Court, but this is not a state office; her position is to represent humanity as a whole. It is precisely not an office giving effect to the will of a particular "people" or "society".

The answer is to situate the right to the truth in its public aspect as integrated with the idea of a just and democratic society, which is presupposed in both non-judicial but also judicial reasoning dealing with responses to atrocity; and is a standard against which to criticise actual experience. "Right" is used metaphorically to express a general non-individuated goal which states should pursue as an underlying constitutional obligation.

Conclusion

The articulation of the right to the truth includes a public aspect: that knowing the truth about atrocity benefits not just individual victims but also a society as

---

Human Rights System' (2016) IX(1) Mexican Law Review 121 (this was the author's concurring opinion in *Rodríguez Vera et al. (The Disappeared from the Palace of Justice) v Colombia* (14 November 2014).

25 The Colombian Constitutional Court (ibid paras 15–18) expressly endorses the right to the truth and involves a challenge to the decision of the Colombian Attorney-General (ibid Ferrer Mac-Gregor at 121–139).

it seeks to come to terms with its past and construct a better future. The significance of the public aspect is not clear. It is hard to make a convincing case that it creates an independent ground of action, unless this is done on the basis of a right to receive information which, at its core, is a political right. But even then, as a political right, this is a right of political actors rather than, in some sense, of society as a whole. It is perhaps best understood as a principle of law which embodies the incidents of a just and democratic society. This is put forward as a general open-textured idea which, nevertheless, is a legal principle which informs judicial reasoning and whose promotion is an aim of adjudication in this context.

This chapter has outlined various arguments and challenges associated with conceptualising the public aspect of the right to the truth as distinct from the individual aspect. Along with the discussion in Chapter 3, we now have a sense of the nature, structure and content of the right to the truth and of some of the issues to which the right gives rise in a general way. In the chapters that follow, we consider the application of the right in various fora and how the nature, structure, content and arising issues have particular form and significance there.

Reference

Ferrer Mac-Gregor E, 'The Right to the Truth as an autonomous right under the Inter-American Human Rights System' (2016) IX(1) Mexican Law Review 121.

5 The right to the truth in different fora

Introduction

We have explored the way in which truth, as the object of a right, is recognised as a background legal norm. We identified a separation argument for "the right to the truth", denoting a general principle or norm which is a widely accepted moral idea grounded specifically on human needs for truth and distinguishable from needs for justice or reparations. As such, the right is a standard against which different practices relating to truth can be analysed. These needs, finding expression as a stand-alone right, support the following as a working definition of the right to the truth. This is a right to (a)(i) an authoritative investigation of both the events and politico-social structures that led to the atrocity and (ii) to the particular circumstances of an individual's suffering; (b) an authoritative reporting or communication of the results of these investigations. The right to the truth would also suggest that (c) an opportunity for victims to narrate their stories needs to be provided. In addition, the right to the truth has significance from a public perspective insofar as it is essential for a just and democratic society to know what happened. In this chapter we consider, in general terms, the presence and effect of the right to the truth in the discourse and jurisprudence associated with international human rights courts, truth and reconciliation commissions and international criminal law trials.

The practices of human rights proceedings, truth commissions, and international criminal trials are not only different from each other in terms of purpose and procedure but also internally complex insofar as there are many different forms of truth and reconciliation mechanisms and different approaches to international criminal law; the different human rights courts draw their authority from differing statutory requirements and operate in different contexts. In this chapter we explore the different purposes and structures of the three practices in relation to how, in their ways, they do or do not give effect to the right to the truth (defined as (a)(i) and (ii), (b) and (c) above). One of the points we analyse here is how the concept of a "right" may have a different meaning and significance in the different contexts. The purpose is to provide some understanding of the basic foundations of these different practices through which comparisons and contrasts can be brought out and which then provide a platform for more detailed expositions in later chapters of the book.

The meaning of truth in context

All three practices – international human rights bodies, international criminal trials and truth commissions – are based on the notion that truth (within differing parameters) is ascertainable to the extent that this is within their respective mandate. The elements of our definition (a) and (b) would point to a conventional correspondence theory whereby the truth of events is ascertained in a synthetic/a posteriori way within certain procedural forms or methods. In addition, the element of truth-telling (c) might be less concerned with the truth in the sense of correspondence theory and more with the psychological satisfaction of the victim and attempts at restoring faith in the rule of law and state institutions.

Much of what is accounted by witness statements, reports, evidence and victims' testimonies before such institutions are descriptive knowledge of what happened. These descriptions can be viewed as true or false. For the purposes of a truth commission's report, the judgment of a criminal trial or the determinations of a human rights court, a judgment is necessary on behalf of those who author it as to what is true. This act of judging contains what the authors of those determinations believe to be true facts that correspond to events that happened at a certain time. As Bertrand Russell said: "although truth and falsehood are properties of belief, they are properties dependent upon the relations of the beliefs to other things";[1] in other words, correspondence between beliefs and facts. This goes back to Aristotle's *Metaphysics*: "To say what is that it is, or of what is not that it is not, is true",[2] which can be described as "a platitude that no one denies"[3] but that has importance nonetheless. In that sense, what the fact-finders of truth commissions, criminal trials and human rights proceedings seemingly have in common is a refutation of the anti-realist or cognitive realist stance that suggests that there are no mind-independent facts of truths. The very notion of a truth commission or fact-finding processes would be undermined by such a starting point. Fact-finders might have sympathy with Rorty's position that criticises the "arrogance of enlightenment" displayed by proponents of correspondence theory, suggesting a softer approach to truth, with the notion of "true" applying to those beliefs upon which we are able to agree. For Rorty, an appropriate synonym to "true" would be "justified".[4] Key to Rorty's conceptualisation of true as justified is "unforced agreement" (coupled with the desire to reduce objectivity to solidarity). He sees, as a representative of the pragmatist position, "the goal of inquiry (in any sphere of culture) as the attainment of an appropriate mixture of unforced agreement with tolerant disagreement".[5]

1 Bertrand Russell, *The Problems of Philosophy* (orig. 1912 Start Publishing 2012) 210.
2 Aristotle, *Metaphysics* 7.27.
3 Simon Blackburn and Keith Simmons (eds), *Truth* (Oxford University Press 1999) at 1
4 Richard Rorty, 'Science as Solidarity' in J Nelson, A Megill and D McCloskey (eds) *The Rhetoric of the Human Sciences Language and Argument in Scholarship and Public Affairs*, (University of Wisconsin Press 1987) at 42 and 45.
5 Ibid 48.

To what extent the word "justified" fulfils the criteria of the right to truth as stipulated earlier is an interesting matter. An account of an investigation by a state might be justified, but whether it satisfies the proof or detail required by victims is not said. To them, from outside the investigative system, the disagreement to that account may be "intolerable", to extend from Rorty's analogy, and therefore not justified. Naturally, as outlined earlier, what is sought to be established by these legal bodies as true is done a posteriori, and the way to ascertain what is true or false is through synthesis of many different pieces of information.

It is in this sense that the South African Truth and Reconciliation Commission, for example, distinguished different types of truth depending on the imparter and utility of the information presented to them. They identified four categories of truth: "factual or forensic truth; personal or narrative truth; social or 'dialogue' truth . . . and healing and restorative truth".[6] In discussions surrounding international trials too, differing truth forms have been distinguished, most notably "historical" and "legal truth".[7] Depending on the forum, the importance of each of these truth categories may vary, but they should be able to fulfil the Rorty criterion of "unforced agreement" and with it be justified.

Whilst the process of fact-finding employed by these institutions differs, they have criteria laid down for their successful appraisal of facts that seek to be rational and methodical. Advance knowledge of such criteria is required. The process is laid out in Rules of Procedure and Evidence, statutes and so forth stipulating the need for a fair procedure, acting in good faith, operating with a standard of proof and reasonable assessment of the presented evidence.[8]

The challenge is to provide a genuine account of facts. But to discover the facts is already to judge that things are to be discovered in a particular way. And they presuppose the impartial observer or adjudicator to observe the methods and processes laid down. Criticism can therefore be voiced on the basis of a predetermined outcome. That said, from within and through that framework which legal systems rely upon, a justified claim, decision or judgment can be arrived at, justified because no one can reasonably disagree, thereby giving some credence to Rorty's understanding of truth, albeit within the rigidity of the system.[9]

Without doubt, the role of fact-finder is a position of significant responsibility, for what is said in the reports or judgments, if believed and if not believed by those outside the legal process, can have profound effects at the individual and

6 Truth and Reconciliation Commission, 'Truth and Reconciliation Commission of South Africa Final Report (Volume 1)' (29 October 1998) at 110.

7 Fergal Gaynor, 'Uneasy Partners – Evidence, Truth and History in International Trials' (2012) 10(5) Journal of International Criminal Justice 1257 and William Schabas, *Unimaginable Atrocities* (Oxford University Press 2012).

8 Rorty, for the arts and humanities, is wary of the paradigm of rationality attached to the sciences, and law and business to a lesser extent, whereby criteria are laid down in advance that need to be satisfied (*supra* note 4 at 39–40).

9 This begs the interesting question whether narrow decisions, such as the 2:1 decision in *Katanga* is 'reasonably justified' since one judge disagreed with the majority in the 'strongest of terms'. This discussion, however, is beyond the scope of our inquiry.

public levels. The outcome of the institutions' processes is also different, as will be discussed in the following section. Similarly, they may make different contributions to the realisation of the right to truth as defined earlier. Examining their impact on the right to the truth is central to this chapter. In the following, we begin with an outline of the role human rights courts play before discussing the role of truth commissions as a transitional justice mechanism and international criminal proceedings.

The role of human rights courts

The mandate

Human rights (as general, if not universal, norms) give three complementary perspectives on the right to the truth. First, they provide the general foundation for the positive implementation of the right. The right to the truth is a human right, which is given effect in various ways such as through human rights treaties (but also, as discussed later, in truth and reconciliation as well as in international criminal processes).

Second, the duties correlating to human rights are primarily on nation states. The institutional means of seeking to enforce these duties is found in global, regional and national juridical bodies. As we shall see here and in later chapters, the positive law, as developed and interpreted, includes the core elements of the right to the truth, such as a state's duty of effective investigation of allegations of atrocity.

Third, as part of any adjudication, a human rights court itself makes authoritative findings of fact which, especially where there has been significant state failure or lack of cooperation, can in the more extreme circumstances be based on their own investigation.

The normative force of human rights adjudication involves giving effect to the correlating duty on states: they are the primary guardians of human rights. One consequence of this is that the interpretation and application of human rights must cohere with the full range of state duties relating to the proper discharge of their legitimate functions. Human rights involves a (usually implicit) theory of a well-ordered society (individualised by history and culture) and of the state's function within it. The consequence of this is that the normative force of particular rights, including those making up the right to the truth, will involve balancing or compromising with legitimate state interests. A few rights (including, of course, the prohibition on torture) are stipulated in positive law as absolute and immune from such compromise,[10] but others, such as a right to receive information, may be limited in respect of legitimate state interests which are accepted as such by the judicial body.

10 Indeed an important question is the extent to which the absolute character of the prohibition on torture extends to its procedural aspect.

There is, however, an obvious theoretical irony: states, through their agents, are the major violators of human rights. Global and regional processes have been created precisely because of this. Furthermore, it is normally only in periods of transition towards greater democracy that these judicial processes can work effectively. But even then, transitional governments may choose not to cooperate. The extent to which grounds of refusal to cooperate are legitimate and on the basis of which elements of the right to the truth can be properly compromised are important judicial questions. The significance of amnesty, truth and reconciliation alternatives and the protection of national security are examples where human rights adjudication can involve not only the identification and rejection of the bogus, bad faith arguments officials may use to stifle investigation and disclosure but also, more interestingly, the seeking of a "fair balance" of the right to the truth with the legitimate interests of the state in a well-ordered society.

The right to the truth is not expressed as a right in any of the great regional human rights instruments. Rather, core content of the right has been guaranteed as a means of making various express rights effective. These may be substantive rights: in particular, the jurisprudence of the European Court of Human Rights (ECtHR) has interpreted the effective protection of both the right to life (Article 2 ECHR) and the prohibition of torture (Article 3 ECHR) as requiring a free-standing "procedural limb" by which the state is under a duty to undertake an effective investigation.[11] Interpretation of the rule of law provisions of human rights instruments may also guarantee core components of the right to the truth. The Inter-American Court of Human Rights (IACtHR) has derived such a duty from both Article 8 ACHR (the right to a fair trial) and Article 25 ACHR (the right to a remedy);[12] similarly Article 13 ECHR (the right to a remedy) under the European system. The indirect recognition of the right to the truth may mean that the full scope of the right to the truth is not always realisable in the human rights context; this applies especially insofar as the right to the truth by definition has a public aspect.

The impartial fact-finders

As said earlier, the duty on states to investigate allegations of atrocity is a norm expressed – if only indirectly – in human rights law, and this duty should be enforced by human rights courts and institutions at the global, regional (to which this discussion relates) and domestic levels. But the right to the truth is also furthered because, as part of the juridical reasoning of the court in coming to its decision, the regional human rights courts will, themselves, give a narrative account of context and go on to describe and explain the events surrounding an alleged breach of a substantive right. Fact-finding and adjudication are to some extent separate functions with a Commission receiving complaints, investigating

11 This was first posited by the European Court of Human Rights in *McCann v United Kingdom* (27 September 1995), see Chapter 7.

12 E.g. *Bámaca-Velásquez v Guatemala* (25 November 2000) para 201.

and making findings of fact which are adopted by the Court. In the European context this system is no longer followed. The Commission was abolished in 1998. Although the court does have investigating powers of its own, its normal position is as reviewer of the state's fact-finding effort. The Inter-American Court is not required to adopt the facts as found by the Commission.

The extent, nature and rigour of their factual findings is a matter for the judges. It is notable that the empowering statutes (e.g. the Statute of the Inter-American Court 1979) or the Rules of Procedure (e.g. Rules of Court ECHR 2018) say little, if anything, on the content and structure of judgments. It will depend upon factors such as the seriousness of the matter and, importantly, may also reflect the extent of the state's failure to investigate and the degree of cooperation enjoyed by the Court. The ECHR, for example, just requires the Court to give reasons for its judgments and decisions, but it gives no further detail on the kinds of matter that should be included or the depth of the analysis that should be required.[13] These are matters for the Court, which reflect both its customs as they have developed but also a more general sense of the character of a compelling and juristically authoritative decision. But there does seem to be an absence of any general legal rules on this matter – a contrast can be drawn here with, for example, domestic English law on the "sufficiency" of reasons given by an inferior tribunal.

Nevertheless, regional human rights courts have developed various approaches to their own investigative and reporting role as they reason towards a decision. For example, in the case of persons who have disappeared after last being reliably seen in the custody of state agents, there is a presumption of state responsibility which can be rebutted only by an effective investigation by the state. Likewise, the circumstances of the case may indicate a breakdown of effective procedures and remedies in the state. In this case the court, whilst insisting that the burden of proof remains with the applicant and that the standard of proof (despite these being "civil proceedings") is "beyond a reasonable doubt" may nevertheless find the burden discharged on the basis of various presumptions that the court makes.

One of the difficulties of human rights courts is the extent to which they must rely on evidence produced for them by the state party. This can be complex for the obvious reason that as the respondent, the state may have an interest in protecting its agents and that, as said earlier, it is the inadequacies of its investigation and report that may be at the centre of the applicant's claim. The state also has a legitimate interest in the peace and security of its population and may seek to resist disclosure on this ground (e.g. because it is pursuing a truth and reconciliation process). For the Inter-American system in particular, it was state responsibility for atrocity and a consequent refusal to investigate and the provision of de facto, if not de jure, impunity for its formal or informal agents that was a major inspiration for its being set up. And its early cases were characterised by a refusal

13 European Convention for the Protection of Human Rights and Fundamental Freedoms (4 November 1950) Article 45 and Rule 56 (European Court of Human Rights, Rules of Court (16 April 2018).

of states to cooperate. The system has been an instrument of transitional justice and the cooperation of partially reformed states with dark histories takes time to develop.[14] Nevertheless, states have duties to cooperate with a human rights court in the sense that a failure to provide proper information can, in itself, be a breach of those rights which protect the rule of law.[15]

As well as “cover-up” failures, there can also be legitimate reasons for a state to seek not to disclose information to its own inquiry, a national court or an international court. Protection of national security interests is the obvious example. The individual approaches of the different human rights courts to this will be discussed later in the book.

Even in the absence of state cooperation, human rights courts may have a considerable range of sources of evidence available to it. Contextual evidence can be provided by the claimant or by third party interveners (or indeed by the respondent state). In cases involving major alleged violations the courts may accept and give significant evidential weight to, for example, NGO reports, relevant journalism, reports of international bodies, evidence of security services activities disclosed through domestic legal processes and so on.[16] This evidence then forms part of the narrative of the judgment and contributes to the reasons for the decision.

Human rights courts may also have their own powers to undertake investigations which are not, therefore, fully reliant on the respondent state. They can include on-site investigations and so on. These are significant powers of the ECtHR, some of the main dimensions of which do not have express statutory authorisation.[17]

Fundamental to the right to the truth is the notion of a disclosure of what happened which is authoritative, which has legitimacy. This applies to all judicial fora. This self-evidently raises issues about the test for authoritativeness. This includes the reasons for a finding being authoritative to an impartial, disinterested observer but also to the claimant even if it does not endorse their allegations. Such reasons are found in the rule of law and the notions of impartiality and independence of the judiciary that are part of it. These are generally recognised judicial standards which apply mutatis mutandis to its own performance. The difficulty is to adjust the application and understanding of those standards in order to make the right to the truth effective without compromising authority. The courts do this, for example, by accepting that in certain circumstances (such as where a person was last seen in the custody of state agents) an absence of reasonable doubt can be based on a rebuttable but unrebutted presumption of state responsibility.

14 E.g. *Velásquez Rodriguez v Honduras* (29 July 1988).

15 An example is in *Husayn (Abu Zubaydah) v Poland* (24 July 2014) and *Al-Nashiri v Poland* (24 July 2014) – two cases involving the ECtHR's reactions to European involvement in extraordinary rendition.

16 See the discussion in Chapter 7 on the extraordinary rendition cases.

17 The issue is discussed in Chapter 7.

A human rights court also gains some authority from being, like all courts, a "forum of principle"[18] in which the principles underlying contentious actions can be considered and judged. Some qualities, such as independence, depend also upon outcomes. Institutional courage, for example, the willingness to make politically unpopular decisions for the sufficient reason that they are compelled by the evidence and the best interpretation of the law. On this issue confidence in necessary qualities and the processes for appointment of the judges is significant. Of particular importance may be the significance of the different legal traditions (e.g. common law and the civilian tradition) and the effectiveness of their coherence in the judicial judgments.

The perception of the authority of an international court can itself be a politically determined matter (as where unjustified claims of partiality are made in order to undermine the jurisdiction of the court); likewise, its authority may be affected by judgments made about the political context within which it operates. This may apply particularly where officials of the court themselves determine the cases to be brought and the investigations to be made – a matter that applies to international criminal courts, where there is a prosecutor, but less to the human rights courts which receive cases on the basis of standard admissibility criteria.

The process

The aim of human rights law is to provide means for the protection of human rights, including the right to the truth, that is effective. Effectiveness means that the domestic courts, if they can, but international courts emphatically, need to approach their procedural rules with flexibility. So, for example, rules on admissibility, such as the exhaustion of domestic remedies, must be adaptable in the light of the domestic political and judicial circumstances.[19]

On the other hand, there are limits to flexibility. The authority of a court also comes from the law which defines its powers and jurisdiction. This may limit its capacity to rule on disappearances that took place before the state party was bound.[20]

Likewise, as indicated earlier, human rights law is an engagement, a dialogue, with the states. The terms of that engagement, it can be suggested, are different depending on the degree to which the state is a tyranny or in transition or has established effective institutions of representative democracy such as are appropriate in a well-ordered society. The right to the truth in a human rights context challenges, in particular, the duty on the state to disclose information. This raises significant problems about how this can be done, if at all, in ways which uphold legitimate public interests protected by the proper exercise of state power.

18 Ronald Dworkin, *A Matter of Principle* (Clarendon Press 1986), see especially Chapter 2.
19 E.g. ECtHR's discussion in *Ilhan v Turkey* (27 June 2000) para 51.
20 Notably *Janowiec and others v Russia* (21 October 2013).

Realisation of the right to the truth

According to the definition at the beginning of the chapter, the right to the truth implies an authoritative investigation of both the events and politico-social structures that led to atrocity and to the particular circumstances of an individual's suffering. It must result in an authoritative reporting or communication of the results of these investigations. We have also identified an opportunity for victims to narrate their stories as an element of the right. As suggested earlier, the regional human rights courts pursue the right to the truth by both seeking to enforce a duty on states to undertake an effective investigation of alleged atrocities and, also, in giving an account of what happened in the context of their own adjudication where the state is alleged to have failed in this duty.

There are a number of issues arising from this which we will discuss in the following chapters. Here we canvass some of the core points.

Empirical evidence of victims' desires and interests suggests that the right to the truth ought also to include a wider exploration of the perpetrators' purpose, motive or excuse. This may be at a general political/ideological level or again the motive of the individual killer. In the human rights context, it may be relevant in explaining why the state abandoned its responsibility of protection in the case of the victims. Victims may want, for example, public exoneration for the activities alleged against them by the authorities. The kind of broader, contextual explanation that is required by this aspect of the victim's right to the truth may not be necessary for the account that is sufficient to discharge the state's duty to investigate or the court's duty to investigate and report in any particular case.

Human rights courts tend to limit their jurisdiction by the exclusion of *actio popularis*. The focus is on the facts and context of the rights claim before them and not on the more general background to that case. Insofar as the courts have identified the nature and scope of the required investigation (by the state party or by themselves), it is limited in respect of this wider reach.[21] Reasoning may also include the desire of victims or others for a particular account of a political struggle. Unless required by the particularities of the case, human rights courts are likely to decline on grounds, inter alia, of avoiding controversy.[22] The broader, historical picture may, however, be necessary to discharge the right to the truth in its public aspect.

Human rights law contains an implicit theory of state responsibilities which is expressed through the idea of positive duties. Specifically, even if the atrocity was not caused directly by state agents (e.g. it was caused by third parties or by the agents of a foreign country), state failures to prevent atrocity or improper cooperation with a foreign country can be the basis of a breach of the Convention and therefore something that needs to be reported on.

21 E.g. UK House of Lords' interpretation of article 2 ECHR in *R (Gentle) v Prime Minister* (2008).

22 E.g. The ECtHR's refusal to name Armenian killings as Genocide in *Perinçek v Switzerland* (15 October 2015).

Human rights courts, when describing the purpose and consequent scope of an investigation emphasise that it should identify those responsible including any officials. There is little space for official impunity allowed in human rights investigations. The failure of the state's institutions to identify (and punish) those with responsibility can of itself be a breach of a Convention right. There is a comparison to be drawn with truth commissions which may be reluctant to name names if to do so would prejudice future prosecutions. The breach comes from the failure or ineffectiveness of prosecution. What is unclear is whether there would still be a breach if prosecution was halted in order to ensure an effective truth and reconciliation process. Since the main focus of human rights law relates to state responsibility, a divide between the specific (who pulled the trigger?) and the general (who ordered it to happen, what was the chain of command, who failed to intervene to prevent it?) may be opened up. This focus may not fully satisfy a victim insofar as she may be concerned with the former and thus disappointed by an investigation which focuses on the latter. On the other hand, the wider sense of the victim's interest in the right to the truth includes the desire to understand and to know why the atrocity happened, and the human rights focus on the higher officials may be helpful here.

But human rights law, unlike international criminal law, is concerned with identifying state rather than individual responsibility. This responsibility may be identified without any naming of names and without any assigned attribution of responsibility. This is a matter for the state and the operation of its criminal law. The failure of the state and its institutions (e.g. prosecution authorities) can be the basis of a violation without the Court itself identifying names. Furthermore, as said earlier, the attribution of state responsibility can be based on presumptions of responsibility and without the precise order of events and personal decisions being identified.

For a state to act compatibly with a relevant Convention right, giving, for instance, the right to life its proper significance, may require an appropriate punishment for those responsible and that can include the need for criminal sanctions against officials and, furthermore, criminal sanctions that reflect the gravity of the breach. Too mild a punishment can, in itself, be a breach of human rights law.[23] The punishment and the refusal to accept official immunity are essential to the legal primacy, the weight and force, given to a human right. But a human rights court itself cannot punish.[24]

An aspect of the right to the truth includes a victim's needs or desires to tell their story in their own words. The state's investigation must give space for victim and/or family but does not give their position any primacy. So far as a human

23 E.g. *Gäfgen v Germany* (1 June 2010) in the ECHR context.

24 This is different at the international criminal level. Here, an argument in support of the unity of law, can be made: the failure by a state to seize the ICC in respect of a person within its jurisdiction could be a violation in itself (e.g. decision in relation to non-state compliance in *Prosecutor v Omar Hassan Ahmad Al Bashir* (6 July 2017).

rights court investigation is concerned, the court will have the applicant's evidence. But in the end, it is the court, with its authority, and on the basis of its duties of impartiality and judicial reason, that gives the authoritative account. This is not the same thing as the victim's account in her or his own words. There is no logical reason why it should even correspond with the victim's views. The rules of court (of the ECtHR at least) do not allow a victim, other than the claimant, to be represented before it. Nor is there a place for public hearings where the court listens to victims.

The remedies of a regional human rights court involve, mainly, the declaration that there has or has not been a breach of human rights. Additional remedies, such as payments in "just satisfaction" are also available. In order to satisfy the right to the truth a wider range of remedies may be necessary. Both the ECtHR and IACtHR are now more imaginative regarding remedies in this context. For example, the court could order a state to make an investigation or undertake a prosecution subject to its own power to refer individuals to the International Criminal Court. They could suggest the use of condemnatory language or, like the IACtHR has done, decide that an appropriate apology be made – directly or as part of an effective response by the state to an alleged breach. Remedies are discussed further in later chapters.

The role of truth commissions

In response to state failure, over the past 30 years, around 40 truth (and reconciliation) commissions with different mandates and legacies have been created. According to the International Center for Transitional Justice, they are "nonjudicial, independent panels of inquiry typically set up to establish the facts and context of serious violations of human rights or of international humanitarian law".[25] They are temporary establishments where the commission's members conduct research and hear a multitude of individual testimonies to uncover the past abuses caused by a regime or through conflict, thus exposing patterns of human rights violations. They are seen as complementing criminal and civil actions. The key premise is that through elucidating the truth about these past gross human rights violations a better, more just, stable and democratic society can be built.[26] In other words, the commission is a starting point for accountability mechanisms,

25 International Center for Transitional Justice, 'Truth Commissions' (2008) www.ictj.org/sites/default/files/ICTJ-Global-Truth-Commissions-2008-English.pdf accessed 14 February 2019. The first ever truth commission was the 1974 Ugandan Commission of Inquiry into Disappearances; this was followed by the internationally significant and better known Argentinian National Commission on the Disappearance of Persons (CONADEP) in 1984, the Chilean and Guatemalan Truth and Reconciliation Commission and the perhaps best known South African Commission to deal with Apartheid (Priscilla Hayner, *Unspeakable Truths. Transitional Justice and the Challenge of Truth Commissions* (2nd edn, Routledge 2011).

26 Louis Bickford, 'Unofficial Truth Projects' (2007) 29(4) Human Rights Quarterly 994.

reparation efforts and government reforms to follow. According to Hayner, a truth commission

> (1) is focused on past, rather than ongoing, events; (2) investigates a pattern of events that took place over a period of time; (3) engages directly and broadly with the affected population, gathering information on their experiences; (4) is a temporary body, with the aim of concluding with a final report; and (5) is officially authorized or empowered by the state under review.[27]

Usually the commission's work is made available to the public, disseminated and discussed.

It is worth distinguishing between truth commissions designed to comprehensively examine large-scale violations of human rights and international humanitarian law on the one hand, and commissions of inquiry on the other. The latter are "independent panels to investigate an incident or situation, issue a report setting out its findings and propose recommendations".[28] They lack, however, in coercive power and cannot compel the production of evidence, relying on state cooperation instead. Typically, the UN Security Council, General Assembly, Secretary-General and Human Rights Council can establish such inquiries. The focus in the following is on comprehensive truth commissions.

The mandate

Whilst official truth commissions are established by a government and are thus an action by the state, they hold fewer powers than courts (though, controversially, the South African Truth and Reconciliation Commission was able to offer individualised amnesty)[29] and therefore, in principle, do neither duplicate nor interfere with the judiciary. In fact, truth commissions are often seen as a complementary mechanism to criminal justice efforts, not a substitute, whereby commissions should be accompanied by prosecutions.[30] This theory, however, has found challenges in practice where the politics of different transitional justice institutions has resulted in rivalry.[31]

27 Hayner *supra* note 25 at 12.

28 Christine Harwood, ''International Commissions of Inquiry as Law-Makers' (2016) *European Society of International Law, Conference Paper Series* No 1/2016 at 3.

29 International Centre for Transitional Justice, 'Truth Commissions II' (2008) www.ictj.org/sites/default/files/ICTJ-Global-Truth-Commissions-2008-English2.pdf accessed 14 February 2019.

30 Ibid.

31 Jasna Dragovic-Soso, 'History of a Failure: Attempts to Create a National Truth and Reconciliation Commission in Bosnia and Herzegovina, 1997–2006' (2016) 20 (2) International Journal of Transitional Justice 292. Examples from Sierra Leone and Timor Leste would suggest that harmonious coexistence of truth commissions alongside judicial mechanisms – the latter usually being equipped with more powers – are rare (William Schabas and Shane

Unlike criminal justice efforts that are focused on the narrow involvement of an individual suspected of having committed a crime, the scope for investigation of truth commissions is usually much broader, permitting investigations into government practices and the responsibility of the state. The South African Truth and Reconciliation Commission, for example, was tasked with recording and acknowledging crimes of apartheid, whereas the Peruvian Truth and Reconciliation Commission was tasked with investigating an internal armed conflict between 1980 and 2000 claiming around 69,000 lives. By contrast, the German *Enquete Kommission* into the Consequences of the SED Dictatorship[32] in Germany and inquiry into overcoming the consequences of the SED Dictatorship in the Process of German Unity conducted a rather scientific investigation without much public participation into state repression geared towards historical correction rather than reconciliation.[33]

Another crucial aim of truth commissions is to focus on victims, their rights, interests and needs. Many victims of gross human rights violations were marginalised in society. Truth commissions are seen as a (visible) vehicle to empower them and educate society about civil rights.[34] In addition to discovering, clarifying, documenting and officially acknowledging abuses through a government sanctioned fact-finding process, truth commissions are also geared towards addressing victims' needs and aiding accountability mechanisms. Their mandate typically includes investigation of institutional involvement in and state responsibility for the crimes committed. Part of the mandate may include the recommendation of reforms, at political or judicial level, for security forces and the educational system, but also recommendations for reparations. Truth commission reports may not only shame and blame past governments for its shortcomings, but they also seek to speak to governments about how to address those past inadequacies. Ultimately, truth commissions, it is hoped, will have a positive impact in promoting a well-ordered society and reconciliation and avoiding future conflict.[35]

The mandate of a commission or its terms of reference may be explicit about the scope and limitations of the commission's remit, or it may provide more generic guidance. The mandate of a commission usually defines its powers, subject matter, geographic and temporal scope of the commission and is created by national legislation, decree or a peace accord.[36] As a result of domestic and international political forces, interferences or negotiations, the mandate can be

---

Darcy (ed) *Truth Commissions and Courts. The Tensions Between Criminal Justice and the Search for Truth* (Springer 2004)).

32 SED stands for the Sozialistische Einheitspartei Deutschlands, the socialist unity party of Germany. It was the governing political party in the German Democratic Republic from 1949 until 1989.

33 Susanne Buckley-Zistel, 'Narrative Truths. On the construction of the past in truth commissions' in S Buckley-Zistel (ed), *Transitional Justice Theories* (Routledge 2014) at 76–84.

34 'Truth Commissions', *supra* note 25 and Bickford, *supra* note 26.

35 Bickford (ibid) at 994.

36 Hayner *supra* note 25 at 75.

restrictive, by, for example, only focusing on enforced disappearances,[37] and in that way limiting the breadth of investigation and subsequent truth to be reported, ignoring other sections of gross human rights abuses. In this respect, the value of truth commission reports has to be qualified depending on the given circumstances, power and remit. Hayner suggests that "as a general rule, terms of reference should be sufficiently broad and flexible to allow investigation into all forms of rights abuses, leaving to the commission the decisions of what specific cases or practices to investigate and report".[38] But truth commissions may have a more restrictive mandate, resulting in a limited truth-value concentrating on a narrow set of crimes.

The impartial fact-finders

In addition to the need for transparency of mandate and powers afforded to the commission, the selection and appointment of commissioners is equally important and has a great impact not only on the report that is created but also on how it is perceived by individuals, sections of society, state authorities and the international community. Hayner goes so far as to suggest that "[p]erhaps more than any other single factor, the person or persons selected to manage a truth commission will determine its ultimate success or failure".[39] Successful management and strong leadership of the entire process is necessary. Similarly, much depends on the selection process of the commissioner to ensure the independence of the commission and public trust in it. The commissioners are involved in the interpretation of the mandate, policy and investigation process and, crucially, determine the content of the final report.

Selection processes increasingly engage the public to gain the necessary support and, as in the example of Sierra Leone, can also include international members.[40] Commissioners should fairly represent a plethora of views and sections of society but also have different areas of expertise, including in human rights. But commissions come in many forms, as the *Enquete Kommission* evidences, where the majority of commissioners came from West Germany, resulting in the criticism that the truth constructed by the commission on the East German past was fashioned based on West German interpretations thereof.[41]

In the commissioner's interpretation of the mandate, self-imposed restrictions on how to implement the mandate may follow giving the work of the commission

37 Like, for example, the Argentine National Commission on the Disappearance of Persons (CONADEP).
38 Hayner *supra* note 25 at 76.
39 Ibid at 211.
40 Ibid at 211–13.
41 Buckley-Zistel *supra* 33 at 82. The commission structure and operation followed the established guidelines for parliamentary commission of inquiry in Germany, with political parties represented equivalent to their representation in parliament as a whole. The successor party to the SED, the Democratic Socialist Party, was represented on the commission with one member. See also Hayner *supra* note 25 at 52.

a particular emphasis. An example is the South African Truth and Reconciliation Commission, where a "consciously reconciliation-oriented atmosphere was created in order to convince those testifying that peaceful coexistence in South Africa was a necessity to which they could personally contribute with their actions and testimonies".[42] Reconciliation was a key goal guiding the interpretation of the commission's mandate, which might give its truth-finding function a particular direction that could cause tension between public and individual truth needs.

The process

Ultimately, it is the commission that decides what is investigated, how information is recorded and what features in the final report. The process comprises the careful research, consideration and analysis of documents. Such documents include testimonies, official records, unofficial records and artefacts. By way of an example, the South African Truth and Reconciliation Commission heard testimonies from over 23,000 victims and witnesses of human rights abuses in public hearings or closed proceedings.[43] Sometimes perpetrators too can testify. Based on these narratives, the final report is fashioned.

To facilitate the process, some information management system is needed to ensure the standardised recording and evaluation of information received. There are a number of challenges associated with documenting the truth: they are strategic, technical and methodological challenges. Determining which documents to collect, record or prioritise depends on the remit of the commission and what particular societal issue of human rights abuses it focuses on. Questions about who to work in partnership with, such as libraries or human rights organisations but also funders, form part of the process. Technical issues include the identification, collection and cataloguing of materials, their organisation and storage, security of staff and collated materials, and preservation of the chain-of-custody, ownership and legal issues surrounding documents. In addition, long-term preservation plans as well as accessibility to the public need to be determined.[44]

Crucially, a commission, according to Hayner, needs to have a clear set of guidelines about what evidentiary standards and level of proof it operates with, and these need to be made explicit in the report, since the report may have severe ramifications for individuals, government sections and parties to the conflict.[45] In her opinion, truth commissions increasingly rely on a "balance of probabilities"

42 Buckley-Zistel (ibid.) at 79. See also Annelies Verdoolaege, 'Dealing with a traumatic past: the victim hearings of the South African truth and reconciliation commission and their reconciliation discourse' (2009) (6)4 Critical Discourse Studies 297.

43 'Truth Commissions II' *supra* note 29.

44 L Bickford and others, 'Documenting Truth', (International Centre for Transitional Justice Report 2009) www.ictj.org/sites/default/files/ICTJ-DAG-Global-Documenting-Truth-2009-English.pdf accessed 14 February 2019.

45 Hayner *supra* note 25 at 222.

standard to come to a finding. Such an approach has found explicit expression by the South African Commission:

> Given the investigative nature of the Commission's process and the limited legal impact of naming, the Commission made findings on the identity of those involved in gross violations of human rights based on the balance of probabilities. This required a lower burden of proof than that required by the conventional criminal justice system. It meant that, when confronted with different versions of events, the Commission had to decide which version was the more probable, reasonable or likely, after taking all the available evidence into account.[46]

The Chilean Commission operated with a "reasonable and honest conviction" approach, considering a multitude of sources to come to such a view:

> The Commission reached a reasonable and honest conviction about each case based on the testimony of the victims' relatives, of eyewitnesses to relevant events, of current and former government agents, uniformed and civilian, including statements by now-retired high and mid-level ranking officers of the armed forces and police and by former agents of state security; press reports; expert testimony and opinion; some visits to the places where events took place; documentation from human rights organizations; official documents and certificates such as birth certificates, death certificates, autopsy reports, voter registration rolls, criminal records, immigration service records about entry into and departure from the country and many other official documents.[47]

The El Salvador Commission required two credible and independent sources to confirm a fact and operated with three different levels of certainty backing a particular finding, stating which of the following three levels of certainty applied for each finding:

1 Overwhelming evidence – conclusive or highly convincing evidence to support the Commission's finding
2 Substantial evidence – very solid evidence to support the Commission's finding
3 Sufficient evidence – more evidence to support the Commission's finding than to contradict it.[48]

46 South Africa TRC Report, *supra* note 6 volume 1, chapter 4 section 155 at 91.

47 Report of the Chilean National Commission on Truth and Reconciliation (University of Notre Dame Press 1993) www.usip.org/sites/default/files/resources/collections/truth_commissions/Chile90-Report/Chile90-Report.pdf accessed 14 February 2019 at 41.

48 Report of the UN Truth Commission on El Salvador. Annex: From Madness to Hope: The 12-Year War in El Salvador (1 April 1993) at 24.

This approach has been criticised since it resulted in convincing evidence that did not meet the threshold of two independent sources being required, being left out of the final report.

Key is that the evidentiary standard applied has to be made explicit to assure transparency and consistency.

Especially if a commission intends to name individuals as wrongdoers, the question arises what due process rules apply. Whether a commission should or should not engage in naming individuals has been subject to debate,[49] but a minimum set of three rules are recommended should a commission choose to reveal names: the individual to be named in a report should be informed of the allegations voiced against her and the commission's intention to name her in the report; an opportunity should be afforded to such individuals to respond (in person or writing) to the allegations expressed and evidence against them, though this might not extend to the full disclosure of the source of the evidence; finally, the report ought to express clearly that its findings do not amount or equate to criminal guilt.[50]

Realisation of the right to the truth

Truth commissions have been recommended as a way to deal with hidden truths but also as a means to address or verify the existence of multiple truths where versions of truths run along ethnic divides.[51] The potential of truth commissions to create a narrative of a particular coloration depending on mandate, strategy and process is undisputed. To what extent this aids the realisation of the right to the truth is thus also somewhat dependent on those parameters. Interestingly, the International Center for Transitional Justice in its advocacy explicitly aligns truth-seeking and truth commissions with the right to the truth in an attempt to anchor such initiatives in international law.[52] Naftali suggests this is to enhance the legitimacy of transitional justice initiatives as it puts them on a firm legal as opposed to moral foundation.[53] Is this alignment justified?

It is fair to say that truth commissions have the potential to offer an authoritative investigation of both the events and politico-social structures that led to atrocity so long as the category of atrocity corresponds with its mandate. Patterns of abuse, state involvement and responsibilities of various parties to the conflict

49 Hayner's view is that 'a truth commission should seek to tell as much of the full truth as possible, including the names of persons responsible for the abuses' (Hayner, *supra* note 25 at 143).

50 Ibid 141. Whether domestic legal remedies such as an injunction would be possible to prevent the naming of individuals is not always clear.

51 Neil Kritz and Jakob Finci, 'A Truth and Reconciliation Commission in Bosnia and Herzegovina: an Idea Whose Time has Come' (2001) 3 International Law Forum 50.

52 International Center for Transitional Justice, 'Truth and Memory' (2017) www.ictj.org/our-work/transitional-justice-issues/truth-and-memory accessed 14 February 2019.

53 Patricia Naftali, 'The Politics of Truth' (2015) December, Revue Québécoise de droit international 101.

can be comprehensively outlined through proceedings and the report. The public element of the right to the truth is thus addressed. In some instances, like the Chilean Commission, for example, this might also mean that individual cases are examined and thus individual suffering – at least to some extent – addressed and acknowledged. However, it is not said that a victim has standing or the right to invoke such an investigation, but a victim may have the possibility to offer testimony (sometimes publicly) and other evidentiary material to the commission. Whether the individual suffering is explicitly acknowledged in a report beyond is a separate matter.

The report that the commission issues can be seen as an authoritative, often public, reporting of the commission's findings. But again the investigations the commission can conduct may not equate to the same level of investigations that state institutions may be able to deliver, for example, the need to account for the fate and whereabouts of a victim might be beyond a commission's scope. States also may be reluctant to share information or open archives should this be to the detriment of those in power. The inability to compel cooperation can severely hamper a truth commission's investigations. That said, the commission's report may present a valuable starting point for further state action to follow: by identifying state obligation towards victims in the form of further investigations, prosecutions and reparations, states may be compelled to act and implement those mechanisms which include steps to realise the right to the truth. In this regard, truth commissions are also seen as contributors to the right to reparations and the right to justice as important transitional justice principles.

As for the right encompassing the opportunity for victims to narrate their story, some form of truth commission, once trust in the institution has developed, may be very well suited to this, offering a safe forum for victims to report and recount their stories.[54] Whilst victims have no standing as such, it is difficult to imagine that their offer to share their story would be turned away by the commission. On the contrary, truth commissions aim to gather testimonies on behalf of victims. In this way victims can be a key contributor to truth commission's evidence gathering whilst at the same time fulfilling a key aspect of the right to truth.

International criminal courts

By default, international criminal courts and tribunals are set up with a view that ascertaining the truth is possible to a certain standard of probability. Primary organs are the judicial divisions comprising pretrial, trial and appeals chambers; the Office of the Prosecutor tasked with analysing jurisdiction, admissibility, investigation and prosecution, and a registry offering administrative support to the court as well as organising witness and victim protection.

According to an early decision of the International Criminal Tribunal for the Former Yugoslavia (ICTY), "[i]nternational criminal justice . . . must pursue its

54 Though truth-telling has the potential of re-traumatisation, as will be discussed in Chapter 8.

mission of revealing the truth about the acts perpetrated and suffering endured, as well as identifying and arresting those accused of responsibility".[55] The truth-seeking function of the Court encompasses a period of investigation and evidence-gathering typically conducted by the Office of the Prosecutor followed by the verification of charges. For the purpose of conducting its investigation into alleged offences, international criminal law mechanisms, unlike their human rights counterparts, operate within the territories of the abusing states, and as such, can gather first-hand access to evidential materials, and interview those which might assist in answering the many questions that victims and their families have in the aftermath of atrocities.[56] Proceedings are held in public, unless security and safety demand closed sessions.

The mandate

The jurisdiction of international criminal institutions like the International Criminal Court is typically "limited to the most serious crimes of concern to the international community as a whole".[57] The mandate is based upon a shared notion of values that the international community has in common, a universal bond that it shares. This mandate encompasses the fight against impunity for those responsible for heinous crimes such as genocide, crimes against humanity and war crimes. At the ICC, a truth-seeking function is placed both on the prosecutor and the judges by virtue of Article 54 and Article 69(3). The prosecutor's investigative duty comprises an obligation to seek to establish the truth, and in particular, to consider whether there might be criminal responsibility under the terms of the statute.[58] The duty, however, is confined to an examination of the crime base and the accused's link to it. Information needed by the victims, such as identification evidence, might be superfluous to the prosecutor's case. In addition, prosecutorial strategy, jurisdictional limits and fair trial requirements may have a restricting effect on the nature of truth uncovered.[59] Therefore, despite the truth-seeking function of the international criminal tribunals, at their core remains the determination of the guilt or innocence of the defendant. Accordingly, the determination and nature of truth which they produce must be focused on that goal. Victims, while viewed as a primary beneficiary of international criminal justice mechanisms, have limited influence on the prosecutorial decisions.

A too narrow an interpretation of the mandate, however, fails to address the number of theoretical underpinnings that have been associated with international

55 *Prosecutor v Karadžić and Mladić* (11 July 1996) at 3.

56 Dermot Groome, 'The Right to Truth in the Fight Against Impunity' (2011) 29(1) Berkeley Journal of International Law 181 at 191).

57 Article 1 of the Rome Statute (Rome Statute of the International Criminal Court (17 July 1998).

58 Ibid Article 54 of the Rome Statute.

59 Margaret deGuzman, 'Choosing to Prosecute: Expressive Selection at the International criminal Court' (2012) 33 Michigan Journal of International Law 265.

criminal trials. Whilst some have doubted the existence of a clear, fruitful purpose of international criminal justice in general,[60] justifications for the presence of international criminal trials typically include retribution, deterrence, rehabilitation, restorative justice and condemnation.[61] The latter includes the notion of courts making clear their condemnation and sense of social solidarity by sending a message of moral outrage to society in an attempt to maintain social cohesion or affirm a common moral order. In that way, if the right to the truth is conceived as a moral principle as opposed to a substantive right, then arguments for a greater victim focus can be made as forming part of international criminal justice's theoretical foundation.

The impartial fact-finders

Selection and appointment of the judges to international criminal institutions is made on criteria of impartiality, integrity, expertise and moral character. Article 13 of the ICTY statute and Article 36(3)(a) of the Rome Statute express this very clearly, with the latter stating that

> judges shall be chosen from among persons of high moral character, impartiality and integrity who possess the qualifications required in their respective States for appointment to the highest judicial offices.[62]

Selection of candidates should take into account the representation of principal legal systems, geography and fair representation of female and male judges.[63] Once appointed, the independence of the judges in the performance of their duties is mandatory.[64]

Former ICC Judge Hans-Peter Kaul described the judge's role as follows:

> The trial judges are thus endowed with a large measure of influence and investigative autonomy during the trial, without it amounting to an inquisitorial system. This special position of the judges helps to increase the chambers' control of the proceedings and at the same time to establish a trial system in which various judicial traditions complement each other. It therefore cannot be said that the criminal procedure of the ICC is either inquisitorial or adversarial. Rather, it is a system sui generis, which will be feinted further by the jurisprudence.[65]

60 E.g. Miijan Damaska, 'What is the point of International Criminal Justice?' (2008) 83(1) Chicago-Kent Law Review 329.

61 For an outline of theoretical frameworks that may justify prosecution and punishment within a domestic context, see Beth Van Schaack and Ronald C Slye, *International Criminal Law and Its Enforcement* (Foundation Press 2007) at 13–18.

62 Rome Statute *supra* note 57 Article 36(3)(a).

63 Rome Statute Articles 36(8)(a)(i), (ii), and (iii).

64 Rome Statute Article 40(1).

65 Hans-Peter Kaul, 'Developments at the International Criminal Court' (2005) 99 The American Journal of International Law 370 at 376.

This new sui generis system, which blends civil law and common law traditions, does however mean that with flexibility of interpretation of the Rome Statute, its object and purpose, judges may come to different views. At other tribunals, including the hybrid tribunals,[66] where domestic and international law is blended, similarly interpretative divergence is always a possibility.

The process

The standard of proof required at international criminal tribunals is "beyond reasonable doubt".[67] Article 66(3) of the ICC, for example, states "[i]n order to convict the accused, the Court must be convinced of the guilt of the accused beyond reasonable doubt". Furthermore, a trial chamber can only convict if satisfied that the accused bears criminal responsibility beyond reasonable doubt based on the entirety of the admitted evidence.[68] It is the prosecutor who has the burden of proof.

The basic format of an international criminal trial (following on from the confirmation of charges) is to hear the opening statements by the parties, followed by presentation of evidence, closing arguments and deliberations, after which the judgment is issued. A reasoned majority judgment is possible. Appeals to the conviction, acquittal or sentence are permissible with the Appeal Chamber affirming, reversing or revising a trial chamber decision. Throughout, fair trial requirements need to be observed during the process. The procedural rules adopt a rather flexible approach to the admissibility of evidence, which reflects the distinctive blend between adversarial and inquisitorial procedural models. Notwithstanding differences in procedural philosophy (collective versus a subjective, party-driven approach), both adversarial and inquisitorial models of adjudication are rooted in the aspiration to ascertain facts on the basis of evidence and ultimately arrive at the truth. At the ICC, victims too may make presentations during the proceedings by virtue of Article 68(3).[69]

Realisation of the right to the truth

The truth-telling function of verdicts, whether a guilty verdict or an acquittal, has been acknowledged,[70] but it has to be pointed out that the right to the truth is

66 Such as the Extraordinary Chambers in the Courts of Cambodia or the Special Tribunal for Sierra Leone.

67 For a definition of 'reasonable doubt' see *Miller* v *Minister of Pensions* (1947) at 373 "Proof beyond a reasonable doubt does not mean proof beyond the shadow of a doubt. The law would fail to protect the community if it admitted fanciful possibilities to deflect the course of justice. If the evidence is so strong against a man as to leave only a remote possibility in his favour, which can be dismissed with the sentence "of course it is possible but not in the least probable" the case is proved beyond reasonable doubt, but nothing short of that will suffice."

68 *Prosecutor v Ntagerura et al.* (7 July 2006) para 278.

69 Rule 89(1) allows for opening and closing statement in order to express victims' views and concerns (International Criminal Court, Rules of Procedure and Evidence (9 September 2002)).

70 *Prosecutor v Ljubičić* (23 December 2008) at footnote 18.

not contained in the ICC statute or any other international tribunal's statute. As alluded to earlier, and in the words of Ruti Teitel, a judgment "is an expression of shared values, at least implicitly",[71] but how it realises the right to the truth requirements is a separate matter. Reflecting on our right to the truth definition, an investigation is conducted by the prosecutor into the events surrounding the charges the accused is alleged to have committed. Investigations into the political and social structures surrounding the crimes and the accused are contextually significant, since the crimes in question require a high degree of cooperation often only possible due to the collaboration of persons in positions of authority and the functioning of an apparatus. But importantly, whilst state parties are obliged to cooperate (Article 86) with the investigation and prosecution, determinations of responsibility are made only regarding the individual defendant.

The investigations resulting in trials are narrow in scope, focused on the accused and his or her involvement in events. This scope may or may not include the particular circumstances of an individual victim and her suffering. To what extent the investigation offers meaningful information to the victim and whether this information can be fully disclosed depends on the given situation. Attempts to expand the breadth of truth-seeking activity and disclosure by the court risks impinging upon the defendant's right to a fair and expeditious trial.[72] In addition, the processes are lengthy and the information gathered through investigations may not be available to victims for many years, which might adversely affect the realisation of the right to truth for those victims.

It is fair to say that the judgments issued by international criminal tribunals would qualify as authoritative, public reporting of the results of the chamber's findings and a determination on what elements of the investigations have been found reliable as far as the defendant is concerned (not necessarily the entire investigations). Through testimonies and victim participation, an opportunity may be given to selected victims to testify. However, this type of testimony before a criminal court may be focused on particular aspects of a victim's experiences and may be ill-suited to their needs.[73] Testifying may not equate to narrating the victim's story. Therefore, rather than being realised as a goal of the proceedings in question, the truth required by victims and their families may emerge as a by-product of the criminal process.

Interestingly at the ICC, pursuant to Article 75, reparations such as restitution, compensation and rehabilitation may be awarded.[74] For the awarding of reparations through the ICC, state parties also have a duty under Articles 75(5)

71 Ruti Teitel, *Humanity's Law* (Oxford University Press 2011) at 199.

72 For a discussion of the tension between the right to a fair trial and victim participation, see Salvatore Zappalà, 'The rights of victims v the rights of the accused' (2010) 8(1) *Journal of International Criminal Justice* 137; Bridie McAsey, 'Victim Participation at the International Criminal Court and its Impact on Procedural Fairness' (2011) 18 *Australian International Law Journal* 105.

73 Eric Stover, *The Witnesses. War Crimes and the Promise of Justice in The Hague* (University of Pennsylvania Press 2005) at 129.

74 Rome Statute *supra* note 57 Article 75(1).

and 109 of the statute to cooperate with those decisions. At the Kampala Review Conference it was expressly recognised that, with regards to victim participation and reparation, a key challenge was

> (ix) Developing mechanisms to address reparations at the national level and help to facilitate victims' rights to truth, justice and reparations, with a particular focus on ensuring access and benefits for women and children.[75]

This admission, coupled with decisions at the court, most notably Judge Steiner's single-judge decision,[76] and academic opinion suggesting a better harnessing and communication of information to render it more useful to victims is needed,[77] indicates that the right to the truth has relevance for international criminal institutions generally and the ICC in particular. Clearly criminal institutions like truth commissions have potential to realise aspects of the right to truth.

Conclusion: the right to the truth in these differing contexts

This brief, preliminary exposition was designed to tease out the differences and similarities in which the right to the truth can be realised.

Human rights courts clearly recognise the right to the truth, predominantly as placing an obligation on states. They also acknowledge the individual and public dimension of the right, and they seek to compel the state to take action in realising the right to truth by way of conducting further investigations and through other remedies. The individual can bring a claim to the court, but society as such cannot. And yet, the public benefit of investigations and knowing the truth is specified. The assessment of evidence brought before a human rights court might fulfil the investigative component of the right to the truth regarding the circumstances and whereabouts of an individual. The right to the truth realisation, however, remains incomplete without implementation of the court's reparative orders by the state. Similarly, human rights courts seemingly fall short of the narrative component. Therefore, whilst human rights courts recognise the right to the truth as a right of individuals and society (possibly derived from other human rights as opposed to a freestanding right), in itself they do not have the capacity to offer the necessary investigation, instead ordering this to be realised by the state. However, this is not to diminish the role of the Inter-American and European Courts: they contribute to the right to the truth through their judgments and findings of fact and in ordering the state to comply with its duty.

75 International Criminal Court, 'The impact of the Rome Statute system on victims and affected communities' Review Conference of the Rome Statute, Discussion Paper, RC/ST/V/INF.4 (30 May 2019), 11 at para 36 a) ix).

76 *Prosecutor v Katanga and Ngudjolo* (13 May 2008).

77 Gaynor *supra* note 7 suggests a part of the judgments outlining events based on a balance of probabilities standard whilst Hayner proposes that the OTP could release a summary report of its findings since the Rome Statute is silent on this matter (Hayner *supra* note 25 at 101).

Truth commissions, set up by states in response to some kind of state failure, also seek to make recommendation to the state to advance the realisation of the right to the truth on behalf of victims and society. Truth commissions, by virtue of their design and purpose, have great potential by themselves to realise the truth explicitly the public element and implicitly the individual aspects of the right to the truth, since they are tasked with investigating past abuses and authoritatively reporting on them. The conducted investigations may sufficiently outline the events and politico-social structures that led to atrocity as well as, in some cases, the particular circumstances of an individual's suffering. Through their victim focus and reliance on victims' testimonies and narratives, they also have the capacity, unlike the human rights court and the international criminal tribunals, to accommodate the victims' truth-telling or narrative element of the right. Whilst truth commissions may not have the right to the truth explicitly as a constituting source in their founding documents,[78] their setup can be seen as a response to the perceived necessity of the right morally if not legally under international law and create, preserve and archive the reports documenting gross human rights violations.

Finally, international criminal crimes, in their focus on individual criminal responsibility, are seen as a vehicle for propagating truth coupled with the sentiment of moral duty to condemn atrocities. Authoritative investigations, along with judicial fact-finding and reporting, are conducted and are likely to address the politico-social structures that led to the alleged individual criminal responsibility; whether the individually relevant component of the right is addressed depends on the scope of the indictment and consequent trial. Similarly, the ability by victims to narrate their story is contingent on the prosecutorial choices. Notably, the right to the truth does not form part of the founding documents for international criminal tribunals. Victims and society have no standing (other than insofar as the court was created to serve them and they are represented by the prosecutor and possibly through victim participation), pointing to a perhaps more principled understanding of the moral desirability of realising the right to the truth as opposed to a rights-based approach.

In the following chapters, we will examine these fora in greater detail to appreciate and fully understand the complexities, relevance and nuances of the right to the truth. The law and practice of Inter-American and European human rights courts, truth commissions throughout the world and criminal justice institutions, including the International Criminal Court, will be examined in the light of the general considerations given in this chapter.

References

Aristoteles, *Metaphysik* (Meiner 1995).
Bickford L, 'Unofficial Truth Projects' (2007) 29(4) Human Rights Quarterly 994.

78 Though some have, see Chapter 8 on truth commissions.

Bickford L and others, 'Documenting Truth', (International Centre for Transitional Justice Report 2009) www.ictj.org/sites/default/files/ICTJ-DAG-Global-Documenting-Truth-2009-English.pdf accessed 14 February 2019.

Blackburn S and Simmons K (eds), *Truth* (Oxford University Press 1999).

Buckley-Zistel S, 'Narrative Truths. On the construction of the past in truth commissions' in Buckley-Zistel S (ed), *Transitional Justice Theories* (Routledge 2014).

Damaska M, 'What is the point of International Criminal Justice?' (2008) 83(1) Chicago-Kent Law Review 329.

deGuzman M, 'Choosing to Prosecute: Expressive Selection at the International criminal Court' (2012) 33 Michigan Journal of International Law 265.

Dragovic-Soso J, 'History of a Failure: Attempts to Create a National Truth and Reconciliation Commission in Bosnia and Herzegovina, 1997–2006' (2016) 20 (2) International Journal of Transitional Justice 292.

Dworkin R, *A Matter of Principle* (Clarendon Press 1986).

Gaynor F, 'Uneasy Partners – Evidence, Truth and History in International Trials' (2012) 10(5) Journal of International Criminal Justice 1257.

Groome D, 'The Right to Truth in the Fight Against Impunity' (2011) 29(1) Berkeley Journal of International Law 181.

Harwood C, 'International Commissions of Inquiry as Law-Makers' (2016) *European Society of International Law, Conference Paper Series* No 1/2016.

Hayner P, *Unspeakable Truths. Transitional Justice and the Challenge of Truth Commissions* (2nd edn, Routledge 2011).

International Center for Transitional Justice, 'Truth and Memory' (2017) www.ictj.org/our-work/transitional-justice-issues/truth-and-memory accessed 14 February 2019.

International Center for Transitional Justice, 'Truth Commissions' (2008) www.ictj.org/sites/default/files/ICTJ-Global-Truth-Commissions-2008-English.pdf accessed 14 February 2019.

International Centre for Transitional Justice, 'Truth Commissions II' (2008) www.ictj.org/sites/default/files/ICTJ-Global-Truth-Commissions-2008-English2.pdf accessed 14 February 2019.

Kaul H-P, 'Developments at the International Criminal Court' (2005) 99 The American Journal of International Law 370.

Kritz N and Finci J, 'A Truth and Reconciliation Commission in Bosnia and Herzegovina: an Idea Whose Time has Come' (2001) 3 International Law Forum 50.

McAsey B, 'Victim Participation at the International Criminal Court and its Impact on Procedural Fairness' (2011) 18 *Australian International Law Journal* 105.

Naftali P, 'The Politics of Truth' (2015) December, Revue Québécoise de droit international 101.

Report of the Chilean National Commission on Truth and Reconciliation (University of Notre Dame Press 1993). www.usip.org/sites/default/files/resources/collections/truth_commissions/Chile90-Report/Chile90-Report.pdf accessed 14 February 2019.

Rorty R, 'Science as Solidarity' in Nelson J, Megill A and McCloskey D (eds) *The Rhetoric of the Human Sciences Language and Argument in Scholarship and Public Affairs*, (University of Wisconsin Press 1987).

Russell B, *The Problems of Philosophy* (orig. 1912 Start Publishing 2012).

Schabas W, *Unimaginable Atrocities* (Oxford University Press 2012).

Schabas W and Darcy S (eds), *Truth Commissions and Courts. The Tensions Between Criminal Justice and the Search for Truth* (Springer 2004).
Stover E, *The Witnesses. War Crimes and the Promise of Justice in The Hague* (University of Pennsylvania Press 2005.
Teitel R, *Globalizing Transitional Justice.* Contemporary Essays (Oxford University Press 2016).
Teitel R, *Humanity's Law* (Oxford University Press 2011).
Truth and Reconciliation Commission, 'Truth and Reconciliation Commission of South Africa Final Report (Volume 1)' (29 October 1998).
Van Schaack B and Slye R C, *International Criminal Law and Its Enforcement* (Foundation Press 2007).
Verdoolaege A, 'Dealing with a traumatic past: the victim hearings of the South African truth and reconciliation commission and their reconciliation discourse' (2009) (6)4 Critical Discourse Studies 297.
Zappalà S, 'The rights of victims v the rights of the accused' (2010) 8(1) *Journal of International Criminal Justice* 137.

6 The Inter-American Court of Human Rights and the United Nations Human Rights Committee

Introduction

Following from our working definition on the right to the truth, in this chapter we will consider the way in and the extent to which aspects of the definition have found expression in the jurisprudence of the Inter-American Court of Human Rights (the Court or IACtHR) and, more briefly, the United Nations Human Rights Committee. The chapter will explore, in particular, the extent of satisfaction of the right to the truth in terms of a state's duty to investigate, the Court's approach to reparations and the significance of its own findings of fact.

Authority

The authority of the Inter-American Court is ultimately derived from the consent of states that accept its authority under the American Convention on Human Rights (ACHR) and specifically acknowledge the Courts "contentious jurisdiction" under Article 62 ACHR. But authority also comes from its acknowledgment of the wider context within which it operates, including the Inter-American Convention on the Forced Disappearance of Persons[1] (in which a duty to investigate is presumed rather than made an express provision), the domestic law of members of the Organization of American States (OAS)[2] and other sources of international human rights law. Its authority also comes from its own judicial practices as a court, its proper regard for its own procedure, and its fairness and its embodiment of judicial virtues such as impartiality. Most profoundly, perhaps, it comes from its understanding of its purpose as a human rights court and its inherent duty to apply the Convention text in a way that achieves this purpose. On these grounds victims, NGOs and others see the point in cooperating with

1 Organization of American States, Inter-American Convention on Forced Disappearance of Persons, (adopted 9 June 1994, entered into force 28 March 1996).

2 For a domestic law example see Fannie Lafontaine, 'No amnesty or statute of limitation for enforced disappearances: the Sandoval case before the Supreme Court of Chile' (2005) 3(1) Journal of International Criminal Justice 469.

the Court and accepting its findings as true, or at least the furthest it is possible to get using human institutions.

This is not the place to describe the general working of the Court.[3] But it should be noted that individual victims do not have direct rights of standing. Individual application is to the Inter-American Commission of Human Rights (the Commission). The Commission, through its procedures, decides which disputes are to be brought to the Court for adjudication (though the cases are brought in the name of the alleged victim).[4] As a stage in its procedure, the Commission reports on the merits of an individual case, and as we shall see, this report forms the basis of the victim's application, though the Court is not limited to ruling only on the specific grounds made by the Commission.

Transitional justice

From early cases, victims have sought the truth in respect of gross atrocities including forced disappearances[5] but also kidnaps, killings and destruction of property, where the fate of individuals is known.

The context of these cases is the often violent political turbulence which occurred in South and Central American states in the last decades of the 20th century. The parties included military dictatorships which had taken control of the state apparatus and political opposition groups of various kinds, including those prepared to use violence and terror. Individual activists, civil society groups, churches and democratic political parties along with families, friends, associates and mere bystanders were also victims. In terms of the right to the truth, the political actions and affiliations of these victims are irrelevant; these are human rights.

Cases involving the right to the truth are unlikely to be brought against dictatorial regimes since they are unlikely to have recognised the Court's authority. They may be brought against a non-dictatorial perpetrator regime insofar as it

3 On the system generally e.g. Laurence Burgorgue-Larsen and Amaya Ubeda De Torres, The *Inter-American Court of Human Rights. Case Law and Commentary* (Oxford University Press 2011); Gerald L Neuman, 'American Convention on Human Rights (1969)' (2010) Max Planck Encyclopedia of Public International Law (online) and Gerald L Neuman, 'Inter-American Court of Human Rights (IACtHR)' (2007) Max Planck Encyclopedia of Public International Law (online). For a general evaluation focusing on impact, and making comparisons with the European system, see James Cavallaro and Stephanie Brewer, 'Regional Human Rights Litigation in the Twenty-First Century: the Case of the Inter-American Court' (2008) 102 The American Journal of International Law 768.

4 Article 61 of the American Convention on Human Rights (Organization of American States, American Convention on Human Rights "Pact of San Jose, Costa Rica" (B-32) (adopted 22 January 1969, entered into force 18 July 1978)). States also have standing. On the Commission see Claudio Grossman, "The Inter-American Commission on Human Rights' (2011) Max Planck Encyclopedia of Public International Law (online). Grossman argues, *inter alia*, that rule changes in the 21st century mean that more cases are referred to the Court. Commission Rules make victims parties to the case.

5 *Velásquez Rodriguez v Honduras* (29 July 1988).

has recognised Court authority. *Velasquez Rodriguez v Honduras* 1988, the first case, was brought against the alleged perpetrator state, which was a civilian successor to military rule. The military government had ratified the Convention in 1977 and been replaced by a civilian government in 1979, which accepted the Court's contentious jurisdiction in 1981 (three days before Velasquez Rodriguez's abduction).[6] Later cases are more characteristic. The right to the truth in the IACtHR has largely been developed, especially in the 21st century in the context of transitional justice, where putatively democratic and rights-respecting regimes have recognised responsibility for the wrongs of the recent past and, to some extent, acted upon this responsibility. But they may also wish to defend peace agreements of various kinds which contain an element of impunity as the price for agreement. It is the limited and incomplete nature of the governments' responses that is in issue in the cases, along with victims' desires for authoritative and judicial declarations of facts and responsibilities, which acceptance by political institutions (i.e. executive and legislature) may not provide sufficient. Cases may begin with the respondent government accepting responsibility under the Convention for the atrocities committed by a predecessor regime and waiving jurisdictional restraints that may prevent the Court making an effective ruling in terms of the right to the truth and other rights. *The Massacres of El Mozote and Other Places v El Salvador* 2012[7] (a series of massacres of hundreds of civilians by El Salvadorian military units in 1981) is a good example.[8] The massacres took place in 1981. El Salvador had ratified the Convention in 1978 but had only accepted the contentious jurisdiction of the Court in 1995. The state (through the president) accepted responsibility in 2010 and made an apology. In its acceptance of the Court's jurisdiction in 1995, El Salvador had made a limitation of jurisdiction, under Article 62(2) ACHR, to the effect that it only accepted responsibility for violation of Convention rights in respect of events started on or after this acceptance in 1995.[9] However, in the context of these proceedings, it waived the limitation of jurisdiction and accepted that the Court could rule on these matters even though they occurred before the instrument of acceptance. Under its Rules, the Court can decide on the sufficiency of any acquiescence by the state of the claimant party's case. In this context it may rule on reparations, close the case on the basis of a friendly settlement or, bearing in mind its responsibility to protect human rights, continue with the case and bring it to judgment,[10] which is what happened in *El Mozote.*

6 See *Bámaca-Velásquez v Guatemala* (25 November 2000) on the abduction, torture and killing of the leader of a revolutionary guerrilla group.
7 E.g. *The Massacres of El Mozote and other Places v El Salvador* (25 October 2012).
8 Ibid paras 17–30.
9 Acceptance of jurisdiction is also possible at the ICC through a declaration under Article 12(3) of the Rome Statute.
10 Organization of American States, Rules of Procedure of The Inter-American Court of Human Rights 2009 (1 January 2010) Articles 62–64.

In the Inter-American context, therefore, satisfying the right to the truth is inherently a part of transitional justice. It may often involve an historical assessment of past events in which the Court completes and corrects the truth-seeking procedures of a reasonably open, democratic and well-ordered respondent state (or at least states which are not military dictatorships) which has acknowledged the facts of the past, the fault of predecessor regimes and that it has remedial duties and responsibilities. This state may be struggling with the political problem of compromising between victims' rights and interests in respect of the truth and other interests, such as those of perpetrators, which may need to be satisfied if there is to be peace. As will be suggested, the question of compromising between truth and impunity is raised in the context of the right to the truth. Conversely victims, in this transitional context, are seeking adequate reparations but above all, an authoritative exposition of the truth, as well as authoritative declarations of the violations of their rights, that only a court expressing the substantive and procedural values of the rule of law can give.

A duty to investigate

There is no express right to the truth in the ACHR. Nevertheless, from early cases, the central idea of the right to the truth, the idea that victims should have knowledge and understanding of what happened to them or their relatives, has been given strong and forceful effect by the Court.[11] The term "the right to the truth" has played an important, if supplementary, role indicating that the ideas behind it have a normative force which helps justify and explain an interpretation of Convention rights which requires the truth to be told. But it has never been treated as a robust, stand-alone right on which a cause of action under the Convention could be directly based,[12] and the Court has resisted the Commission arguments to that effect. The Court's response has been to subsume a state's duty to investigate and disclose the truth within particular express rights in the Convention. The right to the truth may "correspond" to the state's duty to investigate alleged Convention breaches. The duty is an interpretative "concept"

11 Burgorgue-Larsen and Ubeda De Torres, *supra* note 3, Chapter 27; Organization of American States, 'The Right to Truth in the Americas' (13 August 2014) OEA/Ser.L/V/II.152 Doc; Juan Méndez and Francisco Bariffi F, 'Truth, Right to, International Protection' (2011) Max Planck Encyclopedia of Public International Law (online) Part B; Mahmoud Cherif Bassiouni, 'International recognition of victims' rights' (2006) 6(2) Human Rights Law Review 203.

12 E.g. *Castillo Páez v Peru* (3 November 1997) para 86, stating there is no right to the truth expressed in the ACHR and the duty to investigate is sufficiently established otherwise. This position was confirmed in *Bámaca-Velásquez supra* note 6 para 201 where the point is made explicitly in a section of the judgment entitled "The Right to the Truth" or, later, in *"Mapiripán Massacre" v Colombia* (15 September 2005) where "the right to the truth" is a reason the Court gives for requiring a proper investigation, but this is clearly in the context of it being a necessary step in securing proper legal protection for victims through prosecution, punishment and reparations. See Burgorgue-Larsen and Ubeda De Torres *supra* note 3 at 2708–2710.

developed by the Court.[13] By implication the Court also resisted the idea that the speciality of the right to the truth is a public or collective right (this is discussed later in the chapter).[14]

Thus in *Velasquez v Honduras* 1988[15] (involving the kidnapping by men in civilian clothes, torture – witnessed as taking place in military locations – and probable subsequent death of Velasquez), the Court not only found violations of the right to liberty (Article 7), the right to personal integrity (Article 5) and the right to life (Article 4) but also of a procedural duty to investigate such disappearances. This duty on the state to investigate derived from the undertaking and obligation, in Article 1(1), to the effect that states will "ensure" the full and free exercise of Convention rights and freedoms to all persons within their jurisdiction. To give effect to this duty, alleged breaches of any Convention right should be investigated by the state, a duty which applies both to breaches directly by state agents but also to breaches by private parties where the state has a protective or positive duty which it has failed to discharge.[16]

In later cases the foundation of the duty to investigate on the right to legal protection of human rights has been more clearly articulated. Article 1(1) has been read as justifying the view that both the right to judicial protection of Convention rights (Article 25) and the right to a fair trial, with its implied right to access to a court (Article 8), necessarily imply a state duty to investigate breaches of Convention rights. This jurisprudential theory has been developed in cases involving widespread atrocities of the kind dealt with by the right to the truth. It describes a positive duty that states have in order to guarantee Convention rights[17] and, as will be seen, goes beyond investigation and includes prevention and punishment.[18]

In *Bámaca-Velásquez v Guatemala* 2000,[19] the Court accepted that effective judicial protection of rights could require an investigation "to obtain clarification of the facts [...] and corresponding responsibilities" and consequent prosecution. This is in a section marked "right to the truth" and in the context of the Commission's argument that truth is as much a right of society as it is of a victim. The Court kept its focus on individual Convention rights. The right to the truth brought nothing extra but its norms were "subsumed" in the individual rights to judicial protection. In his separate opinion, the president of the Court, Judge Cançado Trindade, stressed the moral importance of truth and argued that finding an investigative duty as inherent in the right to judicial protection of Convention rights was, to gloss his remarks, a proper interpretative move aimed at giving direct respect to a victim's right to the truth. It was a move justified by the "living

13 Ibid *Castillo-Páez* para 86.
14 E.g. *Bámaca-Velásquez supra* note 6 paras 197–202.
15 *Velasquez Rodriguez supra* note 5.
16 Ibid paras 165–176. See also discussion on non-state actors in Chapter 3 *supra* at 69.
17 *García and Family Members v Guatemala*, (29 November 2012) para 130.
18 Ibid para 166 *passim*.
19 *Bámaca-Velásquez supra* note 6.

instrument" doctrine, the purposive evolution of the Convention by the Court conscious of its function of protecting human rights.[20]

At best, this gives thin and partial effect to the right to the truth. There is no discussion in the judgment concerning the content of the right against which the effectiveness of any investigation can be measured. The "operative paragraphs", which contain the Court's orders,[21] require an investigation focused on determining responsibility rather than one indicating the fuller structural and individualised narrative that the right to the truth seems to require. The public aspect of the right to the truth is, perhaps, recognised by the requirement of public dissemination, but little else. In terms of an archive there is nothing expressed. In terms of victims' opportunity for narrative, the Commission held "special hearings to receive the testimony of persons related to the case".[22] These, and hearings held by the Court in the United States, were to receive evidence going to the merits of the case. They were not opportunities for victims to tell their story, and that element of the right to the truth is not satisfied.

Later cases show that the impact of the background right to the truth has led to a more specific and (in terms of remedies) more demanding approach to disclosing the truth. In *Ituango Massacres v Colombia* 2006[23] (law enforcement bodies alleged to have killed, robbed, terrorised and caused displacement of civilians between 1996 and 1997), the investigation duty, still grounded on legal protection of Convention rights, is expressed as "every effort being made to learn the truth of what happened".[24] The state was required to complete effectively the investigations in order to establish (and if necessary punish) not only the killers but also those whose acts or omissions contributed to the state's failure to protect the human rights of its people.[25] In *The Massacres of El Mozote and Other Places v El Salvador* 2012, the right to judicial protection grounds a duty to a "serious, impartial and effective investigation",[26] initiated by the state, done in a reasonable time which depends on the circumstances: in the case of extrajudicial killings, it means done "promptly". The right to the truth is not mentioned in respect of liability but appears to invigorate the range of remedies ordered.

Although the principal ground is the right to legal protection, a duty to investigate has also been established on the cruelty of leaving relatives of disappeared persons in a state of unknowing. This can be a breach of Article 5, the prohibition of inhuman treatment.[27]

20 See Article 31 of the Vienna Convention on the Law of Treaties (adopted 23 May 1969, entered into force 27 January 1980) 1155 UNTS 331 on the duty to interpret a treaty in the light of its "object and purpose".

21 *Bámaca-Velásquez supra* note 6 para 230, see item 8 in operative paragraphs.

22 Ibid para 9.

23 *Ituango Massacres v Colombia* (1 July 2006) paras 283–291.

24 Ibid para 289.

25 Ibid para 399. An effective investigation, however, is not found in the operative paragraphs.

26 Ibid para 219.

27 E.g. *Radilla Pacheco v Mexico* (23 November 2009) para 166. See also *Gomes Lund et al. ("Guerrilha do Araguaia) v Brazil* (24 November 2010) (arbitrary detention, torture and

These and other cases are different from each other, but the general direction of the jurisprudence is clear: the duty to investigate alleged breaches of Convention rights may satisfy the right to the truth but, in Convention terms, it is based on a state's obligation to provide judicial protection of its peoples' rights. There are cases in which the right to the truth, *expressis verbis*, has been argued for by complainants. The Court recognises the right to the truth but where there have been significant domestic procedures for establishing at least individualised truth, including procedures of a judicial character, any flaws in those procedures are included in the general analysis under the right to judicial protection. A ruling specifically on the right to the truth, treated as a freestanding right, will add nothing.[28] The duty to investigate derived from the right of legal protection means that, in the context of forced disappearance at least, the Court has "established the right to the truth in its jurisprudence".[29]

Nature and quality of the duty

To satisfy the right to the truth, the nature and quality of the investigation must, as a matter of law, be sufficient to meet its requirements. In various cases, and with increasing detail, the Court has sought to express these matters. The import is clear; although the principles are developed with regard to the facts and contexts of the different cases, there seems not to be a canonical text, containing all the features of the duty, developed by the Court.

The investigation is conceived as a legal obligation on the state. It must, first, be initiated by the state and conducted under its auspices.[30] Whilst in practice it is likely to be triggered by a complaint or allegation from a victim, in principle it is the event, and it being within the state's jurisdiction, that is sufficient to require an investigation. The positive duty to investigate is not fulfilled by the opportunity for action by others, such as victims bringing civil cases, or depend solely on the evidence that private parties and NGOs can produce. States must ensure that there is an adequate political, administrative and judicial system that is capable of acting on and fulfilling this duty.[31] Second, the investigation must be initiated promptly, though that will depend on the circumstances,[32] and third, be capable

---

forced disappearance, between 1972–75, of 70 persons who were political opponents of the Brazilian military dictatorship 1964–85) para 240.

28 See *García and Family Members supra* note 17 paras 171–177, as an instance.

29 *Radilla-Pacheco v Mexico supra* note 27 para 180 (a forced disappearance in 1974).

30 Cf. *Cabrera García and Montiel Flores v Mexico* (26 November 2010) para 193, where the investigation into alleged torture was initiated by the alleged victim whose actions were commenced more than three months after the events.

31 E.g. *The Massacres of El Mozote supra* note 7 para 247: "an adequate domestic regulatory framework and/or organizing the system for the administration of justice in a way that its operation ensures that serious, impartial and effective investigations are conducted ex officio, without delay".

32 *"Mapiripán Massacre" supra* note 12 paras 217–218.

of resulting, where the findings so indicate, in prosecutions and, if convictions, in proportionate punishment.[33] Investigation is, fourth, a continuing obligation on states which lasts, in the case of disappearances, for as long as the facts of and responsibility for the disappearance is unresolved.[34] Fifth, it is accepted as being an "obligation of means and not of results",[35] but this does not excuse an inadequate or preordained investigation. Finally, since the investigative duty is grounded on the state's obligation to provide effective judicial protection of Convention rights, the investigation must have a judicial character and authority. The Court has many times accepted the credibility of truth commissions and other truth-finding and disclosing procedures, but it is clear that these are insufficient; the victim's right is to know what happened through an authoritative, judicial proceeding,[36] which in the context of the right to the truth (atrocity) will characteristically require a criminal investigation conducted according to the country's constitutional norms. The opportunity for a civil action alone is likely to be insufficient.

The authority of the investigation

The investigation must be prompt and have sufficient authority and resources ("all the means necessary") to be effective, even if the state or powers within the state (such as the military) are uncooperative. It must have powers and authority to be able to access the relevant documents and information on issues such as the whereabouts of victims, the active chain of command, the policies being pursued and so forth. This may include material in the exclusive possession of state agencies,[37] including material in closed state archives or places of detention.[38] Any refusal by the state to produce requested evidence must be justified or the authorities must show that they have taken all available measures to prove that the evidence does not exist. Arguments of national security or confidentiality can

33 E.g. *Cepeda Vargas v Colombia,* (26 May 2010) para 117.

34 E.g. *García and Family Members, supra* note 17 para 134.

35 Ibid para 132. This is a much repeated phrase. The Commission has tried to argue in favour of a more stringent duty: the state must provide answers not just investigate (see Thomas Antkowiak, 'Truth as a Right and Remedy in International Human Rights Experience' (2002) 23(4) Michigan Journal of International Law 990–995; and, for instance, *Cifuentes Elgueta v Chile* (28th July 2009), dissenting opinion of H Keller and F Salvioli). However, it is hard to see this as not being clearly implicit in the duty to investigate in an effective way and in the availability of Article 13 to enable a victim to have access to a report if for some reason the authorities refuse to disclose.

36 E.g. *Zambrano Vélez et al. v Ecuador* (4 July 2007) paras 128–9; *Contreras et al. v El Salvador* (31 August 2011) (systemic abductions of children as part of counter-terrorism policy) para 135.

37 E.g. *Tiu Tojín v Guatemala* (26 November 2008) (on the forced disappearance of mother and daughter in 1990) para 77, *Radilla-Pacheco v Mexico supra* note 27 para 222.

38 On material in places of detention see *Anzualdo Castro v Peru* (22 September 2009) para 135 and archives *La Cantuta v Peru* (29 November 2006) on the kidnapping of students in 1992 para 111.

be attempts to preserve impunity and any such arguments need to be subjected to proper judicial scrutiny.[39] In *Contreras v El Salvador*, the Court required that the different branches of the state cooperate with each other and not to obstruct the investigation.[40] Military proceedings may not satisfy the Court as to effective investigation.[41]

The quality of the investigation

The right to the truth requires that the investigation must not only be "complete" (or "genuine") and "impartial"[42] but also "effective". This should include the "individualized truth", by which victims can know what is sometimes called the "complete truth" about what happened to them or their families. There is no clear or authoritative test for what this might involve and it is clearly context dependent. The Court has referred, as a standard, to the general principles governing investigations into extrajudicial killings in the UN Manual on the Effective Prevention and Investigation of Extra-Legal, Arbitrary and Summary Executions ("the Minnesota Protocol"), which lays down a range of general purposes and standards which such investigations should cover.[43] These are summarised in *Ituango Massacres v Colombia* 2006[44]: those who conduct the investigation must try, as a minimum, to (a) identify the victim; (b) recover and preserve the probative material related to the death to contribute to any possible criminal investigation into those responsible; (c) identify possible witnesses and obtain their statements in relation to the death under investigation; (d) determine the cause, method, place and moment of death, as well any pattern or practice that could have caused the death; and (e) distinguish between natural death, accidental death, suicide and murder. In addition, the scene of the crime must be searched exhaustively, autopsies carried out and human remains examined rigorously by competent professionals using the most appropriate procedures.

But, we suggested in Chapter 3, the right to the truth also involves disclosing the "structural truth" – the duty (likely to be controversial) to explain the historical, political, social and governmental context which may explain (not justify or excuse) why the events took place and thus assist in allocating responsibility

39 See *Myrna Mack Chang v Guatemala* (25 November 2003) (murder of human rights activist allegedly planned and prepared by the military) paras 180–181; the Court adopted the Commission's position.

40 *Contreras et al. v El Salvador supra* note 36 at para 171. See also, *García Prieto et al. v El Salvador* (20 November 2007) para 112; "*Las Dos Erres*" *Massacre v Guatemala* (24 November 2009) (massacres of at least 251 persons in 1982 by a special group in the armed forces) para 144.

41 *Cabrera Garcia and Flores v Mexico supra* note 30 para 197.

42 E.g. *Ituango Massacres, supra* note 23 para 319; cf. para 296.

43 Authority for the use of the Protocol includes *Baldeón García v Peru* (6 April 2006) para 96; *Pueblo Bello Massacre v Colombia* (31 January 2006) para 177, and *"Mapiripán Massacre" supra* note 12 para 224.

44 *Ituango Massacres supra* note 23 para 298.

upwards in the chain of command from the direct perpetrators. Whilst such analysis may have been implicit in the idea of an effective investigation, the Court has, in later cases, begun to stipulate this as a requirement. In *Cepeda Varga v Colombia* 2010[45] the Court held that the investigation should determine "the patterns of collaborative action and all the individuals who took part". It is not enough to confine the investigation to the immediate circumstances of the crime; rather

> it is essential to analyze the awareness of the power structures that allowed, designed and executed it, both intellectually and directly, as well as the interested persons or groups and those who benefited from the crime (beneficiaries) . . . it is not a question of examining the crime in isolation, but rather of inserting it in a context that will provide the necessary elements to understand its operational structure.[46]

The Court refers in this paragraph to the facts of the instant case, and so these remarks could be confined to individual assassinations of senior politicians. However, these remarks indicate the characteristics of an investigation where "structural truth" is required to satisfy the right to the truth.

Ample opportunities for participation by victims and next of kin in the investigation, including criminal and civil proceedings, is important,[47] and must be facilitated by the state, in particular by providing protection for participants who have reason to be vulnerable and fearful. The investigative duty may not be fulfilled if there are indications that victims are restrained from participation in civil or criminal procedures.[48] Participation is not defined. Given that the ground of the duty to investigate is the right to legal protection, the main purpose of victim participation is the collection of evidence to enable criminal or civil justice to be done. The case law does not support "narrative truth", the disclosing by victims of their story in their own words, as an additional purpose. Narrative truth may be appropriate for truth commission procedures, but as indicated earlier, these are not sufficient to satisfy the requirement for an effective investigation with judicial authority. To the extent that narrative truth is an essential aspect of the right to the truth (see Chapter 3), the protection of the right in the context of the Inter-American Court is incomplete.

No freestanding right

The Court, therefore, enforces in its jurisprudence the central element of the right to the truth – the right of victims or relatives to know what happened in terms both of individual and, to some extent, structural aspects. But investigation and disclosure is grounded on the Convention's right to judicial protection

45 *Cepeda Vargas v Colombia supra* note 33.
46 Ibid para 119.
47 E.g. *"Mapiripán Massacre" supra* note 12 para 219.
48 *Ituango Massacres supra* note 23 para 295.

of human rights, and so the purpose of the investigation is not limitable to a victim's interests in the truth. The investigation is necessary to ensure the full scope of judicial protection of rights, such as the right to life or to liberty, and this includes the consequential prosecution of alleged perpetrators and, following conviction, their punishment; it includes proper reparations for victims and can also require access to both civil and administrative procedures. This linking of disclosing the truth with prosecution, punishment and reparations is explicit in the jurisprudence. The "effectiveness" of an investigation in a criminal context is measured not just against disclosure of the truth (and victim satisfaction thereby) but also on the extent to which it identifies perpetrators and thereby enables, by due process, effective punishment.[49] The jurisprudence also makes it clear, especially in cases brought decades after the events, that the investigative duty is necessarily linked to the opposition of international law to formal or informal amnesty or impunity.[50] Conversely, amnesties and other methods of impunity act to prevent criminal investigations and therefore block the right to the truth in the sense of making it harder to discover and disclose what happened and who was responsible.[51]

The public aspect of the right to the truth

As discussed in Chapter 4, international summaries of the right to the truth see it as having a collective or public aspect. The structural and individualised truth is not just necessary for individual victims and their families, but it is also a necessary resource for a society seeking to develop legitimate and democratic institutions as it moves away from military or other forms of dictatorship and oppression and seeks to ensure that past atrocities are not repeated.

The Court has recognised this collective or public aspect of the right to the truth. In *Anzualdo Castro v Peru* 2009[52] (kidnap, disappearance and probably execution by state agents), the Court, in the context of the "right to know the truth in the cases of forced disappearances" held that "it is important that a society knows the truth about the facts of serious human rights violations" and so it is

49 Ibid para 293: the Court must assess, in relation to criminal procedures, "how effective the investigation of the facts has been in determining the truth of what happened, punishing those responsible, and repairing the violations committed to the detriment of the alleged victims" (referring to *The "Mapiripán Massacre" supra* note 12 para 222 and *Pueblo Bello Massacre v Colombia supra* note 43 para 170 which does focus on the purpose of disclosure of the truth.

50 On this principle in general see Dermot Groome, "The Right to Truth in the Fight Against Impunity" Berkeley Journal of International Law, Vol. 29, Issue 1 (2011), 181, 184; Raquel Aldana-Pindell, 'An Emerging Universality of Justiciable Victims' Rights in the Criminal Process to Curtail Impunity for State-Sponsored Crimes' (2004) 26(3) Human Rights Quarterly 605 at 622 *passim*.

51 *Gomez Lund supra* note *27* paras 147 *passim* and 171.

52 *Anzualdo Castro supra* note 38 paras 116 *passim*, 119 and cases cited therein.

a "fair expectation" that the truth about grave violations of human rights should be publicly disseminated. In other cases, making the same point, the reference has been to a "democratic" society.[53]

The public, collective aspect is a necessary but incidental consequence,[54] and not the purpose, of the exercise by a victim of her right to know what happened. As suggested in Chapter 4, it is hard to know how "society", the subject of the public right, can be represented in court.[55] Though the "right to information" (in Article 13, discussed later) can have a political purpose, the right to legal protection is focused on individual victims' rights. It appears, therefore, that the public aspect of the right to the truth is discharged through the way in which legal protection, judicial action, is by definition presumed to be a public matter. It is the duty of a properly legitimate state to administer justice openly and publicly, that grounds the public aspect of the right to the truth in the Inter-American context. This reinforces the suggestion in Chapter 4 that truth disclosure cannot be seen just as a matter of individual right but it is, equally, an incident of the kind of "democratic" (we might say "just" or "well-ordered") society that is, because usually unstated and under-theorised, an inarticulate premise underlying human rights law and the standards applied in the context of transitional justice. The need for truth can be sufficiently justified in terms of the legal obligations of a "democratic society" which treats all its population as equals, and this is inherent in the jurisprudence of the Inter-American Court. The individual right, however, remains of crucial procedural importance since it provides the means by which the state's legal duty towards all its people can be given effect.

Reparations

An effective right must have its remedies. The Inter-American Court determines who the injured parties are and who should receive reparation. These remedies give effect to both the individual and also the public aspect of the right to the truth.

Under Article 63(1) ACHR the Court is to rule that the injured party be guaranteed the enjoyment of the right violated and, where appropriate, order that the consequences of the violation "be remedied" and that fair compensation be paid. The Court has given a wide and evolving definition to Article 63(1) and has developed both pecuniary and non-pecuniary remedies. In respect of the right to the truth and breach of the duty to investigate, the Court has not

53 See Chapter 4, citing *"Las Dos Erres" Massacre supra* note 40 para 149; *Contreras supra* note 36 para 170.

54 "The Tribunal (sic) deems that the right to know the truth represents a necessary effect for it is important that a society knows the truth about the facts of serious human rights violations. This is also a fair expectation that the State is required to satisfy" (*Anzualdo Castro supra* note 38 para 119).

55 See, more generally, Chapter 4.

limited itself to making a declaration that the respondent state's duty to investigate has been breached but has imposed non-pecuniary remedies. It may, as a measure of reparation, make a mandatory order that an adequate investigation be undertaken in order to achieve both the individual and the public aspect of the right to the truth. As exemplified later, it may specify in the reparations section of the judgment special features of the investigation required in any particular case, including those that add to the investigations undertaken by a transitional government.

Reparations may link the investigation to the wider requirements of the right to judicial protection – to be the means not just of identifying what happened but to do so in the context of obtaining the evidence on which perpetrators can be brought to justice. The linkage of the Court's conception of the right to the truth to justice and anti-impunity is clear in the nature and purpose of the reparations ordered.

In *Carpio-Nicolle v Guatemala* 2004,[56] for instance, the Court found a violation of the duty to investigate in respect of the assassination of a journalist and politician along with a number of other persons who were with him. The Court makes express reference to the development of a victim's right to the truth in international human rights law but in the context of a duty to investigate which is, apparently, more wide-ranging in that, first, it may also be a duty owed to society and, second, it is instrumental in the duty to prosecute and punish.[57] Reparation, therefore, appears to satisfy the victim's right to know, society's right to know, and the state's duty to prosecute and punish. But there is no real attempt to differentiate and distinguish these different aspects. The relevant reparation that is ordered is that

> the State must conduct an effective investigation into the facts of the instant case, in order to identify, prosecute and punish those who perpetrated and masterminded the extrajudicial execution of [the victims]. The result of this process must be published, so that Guatemalan society knows the truth.[58]

The Court has developed its jurisdiction so that it can order a wide range of other forms of non-pecuniary reparation.[59] In this, the Court's actions are dramatic and innovative. For example, in *Ituango Massacres v Colombia* 2006,[60] the Court ordered, in addition to the declaration of a violation and financial compensation for pecuniary and non-pecuniary losses, a range of other forms of reparation such as medical treatment and safety for returnees. Relevant to the right to the truth, these included public acknowledgment and apology by the state for its failures, a memorial

56 *Carpio Nicolle et al. v Guatemala* (22 November 2004).
57 Ibid para 128.
58 Ibid para 129, and Operative Paragraph ("Orders") 1.
59 Thomas Antkowiak, 'An Emerging Mandate for International Courts: Victim-Centred Remedies And Restorative Justice' (2011) 47 Stanford Journal of International Law 279.
60 *Ituango Massacres supra* note 23.

plaque and training for officials on their responsibilities.[61] Furthermore, the state was required to publish the facts authoritatively proven in the judgment generally and in relation to individuals.[62] Of particular relevance to the right to the truth is that these mandatory forms of reparation can include a requirement that the state enhances its capacity for an effective investigation.[63] Another example is *Contreras v El Salvador* 2011 (forced disappearance of a number of children between 1981 and 1983), where the Court ordered, inter alia, that the state publish a summary of the judgment, make a public act acknowledging international responsibility, name schools after victims, make an audiovisual documentary and guarantee access to relevant archives.[64] Such remedies satisfy both individual and public aspects of the right to the truth.

These reparative measures can involve considerable expense of the state. They can also have considerable constitutional implications. Directly ordering a state to change its laws has implications for the separation of powers. In *Contreras v El Salvador*, the Court simply "urged" such a change in the laws,[65] but this was not translated into an operative paragraph.

Not all reparative requests are accepted. In *Contreras v El Salvador* 2011, for instance, the Court refused to order that El Salvador establish a website to further the search for missing children.[66] Its grounds were that such had been ordered in another case in a different context which had not yet been evaluated.

In its judgments on reparations, the Court also orders the means by which its remedies (including the non-pecuniary measures for non-pecuniary losses) are to be enforced. For example in *Ituango Massacres*, it specifies dates for completion, methods of payment, restricts attempts at clawback by the state through taxation, makes provisions for minors and so forth. Monitoring is by the Court (through the authority which is "inherent in its attributes") and the case is only closed after full compliance. Under Article 65, the Court submits an annual report to the Organization of American States (OAS), which can include making recommendation in respect of non-compliance.

The Court's own narrative

As well as enforcing the right to the truth through the duty to investigate and the related remedies, the Court, gives effect to the right through the narrative in its judgments. By this, it provides authoritative declarations concerning what happened, socially and individually, and who was responsible at least in the sense of the group or type of person (military, paramilitary groups, etc.) involved. The

61 Ibid paras 405–6.

62 Similar forms of non-pecuniary reparations for non-pecuniary losses are found in other cases such as *"Mapiripán Massacre" supra* note 12 para 294 *passim* or *Moiwana Community v Suriname* (15 June 2005) para 201 *passim*.

63 E.g. *Carpio Nicolle supra* note *56* para 135.

64 *Contreras supra* note 36 operative paras 6–10.

65 Ibid para 219.

66 Ibid para 135.

Court, in performing this role, may have accepted the acknowledgment of the respondent state of its failure to perform its obligations under the Convention but, as permitted by Article 64 of the Rules, continues its judgment in order to give effect to human rights and, in particular, to give an authoritative narrative of what happened. It will also be able to resolve any of the outstanding issues between the parties relating to the extent and fullness of state responsibility. In continuing to give an authoritative account of the truth, the legal merits and the consequences, the Court provides a form of reparation for the victim and contributes to preventing any repetition (in effect recognising both the individual and public aspects of the right to the truth).[67] In *Tojín v Guatemala* 2008,[68] for instance, despite Guatemala's acknowledgment of responsibility and making of a number of reparative steps,[69] the Court proceeded to a full reasoned judgment, mainly in order to establish the full facts in the instant case for the benefit of both the victims and society, and also to resolve the remaining contentious issues. The Court was determined to give a full and accurate account of the disputed facts.[70] Importantly the Court also detailed the duty to investigate Tojín's case in order to show the obstacles, even after transition, to effective investigation, and thus to contribute to the jurisprudence on that issue. Similarly, in *Contreras v El Salvador*,[71] the government, in 2011, accepted human rights responsibility for systematic abductions of children mainly between 1980 and 1984. The Court determined to make an "extensive and detailed examination of the facts" on the grounds that this is an important part of reparation, helps to analyse and clarify the particular violations that took place, and also contributes to prevention of similar outrages happening in the future.[72]

The Court identifies the evidential sources it has used and gives some measure of the probative value of these sources in coming to its authoritative factual conclusions.[73] It is the Commission that brings the case. This is the body with primary (first) responsibility for investigation and fact-finding. Much of the evidence before the Court is based on witness affidavit, expert evidence, evidence from linked cases, or other evidence which the Commission has accepted as true including well-known public facts and declarations evidenced by newspaper articles submitted by the Commission. Its acceptance of a matter as true in the dossier it gives to the Court is likely to be endorsed as true by the Court. It is a source of probative evidence that the Court accepts.

But the Court can itself request evidence to be given and heard in public hearing, which it frequently does.[74] Likewise, evidence as to individual experiences

67 E.g. *Baldeón García supra* note 43 para 56.
68 *Tiu Tojín supra* note 37. The Rules of Procedure in force at the time (1997) were, on this point, of similar effect.
69 Ibid para 23.
70 Ibid para 26.
71 *Contreras, supra* note 36.
72 Ibid. para 28.
73 E.g. ibid para 29 *passim*.
74 Article 58, Rules 2009.

and losses can be accepted but may be summarised if, for reasons of witness safety, the identity of the witness is not disclosed.[75] Evidence that is not contested, whose authenticity is not questioned and which has been presented at the proper procedural opportunity will be accepted as true. From these findings of fact, the Court will declare violations of one or more of the substantive articles of the Convention.

As well as identifying the evidence, the Court states general principles concerning its approach to the probative value of this material. This is *sui generis* in the sense that it is not subject to the full range of "formalities", of "due process" rights, found in an (adversarial) domestic process.[76] An international human rights court is evaluating state action or inaction rather than considering the imposition of criminal penalties or civil remedies on individuals. The Court tends not to name individual perpetrators unless as suspects already identified through the domestic system. The requirements of "legal certainty" and procedural equality between the parties are important. The Court's aim is to analyse on the basis of giving "reasonable credit and weight"[77] to the evidence or subjecting it to "sound criticism"; evaluating the pertinent facts on the basis of "logic" and "experience". The normal burden of proof lies with the applicant but, especially in the case of disappearances, the Court's approach to identifying the facts is consistent with presumptions which the respondent state may then be required to refute[78] (e.g. on the fate of a disappeared person last seen in the custody of the army).[79]

All this comes together in the Court's declaration of what happened and who (at least in group, office or institutional terms) was responsible. A good example is *Ituango Massacres v Colombia* 2006; the Court made a series of findings of fact as to background context of the killings, the rise of paramilitary groups in Colombia, the legal background of the response of Colombia, the events in the areas concerned immediately prior to the massacres and the names of the victims. Importantly, in terms of the victims' right to the truth, the details of individual killings and the impact those killings had on survivors, the history of the particular criminal procedures opened by the Colombian authorities are authoritatively given; likewise, evidence as to compensable losses and so on.[80] The determination of what happens includes a discussion of context (e.g. the social, political and

75 E.g. *Ituango Massacres v Colombia supra* note 23 paras 110 and 125 (65) footnoten 75. Evidence thus kept confidential may, because of fair trial rights, be of limited value if used in other subsequent proceedings, such as criminal prosecutions, as evidence that alleged facts have taken place.

76 "Adversarial" in the broad sense whereby even an "inquisitorial" system must provide proper hearings for both sides based on equality of arms, etc.

77 *Almonacid-Arellano et al v Chile* (26 September 2006 (extrajudicial execution) para 69; *Ituango Massacres v Colombia supra* note 23 para 108.

78 See further, e.g. *Kawas Fernández v Honduras* (3 April 2009) (political murder) para 95; see also *Escher v Brazil* (6 July 2009) (unlawful phone tapping) para 127.

79 *Velasquez Rodriguez v Honduras supra* note 5 paras 130 and 131.

80 *Ituango Massacres v Colombia supra* note 23 para 125(1)-(125) para 125 forms a significant part of the judgment.

economic situation underlying the events) and, more specifically, the political and military responses to these conditions.[81] These judgments are, in effect, models or examples setting a judicial standard for satisfying the right to the truth in detail.

Victims' narrative

The Court goes some way to provide an effective and public forum for victims to tell their stories. Victims can be heard through the testimony they give to the Commission, which may be oral or written, given directly or indirectly through representatives. Likewise, they may give their evidence to the Court directly through public hearing. But it does need to be noted that the ultimate point of these proceedings is to adjudge state responsibility. Victims' evidence is useful as regards information on the alleged violations and on consequences. But the statements are not to be considered in isolation, rather as part of building up the general story.[82] As with any required role for victims in the national investigation, it is unlikely that these international court practices satisfy the idea of "narrative truth". But it is hard to see how developing a procedure designed primarily to give victims a voice would enhance the general purpose of a human rights court.[83]

Article 13

Subsumed within the right to the legal protection of Convention rights, the right to and the disclosure of the truth is linked to prosecution and punishment of perpetrators, to the general opposition in international law to amnesty, as well as to reparations. It does not, in terms of this jurisprudence of the ACHR, stand on its own as a right to know what happened where the idea of relevant knowledge, or the suffering inherent in not knowing, is sufficient to ground an individual right; and the link between knowledge of the past and effective social reconstruction is sufficient to ground a social or public good. It may not matter much in practice, since even though jurisprudentially subsumed in the right to legal protection, the truth is still disclosed. Nevertheless, there would, perhaps, be strength in a *lex specialis* which recognises the distinct, profound human and social interest just in the truth and which would prevail even if the right to legal protection, given its other purposes, is insufficient to effect disclosure.[84]

Given that there is no Convention right to the truth *expressis verbis*, the best candidate for such a right is Article 13: freedom of expression. This includes the "freedom to seek, receive and impart information", which the Court has

81 *Contreras v El Salvador supra* note 36 para 51.
82 *Ituango Massacres v Colombia supra* note 23 para 121.
83 This point is revisited in the conclusion to this book.
84 See James Sweeney, *The European Court of Human Rights in the Post-Cold War Era* (Routledge 2012) 89 *passim* (in the European context).

interpreted conjunctively,[85] so there is a duty on a state to supply the information sought, subject only to the restrictions found in Article 13(2)(a) and (b).[86] In *Barrios Altos v Peru* (2001), the Commission invited the Court to recognise that the "roots" of the right to the truth lay in the right to "seek" and to "receive" public information found in Article 13. Invoking this right would also help to ensure that information was preserved and that public administration was made more transparent. The Court, however, stuck with its view that, whilst not denying the possible relevance of Article 13 for the right to the truth, it had nothing to add in terms of content and effect to the legal protection provisions discussed earlier in this chapter.[87] Even in cases of systematic and unconvincing denial by the military that they did not have the information requested in their archives, the Court's approach was not through Article 13. Rather it stressed that judicial guarantees of legal protection for Convention rights requires that the various branches of the state should collaborate and that investigators need to have sufficient authority and power to get at relevant material wherever found.[88]

The position has changed somewhat in the 21st century and the context of transitional democracy. *Reyas v Chile* 2006[89] concerned individuals linked to a public interest group seeking information about the environmental effects of foreign investments. The Court emphasised the right to receive information in Article 13 both as an individual right but also as a "right" or interest predicated on the democratic character of society and enforceable by, for instance, NGOs and pressure groups. It ordered the information sought to be provided. The Court has followed and developed this interpretation of Article 13 in the context of gross violations of human rights (such as engage the right to the truth). In *Gomes Lund v Brazil* (2010),[90] the particular issue engaging Article 13 was the constant refusal of the Brazilian military to acknowledge the existence of the information requested and to disclose it. The Court declared a breach of Article 13 in relation to Brazil's failure effectively to provide legal protection.[91] It did not order disclosure directly but required an effective criminal investigation which would now benefit from the effect of this judgment on Article 13.

85 *Gomes Lund v Brazil supra* note 27 para 197.

86 Article 13 (2)(a) and (b) permit restrictions on freedom of expression rights if necessary to protect the rights or reputations of others, national security, public order or public health or morals.

87 *Barrios Altos v Peru* (14 March 2001) paras 45–49. See also *Radilla-Pacheco v Mexico supra* note 27 (failure to investigate effectively a forced disappearance in 1974) where the Court expressly declines to rule in respect of Article 13, the need of the authorities to disclose being integrated into the right to justice (para 180); and the leading case *Bámaca-Velásquez v Guatemala supra* note 6 para 201 (the right to the truth is "subsumed" in the rights to justice in Article 8 and 25).

88 E.g. *Contreras v El Salvador supra* note 36 paras 171–173.

89 *Reyes v Chile* (19 September 2006).

90 *Gomes Lund v Brazil supra* note 27.

91 Ibid operative paragraph 6; there is no separate order to disclose, just to continue with the criminal investigation in the light of the present judgment.

Freedom of information in this context is both the right of a victim seeking information pertaining to his or her own position but (in the context of freedom of expression) is also a political right in the sense that the applicant need not have a direct interest or personal involvement in the matter and may "circulate" the information in society – an NGO might use it for purposes of political persuasion and pressure. Article 13 may therefore be especially significant as regards the public aspect of the right to the truth.[92] This, broadly, was central to the position of the Commission in its unsuccessful submissions that the right to the truth should be treated as an independent legal ground.[93] The obvious difficulty of a "social right", what it means and how it can be given specific effect rather than as just a happy consequence of the promulgation of the results of an effective investigation and judicial process, is resolved. Freedom of expression is a public and political right. General defences of the freedom include it as a necessary condition of democracy and of the capacity of presumptively rational and autonomous persons to know of reasons for action in the public sphere and decide whether to act on them or not.[94] In *Gomez Lund v Brazil*, as in *Reyas v Chile* where the point is more emphatic, the public nature of the right to receive information is expressly linked to the necessary conditions of a properly functioning democratic society and is presumed to ensure better, more transparent government.[95] and, consequently, the more effective scrutiny of government actions; and it facilitates greater participation in public affairs. The assumption behind Article 13 is the public disclosure of information.

Most importantly, Article 13 is a vehicle by which institutions of civil society, especially NGOs of various kinds, may have standing to seek information in the public interest as they see it. *Gomez Lund v Brazil* was brought by the Centre for Justice and International Law and Human Rights Watch. Such NGOs may, of course, bring cases to the Commission absent any reference to Article 13, but Article 13, as a right to freedom of expression, is clearly (though not exclusively) orientated towards public promulgation even as far as there being a presumption of public engagement.[96]

There are difficulties with Article 13 in regard to fulfilling the right to the truth. First, it is a right to information held, not to the creation of information and so will not be a satisfactory substitute for the duty to conduct an investigation to discover information.

Second, it is a qualified right. Article 13 permits proportionate restrictions on freedom of expression. Though it expressly forbids any prior censorship,[97] it

92 See Chapter 4.

93 See also *Bámaca-Velásquez v Guatemala supra* note 6 para 197 which urges the social nature of the right to the truth.

94 E.g. Frederick Schauer *Free Speech: a philosophical enquiry* (Cambridge University Press 1982) Part One.

95 *Gomes Lund v Brazil supra* note 27 paras 198 and 199.

96 *Reyes v Chile supra* note 89 paras 84–87.

97 Article 13(2).

permits post-publication liability for various purposes, which include protecting national security and public order. National security can be a legitimate reason to resist disclosure, even to judicial authorities in the course of proceedings, when sensitive material is in issue; protecting informants is another reason. On the other hand, it is obvious that these reasons may be excuses for not disclosing evidence of wrongdoing. Under Article 13, failures to disclose should be analysed against the permitted grounds in Article 13(2)(a) and (b): the "rights or reputations of others" or "the protection of national security, public order, public health or morals".

The Court is clear that the authorities must not abuse the circumstances in which non-disclosure could be justified. In relation to Article 13, the authorities are in breach if they "resort to mechanisms such as official secrets or confidentiality, public interest or national security" in order that disclosure is avoided.[98] But a similar argument also applies to the investigative duty inherent in the right to legal protection of rights (Article 1(1), 8 and 25) – the "state" cannot "hide behind" "official secrets", "confidentiality", "national security" or the "public interest".[99] In the latter context, the point appears in absolute terms, suggesting that the right to legal protection grounds a duty of complete disclosure in the context of an effective investigation into gross human rights abuses which contrasts with the qualified duty under Article 13. In *Myrna Mack Chang v Guatemala* 2003, the Court implies, in the context of the right to legal protection, that any claims to non-disclosure must be subject to close judicial scrutiny albeit without necessary reference to the qualifying grounds in Article 13.[100]

It is unclear which approach is used. A legitimate democratic state might argue that Article 13 is *lex specialis* and failures to disclose should be evaluated not against an unarticulated judicial standard inherent in the right to legal protection but against the allowable purposes and the structured arguments of proportionality in Article 13(2)(a) and (b). In *Gomez Lund*, the breach of Article 13 is in relation to the breach of the rights to legal protection, and these remain the principle ground of the finding and the remedy and thus an apparent merging of the tests.[101] It is likely that, in the context of atrocity, only the weightiest of arguments for non-disclosure will be compatible with the Convention, whether Article 13 is used or not. This indicates the normative force of the right to the truth.

A third reason which limits the impact of Article 13 as a means of giving effect to the right to the truth is the requirement that the investigation and disclosure should be initiated by the authorities and should not be merely conceded at the victim's request. In Article 13, on the other hand, the right to receive follows from the right to seek which requires initiating action by the right holder – the victim or the NGO with standing to apply. Given the absence of an express right

98 *Gomes Lund v Brazil supra* note 27 para 202.
99 *Tiu Tojín v Guatemala supra* note 37.
100 *Myrna Mack Chang v Guatemala supra* note 39 para 181 where the Court adopts Commission reasoning on this point. See also *Gomes Lund supra* note 27 para 203.
101 *Gomes Lund v Brazil supra* note 27 operative paragraph 6.

to the truth in the ACHR this limitation inherent in Article 13 is a not insignificant explanation for the Court's approach of connecting the right to the truth to the right to legal protection and its resistance to the Commission's assertion that the true root of the right to the truth is the right to receive information.

Article 13, therefore, has a role in facilitating the right to the truth particularly in relation to the social aspect of the right. It is, however, subject to important limitations which suggest its role remains one which is ancillary to the development of the rights to legal protection.

United Nations Human Rights Committee

A similar approach to the right to the truth can be found in the case law of the United Nations Human Rights Committee in its "views" on cases brought to it, under the First Optional Protocol, alleging violations of the International Covenant on Civil and Political Rights (ICCPR).

As with the American Convention on Human Rights, the ICCPR contains no express right to the truth nor an express right to an investigation of well-founded allegations of breaches of Covenant rights (including, *a fortiori*, where the factual claim amounts to a crime against humanity: "an atrocity"). Nevertheless, the norms behind the right to the truth, as with the Inter-American Court, are given some degree of effect through a duty to investigate, reparations and the Committee's own narrative.

The duty to investigate

In its communicated "views", the Committee has established a duty on states to investigate claims of atrocity. But, as with the Inter-American Court, this is not grounded, as a right, on the profound interest of the victim or the relative to know the truth but, rather, on the right to legal protection of Covenant rights. A state's duty to investigate allegations of atrocity is a necessary inference from Article 6 of the Covenant (the right to life) or Article 7 (the prohibition on torture), by itself or read in the light of Article 2(3), the victim's right to a remedy. Without the investigation and the disclosure of the truth, there can be no effective legal protection for these rights. This requirement of an investigation is enhanced by reference to the Committee's own General Comments on the relevant article. In *Bautista*,[102] the disappearance and killing of the victim involved a breach of Article 6(1) because of the failure adequately to investigate the allegation. The investigative duty was inherent in Article 6(1) as persuasively glossed in General Comment 6: the state has a duty to "establish effective facilities and procedures to investigate, thoroughly, by an appropriate and impartial body, cases of missing and disappeared persons in circumstances that may involve a violation

102 *Bautista de Arellana v Colombia* (27 October 1995).

of the right to life".[103] Likewise in *Rodriguez v Uruguay* 1994,[104] the duty to investigate a well-founded allegation, of an abduction and torture of the victim by the secret police, was founded on the requirements of Article 7 read in the light of Article 2(3) as so required by General Comment 20,[105] paragraph 14: "Complaints must be investigated promptly and impartially by competent authorities so as to make the remedy effective". This duty applied to the successor regime as much as to the perpetrator regime. In terms of legal form, there was a violation of Article 7 but no separate violation of Article 2(3) which, it seems, is of persuasive, interpretative value in this context.[106]

For cases decided after 2004, the investigative duty of states is generalised. It derives from the gloss in General Comment 31 concerning Article 2 – the general obligations on signatory states. It has replaced General Comment 3, which was focused on the general prospective measures, the "necessary steps", states must take to fulfil general positive obligations under the Covenant and those they might take to inhibit the conditions, such as poverty, in which violations are likely to occur. General Comment 31, on the other hand, contains much more consideration on how to deal with violations. In paragraph 15 it refers, without authority, to the "general obligation to investigate allegations of violations promptly, thoroughly and effectively through independent and impartial bodies", and goes on to suggest that the failure of a state to investigate an allegation of the breach of any of the Covenant rights could, of itself, be a violation of the Covenant. The authority and context for this latter point is Article 2(3), though it can also be seen as a general obligation required to give effect to the Covenant obligations.[107] Article 2(3) is the individuals' right to a remedy. Inherent in this individual right, in the Committee's reasoning, is a duty to investigate any and all allegations of violations. Even so, the Committee is reluctant to find a violation of Article 2(3) based on the failure to investigate, rather the formal breach remains of the substantive articles read in the light of Article 2(3).[108] The remedy, however, is likely to include a duty on the state to conduct an effective investigation.[109] In *Bautista*, the Committee also suggested that Article 14, the right to a fair trial, could also be a context in which the investigative duty could be asserted.[110] The logic of this is not altogether clear, since a victim is not on trial and the Committee accepted

103 UNHRC CCPR General Comment No. 6 Article 6 (Right to Life) (30 April 1982) para 4.
104 *Rodriguez v Uruguay* (19 July 1994).
105 UNHRC, CCPR General Comment 20 Article 7 (Torture) (10 March 1992).
106 For later cases see, for example, *Hero v Bosnia* (28 October 2014) (failure to investigate the disappearance of the authors' husband and father for eighteen years, in the context of the Bosnian war), see para 10.
107 See, for example, *Sassene v Algeria* (29 October 2014) para 7.11.
108 E.g. *Boudehane and Algeria* (24 July 2014) (victims taken away, probably tortured and killed, in the context of the Algerian civil war) where the violation, as recorded in the operative paragraph, remained that of the substantive articles read in the light of article 2(3).
109 See, for example, *Sassene v Algeria supra* note 107 para 9(a).
110 *Bautista de Arellana v Colombia supra* note 102 para 8.6 (there was no violation of Article 14).

that there is no right to compel a prosecution. The applicant's argument was about delays to criminal prosecution which therefore delayed the investigation and promulgation of the truth and so, consequentially, undermined the victim's right. This is not a strong or necessary grounding for the right to the truth and, in any case, no violation of Article 14 was found.

Legal protection of rights is not focused on the truth but on a state's procedural duties, particularly of prosecution and punishment, through which the legal protection of rights is made effective. Truth is obviously instrumental in this rather than being of sufficient independent value to ground a freestanding right. As with the Inter-American approach, the value of truth to victims as a sufficient and complete ground for a right is recognised but only in relation to the relatives of disappeared persons. Not knowing the fate of a loved one is a distinct horror, a distinct cause of "anguish and distress", which, in itself, can be a breach of the Article 7 ICCPR rights of relatives, who may be the "authors" of the claim despite not being the direct victims.[111] This "right to know"[112] is distinct and truth-based. Likewise, the Committee, though joining the general condemnation of amnesties, has done so for the sufficient reason that an amnesty prevents proper investigation and therefore inhibits the emergence of the truth for the individual victim or author/relative; by implication it is the latter that is the dominant interest.[113]

At the same time the Committee's approach suggests that it also adopts the more general position hostile to amnesty for crimes found in international law. In *Rodriguez v Uruguay* 1994, for example, the state party argued that the ending of criminal prosecutions was an appropriate and constitutional means of pursing peace and reconciliation which had been democratically endorsed by referendum and this position of the sovereign people of a state should be respected by the Committee. Furthermore, the amnesty law did not prevent a victim pursuing civil remedies. The Committee rejected these arguments.

As with the Inter-American Court, there is a difficulty in grounding such opposition to amnesty on individual rights to legal protection. Individual remedies do not normally include criminal prosecution. This is a state responsibility, and it is not jurisprudentially offensive to have a public official with powers to prevent or halt private prosecutions. The Committee is emphatic that nothing in the Covenant gives an individual the right to insist on a criminal prosecution.[114] In *Bautista*, such a claim was made in the context to Article 14, the right to a fair trial. It is hard to see how a fair trial can ground a state duty to prosecute.

111 E.g. *Hero v Bosnia supra* note 106 see para 9.6.; *Sarma v Sri Lanka* (16 July 2003).

112 As per Principle 4 of the UNCHR, Report of the independent expert to update the Set of Principles to combat impunity (18 February 2005).

113 *Rodriguez v Uruguay supra* note 104 para 12.3; General Comment 20 *supra* note 195 para 14.

114 See, for example, the terse statement to that effect in *H.C.M.A. [name deleted] v The Netherlands* (30 March 1989) para 11.6; see also *Bautista de Arellana v Colombia supra* note 102 para 8.6.

It is much easier to ground prosecution and punishment on the general duty of states to take necessary measures required to guarantee the Covenant rights of individuals. Nevertheless, in recent cases investigation remains linked to prosecution and punishment. In *Tyan v Kazakhstan* 2017,[115] the Committee found a violation of Article 2(3) in respect of breaches of Article 7. The remedy (i.e. for a breach of Article 2(3)) is not only a proper investigation but also an obligation to "prosecute, try and punish" those responsible.[116] In the context (police beatings of a single individual), there was no question of amnesty, nevertheless investigation, prosecution and punishment are seamlessly linked.[117] General Comment 31, on state duties with particular reference to Article 2, makes it clear that those identified as perpetrators by the investigation required by Article 2(3) should then be prosecuted.[118] This is part of the General Comment considering Article 2(3), which as said, does not obviously extend to criminal prosecutions. It might have been on a sounder jurisprudential footing had it been related to the general duties on states to take "necessary measures" to guarantee Covenant rights, in Article 2(2).

Remedies and the Committee's own narrative

In comparison to the Inter-American Court, the Committee's remedies are less extensive and, especially as regards the social aspect and public promulgation, are less far-reaching. They are also less imperative – the Committee uses Article 2(3) to "urge" the state to undertake an official investigation and to grant proper compensation. Likewise its own reports, whilst giving individualised as well as structural facts, are in comparison relatively short and limited. Of course, the explanation for this lies in the contrasts between the non-judicial procedure of the Committee with the procedures and outcomes of a fully adversarial, judicial process of the Court. The Committee's communications are much shorter than fully reasoned judicial decisions. There is (in the general sense) an adversarial process: the Committee summarises the applicant's (the "author's") case, the response of the state party and the author's own reaction. The Committee considers all the written information made available to it by the individual and the state.[119] These include details of the victim's case, but the Committee tends not to make authoritative findings of fact; rather it "notes" the evidence of the parties

115 *Tyan v Kazakhstan* (6 March – 29 March 2017).

116 Ibid para 11: "Accordingly, the State party is obligated, inter alia, to: (a) conduct a thorough and effective investigation into the author's allegations of torture and, if confirmed, prosecute, try and punish those responsible for the torture of the author".

117 See also *Hero v Bosnia supra* note 106 para 11; *Tharu v Nepal* (3 July 2015) (enforced disappearances) para 11.

118 UNHCR, CCPR General Comment 31 Nature of the General Legal Obligation on States Parties to the Covenant (26 May 2004) para 18.

119 Article 5(1) Optional Protocol: "The Committee shall consider communications received under the present Protocol in the light of all written information made available to it by the individual and by the State Party concerned."

and that, by implication, this provides a *prima facie* case which ought, therefore, to be properly investigated.

Conclusion: the role of the right to the truth

Both the Inter-American Court and the UNHRC can be shown to be giving effect to the norms behind the right to the truth. But, in both contexts, it is characteristically done through a necessary interpretative move concerning the right to legal protection. It is not specifically and sufficiently focused on the need for truth. Although, especially in the Inter-American context, there can be express reference to the "right to the truth", this tends to be more of a section heading rather than the application of a legal principle. These interpretative moves may show that the right to the truth has persuasive legal authority in the sense that it is a general principle of international law.[120] But it remains unclear, as the Court has suggested and Committee implied, whether the right to the truth is supererogatory with nothing to add to what is necessary if the right to the legal protection of rights is to be effective.

The case law suggests that there may be two particular contributions of the right to the truth as independent of the right to legal protection.

First, the background norms of the right to the truth indicate a public aspect. The truth, in the context of atrocity, must be disclosed not just for the victims' sakes but also be publicly disseminated so that it can help form the political discourse of transitioning states. This aspect is recognised in the case law of both Court and Committee. Publicity, of course, is inherent in legal protection of rights and the openness of judicial processes, nevertheless the right to the truth does seem to add more. The public purpose of disclosing truth can be seen, for instance, in the socially imaginative remedies awarded by the Inter-American Court. It is also normal for the Committee to "request" (it has no power to order) the state to publicise the Committee's views on the case which, as mentioned earlier, will have given some degree of authoritative endorsement of the evidence presented to it by the victim and/or the "author". In addition, General Comment 31 notes, at paragraph 16, that appropriate reparation, in the context of remedies required by article 2(3), can involve not only victim specific measures (such as compensation and rehabilitation) but also "measures of satisfaction such as public apologies, public memorials, guarantees of non-repetition and changes in relevant laws and practices".

The individual rights focus of Convention and Covenant do not easily adapt to the public aspect and it has been suggested earlier and in Chapter 4 that articulating the need for truth in terms of the duties inherent in the idea of democratic and well-ordered states, may be more theoretically compelling even if making little practical difference. We have seen that the right to receive information, an element of the right to freedom of expression, may, because it is inherently a

120 As discussed in Chapter 3.

political right, be a better basis for enforcing the public aspect of the right to the truth; but there are strong reasons why this right (e.g. Article 13 ACHR) fails properly to satisfy the requirements of the right to the truth.

A second contribution of the right to the truth is that it be the ground on which a very high degree of normative weight is attached to the state's investigative duty; the point being that this normative weight may be greater in the context of atrocity to which the right to the truth applies; perhaps beyond that attached to legal protection more generally. *Cifuentes Elgueta v Chile* 2009,[121] a UNHRC view, contains a dissent by HRC members Keller and Salvioli which is expressly grounded on the right to the truth. The issue was whether a continuing obligation on a state to investigate disappearances could exist in respect of events (the victim's disappearance in the custody of the security services in 1981) which had occurred before Chile's accession to the Protocol or another earlier date chosen by Chile. The Committee's view was that continuing obligations (such as the duty to search for disappeared persons) could only apply in respect of initial events (e.g. kidnaps) which had occurred after the state accepted responsibility under the Protocol (March 1990 at the earliest).[122]

The dissenters' position was that the extent of continuing obligations was a matter of interpretation by the Committee, that the Committee should approach the matter in terms of the purpose of human rights protection and the idea of the Covenant as an evolutive instrument. In giving this more generous, evolutive, interpretation, the Committee should recognise the new rights and perspectives that have evolved and developed in respect of forced disappearances and these include the right to truth [*sic*].[123] Such rights should influence the interpretation and application of the Covenant. The implication in the context of the case is that the right to the truth is of such weight that it should override any juristically dubious attempt by the state (Chile's declaration) to avoid responsibilities to investigate and punish disappearances over which it has continuing responsibilities. The dissent then goes on to show how the norms of the right to the truth have already influenced the application of the Covenant (the investigative duty under Article 2(3), etc.).

Implicit in this dissent is that the right to the truth enjoys an overriding normative force which (perhaps) is lacking where the investigative duty is grounded simply as a necessary implication of the right to legal protection of rights. The

121 *Cifuentes Elgueta v Chile* (28 July 2009).

122 The Committee upheld its normal position, that the Protocol does not apply to actions occurring before the country accepts responsibilities under the Protocol unless, as in the context of disappearances, there were continuing obligations. The Covenant was in force in Chile in 1981 and the Optional Protocol in August 1992 although Chile accepted obligations under the Optional Protocol for events after March 1990 when democratic government commenced.

123 *Cifuentes Elgueta v Chile supra* note 121, dissenting opinion of Keller and Salvioli, para 20: "The practice of enforced disappearances has given rise to the formulation of new rights and their introduction, through evolutive interpretation, into these general instruments: the right to truth is one example".

inherent investigative duty is usually expressed as an obligation of means; if grounded on the right to the truth, in comparison, it should be seen in more absolute terms tending to be an obligation of results, particularly where the disappeared person was in the custody of the state.[124] Directed by this absolute, results-based conception of the right to the truth, the Committee should not allow (as, perhaps, is easier to accept under the simple inherent investigative duty) state institutions to use any arguments to interfere with the investigation (this might include even well-grounded national security concerns, for example) nor arguments of resources, nor arguments of having done all that can reasonably be expected in the circumstances.[125] The right to the truth, therefore, adds weight and significance to the inherent or inferred duty to investigate making the former into a strong, near absolute right of victims (and perhaps society)[126] to know the truth of what happened.

Despite its focus on truth, the dissent goes on to argue strongly the orthodox linking of truth to prosecution and punishment, which is, as discussed earlier, one of the central requirements of the right to legal protection – there is said to be a false dichotomy between truth and justice.[127] In this latter sense, therefore, the right to the truth adds nothing new.

References

Aldana-Pindell R, 'An Emerging Universality of Justiciable Victims' Rights in the Criminal Process to Curtail Impunity for State-Sponsored Crimes' (2004) 26(3) Human Rights Quarterly 605.

Antkowiak T, 'Truth as a Right and Remedy in International Human Rights Experience' (2002) 23(4) Michigan Journal of International Law 990.

Antkowiak T, 'An Emerging Mandate for International Courts: Victim-Centred Remedies And Restorative Justice' (2011) 47 Stanford Journal of International Law 279.

Bassiouni M C, 'International recognition of victims' rights' (2006) 6(2) Human Rights Law Review 203.

Burgorgue-Larsen L and Ubeda De Torres A, The *Inter-American Court of Human Rights. Case Law and Commentary* (Oxford University Press 2011).

Cavallaro J and Brewer S, 'Regional Human Rights Litigation in the Twenty-First Century: the Case of the Inter-American Court' (2008) 102 The American Journal of International Law 768.

Groome D, 'The Right to Truth in the Fight Against Impunity' (2011) 29(1) Berkeley Journal of International Law 181.

Grossman C, 'The Inter-American Commission on Human Rights' (2011) Max Planck Encyclopedia of Public International Law (online).

124 Ibid para 26 *passim*.

125 Ibid see paras 27 and 29, especially.

126 The public aspect of the right to the truth is introduced but not developed in the dissent.

127 *Cifuentes Elgueta v Chile supra* note 121 – dissenting opinion of Keller and Salvioli, para 33.

Lafontaine F, 'No amnesty or statute of limitation for enforced disappearances: the Sandoval case before the Supreme Court of Chile' (2005) 3(1) Journal of International Criminal Justice 469.
Méndez J and Bariffi F, 'Truth, Right to, International Protection' (2011) Max Planck Encyclopedia of Public International Law (online).
Neuman G L, 'American Convention on Human Rights (1969)' (2010) Max Planck Encyclopedia of Public International Law (online).
Neuman G L, 'Inter-American Court of Human Rights (IACtHR)' (2007) Max Planck Encyclopedia of Public International Law (online).
Schauer F, *Free Speech: a philosophical enquiry* (Cambridge University Press 1982).
Sweeney J, *The European Court of Human Rights in the Post-Cold War Era* (Routledge 2012).

7 The right to the truth at the European Court of Human Rights

Introduction

There is no express "right to the truth" in the European Convention on Human Rights (ECHR). In this it is similar not only to the International Covenant on Civil and Political Rights (ICCPR) but also to the other, UN-grounded regional statements and procedures for the protection of human rights such as the American Convention on Human Rights (ACHR), the topic of Chapter 6, or the African Charter on Human and People's Rights.[1] Nevertheless, as with those systems, there is a significant degree of recognition and enforcement of the core norms of the right to the truth,[2] done through the interpretation and application of express Convention rights.

The European Court of Human Rights (ECtHR or Court) gives effect to the norms of the right to the truth in three ways: enforcing a state duty of investigation, ordering reparations for breach of this duty and in making, in the course of judgment, its own authoritative findings of what happened. It has been suggested that awareness and protection of the norms of the right to the truth is less developed in the European system, its application more restricted, than in the American.[3] This will be examined in the following. Insofar as this is true it is likely to reflect the different contexts of the two systems.

Context

The right to the truth should have effect in the context of gross and perhaps systemic violations of human rights. For the first few decades of its existence, the Court was not (in comparison with the Inter-American Court) required to deal with allegations of widespread, officially sanctioned and policy-driven forced disappearances, massacres and deliberate individual killings. For many of

1 For a brief discussion of the right to the truth under the African Charter, see James A Sweeney 'The Elusive Right to Truth in Transitional Human Rights Jurisprudence' (2018) 67 (2) International and Comparative Law Quarterly 353, in particular at 385.

2 The content of the right to the truth is discussed in Chapter 3.

3 Sweeney *supra* note 1 at 373.

its formative years, western Europe was at peace and the role of the Court was, in effect, to develop the rights element in the constitutional norms of pluralist, democratic societies committed to the rule of law (the condition of membership of the Council of Europe). This is not to undervalue the suffering following from, in particular, the Turkish invasion of Cyprus in 1974, but rather to suggest that there was a different context from the policy-driven breakdown of state protection found in Central and South America. The closest the European Court came to this was in relation to the cases involving the Turkish state reaction to Kurdish terrorism in south-east Turkey. In Greece in 1968 and the Balkans in the 1990s, the Court had no direct role because the parties were not members of the Council of Europe.[4] Since the reunification of Europe, the Court has had to deal with cases reflecting both historical and present issues concerning the transition from communist dictatorships to bourgeois republics. More importantly, it has had to deal with murders, abductions and so forth involving Russian actions in Chechnya and the Caucasus, which are comparable to the actions of South and Central American dictators.

The investigative duty on states

The duty

From some of its earliest cases the ECtHR has required states to undertake an "effective official investigation" into alleged breaches of Article 2 (the right to life).[5] This known as the procedural "limb" or "aspect" of Article 2 and has been applied in the context of the right to the truth.[6] Such an investigative duty has also been applied in relation to credible allegations of breaches of the right not to be tortured or to suffer inhuman or degrading punishment (Article 3).[7] In the case of persons who have disappeared and whose fate is not known, the duty to investigate may arise under Article 2 where the disappearances took place in "life threatening circumstances". This is usually where they were last seen in the custody of armed forces or where there is evidence of widespread detention

4 Greece left the Council of Europe during the period of the military dictatorship.

5 *McCann v United Kingdom* (27 September 1995) – and numerous subsequent cases. Post-1998 Grand Chamber endorsement (in a police shooting case) includes *Giuliani and Gaggio v Italy* (24 March 2011), para 298 passim. See Juliet Chevalier-Watts "Effective investigations under Article 2 of the European Convention on Human Rights: securing the right to life or an onerous burden on a state" (2010) 21(3) European Journal of International Law 701–721.

6 E.g. *Aslakhanova v Russia* (18 December 2012) para 121, itself part of a group of cases involving Russian actions in Chechnya.

7 The article 3 duty was first posited in *Assenov v Bulgaria* (28 October 1998) (police brutality). In *Mocanu v Romania* (17 September 2014) (regarding historical investigations into deaths and ill-treatment during police repression in the final days of the Communist dictatorship) a Grand Chamber confirmed the duty of effective investigation as being well established and applying, mutatis mutandis, to the legal prohibition on arbitrary killing (Article 2) as well as to torture and inhuman or degrading treatment or punishment (Article 3).

and abduction by armed forces.[8] The duty to investigate can also arise under Article 5, in respect of persons known to have been in the custody of the authorities and who have since disappeared.[9] The duty may need to be discharged even in armed conflict and difficult security situations.

The duty arises in respect of sufficiently grounded allegations that state agents or their surrogates had direct responsibility for the atrocities. It has been gradually extended and now seems to create a wider duty on the state requiring the authorities to conduct an effective investigation where outcomes in breach of Articles 2 or 3 (murders, rapes, kidnaps, etc.) are perpetrated by non-state agents.[10] which would include individuals, criminal gangs and paramilitary groups.

Though this duty is expressed as the correlative of an individual victim's human right, it is only incompletely so. There are significant elements of a state duty conceived independently of the victim's will (though embodying general assumptions about victims' interests) and which accord with the requirements of the right to the truth. In particular, the investigation must be initiated by the state of its own volition. This illustrates the "political" element to the grounding of the right to the truth discussed in Chapter 3. The duty is not discharged by a victim's power to bring evidence to support a private prosecution or (as is more likely) a civil action.

For disappeared persons, the investigative duty remains a "continuing obligation"[11] which persists "as long as the fate of the person is unaccounted for".[12] Where it is obvious that an investigation is ineffective, relatives have a duty to apply to the Court in good time, and applications subject to excessive or unexplained delays may be rejected (though the Court accepts that the flaws in an investigation can take time to be exposed). In *Varnava v Turkey* 2009, disappearances took place in 1974; they were eventually investigated by a UN Committee on Missing Persons operating from 1984; the application to Strasbourg was in 1990 which, in the circumstances of difficulties with the Committee, was acceptable.

Standing

Applications on behalf of victims, including of other states, can be brought by one or more High Contracting Parties under the system of collective security

8 *Cyprus v Turkey* (10 May 2001) paras 129–136.

9 Ibid para 147.

10 This is an un-argued extension of the state's duty to investigate alleged breaches of article 3 committed by state agents (*Assenov v Bulgaria supra* note 7 – a police ill-treatment case) made in *M.C. v Bulgaria* (4 December 2003) (a police failure to investigate a rape effectively), paragraph 151 – "such a positive duty [to conduct an official investigation] cannot be considered in principle to be limited solely to cases of ill-treatment by state agents". See the UK case *Commissioner of Police of the Metropolis v DSD* (2018) for discussion. In relation to non-state agents, see our discussion in Chapter 3 on structural truth.

11 *Varnava v Turkey* (18 September 2009) (concerning the disappearances of individual members of the Cypriot armed forces during the active phase of the Turkish invasion of Cyprus in 1974) para 121 and 186.

12 Ibid para 148 (relying on *Cyprus v Turkey supra* note 8 para 136).

embodied in Article 33 – such state applications are rare,[13] though they are appropriate where a member state is protecting the interests of a considerable number of its nationals.[14]

As an individual right to an effective investigation, the right is possessed by a person with standing before the Court under Article 34 – a person, NGO or group that claims to be a "victim" of a violation. A range of other admissibility criteria must also be satisfied (Article 35).

The Court's basic test for being a "victim" is that the applicant must be alive and have been "directly affected" by the alleged breach.[15] Importantly, in the context of the right to the truth, the Court recognises "indirect" victims, including close relatives of deceased direct victims. This applies particularly where the death, disappearance or torture is alleged to be a state responsibility. Close relatives are treated as applicants, not representatives of the victim (the general rule is that, without specific and appointed representation, a case cannot be brought in the name of a deceased person). This flexibility follows from the Court's awareness of the need to avoid an over-formalist approach to its standing and admissibility rules if it is to offer human rights protection which is effective.[16] In *Varnava v Turkey* 2009, nine applications were brought in the name of persons deceased or disappeared in the context of the Turkish invasion of Cyprus in 1974. Each application was linked to a second application by a close relative. A Grand Chamber held that the relatives would be treated as applicants and that it was unnecessary to rule on whether the direct victims could also be applicants.[17] Even a non-relative, but a person closely connected with the direct victim (such as a solicitor who has represented the victims)[18] may be given standing.[19]

Relatives in their own name, Article 3

An investigative duty may also be owed to relatives in their own name as the direct victim. This is on the basis that the agony of relatives faced with an absent or inadequate investigation into, particularly, the disappearance of their loved

13 Between 1956–1999 the Commission considered 17 inter-state cases (all bar 3 before 1959.) Between 1959 and the abolition of the Commission and the coming into being of the full-time Court in 1999, there was one case: *Ireland v UK* 1978. The full-time Court has, since 1999, determined three cases: *Denmark v Turkey* (5 April 2000); *Cyprus v Turkey supra* note 8 and *Georgia v Russia* (3 July 2014) – where various breaches were found against Russia in respect of mass deportations of Georgian citizens).

14 Where states are also members of the European Union, inter-state issues can be addressed using article 7 Treaty of European Union – which require states to respect common European values. Effective action requires unanimity.

15 E.g. *Eckle* v *Germany* (15 July 1982) see para 66.

16 E.g. *Çakici v Turkey* (8 July 1999) and *Bazorkina v Russia* (27 July 2006) (brother and mother of disappeared persons in south east Turkey and Chechnya, respectively).

17 *Varnava v Turkey supra* note 11 paras 111–112.

18 E.g. *SP* v *UK* (20 May 1996).

19 See *Centre for Legal Resources on behalf of Campeanu v Romania* (17 July 2014) for a Grand Chamber summary of admissibility (paras 96–103).

ones, can of itself be inhuman treatment and a breach of Article 3. It derives from the distress, the "anguish of uncertainty" the relatives have suffered as a result of the failure of the authorities to undertake an effective investigation into a disappearance: the "essence of the violation . . . lies in the authorities' reactions and attitudes to the situation when it has been brought to their attention".[20] Where there is a "flagrant, continuous and callous disregard of the obligation to account for the whereabouts and fate of a missing person" and the applicant relatives are left to bear the brunt of discovering for themselves the fate of their loved ones, there can be a breach of Article 3. The breach depends on special factors such as the closeness of the family tie between the relative and the disappeared person and the relative's degree of involvement in the search.[21] Where the authorities have behaved as they should, a breach of Article 3 is unlikely to follow. In *Çakici v Turkey* 1999, for example, the deceased brother's experience was considered to be too remote and relatively uninvolved and there were no aggravating factors flowing from the attitude of the authorities to amount to a breach, in itself, of Article 3.[22]

It is not necessary to show that the state was responsible for the disappearance. Responsibility is based solely on its callous attitude and failure to investigate and respond. The interest being served is the need to know the truth *simpliciter* rather than a broader interest in retribution and in opposing impunity. In this regard, the Court distinguishes between "disappearance" and "confirmed death" cases. A relative's independent right to the truth is based on the agony of not knowing. Where the person is known to be dead, there is no uncertainty, there may be no direct violation of Article 3 suffered by the relative or, at least, these special circumstances will be much more demanding.[23] The distinction between disappearance and confirmed death cases and the special factors which imply the need for relatives to demonstrate suffering over and above the emotional distress normally expected in situations of atrocity, may be a barrier to relatives seeking the truth and an unnecessary limitation to the right to the truth.[24]

The basis of the duty

The duty is grounded in the procedural requirements of the substantive right in issue (normally Articles 2, 3 and 5), although as discussed later in the chapter, the

20 *Varnava v Turkey supra* note 11 para 200.

21 *Cyprus v Turkey supra* note 8 paras 155–158, endorsed by a Grand Chamber in *Varnava v Turkey supra* note 11 para 200.

22 *Çakici v Turkey supra* note 16 paras 98–99. These requirements derive from *Kurt v Turkey* (25 May 1998) where the applicant was the mother of a disappeared person, she suffered deep and long-lasting distress and was met with official inaction. There was a breach of article 3 in her case as well as a breach of article 5 in respect of her son.

23 As in *Janowiec v Russia* (21 October 2013), the surviving relatives of Polish officers massacred in 1940 would have known by 1998, when the Convention came into effect in Russia, that their relatives were dead (paras 177–188).

24 James Sweeney *supra* note 1 at 373–374.

duty may also be grounded on Article 13, the general right to a remedy. There is a superficial contrast with the Inter-American Court of Human Rights, which grounds a similar investigative duty on the general right to legal protection for all American Convention rights.[25] The contrast is superficial, because the purpose and justification for the investigative duty is the same. The investigative duties are proper inferences from the texts of Articles 2, 3 and 5 because they are necessary to ensure the effectiveness of the guarantees in these rights. Effectiveness follows from the states' obligations under Article 1 ECHR to "secure the rights and freedoms" in the Convention for "everyone". Without proper investigations, these prohibitions would be "ineffective in practice".[26] In *Ramsahai v Netherlands* 2008 (police shooting), the Grand Chamber reiterated that the "essential purpose of such an investigation is to safeguard the effective implementation of the domestic laws safeguarding the right to life"[27] and to ensure the accountability of the responsible officials. An effective investigation is also necessary in order to maintain "public confidence in [the state's] adherence to the rule of law and in preventing any appearance of impunity, collusion in, or tolerance, of unlawful acts". For the same reasons, "there must be a sufficient element of public scrutiny of the investigation or its results to secure accountability in practice as well as in theory".[28] Similarly, in respect of Article 3, the purpose of the investigation is to ensure that there has been proper state compliance with the duty not to torture and so forth. This includes consequential, appropriate legal action which is necessary because otherwise this fundamental prohibition would be "ineffective in practice and it would be possible in some cases for agents of the State to abuse the rights of those within their control with virtual impunity".[29] At its heart the investigation is necessary to ensure public confidence in the state's monopoly of legitimate force.[30]

The investigative duty, therefore, is about more than satisfying the victim's (or society's) need for truth. Legal protection of Convention rights necessarily links truth instrumentally with the identification, prosecution and punishment of those responsible: "the national courts should not under any circumstances be prepared to allow life-endangering offences to go unpunished".[31] The ground and driver behind the investigative duty requires all of this and also compensation. It is not limited to giving effect to a freestanding right to the truth. Prosecution and punishment are state functions. Investigation, therefore, is justified as a wider duty predicated on the idea of a properly functioning democratic state, the responsibilities of which are broader than simply duties correlated to individual rights.

25 See Chapter 8.
26 *McCann v United Kingdom supra* note 5 para 161 and numerous subsequent cases.
27 *Ramsahai v The Netherlands* (15 May 2007) para 321.
28 Ibid.
29 E.g. *Gäfgen v Germany* (1 June 2010) para 119.
30 E.g. *Da Silva v United Kingdom* (30 March 2016) (police shooting) para 232.
31 Ibid para 239.

The state's legal and actionable duty to investigate is a necessary implication of or inference from the text of Articles 2, 3 or 5. It does not illustrate the "living instrument" conception of the Convention by which (sometimes controversially) social values are imported in order to guide the Convention's application. The right to the truth appears not as an external value to which the Convention should adjust itself but as something arrived at through normal processes of judicial reasoning.

Transitional justice

The procedural limb of Article 2 applies independently of whether or not there has been a breach of the substantive duty. It can apply in respect of events for which the state was not responsible, and this includes deaths, disappearances and torture by a previous regime, even when these took place before the Convention came into force as a state obligation. This was confirmed by a Grand Chamber in *Silih v Slovenia* 2009,[32] involving a death in hospital occurring over a year before Slovenia recognised the authority of the Convention. The principles were clarified and applied in the context of the right to the truth in *Janowiec v Russia* 2013[33] regarding the effectiveness of Russian investigations into the Katyn massacres of 1940.

A state's obligations to guarantee Convention rights to its population begin on the date when the Convention enters into force in the country ("the critical date"). Actions, omissions and events, including deaths, disappearances and torture that occurred before the critical date cannot be the factual basis for alleged breaches of substantive rights. There can, however, be state responsibility for procedural failures after the critical date which relate to events that took place before it. These include a failure properly to investigate and prosecute in respect of deaths, disappearances and torture which took place before the critical date. There needs to be a "genuine connection" between the death and the entry into force of the Convention, and this is based on two tests. First, the time period between the "triggering event" (the death, disappearance, torture, etc.) and entry into force of the Convention must be reasonably short, and the Court has imposed a cut-off of ten years at most. Second, a significant proportion of the procedural obligations had or should have taken place after the Convention came into force. An investigation "should" have taken place if, after the entry into force of the Convention, new plausible and credible information is made available. Even if no "genuine connection" can be established, the state may still have procedural obligations in respect of pre-critical date events where such investigation is necessary to "ensure that the guarantees and the underlying values of the Convention are protected in a real and effective way"; this is the "Convention values" test. It applies to the most serious violations of rights which are exceptional

32 *Silih v Slovenia* (9 April 2009) paras 153–163.
33 *Janowiec v Russia supra* note 23 para 141 *passim*.

and heinous, and strike at the fundamental values of the Convention and which should be investigated.[34] The test is relevant, therefore, to the context of the right to the truth. But the Convention values test cannot be applied to events which took place before the Convention was first adopted on 4 November 1950.

These tests were applied in *Janowiec v Russia* 2013 in relation to Russia's investigation into the Katyn massacres of Polish officers in 1940. The critical date when the Convention entered into force in Russia was 1998. There was no "genuine connection" because there was no fresh evidence which might, after 1998, have triggered an obligation to investigate. In any case the killings took place more than ten years before 1998. The Convention values test could not be applied because the killings took place years before 1950 when the Convention was first adopted.

The *Janowiec* tests are controversial[35] and were subject to significant dissents. Judge Keller criticised the judgment on the grounds, in effect, of over-formalism.[36] Jurisdictional formalities are allowed to interfere with the need, justified as a legal principle, to investigate and punish the most serious international crimes and give relief to suffering relatives. The right to the truth, given its context, is specifically mentioned as outweighing the jurisdictional limits.

Judge Keller's dissent seems to adopt the right to the truth as a juristic value, external to the Convention, which should nevertheless guide its application. That is in contrast to the jurisprudentially uncontroversial procedural obligation. As the majority implies, adopting external values into the Convention can be controversial, especially if it undermines legal certainty and the basis on which a state knows its actionable obligations under the Convention. There is, of course, something arbitrary about the ten-year limit to a "genuine connection", and perhaps it is true that it was obvious even in 1940 that massacring prisoners was an international wrong. Nevertheless, a state's legal obligations must be knowable even if, thereby, they are less than what is required by moral right and background principle.

The type of investigation

To satisfy the procedural limb of Articles 2, 3 and 5 the effective investigation must aim beyond the simple disclosure of the truth of what happened. It is an instrumental and necessary part of giving full legal protection against violation of the Convention rights. The Court does not specify *in abstracto* the type of investigation. There must be an "adequate response" to the events which may be "judicial or otherwise" but its purpose must be to ensure that proper legal

34 They are the kinds of crimes which, by reference to the Convention on the Non-Applicability of Statutory Limitations to War Crimes and Crimes Against Humanity, should not be subject to limitation.

35 E.g. Sweeney *supra* note 1 who calls the decision "harsh" (at 383–4).

36 Similarly to his dissent in the UNHRC View *Cifuentes Elgueta v Chile*, discussed in Chapter 6.

protection works.[37] Gross violations of the right to life and so forth must be punished, therefore a criminal investigation is likely to be necessary. More extensive investigations such as independent, non-judicial, public or parliamentary inquiries may contribute to overall effectiveness by, for example, better allowing victim and public involvement, or identifying who was responsible in a way that can then be taken up by the prosecution authorities. These latter forms of inquiry may be necessary to satisfy both the procedural obligation and the right to the truth – but not sufficient.

Effectiveness

To be "effective", the investigation must have certain general overall and cumulative characteristics.[38] The investigation must be "independent" in the sense of requiring a lack of hierarchical dependence on the state executive. Public confidence in state institutions is thereby supported. It must be "adequate" in the sense of being able to determine the facts, identify those responsible and provide a basis on which, if necessary, those responsible can be prosecuted and, if convicted, punished. Overall it must be able to provide convincing answers to the legal question which is whether the use of force was justified in terms of the substantive Convention right in issue. Thus *Tagayeva v Russia* 2017 (regarding the multiple deaths consequent on the authority's response to terrorist hostage-taking) involves Article 2 (the right to life). This article, in terms, is not breached by the proportionate use of lethal force. But the state's investigation did not consider important issues relevant to proportionality, such as the appropriateness of the use of indiscriminate weapons.[39]

An effective investigation must have the authority to use appropriate procedures and methods such as, initially, obtaining and securing the evidence[40] and using, inter alia, eyewitness testimony, forensic evidence and, where appropriate, an autopsy to provide a complete and accurate record of injury and an objective analysis of the clinical findings, including the cause of death.[41] The investigation must also have sufficient authority. It must be able to hold state officials to account for their actions and decisions and obtain disclosure of all relevant information.[42]

37 *Da Silva v United Kingdom supra* note 30 para 230.

38 Ibid paras 231–238, giving a full Grand Chamber summary of the requirements for an effective investigation.

39 *Tagayeva v Russia* (13 April 2017).

40 As was done improperly in *Tagayeva supra* note 39, where the clearance of the site took place too quickly meaning that it was impossible to determine the precise cause of death of many victims.

41 Again, in *Tagayeva supra* note 39, the Court held that the investigation's forensic method was inadequate and was consequently insufficient to determine precise cause of death of a third of victims.

42 This can raise important issues of state cooperation, which are discussed later in the chapter.

The quality of the investigation is also a matter for potential review by the Court. The Court uses the language of practical reason: the investigation must involve a "thorough, objective and impartial analysis of all relevant elements". It should do more than merely follow an obvious line of inquiry or be, uncritically, built upon a hasty, initial presumption which leads to a hasty completion. The nature and intensity of scrutiny depends on the context although the Court requires that there should be particular (intense) scrutiny regarding suspicious deaths at hands of state agents. The investigation must be conducted promptly and with reasonable expedition.

Overall, as is often said, the investigation is an obligation of means, not results.[43] This principle is to be treated with caution in the context of the right to the truth, lest it be an excuse for an investigation that lacks the necessary rigour and purpose.[44] The state's duty is to take "whatever reasonable steps they can"[45] to secure the evidence, but apart from that, the state's duty is expressed in imperative terms. There is a margin of appreciation on the specific nature of the investigation but it remains subject to the reviewing powers of the Court which, in the context of the right to the truth, conducts close scrutiny. Finally, the Convention rights involved are not "qualified rights" (such as Articles 9–11) and do not require a balancing exercise between individual rights, the rights of others or the social good.

Investigation and Article 13

Article 13, the right to a remedy, is the basis on which a state can also be under a legal obligation to hold an effective investigation.[46] This obliges states to provide a proper legal procedure to determine "arguable claims" or "complaints"[47] of a breach of a Convention right.[48] The failure to provide a proper investigation can be, in itself, a violation of Article 13 and so separate from violations of the procedural limbs of Articles 2 and 3. Although Article 13 does not expressly mention a duty to investigate, the Court has held that such an investigation is clearly implied.[49]

The relationship of the investigative duty under the procedural limbs of Articles 2 and 3, and under Article 13, is not easy to discover. The Court may find a breach of article 13 on apparently the same grounds as a breach of the procedural

43 *Da Silva supra* note 30 para 233.

44 One of Judge Keller's concerns when a member of the UNHCR, in *Cifuentes Elgueta*, discussed in Chapter 6.

45 *Da Silva supra* note 30.

46 For early cases see Thomas Antkowiak, 'Truth as right and remedy in international human rights expertise' (2001–2) 23 Michigan Journal of International Law 977 at 982.

47 See, for example, *Klass v Germany* (6 September 1978) para 64; *de Souza Ribeiro v France* (13 December 2012) para 78.

48 E.g. *Khashiyev v Russia* (24 February 2005) paras 182–3.

49 *Aksoy v Turkey* (18 December 1996) para 95 *passim*.

obligations under Article 2 or 3.[50] Alternatively it may decline to hold a separate breach of Article 13 on the grounds that the effectiveness of the investigation has been dealt with under Article 2 or 3.[51] Likewise, it may be possible to satisfy Article 13 through the availability of civil remedies which might not be sufficient to satisfy the judicial and punitive requirements of Articles 2 and 3.[52]

The Court has said that Article 13 investigation is "broader" than the procedural wing of Articles 2, 3 and 5. This seems to include the idea that, so long as the lack of a judicially effective investigation is dealt with under the procedural limb of substantive rights, an accumulation of other evidence obtained through a range of types of investigations can satisfy Article 13. In *Tagayeva v Russia* 2017,[53] the failures of the investigation into the Beslan deaths (when Russian forces stormed a school to rescue child hostages) breached the procedural limb of Article 2. But there was no breach of Article 13 because there had been other investigations which, though not sufficient to satisfy Article 2, contributed significantly to the knowledge of victims and their families of what happened. In particular, these were parliamentary inquiries which, though insufficiently judicial and punitive to satisfy the procedural limb of Article 2, provided a great deal of information to allow victims and relatives to get to know what happened. The Court (whilst not denying that Article 13 requires there to be an adequate judicial and punitive remedy) said:

> What appears to be of special importance under Article 13, apart from the compensation mechanisms, is access to information and thus the establishment of truth for the victims of the violations alleged, as well as ensuring justice and preventing impunity for the perpetrators.[54]

Thus Article 13 is seen as giving weight to a range of forms of investigation which focus on disclosure of the truth without necessarily being instrumentally linked to prosecution or reparations. To this degree it may make a distinct contribution to the right to the truth.

Victims' involvement

One of the more controversial and conceptually imprecise ideas attached to the "right to the truth" is victim involvement in the truth-obtaining procedures. This does not mean control but some appropriate degree of involvement.[55] Under

50 E.g. *Assenov v Bulgaria supra* note 7 see para 106 and 117–18.
51 E.g. *Ramsahai v The Netherland supra* note 27 para 363]; *Tagayeva v Russia supra* note 39.
52 The partly dissenting opinion of Judge Zagrebelsky in *Khashiyev v Russia supra* note 48, argued that availability of an effective civil remedy satisfied article 13; the procedural failure was properly attributed to articles 2 and 3.
53 *Tagayeva v Russia supra* note 39.
54 *Tagayeva v Russia supra* note 39 para 627.
55 See in particular Chapter 10 on the role of victims in the International Criminal Court.

the procedural limbs of Articles 2 and 3 the Court has said, without reference to external sources, that an investigation must be "accessible" to victims and relatives to the "extent necessary to safeguard their legitimate interests".[56] In *Oğur v Turkey* 1999,[57] for example, the procedural limb of Article 2 was violated due to the inaccessibility of the case file to close relatives. This is clearly a limited and judicially controlled degree of participation. Participation to safeguard interests is predominantly about access to information. It enables victims to take further steps if they think them necessary for the protection of their interests. It is not a right of control. In particular, given that the investigative duty is necessarily and instrumentally connected with prosecution, the Court has made it clear that there is no right of a victim to have a person prosecuted or punished to a certain level and a "substantial deference to national courts" is allowed on the choice of procedures.[58] Likewise, states are not required to satisfy all requests for investigative measures made by a relative.[59] Participation rights are, therefore, limited. Some victim-focused accounts of the right to the truth emphasise the need for victims to tell their story. Nothing in the investigative duty makes such an opportunity an obligation on states.

Public aspect

The public aspect of the right to the truth (Chapter 4) is discharged, in part, by the principle of public and open justice which should govern the prosecutions and other legal processes consequent on an effective investigation. The Court has always required an effective investigation to have a "sufficient element of public scrutiny".[60] The scope and nature of this scrutiny depends upon case circumstances. In particular, the sufficiency of public scrutiny can be limited by legitimate concerns to protect sensitive material from public disclosure if other investigations or individuals might be prejudiced. Fuller public disclosure may have to wait for other procedures outside those strictly required to fulfil the investigative duty.[61] Such restrictions on openness can lead to potential tension with the full requirements of the right to the truth, the distinctive point of which may be disclosure to victims in almost all situations;[62] and victims could not easily be prevented from making further public disclosure undermining investigation and prosecutorial confidentiality. A tougher attitude, more reflective of the needs of the right to the truth, is taken by the Court in respect of state cooperation with the Court (see below) – but this involves disclosure of information to the Court,

56 *Da Silva v UK supra* note 30 para 235.
57 *Oğur v Turkey* (20 May 1999)
58 *Da Silva v United Kingdom supra* note 30 para 238.
59 *Giuliani and Gaggio v Italy supra* note 5 para 304.
60 Ibid para 303
61 Ibid para 304.
62 As in Judge Keller's dissent in *Cifuentes Elgueta v Chile*, discussed in Chapter 6.

which the Court can keep confidential, rather than public disclosure in the context of a state investigation.

The Court has consistently turned its face against *actio popularis*. An applicant, as we have seen, must have been directly affected or a close relative and cannot be a public official somehow representing society. Given this, the investigative duty does not correlate to a social right in any meaningful sense. It is a victim's right correlating to a state duty with social consequences.

Article 10

The ground on which an action might be brought, by someone not a direct victim, and in order to have information disclosed where the point is to make it socially available, could be Article 10: the right to freedom of expression. Article 10 is a political right in the sense that one of its main purposes is to facilitate democratic deliberation on public affairs. Although Article 10 includes a right "to receive" information this has, in the past, usually excluded a right to receive from an unwilling provider.[63] The Court has begun to move to the position in which it can be a breach of Article 10 if a public authority refuses to disclose information in its possession to an applicant if the information relates to matters of public interest and the applicant is a media outlet, NGO and so forth, seeking the information in order to make it public (*Magyar v Hungary* 2016).[64] The information must be ready and available, so this is not a basis for compelling an investigation in the first place. Furthermore, Article 10 is a qualified right, so disclosure can be limited under the terms of Article 10(2).

There have been cases where Article 10 has been proposed as a ground of action in the right to the truth context. This has been rejected as manifestly ill-founded as not providing an analytical framework which introduces distinctive factors from the investigative duties inherent in Articles 2, 3 and 5 and also 13.[65] These cases were decided prior to the Grand Chamber's endorsement and specification of a qualified right to receive information from an unwilling provider in *Magyar*. *Magyar* grounds a tentative suggestion that Article 10 could raise distinct issues where the aim is to enforce public disclosure of available information in order to contribute to public understanding of the truth concerning atrocities of many years back and where amnesty and other provisions have prevented the disclosure of available information.[66]

63 Unlike under Article 13 American Convention of Human Rights, there is no right to "seek" information in Article 10; see Chapter 6.

64 *Magyar Helsinki Bizottság v Hungary* (8 November 2016) see especially para 156 *passim*.

65 *Al Nashiri v Poland* (July 2014) para 580, where the social aspect is explicit; follows *El Masri v Macedonia* (12 December 2012) paras 264–5.

66 *Reyes v Brazil* Judgment of November 24 2010 discussed in Chapter 6.

Reference to the right to the truth

In the European case law the investigative duty inherent in Articles 2, 3 and 5 and also 13 is not normally stated as an expression of the right to the truth. Unusually, in *El-Masri v Macedonia* 12 December 2012,[67] the Court did, in one paragraph,[68] relate the procedural limb of Article 3 to the victim's "right to the truth".[69] The case involved "extraordinary" illegal rendition and clearly had major political and social aspects relating to the "war on terrorism". In the paragraph, the Court referred to the submissions of authoritative interveners such as the UN High Commissioner for Human Rights and NGOs including Redress and Amnesty International and the International Commission of Jurists. It found a violation by Macedonia of the procedural limb of Article 3. Macedonia's ineffective investigation was sufficiently established by reference to the contextually dependent requirements of an effective investigation that satisfies the procedural limb. The Court suggests that the right to the truth as a principle of international law could have provided an additional reason for the violation of Article 3 but it is clear that, absent this, the result would have been the same.

Four judges argued that the Court should have made a direct declaration that Macedonia had violated the applicant's right to the truth which should have been made in the context of the violation of Article 13. They argue that this is the appropriate basis for finding a failure to provide an adequate remedy in the context of the most serious and basic human rights violations. Inherent in this position is an intuitive distinction between ordinary violations and those whose "scale and seriousness" engages universal international law and the right to the truth. Reading Article 13 in this way does not involve a change in the substance of the law. Rather, giving the right to the truth as the reason for a violation of the right to a remedy in this context, gives a "renewed light" to the well-established position. In doing this, the Court will also be expressly associating itself to a significant trend in international law. In not doing it, the Court has been "timid" and over-cautious".[70]

But two judges[71] disagreed as to the appropriateness of the original reference in the judgment to the right to the truth. The grounds involve the argument that Convention rights in law are clearly predicated on the direct victim, who is the

67 *El-Masri v Macedonia supra* note 65.

68 Ibid para 191. The same argument is made in the related case: *Al Nashiri v Poland supra* note 65.

69 See Federico Fabbrini, 'The European Court of Human Rights, Extraordinary Renditions and the Right to the Truth: Ensuring Accountability for Gross Human Rights Violations Committed in the Fight Against Terrorism' (2014) 14(1) Human Rights Law Review 85–106.

70 *El Masri v Macedonia supra* note 65 – concurring opinion of Judges Tulkens, Spielmann, Sicilianos and Keller.

71 *El Masri v Macedonia supra* note 65 – concurring opinion of Judges Casadevall and López Guerra.

sole subject of the right to an effective investigation under Articles 2 and 3. The majority's reference to the right to the truth (as in the other sources of international law) suggests that it is there in part to serve the broader public interest. But in the judges' view, the victim's right to an effective investigation exists, under the procedural aspect of Article 3, irrespective of whether the issue is significant in a socio-political context.

This dispute about the place of the right to the truth in Convention jurisprudence illuminates the issue of the particular contribution that the right would make were it to be an express part of Convention jurisprudence. There seem to be three general points that are made by commentators and judges.

First is the formal argument that a recognition of the right to the truth might better align the European Convention with developments in international law and regional enforcement.[72] But this is not form for form's sake. Such an express alignment with the concepts of international law would strengthen real rights in the circumstances of current and historical atrocities.

Second, the right to the truth has an express and clear public aspect. This is made clear by the Court in the reference to the right in *El Masri v Macedonia* 2012 and also in another rendition case, *Husayn v Poland* 2014, where the "right to the truth" belongs, in the context of serious abuse, not just to the direct victim but to other victims and society.[73] The practical significance of this is not clear since, absent any reference to the right to the truth, the reasoning behind the investigative duty already requires public scrutiny in order to uphold public confidence in the rule of law and prevent impunity.[74] A secret criminal trial or an investigation that was private between victims and the state would be unlikely to satisfy Article 2, 3 or 13. In the context of widespread and serious abuse, the social and political importance of knowing the truth can be a reason supporting finding a violation of the procedural limb.[75]

Third, the right to the truth taken as a judicial principle of high persuasive authority gives a court legally compelling grounds for limiting legal provisions which may otherwise act to restrict the effectiveness of any investigation. Statutes of limitations can have this effect, and their role in prevention of investigation of and redress for major abuses could be helpfully weakened by the right to the truth.[76] The Court's own principles for determining its jurisdiction *ratione temporis* should likewise be applied in ways that give effect to the ban on impunity

72 Judge Tulkens et al. *supra* note 70; Judge Ziemele *et al* partially dissenting in *Janowiec v Russia supra* note23 refer to the "clear trend" in international law; see also James Sweeney *supra* note 1 at 32–33.

73 *Husayn v Poland* (24 July 2014) para 489; see also Al *Nashiri v Poland supra* note 65 para 495.

74 See *Ramsahai v The Netherlands supra* note 27, quoted earlier. Upholding the rule of law is expressly referred to in *Husayn v Poland supra* note 73 para 489.

75 E.g. *Association "21 December 1989" and others v Romania* (24 May 2011) paras 134 and 142.

76 *Mocanu v Romania supra* note 7, the concurring Opinion of Judges Pinto de Albuquerque and Vučinić uses sources of the right to the truth in the context of an argument that statutes of limitations on crime, though normally proper, do not apply to gross abuses.

and the language of the right to the truth.[77] Similarly, the right to the truth justified reading down the scope of amnesty laws so that they do not inhibit the investigative duty.[78] In these footnoted cases it is really only *Janowiec v Russia* 2013 where the right to the truth, as understood by the dissenters, might have added something extra and made a difference to the outcome; though, as discussed earlier, it remains controversial whether the virtual abolition of jurisdictional rules in the context of war crimes and crimes against humanity is consistent with the rule of law.

Reparation

The right to know the truth must be effective. It is linked to general rights to reparations, but it is the effectiveness of rights to get at the truth in the context of gross violations which is the focus of concern in this section – specifically the nature and effectiveness of the remedy ordered for failing to conduct an effective investigation.

There is a limit to effective remedies in this context since regional human rights systems, such as the European and Inter-American Conventions and Courts, rely on the cooperation of contracting states. States which are directly complicit in gross abuse may, assuming they are contracting parties, simply ignore their obligations, denounce membership or be (indirectly) expelled.[79] Under ECHR, denunciation does not release a state from any liabilities it has already incurred, and this seems to be true, as well, of expulsion.

Effectiveness of remedies, therefore, implies an element of underlying cooperation by states which accept they have obligations under the Convention and that the political costs of leaving continue to outweigh those of staying of staying.

The European Court's principal remedy is declaratory: it declares a breach of the Convention leaving the state to fulfil its obligation under Articles 1 and 46 to repair the violation. States have primary discretion over this. Supervision of the state response is by the Committee of Minsters, though the Court can also have a role in enforcement. Under Article 46, it can rule, on the basis of a reference from the Committee of Ministers, on whether a state has fulfilled its obligation to abide by the final judgment of the Court.

The Court may also, under Article 41 ECHR, order "just satisfaction" insofar as any domestic remedies for the proven breach are inadequate. Just satisfaction has been understood and applied by the Court in financial terms. It covers both

77 E.g. *Janowiec v Russia supra* note 23, partly dissenting opinion of Judges Ziemele, de Gaetano, Laffranque and Keller (discussed earlier). For these judges the right to the truth undermines the Court's argument that there was no post-accession procedural duty on Russia to investigate the Katyn massacres and this is reinforced by the right to the truth's focus on the social need to know of and come to terms with its past (paras 9 and 24).

78 *Margus v Croatia* (27 May 2014) where the right to the truth is referred to as part of a survey of international law on amnesty, para 64).

79 Article 58 ECHR and Article 8 of the Statute of the Council of Europe. Greece denounced in 1969.

"pecuniary" and "non-pecuniary" losses which may include payments for pain and suffering. Notoriously the latter has been determined on what is called an "equitable basis" rather than on the more specific financial schema of losses found in domestic law of torts and obligations. Typically, cases engaging the right to the truth involve violations of more than one Convention right, and it is not possible to allocate some portion of non-pecuniary losses to, specifically, the failure of the respondent state to conduct an effective investigation. In *Husayn v Poland* 2015 (illegal rendition) there was a violation of Articles 3, 5, 8 and 6(1), including a failure to investigate. On an equitable basis the Court awarded EUR 100,000 plus tax for non-pecuniary damages consequent on all the violations. Where the investigative failure is a significant part of the breach, the non-pecuniary just satisfaction can be quite significant. In *Vasilyev v Russia* 2009,[80] an inadequate police investigation into a street attack must have engendered "emotional feelings of distress, frustration, injustice, and prolonged uncertainty";[81] the non-pecuniary award was EUR 78,000.

The basis of such awards in the right to the truth context has been explored by a Grand Chamber in *Varnava v Turkey* 2009[82] (the continuing failure of the Turkish authorities to investigate the disappearance of Cypriot soldiers captured during the Turkish invasion of Cyprus in 1974). Although there is no express provision in the Convention for "non-pecuniary or moral damage" and a declaration will often be sufficient, there are cases in which something more is required; specifically "evident trauma, whether physical or psychological, pain and suffering, distress, anxiety, frustration, feelings of injustice or humiliation, prolonged uncertainty, disruption to life, or real loss of opportunity" and cases involving severe impact on the moral well-being of the applicant. This is emphatically not to give some "financial comfort" or "sympathetic enrichment" to the applicant. The amounts are based on the Court's general view of the "equity" of the situation.[83] In this cases, EUR 12,000 was awarded to each applicant.

A declaration and a compensatory financial payment does not, of itself, provide for the truth to be disclosed. The Court does not have a direct power derived, expressly or by necessary implication, from the Convention, to order an investigation or other remedies related to the obtaining and disclosing the truth. Here there is a contrast to be made with the Inter-American Court of Human Rights which, under the American Convention has felt able to order, as express provisions in the "operative paragraphs", an investigation and also other steps relating to disclosure which states must perform.[84]

80 *Vasilyev v Russia* (17 December 2009)

81 Ibid para 170

82 *Varnava v Turkey supra* note 11.

83 Ibid para 224. For a general review of Strasbourg case law see the UK case (in the Court of Appeal) *D v CPM* [2014] EWHC 2493 (inadequate police investigation of a number of rapes).

84 E.g. *Carpio-Nicolle v Guatemala* (22 November 2004) para 115 "Orders", No 1. The matter is discussed further in Chapter 6.

Article 46 and state cooperation

There are limited circumstances in which the European Court does order particular remedial measures especially where a fundamental right is subject to ongoing violation and a specific action needs to be taken.[85] Generally, however, there is no power of direct ordering of an investigation or other truth-specific remedy. But the Court has begun to indicate the kinds of measure that states should adopt in order to fulfil their obligations, including in the right to the truth context. These indications are to assist the states (who have a duty of cooperation under Article 46) but also the Committee of Ministers. The Committee's supervision has a dialogic quality in which, inter alia, it considers the adequacy of any individual or general measures taken to remedy the Convention breach.[86] The Court has frequently said that, as well as paying any just satisfaction ordered, states must also "adopt the necessary general and/or, where applicable, individual measures" required to give effect to the judgment and prevent future violations.[87] The Court has given itself the power to issue, within the judgment's text, "guidance" on what those general or individual measures should be.[88]

There is a so-called pilot procedure where the applicant is a member of a group affected by a statute or other rule of law which is incompatible with the Convention and is generating a large number of complaints. The Court may suspend pending cases whilst the state, on the basis of a timetable, makes the necessary changes.[89] But beyond this, in what it calls "exceptional circumstances", the judgment's text may contain deliberate "indications" and "pointers" to what states should do and the Committee of Ministers should insist upon. The "holding" paragraphs simply specify the grounds of the violation and any just satisfaction but not further remedies.[90] The Court sees these indicators and pointers as reflecting the obvious remedy for the breach. Given this obviousness, these cases tend to be ones in which there is a concern about state cooperation. In

85 E.g. *Assanidze v Georgia* (8 April 2004) where the applicant was illegally detained in violation of article 5; clause 14(a) of the holdings requires that the state should seek his immediate release.

86 See, in particular, Rule 6, *Rules of the Committee of Ministers for the supervision of the execution of judgments and of the terms of friendly settlements.* 2006, amended January 2017.

87 E.g. *Al Nashiri v Poland supra* note 65 para 586.

88 Council of Europe European Court of Human Rights, Registry, Rules of the Court, August 2018 contain the Practice Directions issued by the Court and the Practice Direction on Just Satisfaction (issued 28 March 2007) authorises the guidance (para 23). See Linos-Alexander Sicilianos, 'The Involvement of the European Court of Human Rights in the Implementation of its Judgments: Recent Developments Under Article 46 ECHR' (2014) 32(2) Netherlands Quarterly of Human 235–262, section 3.3.

89 E.g. *Greens v United Kingdom* (23 November 2010) (prisoners' rights to vote).

90 E.g. in *Al Nashiri v Poland supra* note 65 the Court "requires" (para 589) that, in order to discharge its duty under Article 46 and in the context of a continuing risk, the state seek assurances from the US government (to whom the applicant had been unlawfully transferred) that he would not be subject to the death penalty; the operative paragraphs identify that the risk of the death penalty is one of the grounds for holding that there was a violation but they do not contain an order requiring assurances to be sought.

Varnava (above), Judge Spielmann, in a joined concurring opinion, argued that such necessary measures should not only be spelled out in the part of the judgment dealing with state obligations under Article 46, but should also be specified in the holding paragraphs. Nevertheless, the language of such guidance tends to be imperative whether or not contained in the holdings paragraphs. Article 46(4) authorises the Committee of Ministers to apply to the Court for a ruling on whether there has been compliance and failure to give effect to the guidance is a strong indicator that Article 46 has been breached.

This "guidance" on general and individual measures necessary for proper implementation of a judgment can reflect the right to the truth, such as by requiring an effective investigation to be undertaken (and not just declared not to have been done). In *Abuyeva v Russia* 2010, the Court was faced with a clear and continuing refusal of the Russian authorities to hold an effective investigation into civilian deaths caused by military actions in Chechnya. Having earlier declined to order such an investigation, the Court, applying Article 46, now took a more imperative line, more or less instructing the Committee of Ministers to insist that one should be undertaken.[91]

In *Tagayeva v Russia* 2017,[92] the Court went significantly further. It found that investigations into the deaths caused by the way the authorities ended the Beslan siege was seriously ineffective. The Court's "guidance" goes beyond requiring a proper investigation; it indicates a range of measures that the authorities should take in order to provide reparation including the pursuit of non-judicial measures for getting at the truth, public condemnation, better training for officials, redrafting of legal basis for cooperation between state agencies, clear formulation of legal rules for use of lethal force and memorials. *Tagayeva* followed another Chechnya case, *Abakarova v Russia* 2015.[93] The Court indicates here that the continual failure properly to investigate should be addressed by a raft of measures such as (in the context of a failed criminal investigation) the use of non-judicial means for collecting information (e.g. the parliamentary inquiries also discussed in *Tagayeva*). More innovative measures are also included such as public acknowledgment and condemnation of violations.[94] State compliance also requires better dissemination of information and deeper involvement of victims. In summing up, the Court insists that it is "incumbent" on the Committee of Ministers to pursue these measures in its enforcement of this and earlier judgments.

Thus the Court, at least in exceptional circumstances where state cooperation under Article 46 is in issue, gives effect to the norms of the right to the truth, not just by declaring a breach of the investigative duty but by recognising the

91 *Abuyeva v Russia* (2 December 2010) "it [the Court] considers it inevitable that a new, independent investigation should take place". See also *McCaughey v United Kingdom* (16 July 2013) para 145 – requiring the procedural obligation of Article 2 to be performed "expeditiously".

92 *Tagayeva v Russia supra* note 39.

93 *Abakarova v Russia* (15 October 2015)

94 Ibid see para 112.

obvious (that there needs to be an effective investigation) but sometimes the less than obvious further measures that the victims' and society's right to the truth requires. In these circumstances it is prepared to give indications – almost instructions – to the Committee of Ministers on what to require of the state if it is to fulfil its obligation, in Article 46, to "abide by the final judgment". Legally these are guidance, but they have an authority that cannot be ignored.[95]

An authoritative declaration of what happened

In the text of its judgments, the Court makes authoritative findings of fact and thus may partially fulfil a victim's right to know what happened. These findings, though significant, may not be sufficient fully to satisfy the right to the truth. The right to the truth (as discussed in Chapter 3) requires a complete authoritative account of what happened, which satisfies the need for both individualised and structural truth and fulfils both individual and public aspects of the right.

First, there is little by way of legal framework governing the content of any judgment by the Court. The rules that the Court is required, as a matter of law, to follow are scant as to the content of the judgment. Article 45 ECHR requires the Court to "give reasons" for its decision, and this has been embodied in the Rules as requiring a "decision . . . followed by reasons";[96] Rule 74 requires, inter alia, any decision to give an account of the facts and reasons from a point of law for its decisions.[97] The structure of judgments tends to be uniform (with sections on the facts, the law, the arguments of the parties and the Court's assessment, which is normally in two parts – an exploration of general principles and the application of these principles to the facts of the case). Other than that, the content of a judgment, what counts as an adequate account of the facts and adequate reasons, is a matter of unarticulated principles of judicial reasoning left to the Court's conception of its duties in the context of the case. The degree of detail of the factual description given by the Court, its scope, the extent to which it engages with the underlying political and historical context, the extent to which it traces chains of command or focuses on local decision-taking, and so on are not directly matters of law. If the right to the truth requires, as it were, a checklist of such matters to be dealt with as of right, as legally enforceable requirements, the way the Court gives its reasons may not be sufficient. Certainly (except rarely, as indicated earlier) the content of adequate reasons is not expressly motivated by a need to give effect to the victim's right to the truth.

Second, it is the respondent state, not the Court, which is the primary finder of fact; the Court's focus is predominantly on state responsibility. It will often act

95 For full discussion see Sicilianos *supra* note 88; Antkowiak *supra* note 46, suggests (mainly in the context of the Inter-American Court) that the added point of the right to the truth might lie in the provision of a wider range of remedies.

96 Council of Europe European Court of Human Rights, Registry, *Rules of the Court* (1 August 2018) Rule 56.

97 Ibid Rule 74 (f) and (h).

on the basis of agreed facts between the parties. Any additional fact-finding role of the Court can be controversial, since the state may object that the principle of subsidiarity is undermined by the Court taking over this role. The Court has a reviewing role over the facts and rejects any claim that states enjoy a monopoly over fact-finding.[98] It is prepared to make findings of fact based on information available to it and on various implications and presumptions therein. In *Cyprus v Turkey* 2001, for example, the fact-finding aim was not to establish what happened to the direct victims but to measure the effectiveness of the investigation[99] into that matter. Nevertheless, there are significant findings of fact, general and specific, relating to the particular victims. Likewise, in cases involving disappearances in Chechnya under Russian occupation, the focus tends to be on the inadequacies of investigations.[100] But close scrutiny is given and findings of individual fact are made. What is less apparent in the judgments is the kind of general background account with attribution of responsibility that the "structural" aspect of the content of the right to the truth requires. Nor will there generally be findings of individual responsibility given that these are the purpose of the criminal investigation whose adequacy the Court supervises. Much turns on the nature of the case. The cases on illegal rendition, for example, contain a considerable amount of information, given with the authority of the Court, about rendition in general terms as background to the individual application.[101]

Third, although the Court does have authority to conduct its own investigations, it will normally not have the resources for this. It relies, therefore, on its understanding of the facts as discovered through various sources provided to it as part of an adversarial process. The obvious problem is that, if the state has conducted an effective investigation, there is nothing gained by the Court's own assessments but, if no such investigation has been conducted, the Court may have only limited information on which it can make findings of fact. What the Court does not have (in contrast to the Inter-American Court of Human Rights) is an authoritative statement of facts given by a judicial organ whose role includes fact-finding and which has standing before the Court.[102]

The grounds of proof

Where there has been no, or only an inadequate, investigation the Court can have before it several sources of evidence, mainly evidence submitted by the applicants, the state and third-party interveners. This can include personal experiences, expert opinion, the views of NGOs, officially disclosed documents and matter that is in the press and public domain. In the unlawful rendition case *Husayn v*

98 E.g. *Al Nashiri v Poland supra* note 65 where the Polish government's claim on subsidiarity (para 340) is, by implication, rejected.

99 *Cyprus v Turkey supra* note 8 para 22 and 121.

100 E.g. *Aslakhanova v Russia supra* note 6.

101 *Al Nashiri v Poland supra* note 65 contains thirty-seven paragraphs of background.

102 This role was played, largely, by the European Commission prior to 1998.

Poland 2014, for example, the evidence included limited information supplied by the Polish authorities and, supplied by the applicant, media reports and some other materials in the public domain, NGO investigations and the reports by Senator Marty under the auspices of the Council of Europe and, also, disclosed, albeit redacted, Central Intelligence Agency (CIA) documents. This amounted to a large amount of information available for the Court to assess.[103] The court will also have the government's responses.

In the light of such evidence and in particular where there has been a failure of state cooperation, or the state has failed to refute allegations made, the Court is prepared to draw whatever inference it thinks appropriate. The standard of proof remains "beyond reasonable doubt", but the Court is clear that this is an autonomous Convention standard not to be equated with, for example, reasonable doubt in domestic criminal law. The Court will draw conclusions and make findings of fact. The basis for doing this has been restated by a Grand Chamber in *Baka v Hungary* 2016. The Court's conclusions are based on the

> free evaluation of all evidence, including such inferences as may flow from the facts in their entirety and from the parties' submissions . . . proof may follow from the coexistence of sufficiently strong, clear and concordant inferences or of similar unrebutted presumptions of fact.

This approach to proof is flexible "taking into consideration the nature of the substantive right at stake and any evidentiary difficulties involved".[104]

The burden of proof

The Court is aware that an applicant may find it very hard to prove a case to the "beyond reasonable doubt" standard in situations in which gross violations of human rights are alleged. If an applicant can make a prima facie case, the Court is prepared to shift the burden of proof in certain situations.[105] The Court may make inferences from the state's failure to produce contrary evidence or a convincing explanation, especially where the knowledge of what happened is clearly within the control of the state and its agents. In these situations the Court accepts that evidence may be "circumstantial" but, nevertheless, sufficiently compelling for an authoritative declaration of the facts of what happened. The Court can make a finding of lack of cooperation or obstruction by the state, which may be both a breach of Article 46 and also a ground for making presumptions about facts (such as the fate of an individual last seen in the custody of police). Likewise a state is taken to know if stories circulating in the press and media indicate possible breaches of Convention rights and should undertake investigations. A failure to investigate such notorious issues can lead to a finding of a lack of cooperation.

103 *Husayn v Poland supra* note 73 paras 42–170.
104 *Baka v Hungary* (23 June 2016) para 143 and cases cited thereto.
105 Ibid.

Where the evidence suggests an inadequate investigation, the Court may make authoritative findings based on its own analysis of facts which have emerged. *Tagayeva v Russia* 2017, for example, contains extensive summaries of various reports into the Russian authorities' responses to the Beslan hostage-taking. This analysis enables the Court to find, for example, that there was no adequate planning in respect of the known threat in the area.[106] But the Court's role is focused on whether the state has properly discharged its duty to investigate. As *Tagayeva* demonstrates, vital aspects of the right to the truth, in particular the precise fate of individual victims (which in many cases would be no more than the last sightings of individuals whose remains had not been discovered and may have been burnt beyond recognition) cannot be authoritatively given.

Court's own inquiry or investigation

The Court may simply rely on its own evaluation of the available evidence presented to it by the parties and by third-party interveners. However, Article 38 empowers it to undertake its own investigation. This includes powers to seek information from the respondent state or other sources. In respect of this investigation, there is an obligation on the respondent state "to furnish all necessary facilities", which has been understood as imposing a general duty to cooperate.

Since 1998, responsibility for fact-finding lies with the Court. The number of independent investigations, in particular on-the-spot investigations, has dropped considerably from the days of the Commission. A major reason for this is the greater acceptance, reflecting the principle of subsidiarity, by the Court of primary state responsibility for fact-gathering. Failures to provide sufficient information can be dealt with, as indicated earlier, on the basis of the burden of proof and presumption.[107]

Article 38 gives authority to undertake an investigation "if need be", and this power has been clarified in an expansive way by an Annex to the Rules which was inserted by the Court in October 2003. These Rules, inter alia, allow the Chamber seized with the application to use any investigative measure that may clarify the facts. This includes the Chamber inviting documentary evidence and holding proceedings in which experts, witnesses and any other person can be heard and questioned (by the Chamber or by delegation and also, with the consent of the Court, cross-examined by parties and their advocates);[108] in particular, they authorise the Court to institute on-site investigations conducted by itself or by delegates, and these investigations enjoy the Court's full authority. The powers of delegates to question and allow cross-examination are also enjoyed by a Chamber. These hearings are in private unless the Court decides otherwise.

106 *Tagayeva v Russia supra* note 39 para 491.
107 On fact-finding generally see Michael O'Boyle and Natalia Brady "Investigatory Powers of the European Court of Human Rights" (2013) 4 European Human Rights Law Review 378.
108 Council of Europe European Court of Human Rights, Registry, *Rules of the Court* (1 August 2018) Annex to the Rules (concerning investigations) Rule A7,2.

From the point of view of the victim's right to the truth, though these powers authorise methods of fact-finding that might enable a convincing and full account of what happened to be achieved, they make no specific reference to victims, who have no special status before the Court. It is at the Court's discretion whether victims be examined, and victims have no rights embodied in the Rules, nor are there any specific provisions in the Rules for their protection or well-being other than a power to examine them in the absence of other parties. Unless ordered otherwise, the hearings are in private, and thus the interest of victims in stating their case in their own way ("narrative truth") is not protected. Of course, direct victims will have the rights of applicants generally; the problem here relates to the situation of victims in relation to investigations and hearings when the Court is seeking evidence of the truth beyond that which the applicants were able to produce themselves.

The authority to make these Rules is Article 25(d) ECHR, which empowers the Plenary Court to "adopt the rules of the Court".[109] The meaning or application of the Rules can be challenged in the course of proceedings, and a Chamber's understanding challenged through a referral to the Grand Chamber under Article 43. Whether such procedures would be consistent with judicial independence is an open question. Whether there ought to be a public administrative law and process of international tribunals goes beyond the subject of this book, but given the absence of any special status for victims in the Rules relating to investigations, it is a point of relevance to any discussion. In *Al Nashiri* 2015, the Court held that the lack of rules (here relating to confidential material) did not release states from the duty to follow the Court's established practices;[110] in principle, the Court could develop appropriate practices in relation to victim participation in investigations.

State cooperation

In the course of its examination of the case, a Chamber may seek information from the respondent state. Failure to cooperate can be for reasons which disclose bad faith and a desire to cover up failures or may be for legitimate reasons, such as protecting confidential information which it has agreed not to disclose or which, for some other reason, it would be illegal to disclose.

Failure of state cooperation can involve a breach of Article 38. The legitimacy or otherwise of the state's reasons for not cooperating are decided, ultimately, by the Court which, in regard to Article 38, is master of its own procedure. It has "complete freedom" in assessing the value of the evidence presented to it and alone decides what other evidence should be produced to enable the proper examination of the case. States must, under Article 38, comply with its

109 *Al Nashiri v Poland supra* note 65 para 371 – that the Rules are not merely internal guidance but derive from a Treaty given power.

110 Ibid.

requirements.[111] The fact that an applicant is denied by the domestic authorities his or her wish to disclose sensitive material to the Court will not, without the Court's request, breach Article 38.[112] The Court, as master of its own procedure, will decide on potential relevance and weight and whether, on balance, disclosure is required, domestic unlawfulness notwithstanding. However, the Court is aware of its position as an international human rights court. It is not competent to act as a fourth tier of appeal from the national courts. Its focus, therefore, is on the adequacy of the domestic legal procedures by which the reasons for a refusal to disclose are assessed.

There can be a breach of Article 38 even though there has been no breach of a substantive right. In *Janowiec v Russia* 2013,[113] the continual refusal of the Russian authorities to supply the Court with the text of the decision to discontinue the criminal investigation (which began in 1990) into the Katyn massacres and the court documents therein, was a violation. The fact that, under Russian law, disclosure to an international body was unlawful and that the Russian view was that the ECtHR had insufficient procedures to protect confidentiality was not sufficient to prevent a finding that Article 38 was breached. The Russian court had not properly examined the executive decision to keep the information gathered from the investigation secret for 70 years and balance this against the other interests involved (the public interest in transparency and the private interests of the relatives of victims).

The state's purported reason to refuse disclosure may be based on national security reasons. The Court is aware that it is "ill-equipped" to challenge any refusal to disclose under domestic law. But it has a duty to satisfy itself that any national security or confidentiality argument is based on "reasonable and solid" grounds. It will examine the credibility of the domestic legal provisions for determining disclosure in the light of the government's confidentiality claims.[114] Its position is uncompromising. Even where the national security or confidentiality grounds are legitimate, it can seek the evidence subject to closed material provisions such as redaction or a summary. Furthermore, it can use Rule 33(2) to classify the documents as confidential and not available for public scrutiny. In extreme situations it can hold private hearings under Rule 63(2). The Court is clear and imperious: states cannot refuse to comply with the Court's request for information because of their own laws on confidentiality or because they mistrust the Court's own procedures to protect the confidentiality of information lodged with it. There is, it is claimed, ample evidence that the Court has robust procedures for protecting confidentiality and will give appropriate guarantees.[115] In

111 *Al Nashiri supra* note 65 para 363.
112 In *R (Yam) v Central Criminal Court* (2015) UKSC 76 the UK Supreme Court took the view that an applicant to the European Court of Human Rights had no Convention derived right to submit evidence that it would otherwise be unlawful to disclose.
113 *Janowiec v Russia supra* note 23, discussed earlier.
114 See, in particular, *Janowiec v Russia supra* note 23 para 214.
115 *Al Nashiri v Poland supra* note 65 paras 365–366, 367 and 371, and cases cited therein.

this context there is no balancing judgment for the Court to make between the national security grounds (which it is not well placed to judge) and the need to guarantee the applicant's human rights. Irrespective of their constitutions, states must set aside their laws in this situation. But, as said earlier, disclosure is private to the Court and hardly satisfies the right to the truth.

Conclusion: fulfilling the right to the truth

As suggested earlier, awareness of the right to the truth may justify the Court in strengthening the normative force of some of its rules and procedures, such as those relating to state cooperation and jurisdictional limits.[116] But as *Janowiec v Russia* demonstrates, the Court limits itself by the requirements of the rule of law in a way that does not satisfy some commentators who want the right to the truth to have a more overriding power.

Similarly, in relevant cases, the Court makes extensive findings of fact. But it does this in the context of being a reviewing court and secondary fact-finder. Furthermore, a judgment's content is to some degree discretionary. A legal "right" to the truth might justify a more structured and rule-based approach in order to ensure that both the individual and the structural requirements of the right are satisfied.

Victims are inclusively defined and should have participation rights in domestic proceedings. But these can be limited to the victims' interests. The Court's primary concern is with state responsibilities generally, though this assists with guaranteeing the social aspect of the right. As regards its own investigations, however, there is a strong case for strengthening the position of victims if the right to the truth is to be satisfied.

Remedies, prima facie, are inadequate since the Court has no direct authority to do more than declare a breach and order financial restitution. Nevertheless, it is increasingly willing to issue guidance which in effect indicates other remedial measures that should be taken.

The Court's own findings of both individual and structural fact can themselves be major contributions to the truth, as the "extraordinary rendition" cases illustrate. These findings and the investigations they reflect are particularly important when there is a failure of state cooperation. The Court is uncompromising in its insistence on full cooperation even when a state has legitimate grounds for reticence. In the end, however, it is for the Committee of Ministers to decide on appropriate action.

In general, however, the European Convention, as interpreted by the Court, goes some considerable way towards giving effect to the definition elements of the right to the truth by imposing a duty on states to investigate in indicative situations; the granting of remedies and, in its judgments, making findings as to what happened.

116 State cooperation is also something that is discussed in the context of the ICC in Chapter 10.

References

Antkowiak T, 'Truth as right and remedy in international human rights experience' (2001–2) 23 Michigan Journal of International Law 977.

Chevallier-Watts J, "Effective investigations under Article 2 of the European Convention on Human Rights: securing the right to life or an onerous burden on a state" (2010) 21(3) European Journal of International Law 701.

Fabbrini F, 'The European Court of Human Rights, Extraordinary Renditions and the Right to the Truth: Ensuring Accountability for Gross Human Rights Violations Committed in the Fight Against Terrorism' (2014) 14 (1) Human Rights Law Review 85.

O'Boyle M and Brady, 'Investigatory Powers of the European Court of Human Rights' (2013) 4 European Human Rights Law Review 378.

Sicilianos, L-A. "The Involvement of the European Court of Human Rights in the Implementation of its Judgments: Recent Developments Under Article 46 ECHR" (2014) 32 (3) Netherlands Quarterly of Human Rights 235–262.

Sweeney J, 'The Elusive Right to Truth in Transitional Human Rights Jurisprudence' (2018) 67 (2) International and Comparative Law Quarterly 353.

8 Truth commissions and the right to the truth

Introduction

Advocates of truth commission consider the right to the truth as a key reason to establish truth commissions.[1] With the increase in numbers of truth commissions as an alternative or a complementary action to criminal justice,[2] they have been firmly established as a popular transitional justice[3] mechanism and thus warrant further attention in terms of their relationship with the right to the truth. This chapter will examine truth commissions and their potential to satisfy individual and public aspects of the right to the truth. It is concerned with victim involvement and their testimony in the truth-finding process as well as the challenges associated with investigating but not prosecuting. Investigations may lead to serious implications for those who feel accused by allegations, but does the right to the truth imply that prosecutions have to follow? The chapter will also focus on the potential stepping stone truth commissions represent in working towards prosecutions and reparations to fully appraise their significance for the right to the truth.

"An important step in realizing the right to truth"[4]

Countries emerging from conflict, repressive regimes, civil war and past abuses struggle with question on how to move forward: whether the strategy should

1 E.g. Priscilla Hayner, *Unspeakable Truths. Transitional Justice and the Challenge of Truth Commissions* (2nd edn, Routledge 2011 at 24; Patricia Naftali, 'Crafting a "Right to truth" in International Law: Converging Mobilizations, Diverging Agendas?' (2016) XIII Champ penal/Penal field 1.

2 For a multitude of debates on the subject, see William Schabas and Shane Darcy (ed) *Truth Commissions and Courts. The Tensions Between Criminal Justice and the Search for Truth* (Springer 2004)).

3 As are semi-official inquiries and non-official truth commissions (e.g. Louis Bickford, 'Unofficial Truth Projects' (2007) 29(4) Human Rights Quarterly 994 and Hayner *supra* note 1). Truth Commissions are part of the post-conflict models of transition (The Rule of Law and Transitional Justice in Conflict and Post-Conflict Societies. Report of the Secretary-General, (23 August 2004)).

4 Guidance note of the UNSG, United Nations approach to Transitional Justice (March 2010) at 8.

include digging up the past or burying it instead,[5] whether it involves domestic trials, international trials, truth commissions, other forms of justice mechanisms or not. As we have seen in Chapter 5, different institutions with differing mandates and truth-seeking parameter will make differing contributions to truth-finding. Some initiatives may be compatible; others perhaps may result in more conflicting relationships. Prosecutions and human rights court adjudications, however, are more likely to concur than disagree with truth commission interpretations, though divergences are conceivable. In principle, each of these mechanisms is (and should be) independent. They are not a repeat of the same exercise designed to confirm results but a separate, new investigation, and often they operate at different times.[6]

In fact, the Inter-American Court of Human Rights has made explicit reference to the work of truth commissions in its case law, appraising such mechanisms:

> The Court deems that the establishment of a Truth Commission – depending on its object, proceedings, structure and purposes – can contribute to build and safeguard historical memory, to clarify the events and to determine institutional, social and political responsibilities in certain periods of time of a society. The recognition of historical truths through this mechanism should not be understood as a substitute to the obligation of the State to ensure the judicial determination of individual and state responsibilities through the corresponding jurisdictional means, or as a substitute to the determination, by this Court, of any international responsibility. Both are about determinations of the truth which are complementary between themselves, since they all have their own meaning and scope, as well as particular potentialities and limits, which depend on the context in which they take place and on the cases and particular circumstances object of their analysis. In fact, the Court has granted a special value to reports of Truth Commissions as relevant evidence in the determination of the facts and of the international responsibility of the States in various cases which has been submitted before it.[7]

Truth commissions can generate findings that are of great value to judicial mechanism, like the Inter-American Court of Human Rights with the court taking such findings into account. But crucially, from the outset, a truth commission cannot release the state from undertaking obligations such as conducting full

5 E.g. Hayner *supra* note 1 at 4.

6 Some publications speak about "sequencing" and "timing" of transitional justice mechanisms. See, for example, Sam Szoke-Burke, 'Searching for the Right to Truth: The Impact of International Human Rights Law on National Transitional Justice Policies' (2015) 33(2) Berkeley Journal of International Law 526; Laurel Fletcher, Harvey Weinstein and Jamie Rowen, 'Context, timing and the dynamics of transitional justice: A historical perspective' (2009) 31(1) Human Rights Quarterly 163.

7 *Zambrano Vélez et al. v Ecuador* (4 July 2007) para 128.

investigations, communicating results, prosecuting perpetrators and the granting of reparations through the appropriate judicial mechanisms:

> [N]otwithstanding the potential contributions of the said Truth Commission to the knowledge of the facts, the State must fulfill its obligations to investigate and punish, through the relevant judicial means, all the facts constituents of human rights violations established in this Judgment. As such, the State must take into account the different aspects of the case which were decided by this Court in the present Judgment, including the considerations made regarding the victims, the rights held as violated and the determination of the seriousness and magnitude of the said violations.[8]

In other words, the establishment of a truth commission may be a welcome and beneficial mechanism. However, the state still needs to fully comply with its duties and responsibilities under international human rights law, including the judgments of the regional human rights courts.

We outlined in Chapter 2 that, under international law, there is an obligation placed on states to conduct investigations, and this is what truth commissions have been understood to be: "an official investigation into a past pattern of abuses".[9] In the Guidance note of the UN Secretary-General on transitional justice, this link is clearly spelled out:

> Truth-seeking processes assist post-conflict and transitional societies investigate past human rights violations and are undertaken by truth commissions, commissions of inquiry, or other fact-finding missions.[10]

They, through mapping and documenting the gross human rights violations, are "an important step in realizing the right to the truth".[11] Furthermore, the note suggests that critical elements in the realisation of the right to the truth are the provision of domestic archive systems and effective victim and witness protection.[12]

Whether such categorical assertion and supportive view of truth commissions is justified is a matter of debate and is increasingly questioned for want of corroborating evidence.[13] It has been suggested that governments have sought to hide behind these transitional justice mechanisms to promote injustices and partial

8 Ibid para 129.
9 Hayner *supra* note 1 at 17.
10 Guidance note of the UNSG, United Nations approach to Transitional Justice *supra* note 4 at 8.
11 Ibid.
12 Ibid at 8.
13 E.g. Clark lamenting the lack of known impact of transitional justice initiatives (Janine Natalya Clark 'Transitional Justice, Truth and Reconciliation: An Under-Explored Relationship', 11 (2011) 11 International Criminal Law Review 241.

accounts, if politically opportune.[14] In the following we test truth commissions' operationalisation and contribution against our working definition of the right to the truth.

Working towards the public aspect of the right to the truth

Reference to the right to the truth has found expression in some truth commissions' mandates and reports. The El Salvadorian truth commission was tasked with "investigating serious acts of violence that have occurred since 1980 and whose impact on society urgently demands that the public should know the truth",[15] expressing the right implicitly. The Guatemalan Agreement to establish a Commission states:

> Whereas the people of Guatemala have a right to know the whole truth concerning these events, clarification of which will help avoid a repetition of these sad and painful events and strengthen the process of democratization in Guatemala.[16]

This statement links the right to a process of political transformation towards a stable democracy. The Peruvian decree considering the proposal for the creation of the truth commission speaks of

> the painful process of violence experienced by the country in the last two decades should be fully clarified, it should not remain forgotten and that the State should guarantee the right of society to the truth.[17]

The commission's 8,000-page final report released in August 2003 echoes a public right to the truth by reiterating the link of the truth commission's creation to a society's right to know the truth about ones history as an internationally recognised right.[18] There are other examples: Méndez reports that the 2002 Panama report explicitly refers to the right to the truth ("*derecho a la verdad*").[19]

The 2011 Law to establish a National Truth Commission in Brazil speaks of a "*direito à memória e à verdade histórica e promover a reconciliação nacional*"[20] – the

14 Cyanne Loyle and Christian Davenport, 'Transitional Injustice: Subverting Justice in Transition and Postconflict Societies' (2016) 15 Journal of Human Rights 126 at 127
15 El Salvador: Mexico Peace Agreements – Provisions Creating the Commission on Truth (27 April 1991) Article 2.
16 Agreement on the Establishment of the Commission to Clarify Past Human Rights Violations and Acts of Violence that have Caused Guatemalan Population to Suffer (23 June 1994)
17 Peru: Supreme Decree, No. 065–2001-PCM (4 June 2001).
18 Peru: Truth Commission Report, Vol 1 (28 August 2003) Introduction at 28.
19 Juan Méndez, 'The Human Right to Truth. Lessons Learned from Latin American Experiences with Truth Telling' in Borer T A (ed), *Telling the Truth: Truth Telling and Peace-Building in Post-Conflict Societies* (University of Notre Dame Press 2006) 115 at 133.
20 Brazil: Law No. 12.528 (18 November 2011) Article 1.

right to memory and historical truth in an attempt to promote national reconciliation.

The emphasis in these examples is on the public dimension of the right and recording of history[21] (also with a view to transitioning towards a democracy) which is consistent with the reading of transitional justice that seeks to advance democracy[22] as part of the process.

Working towards the individual aspect of the right to the truth

Tunisia's and Kenya's efforts to address past violence include a more individual-focused notion of truth-seeking. Article 2 of Tunisia's "Organic Law on Establishing and Organizing Transitional Justice" states that "revealing the truth about the violations is a right guaranteed by law to every citizen taking into consideration the respect of the victims' interests and dignity and the protection of private information".[23] Article 4 then spells out what is meant by this truth-finding:

> Revealing the truth shall consist of a series of methods, procedures and research used to dismantle the authoritarian system by identifying and determining all the violations as well as determining their causes, conditions, sources, surrounding circumstances, and repercussions. In cases of death, missing persons, and enforced disappearance, it shall uncover the fate and whereabouts of the victims as well as the identity of the perpetrators and those responsible for such acts.[24]

In addition to this provision, which contains a number of elements that satisfy the public and individually relevant information required by our definition of the right to the truth, the preservation of memory is acknowledged as a duty of the state and a right predicated on future Tunisian generations[25] – thus echoing part of Principle 3 on preserving memory for educational purposes of the Updated Principles on Impunity.[26]

Kenya's "Truth, Justice and Reconciliation Commission Bill of 2008", whilst not stating the right to the truth explicitly, is interesting as it seeks to provide much of what we have established in our working definition of the right to the truth. The Kenyan mandate stipulates, inter alia, to establish "an accurate,

21 Habermas in the context of the German "Historikerstreit", for example, suggested that whilst there is no satisfactory theoretical answer to the question whether one can learn from history, he nonetheless contends that one can learn how not to do things (Jürgen Habermas, *Die Normalität einer Berliner Republik – Kleine Politische Schriften VIII* (Suhrkamp 1995).

22 Bronwyn Anne Leebaw, 'The Irreconcilable Goals of Transitional Justice', (2008) 30 Human Rights Quarterly 95.

23 Tunisia: Organic Law No 2013–53 Establishing and Organising Transitional Justice (24 December 2013).

24 Ibid.

25 Ibid Article 5.

26 Report of the independent expert to update the Set of Principles to combat impunity (18 February 2005) Principle 3 (hereinafter Updated Principles on Impunity).

complete and historical record of violations and abuses of human rights and economic rights", including the circumstances of events, taking into account the views of victims and alleged perpetrators, identifying and recommending prosecution of those deemed responsible for gross human rights violations, investigating the whereabouts of victims and identifying victims of violations including suggestions for redress whilst also educating and engaging the public.[27] The bill suggests comprehensive investigations into the events leading to systematic and individual violations, identifying victims and perpetrators whilst providing a platform for candidly hearing and telling the truth of all involved and contemplating remedies.

According to Méndez and Bariffi, the Chilean Commission also worked towards fulfilling the obligation the state owes to individual victims and families of the disappeared in uncovering the fate and whereabouts of those victims of state abuse.[28] Article 1 of the Supreme Decree No. 355 on the "Creation of the Commission on Truth and Reconciliation" requires the establishment of a complete picture of events and circumstances and the gathering of evidence to identify victims individually and uncover their fate and whereabouts.[29] In Argentina too, one focus of investigations was to clarify what happened to those who disappeared between 1976 and 1983 and uncover the facts involved in those cases, including the locations of the bodies.[30] Another approach can be seen in Morocco's commission founding charter, where no mentioning of the right to truth is made, though as part of the definition of the crime of "forced disappearance" the refusal to inform relatives is listed as forming part of the crime.[31] In addition, the text makes reference to memory preservation as well as the state's compliance with international law,[32] thus situating the truth-seeking exercise within the wider human rights context framing the mandate of this particular commission.

Whether a mandate translates into reality is, of course, an entirely different story. For the case of Morocco, for example, Hayner reports that great disappointment was felt by victim groups and human rights activists about the limited information provided on the fate of missing persons and location of their remains, despite confirmation of 742 disappeared persons being dead.[33] The point here is that the founding principles of many a truth commission are predicated on the belief that elements of the right to the truth can (and should) be realised, recognising state obligations in this regard which the commission as an authority created by the state can take on. Formally and normatively, the capacity to offer

27 Kenya: Truth, Justice and Reconciliation Commission Bill (28 November 2008) Article 5(a), (b), (k), (o); Article 6(a), (c), (i).

28 Juan Méndez and Francisco Bariffi, 'Truth, Right to, International Protection' (2011) Max Planck Encyclopedia of Public International Law (online).

29 Chile: Decree No. 355 'Creation of the Commission on Truth and Reconciliation' (25 April 1990).

30 Argentina: Decree No. 187/83 (15 December 1983)

31 Morocco: Dahir (Royal Decree) No. 1.04.42 (10 April 2004) Article 5.

32 Ibid.

33 Hayner *supra* note 1 at 44.

(1) an authoritative investigation of both the events and politico-social structures that led to atrocity and (2) to the particular circumstances of an individual's suffering is enshrined in truth commission mandates (subject to restrictions in focus).

Tensions between individual and public aspects

Commenting on the right to the truth in relation to enforced disappearances contained in the Declaration on the Protection of All Persons from Enforced Disappearances,[34] the working group draws an interesting distinction: whilst it is an apparently absolute right without limitation or derogation for relatives of the enforced disappeared to know the truth of the fate and whereabouts of those who disappeared,[35] that is the individualised truth, the right to the truth about the circumstances – however, is not absolute.[36] The latter element – more akin to what we describe as the "politico-social structures" that led to the event and public truth – is substantiated through the point that state practice includes hiding part of the truth if it deems it to "facilitate reconciliation".[37] In this interpretation (which stands in contrast to that offered by the UN 2006 Study on the Right to the Truth),[38] there is an element of discretion that the state may exercise in deciding what it wishes to publicly investigate and disclose regarding past abuses, but there is no such discretion for the obligation to take all necessary steps (through forensic expertise, investigative and scientific methods) to find a disappeared person (though there is no absolute obligation of results). In some regards this distinction is understandable resulting from well-known debates about the tensions between "truth versus peace"[39] or "truth versus justice"[40] and, in an attempt to build lasting peace, insisting on truth and justice may not be an immediate peace broker. There may also be some logicality in this difference in obligation, since investigating the particular circumstances is a necessary step to build the bigger, structural picture of the circumstances and patterns leading to the many abuses – which may, perhaps, at a later time, be made available to the wider society. Whilst the individual investigation results need to be recorded

34 Declaration on the Protection of All Persons from Enforced Disappearances (12 February 1993).

35 Report of the Working Group on Enforced or Involuntary Disappearances, General Comment on the Right to the Truth in Relation to Enforced Disappearances (26 January 2011) para 4.

36 Ibid para 8.

37 Ibid.

38 Promotion and Protection of Human Rights. Study on the Right to the Truth (8 February 2006) at para 60 (hereinafter 2006 Study on the Right to the Truth).

39 E.g. Tristan Anne Borer, 'Truth Telling as a Peace-Building Activity. A Theoretical Overview' in Borer T A (ed), *Telling the Truth: Truth Telling and Peace-Building in Post-Conflict Societies* (University of Notre Dame Press 2006) 1–57.

40 E.g. Hayner *supra* note 1, especially chapter on 'Truth and Justice: A Careful but Critical Relationship' (91–109).

and communicated, the broader structural truth, however, may not need to be publicly reported.

Pragmatically, therefore, a conception of the right to the truth of this kind may make sense, especially since transitional justice institutions like truth commissions aim to challenge the legitimacy of prior regimes and practice whilst establishing their own legitimacy.[41] A state-given mandate of a truth commission has to be viewed in the context of trying to maintain a degree of order and future institution-building. Hayner identifies four common reasons for not engaging in formal truth-seeking exercises: (1) the fear of adverse consequences and resurfacing of violence, (2) lack of political will and lack of independent civil society, (3) prioritising survival and rebuilding, and (4) "some societies have alternative mechanisms that they turn to, which make national, official truth-seeking unnecessary or undesirable, or a culture that eschew confronting conflict directly".[42]

In such a conceptualisation, however, the notion of "the right to the truth" may take on two separate and not necessarily compatible meanings: on the one hand, it includes the absolute "right to truth as far as individual incidents are concerned"; on the other hand, it includes a qualified "right to some truth as determined by the given situation". This, however, can be interpreted as not being truth at all but rather a "politically and socially deemed opportune version of events to facilitate the realisation of a particular future". It is a formula where the "particular future" may function as a variable for many ideologies. The very notion of discretionary investigative powers undermines the conception of truth. To suggest that a state whose obligation it is to uncover state-done wrongs is to determine what wrongs to include and what not and to label this exercise a "truth-finding mission" is to engage in a potentially highly relativistic notion of truth, if not risking a leap into the opposite of truth, namely falsehood or deceit. This criticism notwithstanding, which seems inherent to truth commissions and the societal aspect of the right to the truth, the examination of the relationship of the right to the truth and the truth commission processes is still warranted, since the process of truth-finding, once established, ought to be guaranteed as an independent process, though, quite naturally, there is always the fear that the work of truth commissions may reflect the prejudices of their framers.[43]

41 Bronwyn Anne Leebaw, 'The Irreconcilable Goals of Transitional Justice', (2008) 30 Human Rights Quarterly 95 at 97. For international criminal purposes this rationale may be less convincing since they operate outside the domestic sphere.

42 Hayner *supra* note 1 at 196. See also Ignatieff who points out that peace and stability within a state are mandatory prerequisite to guarantee other rights (Michael Ignatieff, 'Human Rights as Idolatry', The Tanner Lecture on Human Values (Princeton University 4–7 April 2000).

43 Jonathan Tepperman, 'Truth and Consequences' (2002) March/April Foreign Affairs 128.

Witness testimony

One element of our working definition is that the right to the truth encompasses the opportunity for victims to narrate their story. This is a reflection of the need for survivors of gross human rights to relate their experiences – also perhaps independently from an official process.[44] "Truth commissions", according to Hayner, "seem to satisfy – or at least begin to satisfy – a clear need on the part of some victims to tell their stories and be listened to".[45]

At the same time, it offers a society, which may have diminished trust in the ability of the state to provide accurate and reliable information about human rights abuses, an alternative source of information. As we have seen in earlier chapters, the right to the truth has commonalities with the right to information, which includes not only the right to seek and receive information but also the right to impart it. Whilst it has been suggested that victims providing testimony to truth commission seldom learn new aspects of their own case, in doing so,[46] personal truth-telling places survivors in a more proactive role in the achievement of a broad, public truth. This is congruent with commentators' argument seeing the state to be in a better position to satisfy the individual truth, whereas truth commissions are perhaps better placed to offer the structural element.[47]

Truth-telling by survivors of gross human rights violations or "narrative truth" as a form of truth in the transitional justice context was expressly acknowledged and sought through the process of the South African Truth and Reconciliation Commission.[48] Interestingly, within the South African Truth and Reconciliation Commission the emphasis on narrative truth was based upon an individually therapeutic or restorative rationale rather than on any perceived benefit to society as a recipient of truth. In that sense, truth-telling to fulfil the public aspect of the right to the truth may not have been a primary rationale, despite many of such testimonies having been given in public. The opportunity to narrate one's story does not stipulate whether this has to take place as a public affair. Offering a statement to a commission officer (or a state representative outside the truth commission) may satisfy this requirement and be a safer option to providing testimony in the full view of the public and television cameras.

It is also possible to create commissions which are victim-centred inquiries but which lack the large-scale testimony element. Through restricted mandates, participation of victims can be intentionally or unintentionally excluded

44 "Many human rights workers and journalists report what seem to be a very basic need by victims to recount their stories of violence and survival, entirely independent of any commission or official process." (Hayner *supra* note 1 at 147)

45 Ibid at 153, though counter-anecdotes can also be found.

46 Ibid at 21.

47 Szoke-Burke *supra* note 6 and Hayner *supra* note 1.

48 E.g. Stephen Ellis, 'Truth and Reconciliation Commission of South Africa Report, Volumes 1–5. Pretoria: Government Printer, October 1998' (2000) 42 Transformation 61.

or silenced.[49] Commissions therefore do not *ipso facto* work towards offering an opportunity to victims to realise the element of the right to the truth, that is to tell their story – though in reality most do and rely on victims as a source of information. But many commissions do not have the power to compel attendance of witnesses. Naturally, a difficulty with survivor testimony lies in verifying the information they offer. The fact that survivors may continue to suffer the impacts of psychological trauma, which in turn can negatively affect the ability of the individual to recall their experiences and to construct and articulate a clear, coherent account of their experiences, also needs to be taken into consideration.

In any event, the state has an obligation to provide protection and assistance to victims, witnesses and interested persons.[50] Such safeguarding is key, since investigating and testifying may provoke threats or even attacks on behalf of those who have a keen interest in preventing successful fact-finding. Necessary measures need to be put in place to protect interested parties from ill-treatment, intimidation or reprisal. Such protective measures may be implemented by the commission, acting on the state's behalf.

Contribution to public and individual truth

The impetus of some truth commissions may be public truth oriented rather than focused on the individual and lacking in specificity when it comes to individual victims and their fate. But there are also examples where both aspects can be achieved. The following summary of a case, the killing of the Archbishop of San Salvador, from the El Salvadorian Report "From Madness to Hope", which took into account 2,000 statements in relation to 7,000 cases,[51] recounts the commission's findings.

1. Former Major Roberto D'Aubuisson gave the order to assassinate the Archbishop and gave precise instructions to members of his security service, acting as a "death squad", to organize and supervise the assassination.
2. Captains Alvaro Saravia and Eduardo Avila, together with Fernando Sagrera and Mario Molina, were actively involved in planning and carrying out the assassination.
3. Amado Antonio Garay, the driver of former Captain Saravia, was assigned to drive the gunman to the Chapel. Mr. Garay was a direct witness when, from a red, four-door Volkswagen, the gunman fired a single high velocity .22 calibre bullet to kill the Archbishop.
4. Walter Antonio "Musa" Alvarez, together with former Captain Saravia, was involved in paying the "fees" of the actual assassin.

49 Loyle and Davenport *supra* note 14 at 131.

50 General Comment on the Right to the Truth in Relation to Enforced Disappearances *supra* note 35 para 10.

51 According to Hayner, secondary sources revealed a further 20,000 additional victims as part of the commission's efforts (Hayner *supra* note 1).

5 The failed assassination attempt against Judge Atilio Ramírez Amaya was a deliberate attempt to deter investigation of the case.
6 The Supreme Court played an active role in preventing the extradition of former Captain Saravia from the United States and his subsequent imprisonment in El Salvador. In so doing, it ensured, inter alia, impunity for those who planned the assassination.[52]

The report goes on to describe the actual assassination as follows:

> On Monday, 24 March 1980, the Archbishop of San Salvador, Monsignor Oscar Arnulfo Romery y Galdámez, was celebrating mass in the Chapel of the Hospital de la Divina Providencia when he was killed by a professional assassin who fired a single .22 or .223 calibre bullet from a red, four-door Volkswagen vehicle. The bullet hit his mark, causing the Archbishop's death from severe bleeding.[53]

Whilst this example may not be representative of truth commission findings and though limitations on resources might not permit this level of detail for each case investigated, it nonetheless clearly outlines how elements of the right to the truth can be satisfied: the details of what happened to the victim, cause and manner of death, are clearly accounted for, including the names of those responsible. They spell out the level of organisation required to commit the actual offence and the chain of command behind the act; the fact that there was a decoy to sidetrack any investigation in the immediate aftermath of the killing reinforces the strategic elements employed in orchestrating the assassination, including a cover-up operation. The account also alludes to a failure on behalf of the judiciary in working towards accountability, instead colluding in impunity. From the commission's summary of one individual's killing, a greater picture emerges as to how the political sphere and the judiciary may have operated to avert accountability, sanctioning criminality.

Furthermore, through investigations, an archive of information is created which may be accessible to family members to help gather necessary elements of the right to truth. Therefore a contribution to the individual and public truth elements is made.

Naming names

The preceding example leads to the important discussion on truth commissions naming or not naming perpetrators in their report. For Hayner, "[n]aming names is part of the truth-telling process, and is especially important when the judicial

52 From Madness to Hope: The 12-Year War in El Salvador (1 April 1993) at 119.
53 Ibid. Similar evidence can be found in Inter-American Human Rights cases, e.g. *Ituango Massacres v Colombia* (1 July 2006), VIII Proven Facts para 125, specifically para 125(36) on the death of William de Jesús Villa García.

system does not function well enough to expect trials".[54] The 2006 Study on the Right to the Truth echoes the need to know who those involved in the abuse were, with the report stating that

> [t]he right to truth implies knowing the full and complete truth as to the events that transpired, their specific circumstances, and who participated in them, including knowing the circumstances in which the violations took place, as well as the reasons for them.[55]

Naming perpetrators poses significant challenges for truth commissions for due process reasons, but also for security purposes, which the study also acknowledges. Even with a presumption of innocence,

> [t]here is a potential problem [...] where perpetrators are named pursuant to an extrajudicial mechanism such as a truth commission, given that not all truth-seeking processes apply due process guarantees.[56]

The working group on enforced disappearances refers to this issue too, and whether not naming perpetrators falls within the discretionary ambit of the right to the truth where the right to know the truth about circumstances of the violations are not absolute. However, noting Article 14 of the Declaration on the Protection of All Persons from Enforced Disappearances,[57] the working group makes it clear that the state has an obligation to bring any person alleged to have perpetrated an enforced disappearance before the relevant authorities.[58] Even if truth commissions do not name perpetrators, the state is still under an obligation to prosecute those alleged to be responsible. This requirement has since been codified in Article 11(1) of the International Convention for the Protection of All Persons from Enforced Disappearance:

> The State Party in the territory under whose jurisdiction a person alleged to have committed an offence of enforced disappearance is found shall, if it does not extradite that person or surrender him or her to another State in accordance with its international obligations or surrender him or her to an

54 Hayner *supra* note 1 at 121.

55 2006 Study on Right to the Truth *supra* note 38 para 3.

56 Ibid para 39. In her discussion on "the politics of truth" Naftali interprets this to mean that the authors of the study favoured prosecutions over the use of truth commissions in realising the right to truth (Patricia Naftali, 'The Politics of Truth' (2015) December, Revue Québécoise de droit international 101 at 111).

57 Declaration on the Protection of All Persons from Enforced Disappearances (12 February 1993).

58 General Comment on the Right to the Truth in Relation to Enforced Disappearances *supra* note 35 para 8.

> international criminal tribunal whose jurisdiction it has recognized, submit the case to its competent authorities for the purpose of prosecution.[59]

In that regard, knowing who perpetrated the crime seemingly forms part of the right to the truth, making prosecutions a necessity. That said, the working group also noted on the subject of prohibition of amnesty its position that amnesty may be a possibility if an amnesty leads to the termination of a disappearance. In essence, according to the working group, therefore, there may be instances where the "right to the truth" may lead, in exceptional circumstances, to a limitation of the "right to justice" and vice versa – though not if the enforced disappearance amounts to a crime against humanity.[60] This phrasing is somewhat curious. If there is a restriction on the right to know the names of the perpetrators, then that logically may lead to the possibility that the right to justice is also circumvented, since prosecutions are perhaps less likely to follow (though it is possible to contemplate a temporary non-disclosure, pending investigative proceedings). Nonetheless, a limited right to the truth can result in a limited right to justice. Curtailing the right to justice (i.e. offering amnesties) for the purposes of advancing the right to know the truth (and potentially facilitate the return of those missing) is different: curtailing the right to justice can positively impact on knowing details about the events and it may still mean that the names of the perpetrators are known (i.e. the full realisation of that aspect of the right to the truth). Extending amnesties and naming perpetrators in a truth report are separate matters. In contrast to the working group's position, the 2006 Study on the Right to the Truth advocates that amnesties should "never be used to limit, deny or impair the right to the truth".[61] Naftali explains this difference in interpretation by the fact that depending on whether truth commissions or trials are the preferred route to satisfy the right to the truth, a slight variation of the absolute versus not absolute content is proffered.[62] In her view, the rhetoric utilised by legal lobbyists and truth activists to drive the legal crafting of the right is masking its ambivalence and "polyphony", especially when contrasting between truth commissions and international criminal prosecutions.[63] If a retributive approach to truth-finding is offered, then naturally naming perpetrators is implicit and amnesties are not an option. Where, however, truth-seeking and reconciliation are at the fore, then first, naming perpetrators in a non-judicial forum requires safeguards, and second, amnesties are perhaps conceivable as part of a more conciliatory path.

59 International Convention for the Protection of All Persons from Enforced Disappearance, Article 11(1).
60 General Comment on the Right to the Truth in Relation to Enforced Disappearances *supra* note 35 para 8.
61 2006 Study on Right to the Truth *supra* note 38 para 60.
62 Naftali *supra* note 56.
63 Ibid at 127–128.

The case is not settled for truth commissions and their duty to name names. The OHCHR's "Rule-of-Law Tools for Post-Conflict States: Truth Commissions" suggest that

> [t]here are legitimate reasons why a commission may choose not to name the wrongdoers or to name only those most responsible or most senior in the chain of command. These may include concerns for the security of witnesses or the safety and security of those named, especially if justice is not expected in the courts.[64]

Practice of truth commissions demonstrates that a number operate without naming names. In fact, the Morocco, Chile and the Solomon Islands Commissions were forbidden from naming perpetrators. In contrast, the Argentinian Commission presented a list of 1,351 military, civilian and religious leaders to the president.[65]

Protecting the civil rights of alleged perpetrators is a serious one, since it is important for the credibility of the commission and how it views its work within a wider human rights framework, including the Covenant on Civil and Political Rights and Article 14 requirements for a fair, public trial, presumption of innocence and other fair trial guarantees. Truth commissions, by definition, are not tribunals, nonetheless, a minimum of due process rules is required if a commission is to name individual alleged perpetrators. All of this is time-consuming. And there are those that caution against a uniform set of criteria of due process, as even in well-established domestic contexts such as the United States, it is a flexible concept whose definition depends on the context.[66] Ways to circumnavigate some issues may include a commission summarising the "evidence before it, including names mentioned by witnesses where they hold credibility, without stating firm conclusions on each individual's culpability".[67] At times it may be easier in terms of lacking evidence, security concerns and political ramifications to say what crimes occurred without actually saying who committed them. The flip side to this approach is that to a more absolutist reading of the right to the truth, elements of it are not fulfilled by those truth commissions.

Working towards prosecutions

As noted before, the discourse on truth commissions vis-à-vis criminal prosecutions sees the former as also serving as a first step towards the latter. This

64 Rule-of-Law Tools for Post-Conflict States: Truth Commissions (2006).

65 Hayner *supra* note 1.

66 Sanford Levinson, 'Trials, Commissions and Investigating Committees. The Elusive Search for Norms of Due Process' in Rotberg R and Thompson D (eds) *Truth v. justice: The morality of truth commissions* (Princeton University Press 2000) 211. In some UK contexts, the "balance of probability" standard of proof (oft employed by truth commissions) can also demand a very high standard of proof (*In re H (Minors)* (1996) as per Lord Nicholls)

67 Hayner *supra* note 1 at 143.

has not always been the case. When truth commissions were emerging in the 1980s, prosecuting heads of states for human rights violations committed whilst in office was a far-fetched idea and barred by immunity under international law. There were few domestic trials and international human rights litigation not well established.[68] Since then, with the cases of Pinochet, Milošević, the indictment of Omar Al-Bashir and through human rights courts, alternate avenues have opened up to ensure justice is served, especially when transitional justice efforts are framed by the right to the truth, right to justice, right to reparation and right to non-repetition. The international routes available are even more important, since the failings of the judiciary may be part of the systemic problems allowing the past abuses to take place without accountability.

This point came to the fore at the Inter-American Court in the Case of *Almonacid-Arellano et al. v Chile*,[69] where the Court concurred with the Chilean Truth Commission's assessment that the truth ('historical truth') contained in the commission report is not a substitute for a state's duty to arrive at the truth through judicial proceedings, including the punishment of those responsible. The Chilean report wrote:

> From the standpoint of prevention alone, this Commission believes that for the sake of achieving national reconciliation and preventing the recurrence of such events it is absolutely necessary that the government fully exercise its power to mete out punishment. Full protection of human rights is conceivable only within a state that is truly subject to the rule of law. The rule of law means that all citizens are subject to the law and to the courts, and hence that the sanctions contemplated in criminal law, which should be applied to all alike, should thereby be applied to those who infringe the laws which safeguards human rights.[70]

Naturally, and as evident from the Chilean report, truth commissions have a different mandate to trials, but there may be some overlap. Truth commissions not only have, at times by virtue of their mandate, the possibility to suggest reforms of the judicial system but also to have some collaborative agreement with the prosecuting authorities of the country. The passing on of information may constitute a step towards potential proceedings in a criminal court. And this threat of prosecutions may be important to reveal truth aspects that remain hidden from a truth commission where alleged perpetrators are not compelled to tell the truth.[71] The Peruvian Truth Commission is oft cited as a prime example of this, since it presented 47 fully developed cases to the prosecutor's office, though of

68 Tepperman *supra* note 43 at 142.

69 *Almonacid Arellano et al. v Chile* (26 September 2006).

70 Chile: Report of the Chilean National Commission on Truth and Reconciliation, (Rettig Report) February 1991, available at www.usip.org/sites/default/files/resources/collections/truth_commissions/Chile90-Report/Chile90-Report.pdf at 1113.

71 Nancy Combs, *Guilty Pleas In International Criminal Law: Constructing A Restorative Justice Approach* (Stanford University Press 2007).

the prosecutions that followed, few resulted in convictions.[72] That said, Peru's constitutional court confirmed the right to the truth and the inapplicability of statutes of limitation in cases pertaining to disappeared persons, paving the way for prosecutions and recognition of victims' rights.[73] South Africa's Truth and Reconciliation Commission also urged for prosecutions based on the files it had collated during its investigations but no-one recommended by the commission was prosecuted.[74] Discrepancy in evidentiary standards and differing lines of questioning in truth commission settings as well as lack of political will have been the main explanations for scant prosecutorial results.

Another issue that may adversely affect the potential for prosecutions with an impact on the realisation of the right to the truth is that talking to a commission is viewed differently than testifying in court. Hayner gives an example from Uganda, where witnesses retracted their evidence:

> Even the commission found that witnesses would sometimes return after a hearing to withdraw their testimony, flatly denying what they had said even when it was recorded on video- or audiotape. It was clear they had been pressured to recant their story, particularly if they named perpetrators. Certainly witnesses felt even more hesitation to go to court to help put someone in jail.[75]

The propensity to testify in court may also, as we will also see in the following chapters, be diminished and thus negatively impact on the ability to narrate their story.

Reparations

As discussed in previous chapters, the right to the truth, in itself, is a form of reparation. Truth commissions, if not conceived as a reparative measure in itself, are often designed to bring reparative benefit at the individual and societal level. They may recommend economic assistance to victims in the form of pensions or employment; educational, health and housing benefits; vetting; restitution of confiscated property; symbolic reparations in the form of memorials; and apologies.[76]

72 According to Gonzelalez Cueva, the Peruvian Truth and Reconciliation Commission in 2002 set up a Special Investigations Unit tasked with organising legal cases to be presented to the attorney General's office for consideration (Eduardo González Cueva, 'The Contribution of the Peruvian Truth and Reconciliation Commission to Prosecutions' in Schabas W and Darcy S (eds), *Truth Commissions and Courts. The Tensions Between Criminal Justice and the Search for Truth* (Springer 2004) 55. Hayner *supra* note 1 at 282 and Méndez *supra* note 19 at 135–138.

73 Hayner *supra* note 1 at 38.

74 Ibid at 281

75 Ibid at 98.

76 As can be ordered by the Inter-American Court of Human Rights.

The right to the truth has an inherent link with such measures, perhaps most notably with education, preserving archives and memorialisation since this forms part of Principle 3 of the Updated Principles and the duty to preserve memory.[77] In addition, the Basic Principles stipulate the "[i]nclusion of an accurate account of the violations [...] in educational material at all levels".[78] This latter provision stresses the need for inclusion of truthful accounts for educational purposes which, in turn, is compatible with the functions of memorialisation. This requirement for a truthful account is in an interesting juxtaposition to the "non-absolute" public element of the right to the truth, as proffered by the UN Working Group on Enforced Disappearances. In this reading, engaging with education and memory preservation has thus also a duty to work towards avoiding falsehood, limiting the scope of flexibility and discretion of transitional justice mechanisms. Otherwise lessons of exclusion, limited remembering, restricted debate and continued autocracy might be perpetuated. The public aspect of the right to the truth should therefore not be compromised by truth commissions designed in their focus to consolidate the power of incumbent governments.[79]

Apart from these rather general examples of reparative benefits that may follow from a truth commission and are allied to the right to the truth, there is another very poignant example of a contribution to the right to the truth: the Argentinian instigated legal category of "forcibly disappeared".[80] This category of "forcibly disappeared" is important, as it is considered legally equivalent to a death for civil purposes but it is not a declaration of death. Law No. 14,321 of 11 May 1994 allows families to process wills, deal with the disappeared's estate and inheritance matters, but the possibility of "reappearance" of the individual remains open. Such a declaration inherently acknowledges state involvement or responsibility for the individual's death (unlike a mere death certificate), since the crime of enforced disappearance, as per Article 2 of the Convention, defines enforced disappearance as

> the arrest, detention, abduction or any other form of deprivation of liberty by agents of the State or by persons or groups of persons acting with the authorization, support or acquiescence of the State, followed by a refusal to acknowledge the deprivation of liberty or by concealment of the fate or whereabouts of the disappeared person, which place such a person outside the protection of the law.[81]

Through the establishment of this category an acknowledgment is made, first, that the crime of enforced disappearance is in itself an infringement of the right

77 Updated Principles on Impunity *supra* note 26.
78 Ibid Principle 21(f).
79 Loyle and Davenport *supra* note 14.
80 Hayner *supra* note 1 at 171 and 280 (Appendix).
81 International Convention for the Protection of All Persons from Enforced Disappearance, Article 2.

to the truth by refusing to provide information on the disappeared, and second, that the state has had a role to play in the crime.

Truth – costs and benefits?

It is worth reiterating that the starting point for a right to the truth is needs-based. The inquiry is about how, where and to what extent this right can be realised in differing fora. The impact of knowing the truth, whether positively, negatively, societally or individually felt, is a separate matter. However, it seems apt to make a number of cautious remarks with regards to truth commissions, the right to the truth and potential impact claims to ensure the context of the right is captured.

Psychological cost, morality and substantiation

Crucially the central aim of truth commissions (or the right to the truth) is not therapy. Instead truth commissions may present a one-time opportunity to reveal one's personal experience, often before persons the survivors never met before and are unlikely to meet again.[82] As such, the process may or may not be psychologically beneficial for those involved in it.[83]

There are anecdotes to substantiate a variety of claims[84] and after scathing criticism[85] of the literature on transitional justice claiming positive effect without actually measuring impact, there are now studies examining the effect of transitional justice measures, including truth commission.[86] It seems that

> when a TRC is perceived as fulfilling important functions related to the knowledge of the truth, and when their report contributes to further activities in seeking justice by civil society, then a TRC is positively valued.[87]

The quote comes from a comparative study on Chile, Peru and Argentina. Interestingly, Argentina rejected outright the idea of reconciliation and yet the truth and reconciliation commission (TRC) there has been viewed to have made a

82 Hayner *supra* note 1 at 147.

83 This includes staff working for Truth Commissions.

84 One account speaks of a mother from South Africa whose son was killed; she had been strong advocate for the right to know the truth. However, on knowing what actually happened to her son this may, in the end, have been too much for her to bear (Hayner *supra* note 1 at 150).

85 Clark *supra* note 13 and David Mendeloff, 'Truth-Seeking, Truth-Telling, and Postconflict Peacebuilding: Curb the Enthusiasm?' (2004) 6 International Studies Review 355.

86 E.g. James Gibson, *Overcoming Apartheid: Can Truth Reconcile a divided Nation?* (Sage 2004) and Manuel Cárdenas, Darío Páez, Maintane Arnoso, Augustín Espinosa, 'Determinants for Approval the work of Truth Commissions in the Southern Cone: A comparative study' (2016) 31(3) International Journal of Social Psychology 423.

87 Ibid at 439.

positive contribution. On the other hand, the South African commission operated with the hypothesis that truth was going to work towards reconciliation. In his research, Gibson offers two conclusions on the South African experience: the minimalist version suggests "that the truth and reconciliation process has done little to harm race relations in South Africa; the maximalist conclusion is that the truth process has actually caused a salutary change in racist attitudes".[88] However, for black South Africans, the study found truth not to lead to reconciliation or vice versa.[89] The record of truth commissions is thus not only patchily understood but also dependent on what the mission of a truth commission was and thus not easily comparable or transferable, making it difficult to draw inferences.

Families have invoked the right to the truth for humanitarian purposes (to alleviate suffering), sometimes with reference to cultural and religious reasons too.[90] However, in different contexts, truth commission-instigated truth-finding and truth-telling may not be equally morally convincing: it may run counter to local understanding of healing and reconciliation and thus compromise or neutralise those efforts if the truth commission's design and set-up does not reflect or is not situated in that particular social understanding and cultural tradition.

Truth and acceptance

The right to the truth does not explicitly say that the truth needs to be accepted and acceptable to the "right-bearer", unless there are critical gaps or inconsistencies in the investigations which would not satisfy the right to the truth requirements. And yet, returning to the notion of education and memorialisation, societies as a whole have the right to preserve their memory of the past. Preservation of a particular narrative will be more successful if it is actually accepted. And in fact, collective memory presupposes a "socially accepted understanding of the meaning of the past".[91] But acceptance of a particular narrative or indeed the emergence of a dominant narrative is not a given. Clark suggests that the problem of multiple, contested and unacknowledged truths is downplayed or overlooked by transitional justice discussions. In her research, conducted in the Balkans, she has come across "various forms of denial"[92] along ethnic divides. Méndez too, in his appraisal of Latin American experience with truth-telling, notes that truth commissions there did not investigate ethnicity as part of human rights violations, nor did they formulate recommendations to overcome ethnic division or indeed racism.[93] Therefore, their work and impact on individuals and

88 James Gibson, 'Does the Truth lead to Reconciliation?' 2004 48(2) American Journal of Political Science 201 at 215.
89 Ibid at 215
90 E.g. Naftali *supra* note 1.
91 See Gibson *supra* note 88 at 204.
92 Clark *supra* note 13 at 248.
93 With the exception of Guatemala's war against indigenous people (and Méndez *supra* note 19 at 116.

society, he argues, has to be considered in this light. The challenge of getting sections of society to "buy into" the process has been noted as a challenge for the South African Truth and Reconciliation Commission too, with Archbishop Desmond Tutu acknowledging that "one of the greatest weaknesses in the Commission was the fact that we failed to attract the bulk of the white community to participate enthusiastically in the Truth and Reconciliation process".[94]

In countries such as Bosnia and Kosovo, where the scars of conflict are still keenly felt along ethnic lines, it is not at all clear whether a particular narrative is emerging, let alone accepted, that will offer a way to peacefully coexist. For the contemplated but failed Bosnian Truth Commission, it seems that attempts to create an official state-legitimising narrative did not resonate with the population, civil society (including victim associations) or political leaders.[95] There may be too many competing truth actors or truth versions (as opposed to one factual account), or perhaps it is still too early to tell – too early to grapple with the complexities. Michael Scharf, in the context of post-Nuremberg Germany, seeks to dispel what he calls "[o]ne of the modern myths of Nuremberg",[96] whereby the German population allegedly accepted legitimacy and judgments of the Nuremberg Tribunal. In fact, opinion polls conducted by the US Department of State between 1945 and 1958 show evidence quite to the opposite, with the trials having failed to "re-educate" West Germans at the time. Today, most international criminal law books see Nuremberg as a founding moment of the discipline, and the question of Germany's guilt is largely settled.

The point to stress here is that even if the right to the truth is realised in truth commissions, the effect of the realisation can have a multitude of consequences. One such consequence may be the rejection of the very realisation of the right to the truth on behalf of those who hold the right, whether collectively or as individuals.

Conclusion: forward and side-steps

Truth commissions can be a step towards addressing elements of the right to the truth, especially where gross human rights abuses were pervasive and perpetrated through state structures. Truth commissions can be state-initiated processes (most likely by a successor government), though often with external support and/or pressure. It is worth recalling, however, that the application of the right to the truth is not limited to instances of societal transition, and where isolated abuses occur, or where systematic abuse occurs within an ongoing, oppressive environment, alternative avenues for pursuing the right will be necessary.

94 Desmond Tutu, *No Future Without Forgiveness* (Rider 1999) at 184.

95 Jasna Dragovic-Soso, 'History of a Failure: Attempts to Create a National Truth and Reconciliation Commission in Bosnia and Herzegovina, 1997–2006' (2016) 20 (2) International Journal of Transitional Justice 292.

96 Michael Scharf, 'Slobodan Milošević' in Schabas W (ed), *The Cambridge Companion to International Criminal Law* (Cambridge University Press 2016) at 309.

Although truth commissions may include an individual element, their outlook is often collective, and as a result, may not be able to generate the level of detail required to satisfy the right to the truth requirements in individual cases. At the same time, however, advocates for the right are not unanimous in what the right's non-derogable aspects are: the public element may be perceived as discretionary, allowing flexibility to truth commissions' mandate of investigative scope; and on the issue of naming names relevant information may be withheld, contravening some conceptions of the right to the truth. In that sense, and dependent on politico-social circumstances, advocates seek to inject some flexibility into the right so that it can be moulded to suit different agendas.

The positive aspect of such flexibility within the concept is that no uniform truth commission model for truth-finding has emerged. In fact, Hayner suggests that

> [t]here has been rather a healthy practice of closely studying other experiences, incorporating some of the more useful elements, while crafting something new and different, basing the new inquiries in national needs and historical contexts.[97]

The right to the truth as a legitimising, mostly morally persuasive and yet flexible right, may have served this purpose.

Yet, whilst commissions are usually established by the state, their contribution to the right to the truth by virtue of their investigations, process and report are a potential step in working towards further realisation of the right to the truth (namely through prosecutions). However, they lack legal force: any recommendation by the commission that the state concerned conduct thorough forensic examination, prosecutions or reparations are typically not legally binding and hence may go unrealised. Sadly, in the case of Jeremías Osorio Rivera, for example, such recommendations were ignored. Whilst the Peruvian Truth Commission had asked the state authorities to conduct an effective investigation,[98] the Inter-American Court found that

> the whereabouts of Jeremías Osorio Rivera remain unknown and, to date, the State has not taken any steps to discover the victim's whereabouts, but continues to deny that an enforced disappearance occurred.[99]

Like so many countries, Peru is still grappling with its past, as evidenced by recent legislation[100] on forensic excavation processes, something originally developed by the Peruvian Truth Commission, pointing to the potentially very long road to truth-finding.

97 Hayner *supra* note 1 at 236.
98 *Osorio Rivera and family v Peru* (26 November 2016) para 246.
99 Ibid para 249.
100 Peru: Law No 30470, 22 June 2016. The legislation entitled 'Ley de búsqueda de personas desaparecidas durante el período de violencia 1980–2000' was approved by congress in June 2016.

References

Bickford L, 'Unofficial Truth Projects' (2007) 29(4) Human Rights Quarterly 994.

Borer T A, 'Truth Telling as a Peace-Building Activity. A Theoretical Overview' in Borer T A (ed), *Telling the Truth: Truth Telling and Peace-Building in Post-Conflict Societies* (University of Notre Dame Press 2006).

Cárdenas M, Páez D, Arnoso M and Espinosa A, 'Determinants for Approval the work of Truth Commissions in the Southern Cone: A comparative study' (2016) 31(3) International Journal of Social Psychology 423.

Clark J N, 'Transitional Justice, Truth and Reconciliation: An Under-Explored Relationship', 11 (2011) 11 International Criminal Law Review 241.

Combs N, *Guilty Pleas In International Criminal Law: Constructing A Restorative Justice Approach* (Stanford University Press 2007).

Dragovic-Soso J, 'History of a Failure: Attempts to Create a National Truth and Reconciliation Commission in Bosnia and Herzegovina, 1997–2006' (2016) 20 (2) International Journal of Transitional Justice 292.

Ellis S, 'Truth and Reconciliation Commission of South Africa Report, Volumes 1–5. Pretoria: Government Printer, October 1998' (2000) 42 Transformation 61.

Fletcher L, Weinstein H and Rowen J, 'Context, timing and the dynamics of transitional justice: A historical perspective' (2009) 31(1) Human Rights Quarterly 163.

Gibson J, 'Does the Truth lead to Reconciliation?' 2004 48(2) American Journal of Political Science 201.

Gibson J, *Overcoming Apartheid: Can Truth Reconcile a divided Nation?* (Sage 2004).

González Cueva E, 'The Contribution of the Peruvian Truth and Reconciliation Commission to Prosecutions' in Schabas W and Darcy S (eds), *Truth Commissions and Courts. The Tensions Between Criminal Justice and the Search for Truth* (Springer 2004).

Habermas J, *Die Normalität einer Berliner Republik – Kleine Politische Schriften VIII* (Suhrkamp 1995).

Hayner P, *Unspeakable Truths. Transitional Justice and the Challenge of Truth Commissions* (2nd edn, Routledge 2011).

Ignatieff M, 'Human Rights as Idolatry', The Tanner Lecture on Human Values (Princeton University 4–7 April 2000).

Leebaw B A, 'The Irreconcilable Goals of Transitional Justice', (2008) 30 Human Rights Quarterly 95.

Levinson S, 'Trials, Commissions and Investigating Committees. The Elusive Search for Norms of Due Process' in Rotberg R and Thompson D (eds) *Truth v. justice: The morality of truth commissions* (Princeton University Press 2000).

Loyle C and Davenport C, 'Transitional Injustice: Subverting Justice in Transition and Postconflict Societies' (2016) 15 Journal of Human Rights 126.

Méndez, 'The Human Right to Truth. Lessons Learned from Latin American Experiences with Truth Telling' in Borer T A (ed), *Telling the Truth: Truth Telling and Peace-Building in Post-Conflict Societies* (University of Notre Dame Press 2006) 115.

Méndez J and Bariffi F, 'Truth, Right to, International Protection' (2011) Max Planck Encyclopedia of Public International Law (online).

Naftali P, 'Crafting a "Right to truth" in International Law: Converging Mobilizations, Diverging Agendas?' (2016) XIII Champ penal/Penal field 1.

Naftali P, 'The Politics of Truth' (2015) December, Revue Québécoise de droit international 101.

Schabas W and Darcy S (eds), *Truth Commissions and Courts. The Tensions Between Criminal Justice and the Search for Truth* (Springer 2004).
Scharf M, 'Slobodan Milošević' in Schabas W (ed), *The Cambridge Companion to International Criminal Law* (Cambridge University Press 2016) 295.
Szoke-Burke S, 'Searching for the Right to Truth: The Impact of International Human Rights Law on National Transitional Justice Policies' (2015) 33(2) Berkeley Journal of International Law 526.
Tepperman J, 'Truth and Consequences' (2002) March/April Foreign Affairs 128.
Tutu D, *No Future Without Forgiveness* (Rider 1999).

9 International criminal trials

Introduction

The political background to the right to the truth is the failure of state institutions to deal, through their own criminal and civil processes, with atrocities. International criminal proceedings, whilst initiated by supra-national institutions, are not meant to prosecute states but rather individuals, and therefore would not be able to address the right in this way. In addition, there is no mentioning of the right to the truth in any of the founding documents for international criminal tribunals. So why have prosecutions been identified as key realisers of a right to the truth in their fight against impunity?[1]

Within the transitional justice discourse, advocates of international criminal trials believe that prosecutions

> will help communities rebuild because trials support one, if not all of the following goals: (1) to discover and publicize the truth of past atrocities; (2) to punish perpetrators; (3) to respond to the needs of victims; (4) to promote the rule of law in emerging democracies; and (5) to promote reconciliation.[2]

Academics propose that the main reasons for prosecutions and trials include truth, accountability, reconciliation and reparation.[3] with others wishing to add reformation of institutions to this list.[4] Effective prosecutions, in a maximalist

1 E.g. Dermot Groome, 'The Right to Truth in the Fight Against Impunity' (2011) 29(1) Berkeley Journal of International Law 175; Sam Szoke-Burke, 'Searching for the Right to Truth: The Impact of International Human Rights Law on National Transitional Justice Policies' (2015) 33(2) Berkeley Journal of International Law 526; and Promotion and Protection of Human Rights. Study on the Right to the Truth (8 February 2006) at 14 (hereinafter 2006 Study on the Right to the Truth).

2 Laurel Fletcher and Harvey Weinstein H, 'Violence and Social Repair: Rethinking the Contribution of Justice to Reconciliation' (2002) 24 Human Rights Quarterly 573 at 586. Fletcher and Weinstein do not endorse this view.

3 Stephen Parmentier, 'Global Justice in the Aftermath of Mass Violence. The Role of the International Criminal Court in Dealing with Political Crimes', 13th World Congress of Criminology. Reducing Crimes and Promoting Justice: Challenges to Sciences, Policy and Practice (10–15 August 2003).

4 Briony Jones, Elisabeth Baumgartner and Sidonia Gabriel, 'A Transformative Approach to Dealing with the Past' (February 2015) Swiss peace.

view of impact, are thought to satisfy the victims' desire for retribution, prevent individuals from seeking retaliation for what they suffered and avoid a repetition of the injustices.[5] Judges themselves paraphrased the multifold objectives of punishment for breaches of international law, prevention and improvement of the rule of law voiced by the Security Council when setting up the International Criminal Tribunal for the Former Yugoslavia.[6]

Allied to these objectives, the ICTY was also believed to contribute to the restoration and maintenance of peace by removing those most responsible from being able to continue the armed conflict and to ensure that individual responsibility would avoid collective responsibility and blame associated to ethnic or political groups from emerging.[7] This arguably inflationist representation of what international criminal prosecutions may achieve amid scant empirical substantiation has been criticised.[8] But even with a modest belief that "[p]roceedings focused on individual criminal responsibility represent a form or reaction oriented toward both establishing the truth and punishing the individual criminal perpetrator",[9] the notion of truth can take centre stage for those advocating for criminal prosecutions. In that sense, trials are believed to contribute to a notion of truth through producing a record of the causes of conflicts, the responsible actors and parties, as well as the events themselves.[10] However, the truth-finding during trials is narrowly framed:

> The truth-seeking process in the ad hoc tribunals is bounded by the criminal responsibility of the individual before the court with respect to the specific crimes charged. The parameters of the exercise are no broader. An international criminal trial will not inquire or adjudicate matters not directly related to the crimes charged in the indictment; it will not inquire or adjudicate the responsibility of those other than the persons charged in those crimes unless absolutely necessary.[11]

But in seeking to come to a determination in accordance with the charges, what is "absolutely necessary" in terms of context is significant and subject to interpretation. During international criminal trials various aspects of truth-finding come together. Crucially, the truth-seeking function of the Court begins prior to the conduct of any trial, and includes a period of investigation, evidence-gathering

5 Beth Van Schaack and Ronald Slye, *International Criminal Law and Its Enforcement* (Foundation Press 2007).
6 *Prosecutor v Momir Nikolić* (2 December 2003) para 59.
7 Ibid para 60.
8 E.g. Janine Natalya Clark, *International Trials and Reconciliation: assessing the impact of the international criminal tribunal for the former Yugoslavia* (Routledge 2014) and Fletcher and Weinstein (*supra* note 2)
9 Van Schaack and Slye *supra* note 5 at 7.
10 E.g. Michael Scharf and Paul Williams, 'The Functions of Justice and Anti-Justice in the Peace-Building Process' (2003) 35 Case Western Reserve Journal of International Law 161.
11 Groome *supra* note 1 at 186.

and verification of charges. In fact, as an order by the co-investigating judges at the Extraordinary Chambers makes clear, these investigations are important to the suspects and the victims, who otherwise would be "deprived of their right to be heard, their right to justice, their right to the truth and their right to reparations".[12]

For the purpose of conducting its investigation into alleged offences, international criminal law mechanisms, unlike their human rights counterparts, operate within the territories of the state where the abuse happened, seeking first-hand access to evidential materials, including those which might assist in answering the many questions that victims and their families have in the aftermath of atrocities.[13] Successful investigations are contingent on the appropriate state cooperation, which is not always there.

Trials seek to establish a historical record (historical truth) about the circumstances, structures and succession of events;[14] they engage forensic investigations and experts to present forensic truth;[15] they allow testimony of individual victims to offer narrative truth;[16] and the Chambers, after thorough deliberation (and within the constraints of the indictment, statutory provisions, rules and regulations, etc.) pronounce on the innocence or guilt of the accused (legal, procedural or juridical truth). These components, though lacking precise definitions, have the potential, in different ways, to work towards the individual and public elements of the right to the truth, despite being a by-product[17] of the criminal process. They are, however, not fixed categories. Instead there may be overlap

12 *Case 003 against Meas Muth and Sou Met* (2 December 2011) para 7.

13 Groome notes that '[t]he ability of an international prosecutor to collect evidence from a variety of sources is an important tool in truth-seeking, and one not ordinarily available to individual complainants in human rights cases' (Groome *supra* note 1 at 191). However, as the Kenyatta case has shown, state cooperation is vital to allow for in-country evidence collection and investigation.

14 E.g. Fergal Gaynor, 'Uneasy Partners – Evidence, Truth and History in International Trials' (2012) 10(5) Journal of International Criminal Justice 1257 and William Schabas, *Unimaginable Atrocities* (Oxford University Press 2012).

15 The South African Truth Commission distinguishes four notions of truth: factual or forensic truth; personal or narrative truth; social or "dialogue" truth and healing and restorative truth. In its definition of forensic truth questions such as "what happened to whom, where, when and how, and who was involved?" are answered and information about the "context, causes and patterns of violations" ascertained (Truth and Reconciliation Commission, 'Truth and Reconciliation Commission of South Africa Final Report (Volume 1)' (29 October 1998) at 110).

16 Survivor truth-telling or "narrative truth" is recognised as a form of truth in the transitional justice context. E.g. Stephen Ellis, Ellis S, 'Truth and Reconciliation Commission of South Africa Report, Volumes 1–5. Pretoria: Government Printer, October 1998' (2000) 42 Transformation 61.

17 In *Prosecutor v Milutinović et al.* this was expressly stated: "[c]oincidentally, the narrative of this Judgment includes information which may help to provide a fuller understanding of events in 1998 and 1999 in Kosovo. This Judgment is, however, simply one element in an array of material from which historians will derive a complete historical record." (*Prosecutor v Milutinović et al.* (26 February 2009) para 4). See also Richard May and Marieke Weirda, 'Evidence before the ICTY' in May R, Tolbert D and Hocking J (eds) *Essays on Procedure and Evidence: In Honour of Gabrielle Kirk McDonald* (Kluwer 2001).

between each of the named truth types, and in fact the distinction may be entirely artificial as they all pertain, ultimately, to one big court record. A legal finding will incorporate historical records, forensic information and victim testimony. Conversely, a judgment can itself become a historical record. In order to give greater specificity to what a trial can offer in terms of the realisation of the right to the truth, a differentiation between these four types seems useful as they each capture particular values (historical, forensic, narrative and juridical) linked to the right to truth.

Once more, we seek to test our working definition of the right to the truth against the processes of international criminal trials before turning our attention to the International Criminal Court. Instead of focusing predominantly on statutes, Rules of Procedures and decisions or indeed the various stages in proceedings (investigations, pretrial, trial and appeal), in this chapter we seek to have a more general outlook at the possibilities of truth realisation in international criminal proceedings, since there have been a number of such endeavours.[18] Therefore, the chapter discusses the truth potential of international trials thematically under the headings of historical truth, forensic truth, narrative truth, and legal truth.

Historical truth

Judge Schomburg emphasised the importance of truth in the context of justice: "there is no peace without justice; there is no justice without truth, meaning the entire truth and nothing but the truth".[19] This is an argument oft raised by the inquisitorial system which considers getting as closely as possible to the truth to be at its core. International criminal trials in their totality have been seen as a conduit if not a creator of a historical record,[20] with those involved in trials playing, willingly or unwillingly, a role in producing such a record. This has been made explicit by judges inside and outside the courtroom.[21] For example, in addition to the list of objectives for international criminal proceedings provided earlier, the Trial Chamber in the Momir Nikolić case also added another purpose to international criminal trials:

> through public proceedings, the truth about the possible commission of war crimes, crimes against humanity and genocide was to be determined, thereby establishing an accurate, accessible historical record.[22]

18 E.g. In addition to the ad hoc tribunals, tribunals have been created in Cambodia, Sierra Leone, East Timor and Lebanon.

19 *Prosecutor v Deronjić* (30 March 2004), Dissenting Opinion of Judge Wolfgang Schomburg para 6.

20 Gaynor *supra* note 14 at 1258.

21 Most famous in this regard is probably Cassese's address to the UN General Assembly on 4 November 1997 (Address of ICTY President Antonio Cassese to the UN General Assembly, (4 November 1997) at 2). See also, May and Weirda *supra* note 17 and Patricia Wald, 'Foreword: War Tales and War Trials' (2008) 106 Michigan Law Review 901.

22 *Prosecutor v Momir Nikolić* (2 December 2003) para 60.

The creation of a detailed historical record through trials was discussed here in relation to a guilty plea by the defendant resulting in the lack of a public trial. One of the questions posed was whether under circumstances of plea bargaining a complete historical record could be established – an issue which we will return to in later discussion. Other chambers have sought to avoid discussions on political and historical backgrounds, instead seeing their purpose more restrictively:

> The function of the Trial Chamber is to do justice in the case at hand and while this naturally involves presenting its findings in context, we will limit this background section to those facts which are necessary to situate the evaluation of the present case.[23]

Engagement with the historical context, when trying high-ranking individuals, however, is inevitable. In the landmark verdict on Radovan Karadžić, the Trial Chamber, in its 2,615-page strong judgment, devotes some 150 pages to the backgrounds relating to the case, offering insights into the historical context, the relevant Bosnian Serb political, constitutional, military and police structures, the justice system and international peace negotiations, ending with the Dayton Agreement.[24] In short: the role of the state needs to be understood. All this is laid out before findings regarding incidents in particular municipalities, in line with the indictment, are made. Particular attention is paid to Sarajevo, including, for example, sniping, shelling, and the siege of the city,[25] as well as Srebrenica (we shall return to this later in relation to forensic truth).[26] Elements of the judgment, therefore, suggest that an authoritative fact-finding into the politico-social structures that led to atrocities perpetrated was conducted. Karadžić was found guilty on ten counts, including genocide in Srebrenica; persecution, extermination, murder; deportation and inhumane acts of forcible transfer as crimes against humanity; as well as murder, terror, unlawful attacks on civilians and hostages taken as violations of the laws or custom of war. For crimes against humanity, the systematic or widespread nature of the crime form part of its characterisation, and therefore a prosecutor has to investigate and produce evidence on the extent of organisation, scale and policy elements by virtue of proving the very charge.

Whether the trial offers information on the particular circumstances of an individual's suffering depends on the charges and focus of the trial. Testimony offered by victims and other evidence that featured in a trial may become part of the (historical) trial record in the sense that they are filed in the tribunal's archive. However, if not contained in the judgment, it may lack the *authoritative* public recording element of the fact-finding exercise.

Gaynor suggests that the term "historical record" for the purposes of international criminal proceedings can mean a number of things: it can be interpreted to

23 *Prosecutor v Delalić et al.* (16 November 1998) para 88.
24 *Prosecutor v Karadžić* (25 March 2016).
25 Ibid volume III of the judgment.
26 Ibid volume IV of the judgment.

mean the trial judgment itself (which we suggest to be the legal or juridical truth based upon the examination of evidence before the Chambers), the evidence admitted during a trial or the totality of materials produced and archived by a tribunal.[27] Regardless of which view is adopted, limitations on what is submitted to a tribunal naturally apply by virtue of the court's jurisdiction, indictment of a given case, prosecutorial strategy and discretion,[28] confidentiality requirements, trial management on behalf of the judges, plea agreement process and admissibility rules.[29] These factors have profound impact on what is generated in terms of a historical record and in this regard are relevant to the realisation of the right to the truth, especially its public element and pertaining to collective memory.

Interestingly, an appeal for a comprehensive view of the truth and the creation of a historical record that encompasses inquiries into the broader socio-historical context of a conflict have been made by both parties to the proceedings as and when it suits their strategic purposes.[30] Defendant Radovan Karadžić argued for a broad investigation into the Srebrenica events and Yugoslav wars. In an exchange with Judge Kwon, he argued for the need for truth as akin to a collective need through his use of the first person plural:

> We have to establish all the facts of the events and actually shed full light on the events in Srebrenica. So it is very important where the weapons came from and it is important because we want to show and we want to question how unbiased can representatives of such countries be as witnesses in this trial.[31]

Judge Kwon, however, sought to limit the presentation of evidence to what is legally relevant to the charges, reminding Mr Karadzic of the scope of the point in question:

> Mr. Karadzic, it is one thing that there's a legitimate cause in waging a war, but it's totally a separate matter how it is waged. So in this regard,

27 Gaynor *supra* note 14.

28 Office of the Prosecutor, The ICC Prosecutorial Strategy 2009–2012 (1 February 2010) states that its "mandate does not include production of comprehensive records for a given conflict" which is somewhat in contrast to the purpose given to the ICTY which was tasked with a geographically and temporally defined jurisdiction, though the ICC strategy suggests that a representative approach is taken that would reflect "the gravest incidents and the main types of victimization" (ibid, para 20). At the ICTY the prosecutor is not required to investigate exonerating circumstances, whereas under the Rome Statute (Article 54(1)(a)) the prosecutor is under the obligation to pursue both incriminating and exonerating lines of inquiry equally.

29 For a discussion on each point, apart from trial management, see Gaynor *supra* note 14.

30 An example of this is defence counsel Dr Otto Freiherr von Lüdinghausen (representing the accused Konstantin Freiherr von Neurath) International Military Tribunal, Nuremberg Trial Proceedings, Vol. 19 (23 July 1946) also reported in Schabas *supra* note 14.

31 *Prosecutor v Karadžić* (15 February 2010) at 765. Later that day Mr Karadzic repeated his question by insisting on a broader evidence base: "How else could we establish the truth and pass a sentence if we do not have that evidence as well?" at 779.

> Mr. Karadzic, I would like to remind you that the purpose of this trial is to judge whether you are guilty of charges as alleged in the indictment. And this is not an opportunity for you to produce a white book of all the events that took place at the time. And I would advise you to concentrate on defending yourself against the charges in the indictment.[32]

Asking for potentially valuable information on why a certain chain of events was triggered and what role each party played can be of interest for the realisation of the right to the truth, it is unlikely to result in direct answers through the court processes. Though a number of historians have presented expert evidence before international tribunals,[33] there are several reasons for curtailing requests for too much historical background: the demands fall beyond the jurisdiction of a tribunal (individual responsibility is at issue – not collective or state responsibility and individual responsibility for the way a war is fought is examined not the involvement of other parties); it would be unfair to the defendant to require investigations into allegation beyond the crimes with which he or she is charged; causes of war may be irrelevant and the prosecutorial strategy might mean that the focus lies on charges that the prosecution is more likely to successfully prove. In addition, it could be that historical evidence does not meet the admissibility standards of a tribunal.[34]

All this, in turn, may mean that the pattern of crimes emerging from tribunals' jurisprudence and publicly accessible records might not be a true reflection of crimes perpetrated on the ground, as critics have pointed out in the aftermath of the Lubanga case but also in relation to the Balkans. Crimes of sexual violence, for example, tend to be challenging to prove,[35] with witnesses unwilling to come forward, so that the record of indictments with corresponding legal findings may not adequately reflect the realities or what historians describe.

There are other concerns raised that would diminish the historical truth value of tribunals. The death of a defendant results in the end of proceedings, as in the Milošević case, meaning that proceedings come to a halt and with it relevant additions to the historical record, leaving it incomplete. The burden of proof "beyond reasonable doubt" that is placed on the judges might mean that certain determinations of legal facts beyond reasonable doubt cannot be made. One such prominent example is the acquittal of Colonel Bagosora, believed to have been an architect of Rwanda's architect on the charge of conspiracy to commit genocide. The Trial Chamber said in its ruling on Bagosora

32 Ibid at 765.

33 E.g. Schabas *supra* note 14 at 158.

34 At the ICTY, admissibility of expert evidence can be denied on grounds of unreliable methods (Rules of Procedure and Evidence (8 July 2015) Rule 95); issues of fairness of the trial (Rule 89 D); or lack of probative value (Rule 89 C).

35 Ellie Smith 'Investigating Rape at the International Criminal Court: The Impact of Trauma', 2012 (2) Issues in International Criminal Justice 99.

and his co-defendants that more than one plausible inference existed for the presented evidence:

> The Chamber certainly accepts that there are indications which may be construed as evidence of a plan to commit genocide, in particular when viewed in light of the subsequent targeted and speedy killings immediately after the shooting down of the President's plane. However, the evidence is also consistent with preparations for a political or military power struggle and measures adopted in the context of an on-going war with the RPF that were used for other purposes from 6 April 1994. Consequently, the Prosecution has not proven beyond reasonable doubt that the only reasonable inference to be drawn from the evidence is that the four Accused conspired amongst themselves or with others to commit genocide before it unfolded from 7 April 1994. The Chamber has acquitted them of the count of conspiracy.[36]

Such a wording, whilst closing the door on the legal finding on conspiracy to commit genocide, nonetheless leaves open the door for historical conclusions that would find it plausible, based on the evidence, that the defendants were in fact conspiring to commit genocide as opposed to political power plotting. Whilst the Chamber cannot come to such a conclusion, victims seeking to understand the events leading up to the Rwandese genocide, may find the information compelling – though to what extent victims actually engage in these records is a separate matter.[37]

However, there are also occasions where seemingly uncontroversial historical records can be created. This is despite the defence team's primary loyalty lying with their client and not the espousing of truth.[38] In the case of Kalimanzira, the Trial Chamber emphasises that both the "defence and prosecution evidence, when viewed in combination as a whole, provides a broader historical record of the killings at Kabuye hill",[39] and that in fact the defence evidence supported the prosecution case in that regard. This would represent a unified view of this particular event which not only withstood the test of probative value but was acceptable to both parties to the proceedings.

Finally, the issue of guilty pleas and plea bargaining has cast a substantial doubt over the achievement of a historical record, especially as plea agreements will not result in a full public trial where evidence is received and testimonies are given. It also has adverse consequences for narrative truth insofar as victims are rarely

36 *Prosecutor v Bagosora et al.* (18 December 2008) para 13–14.

37 Following the *Karadžić* verdict, Dov Jacobs questioned, inter alia, the value of a 2,615-page strong judgment and the "usefulness of international judgments generally" (Dov Jacobs, '6 Quick Thoughts on the Karadzic Judgment' https://dovjacobs.com/2016/03/25/6-quick-thoughts-on-the-karadzic-judgment/ accessed 14 February 2019).

38 Gaynor *supra* note 14.

39 *Prosecutor v Kalimanzira* (22 June 2009) para 386.

called to testify in plea agreements.[40] In this sense the chamber acknowledged that a

> public trial, with the presentation of testimonial and documentary evidence by both parties, creates a more complete and detailed historical record than a guilty plea, which may only establish the bare factual allegations in an indictment or may be supplemented by a statement of facts and acceptance of responsibility by the accused.[41]

Therefore, the completeness of historical records is questionable in these circumstances, especially since plea bargain agreements are entered for motives other than to advance the truth (though pleading guilty may come also at a security cost to the defendant and his/her family). Nonetheless in the case of Momir Nikolić, despite controversies surrounding earlier untruthful statements by the defendant,[42] the judges found that his guilty plea was significant since it recognised the crimes that were committed in Bosnia, thus contributing to the historical truth.[43] Similar remarks have been made in relation to other defendants, with the Trial Chamber quoting the prosecution in the Biljana Plavšić case, saying that "an unprecedented contribution to the establishment of truth and a significant effort toward the advancement of reconciliation" was made.[44]

Guilty pleas often go hand in hand with apologies on behalf of the defendant. The ICTY considers apologies and expressions of remorse as mitigating factors in sentencing, thus creating an incentive for defendants to do so – which is, of course, not without controversy.[45] The ICTY lists 20 plea agreements and 19 videos of guilty statements, some including an apology.[46] Plea bargains can facilitate defender truth-telling of facts only known to him/her, and if related to lower-ranking perpetrators, this might reveal important information on what crime was perpetrated, in what manner, by whom, for what reason and who the victims were. In this regard, a contribution to an acknowledgment of criminal wrongdoing and the patterns thereof may be offered, whilst the specifics about victims, numbers and the disposal of bodies may be discerned, thus fulfilling important

40 *Prosecutor v Momir Nikolić* (2 Dec 2003) paras 61–62.

41 Ibid para 61.

42 The defendant had initially told prosecutors that he had been involved in two major executions at Sandići meadow and the Kravica warehouse as part of the Srebrenica massacre, when, in reality, he was not present at the time of executions. According to Combs, "Nikolić admitted lying soon after he had done so and said that he had fabricated the story because he had so wanted the plea agreement to succeed." (Nancy Combs, *Guilty Pleas In International Criminal Law: Constructing A Restorative Justice Approach* (Stanford University Press 2007) at 194).

43 *Prosecutor v Momir Nikolić* (2 Dec 2003) para 65.

44 *Prosecutor v Plavšić*, (27 February 2003) para 67.

45 Combs *supra* note 42 at 145.

46 ICTY, 'Statements of Guilt' (no date) www.icty.org/en/features/statements-guilt (accessed 16 January 2019).

elements of the right to the truth for the individual survivor and the public. The case of Dragan Nikolić, during a sentencing hearing, is illustrative of this point. After being asked by a witness, without invitation, as to the whereabouts and burial place of her sons, and following a closed session and lawyer consultation, the defendant made the following statement:

> As far as her sons are concerned, as far as I heard – because I wasn't there when it happened – on the 30th of September, I believe, together with a group of about 40 people, they were taken to Debelo Brdo and liquidated. From that group, I remember – and I can say this because I know this lady and her sons and I remember that group of people – I remember that this group included mainly people who had previously said that they wanted to stay in Vlasenica. Most of them were locals from Vlasenica, people whom I knew and some of them were my friends. That's why I remember them. And it was in this group of people that Enis and Bernis,[47] this lady's sons, were. I knew them well. And from what I heard, there were liquidated – they were liquidated on that site. I don't know how far the exhumations have gone. And as the lady says, all their ID's were removed. I don't know if anything was found on the bodies; maybe some clothing. And if I remember her sons well, one of her sons was wearing a denim jacket and trousers. And should there be an exhumation, perhaps he could be recognised by his clothes. And if an exhumation takes place, I believe that's where her sons would be found.[48]

Naturally, this information can also provide important leads for further investigations and have an impact on consequent truth-finding and truth realisation. The information offered by the defendant has since been acknowledged by the judgment in *Karadžić*, stating that 41 non-Serb detainees from the Sušica camp "were taken away and killed by the Bosnian Serb police at Debelo Brdo".[49] When, however, such information and detail of events and on victims is not offered or corroborated, this may result in disappointment on behalf of the victims and their families.[50] To avoid such a response and show respect to the victims and their families, the prosecutor, in the guilty-plea hearing of Banović, read out the names of the victims from the Keraterm camp since "ultimately these proceedings are

47 In the Karadžić verdict the sons, together with 39 others, are named as Bernes Hadžić and Enes Hadžić. Of these named individuals, 18 are said to have been identified. On the list provided to the court in the 'Updated Table 2 to the Report of Amor Mašović' the names of Bernes Hadžić and Enes Hadžić do not appear (*Prosecutor v Karadžić* (25 March 2016) footnote 4173 at 490–491).

48 *Prosecutor v Dragan Nikolić* (Trial Transcript) IT-94-2 (3 November 2003) at 256–257.

49 *Prosecutor v Karadžić* (25 March 2016) para 1212.

50 This is reported to have been the case when Darko Mrda, as part of his plea agreement, did not reveal the burial locations of victims relating to the Koricanske Stijene massacre (Combs *supra* note 42 at 196)

about people who suffered at the Keraterm camp",[51] thus giving the proceedings a victim focus that is publicly accessible.

This exposition of detailed information on individual victims offered by the defendant during guilty pleas, logically leads on to the discussion of forensic science in the next section. However, to summarise the contribution of historical truth for the purposes of the right to the truth, it is fair to say that the historical truth offered as part of international criminal proceedings, in their official records and judgments, is likely to result from an authoritative investigation that includes the politico-social structures that led to the crimes committed. This will include information on particular individuals and circumstances which may be revealed during proceedings, court documents or jurisprudence. In that sense important public aspects of the right to the truth, including public reporting or communication of the investigations and fact-finding, is made so long as – and this is a key proviso – it is framed adequately by the indictment.

Forensic truth

By forensic truth, we understand the information expertly generated for use in a public forum, such as a court. The purpose of forensic truth in this context is to generate findings related to questions such as "what happened to an individual, where, when and how?"; and second information about the reasons, circumstances and patterns of the events leading to the perpetration of a crime. In line with admissibility requirements, such evidence can be denied admissibility for use of unreliable methods; issues of fairness of the trial; or lack of probative value.[52]

Forensic truth is particularly pertinent to the right to the truth, since it has the potential to provide the information needed to realise the individual aspect of the right to the truth. This is reflected in provisions of customary international law and on missing persons which suggest that following burial forensic excavations and investigations, including DNA tests, carried out by specialists,[53] may facilitate identification.[54] Similarly, patterns of crimes, factors corroborating the legal categorisation of crime, how and where they were perpetrated and through what means can emerge through such forensic work.

At the ICTY, there are ample examples of the use of forensic truth in criminal proceedings. In *Karadzic*, the Trial Chamber examined the forensic evidence and data on the missing presented to it and "found that at least 5,115 men were killed by members of the Bosnian Serb Forces in July 1995 in Srebrenica".[55] The cause and manner of death were also discussed. The judges are acutely aware of the

51 *Prosecutor v Banović* (3 September 2003) at 111.

52 Rule 95, Rule 89(D) and Rule 89 (C) before the ICTY.

53 International Committee of the Red Cross, 'Guiding Principles/Model Law on the Missing', 2009, available at www.icrc.org/en/document/guiding-principles-model-law-missing-model-law, Commentary to article 21 at 46 and 48.

54 Jean-Marie Henckaerts and Louise Doswald-Beck, *Customary International Humanitarian Law, Volume I: Rules* (Cambridge University Press 2006) Rule 114.

55 *Prosecutor v Karadžić* (25 March 2016) para 5519.

importance of naming and, through it, acknowledging the loss of life, with Judge Schomburg stating that "it is of high importance and relevance that the names of those killed at that time are mentioned in open court",[56] though this information may not, strictly speaking, be necessary for the determination of innocence or guilt of the accused.

Similarly, in the case of *Prosecutor v Mrkšić et al.*, where three defendants stood accused of the abuse and execution of individuals who had been taken prisoner from the Vukovar hospital in November 1991, the identification of individual victims and an assessment of the causes of death was not necessary to the determinations of charges. However, following investigations into the mass grave at Ovčara, the vast majority of victims were named and the cause of death expressly identified. In a significant number of cases, ill-treatment prior to death was also documented. The names of those killed in the massacre were included in a schedule to the tribunal's judgment in the case, indicating a mindfulness to the needs of the victims and their families.[57] Expert testimony on the suffering of those surviving was also heard in other cases, contextualising the value of this level of truth information for victims and survivors.[58]

Forensic investigations of the type that featured during criminal proceedings have been conducted under the auspices of the respective court. In that sense, an authoritative investigation ought to be guaranteed. Whilst forensic investigations examine particular events, including the circumstances of an individual's suffering, they may, through inference, also reveal relevant information about the patterns of abuse. Forensic truth, in that way, can make a contribution to the structural elements of the right to the truth. These investigations' results are compiled in a report that ought to be accessible to others, intelligible, clear and unambiguous as well as explaining all the important scientific findings,[59] and they are publicly reported in court, but they only receive their "authoritative backing" when accepted by the judges (through what we call legal/judicial truth). Similarly, forensic truth does not offer an opportunity for victims to narrate their story in a public forum. Forensic truth might, however, corroborate such narratives on behalf of victims and become part of the historical truth (above).

Narrative truth

In our understanding of the right to the truth, it also implies an opportunity for victims to narrate their stories.[60] This places survivors in a more proactive

56 *Prosecutor v Deronjić* (30 September 2003) at 79.

57 See also *Prosecutor v Milutinović et al.* whose judgment gives a detailed list of the findings regarding the charges, including forensic examination of victims (*Prosecutor v Milutinović et al.* (26 February 2009) Vol. 2).

58 E.g. *Prosecutor v Krstić* (Judgment) IT-8–33 (2 August 2001) para 93.

59 For a description of what a report should contain see Marc Skinner, Djordje Alempijevic and Marija Djuric-Srejic 'Guidelines for International Forensic Bio-archaeology Monitors of Mass Grave Exhumations' (2003) 134(2) Forensic Science International 81 at 91–92.

60 See Chapter 3 and the section there on narrative truth.

role not only with regards to their own individual story but also in light of the contribution they can make to structural truth. We have noted how this is important in fora where state abuse is at issue since victims may be able to offer accurate and reliable information. Within the confines of a criminal judicial mechanisms, the role of victims is typically that of a witness (we turn to victim participation as a feature of the International Criminal Court in the next chapter).

In the courtroom, victims are required to respond to a series of questions about a defined and limited set of circumstances that may not give them the ability to recount their stories as they would perhaps have liked to. Instead they are expected to recount horrific memories relating to the events in question and undergo a public challenge to the veracity of their account. The realities of testifying in court may therefore be "ill-suited for the sort of expansive and nuanced story-telling so many witnesses yearn to engage in".[61] Testimony of that type may not meet the psychological desire to narrate ones story and therefore will fail to provide the necessary restorative element which forms the individual aspect of survivor narrative.[62] Nor may all traumatised victims be able to recall and account their story fully, since their memory may be affected. The chamber in *Karadžić*, for example, described its assessment of all witness testimonies, including victims, as follows:

> In its evaluation of witnesses testifying viva voce or pursuant to Rule 92 ter, the Chamber had regard to, inter alia, the demeanour of witnesses, as well as to the passage of time since the events charged in the Indictment and its possible impact on the reliability of the evidence. With regard to all witnesses, the Chamber also assessed the probability and the consistency of their evidence as well as the circumstances of the case and corroboration from other evidence.[63]

Nonetheless, many victims have made the (at times very long) journey into the court room to face the perpetrator, the defence team, judges and prosecutors to account their experiences. Witness O, who appeared in the *Krstić* trial, was one such victim-witness. He testified on the Srebrenica massacre, as he had survived the shooting at an execution site and managed to escape.[64] He recounted his ordeal pointing to the systematic efforts that went into the killings. At the end of his testimony, he was asked by Judge Rodrigues: "Is there anything else that you would like to say and that you have not had a chance

61 Eric Stover, *The Witnesses. War Crimes and the Promise of Justice in The Hague* (University of Pennsylvania Press 2005) at 129.

62 E.g. Judith Herman, *Trauma and Recovery: The aftermath of violence – from domestic abuse to political terror* (Basic Books 1997).

63 *Prosecutor v Karadžić* (25 March 2016) para 11.

64 *Prosecutor v Krstić* (13 April 2000) at 2859–2935.

to say?"[65] demonstrating the mindfulness of allowing the victims at least some scope to add, following the examination-in-chief and cross-examination, additional elements they feel are important. Others, like Habiba Hadžić, a former detainee at Sušica camp who asked Dragan Nikolic a question, or Emir Beganović, a former detainee at the Omarska camp testified before the tribunal (in the *Dusko Tadić* case and later in 2000 in the *Kvočka et al.* case) to recount their horrific experiences also on behalf of those who had perished during such circumstances.

In his study on witnesses before the ICTY, Stover argues that, in addition to seeking retributive justice and alleviating the psychological pain, it is also the notion of fulfilling a moral duty that seems to be of great importance for those choosing to testify.[66] Stepakoff et al. anchor this obligation in the moral judgments of distinguishing right from wrong which compels witnesses to testify. Within this notion of fulfilling a moral duty, three further aspects are relevant findings from the literature: the desire on behalf of witnesses "1) to make known the truth; 2) to prevent future war crimes; and 3) to honor victims".[67] In their own study into witnesses testifying before the Sierra Leonean Special Tribunal, the response given most frequently by participants was "to denounce wrongs committed against me during the war" followed by "to contribute to public knowledge about the war".[68] In this regard, victims who testify may see themselves as contributors to the right to truth realisation by advancing the public, eventually authoritative, acknowledgment of their own suffering and that of others.

Insofar as the opportunity to narrate one's story forms part of the right to the truth, international criminal trials will offer aspects of this to certain victims, so long as it is in relation to the indictment. Furthermore, the number of victim witnesses appearing before criminal trials is limited. In this regard, the possibility to realise narrative truth is limited too for international criminal tribunals. As we will see in the next chapter, the ICC has struggled to find a way to adequately represent hundreds of victims of crimes, let alone give them a voice in the trials. As a result, to the extent that survivor narrative falls within the remit of the right to the truth, alternative and more appropriate fora for this form of truth-telling, including, for example, through the establishment of a specific victims' forum or an oral histories public documentation and archiving mechanism, are needed.

65 Ibid at 2935.

66 E.g. Stover *supra* note 61 and Eric Stover, Mychelle Balthazard and Alexa Koenig, 'Confronting Duch: Civil Party Participation in Case 001 at the Extraordinary Chambers in the Courts of Cambodia' (2011) 93 International Review of the Red Cross 503.

67 Shanee Stepakoff, Shawn Reynolds, Simon Charters and Nicola Henry, 'Why testify? Witnesses' Motivations for Giving Evidence in a War Crimes Tribunal in Sierra Leone' (2014) 8 International Journal of Transitional Justice 426 at 431

68 Ibid at 426. The study encompassed 200 individuals testifying for the defence as well as the prosecution and included victims, insiders and child combatants. Nonetheless, the desire to contribute to the establishment of the truth seems to prevail across the participant groups.

Legal truth

Tribunals seeking to make detailed findings about political and social events have, of course, been criticised as not producing the "best approximation of history".[69] What they do produce, beyond the trial record, are judgments at trial or appeal level. These legal findings are what we call the "legal truth" pronounced to a high standard of proof. Some of these findings may be of historical interest. And in fact, the judgment in the landmark case of Radovan Karadžić, the highest ranking official to be tried in the 23-year history of the ICTY, is likely to go down in international criminal law, if not history, books. It confirms the atrocities committed in Bosnia's war from 1992 to 1995. Of the 11 counts that Mr. Karadžić was indicted for, he was found not guilty on the first count of genocide in certain municipalities, but guilty for all the other ten counts, including genocide in Srebrenica; persecution, extermination, murder; deportation and inhumane acts of forcible transfer as crimes against humanity; as well as murder, terror, unlawful attacks on civilians and hostage taken as violations of the laws or custom of war.[70] A 40-year sentence was the result of this guilty verdict. In 2017, General Mladić's case ended in a similar conviction.[71]

Once again, it is worth remembering that the scope of a trial is based on the selection of charges, incidents and modes of liability on behalf of the prosecutor based upon the materials and facts before her. And at the ad hoc tribunals, the prosecution "will not submit to the court evidence that does not support the prosecution case, however historically significant it might be".[72] This is to avoid entanglement in political antagonisms since the capacity of trials to further general knowledge about broader, historical events has raised significant scepticism.[73] As truth commissions, tribunals have been created within a particular political context. They exist because of political will and the events that preceded them. Just as the charge of victor's justice has been raised against the Nuremberg Tribunal, defendants before international criminal tribunals have tried to argue a lack of legitimacy and legality for the UN-backed trials,[74] allegedly compromising

69 Judge Wald is referring to her experience at the ICTY where a considerable proportion of judgments focused on the nature and cause of the conflict. (Patricia Wald 'The International Criminal Tribunal for the Former Yugoslavia Comes of Age: Some Observations on Day-To-Day Dilemmas of an International Court' (2001) 5 Journal of Law & Policy 87 at 116–117). Although she is cautious about the historical value of the ICTY judgment, she hopes that the ICTY will make a contribution to publicising the awfulness and atrocities of armed conflict and the impact war has on civilians. In that sense, she may be seen to agree with expressive theory of morally condemning such atrocities.

70 *Prosecutor v Karadžić* (25 March 2016) paras 6000–6010.

71 *Prosecutor v Mladić* (22 November 2017).

72 Gaynor *supra* note 14 at 1272. This is in contrast to the Rome Statute, Article 54(1)(a).

73 E.g. Martti Koskenniemi, 'Between Impunity and Show Trials' in Frowein J and Wolfrum R (eds) *Max Planck Yearbook of United Nations Law* (Martinus Nijhoff Publishers 2002) 1.

74 E.g. *Prosecutor v Tadić* (2 October 1995), Part II: Unlawful establishment of the international tribunal, para 9 onwards; *Prosecutor v Milošević* (8 November 2001). Karadžić called the ICTY a "court of NATO" (*Prosecutor v Karadžić* (29 August 2008) at 31.

their ability of independence and objectivity. In this regard, the findings of such trials can remain contested between the parties to the former conflict.[75]

Nevertheless, the International Court of Justice has clearly expressed its faith in the judgments and that "it should in principle accept as highly persuasive relevant findings of fact made by the Tribunal at trial".[76]

It ought to be remembered that judgments operate with a particular level of proof (beyond reasonable doubt) unlikely to be employed by historians, though the actual verdicts may not be as effortlessly processed as historical accounts: the readability of judgments coupled with their length and technical detail (especially in appeal decisions) are not (to put it mildly) to everyone's liking or indeed easily understandable by a lay person. That said, the media frenzy around the highly anticipated *Karadžić* verdict also demonstrates an acute interest in the outcome of such trials. Not everyone may have read the actual judgment, but the summaries of judgments are usually available and much easier to digest, as are the ICTY's case information sheets prepared for each individual defendant.[77] In addition, tribunals have archives accessible to researchers, outreach activities, dedicated web portal and regional programmes to disseminate the work of the courts. For those interested in individual names and stories, as discussed earlier, they can appear in judgments. To many commentators, and no doubt victims, the verdict identifies Radovan Karadžić as utilising extermination, torture, rape, forced deportation and persecution as a way to create an ethnically pure Serb state within the territory of Bosnia at the costs of Bosnian Muslims and Croats,[78] offering an evidence-based link between Karadžić's policy and the destruction, death and suffering amid the conflict.[79]

What do judgments offer towards the realisation of the right to truth? First and foremost, looking at the expanded version of the right to the truth definition, which includes the naming of the perpetrators, judicial verdicts are significant since they establish individual criminal responsibility beyond reasonable doubt, as well as naming in the judgment associates if it is not a joined trial.[80]

75 This is evident in the mixed reactions to the Karadžić verdict where "political and ethnic divisions were on display" (Rodolfo Toe, 'Bosnian Media Split Over Karadzic Verdict' Balkan Transitional Justice (26 March 2016)).

76 ICJ, Case Concerning Application of the Convention on the Prevention and Punishment of the Crime of Genocide (Bosnia v Serbia) (26 February 2007) para 223.

77 ICTY, The Cases www.icty.org/en/action/cases/ accessed 14 February 2019. However, the ICTR's legacy website has no such different pieces of information.

78 Refik Hodzic, 'Post-Karadzic Bosnia and Herzegovina: The End of the Criminal Justice Era' (4 November 2016) www.ictj.org/news/karadzic-bosnia-herzegovina-criminal-justice#.VwvL_wtXbgc.twitter (accessed 14 February 2019).

79 Denisa Kostovicova, 'The Karadzic verdict: How the trial played out and what it means for Bosnia' http://blogs.lse.ac.uk/europpblog/2016/03/24/the-karadzic-verdict-how-the-trial-played-out-and-what-it-means-for-bosnia/ (accessed 14 February 2019).

80 There is a section in the Karadžić judgment on the knowledge and acts of named alleged members of the Joint Criminal Enterprise (*Prosecutor v Karadžić* (25 March 2016) para 1224–1254).

These judgments are de facto predicated on an investigation and are authoritative through their process.

In addition, they contain information that is relevant to individuals whose suffering may be included, described or acknowledged in the judicial documents, whether that is relating to rape, torture, cruel treatment, killings, detention, shelling, sniping or otherwise. This includes the impact and lasting effects of suffering on the survivor population. In *Krstić*, the trial chamber explicitly referred to the Srebrenica syndrome, thus implicitly acknowledging the very rationale for the right to the truth as well as establishing the "not knowing" as part of the crime of genocide, since it constitutes serious mental harm.

> One of the primary factors giving rise to the [Srebrenica] syndrome is that, with few exceptions, the fate of the survivor's loved ones is not officially known: the majority of men of Srebrenica are still listed as missing. For Bosnian Muslim women it is essential to have a clear marital status, whether widowed, divorced or married: a woman whose husband is missing does not fit within any of these categories. Moreover, on a psychological level, these women are unable to move forward with the process of recovery without the closure that comes from knowing with certainty what has happened to their family members and properly grieving for them. The Trial Chamber also heard of the collective guilt experienced by women because they survived the events in Potočari and their husbands, brothers and fathers did not.[81]

Similarly, structural information is revealed about the scale, targets and methods associated with international crimes. This is significant, since some of these facts and events can be highly disputed and politically charged. This includes, for example, the movement of populations during a conflict, the use of child-soldiers, the siege of a city like Sarajevo, the running of a prison like Tuol Sleng in Phnom Penh,[82] the role of the media broadcasts in conflict[83] or numbers of victims in a given conflict area, as was at issue in *Karadžić* and the Srebrenica massacre.[84]

Finally, the judgments also allude to the many witnesses (in text and in footnotes) that have come before the chambers to testify. Their contribution to the findings, their credibility or non-veracity is discussed and contextualised by other evidence presented. This includes the narrative truth expressed by victims, which then becomes part of an authoritative account.

81 *Prosecutor v Krstić* (2 August 2001) para 93. See also Karadžić judgment (*Prosecutor v Karadžić* (25 March 2016) para 5664) on the serious mental harm inflicted on the surviving family members and loves ones of those killed.

82 *Case 001 against Kaing Guek Eav alias Duch* (26 July 2010) page 42 onwards.

83 *Prosecutor v Haimana, Barayagwiza and Ngeze* (3 December 2003).

84 *Prosecutor v Karadžić* (25 March 2016) pages 2303–2342.

Conclusion

Justice Jackson famously said that the Nuremberg prosecutions were to provide "undeniable proofs of incredible events".[85] In an early decision of the International Criminal Tribunal for the Former Yugoslavia, the ambition of international criminal justice is to "pursue its mission of revealing the truth about the acts perpetrated and suffering endured, as well as identifying and arresting those accused of responsibility".[86] The preceding discussion has demonstrated that criminal trials have a potential to contribute to various forms of truth; they can accrue information of historical value, engage forensic and expert investigations to create seemingly scientific and objective information to facilitate a just outcome and be mindful of victims and human rights discourses as part of their processes, yet they are founded on the tradition of legal positivism. They are, however – at least the ad hoc and hybrid tribunals – created through a political, albeit legally validated, process.

The question that also arises is whether international criminal trials can function as an extension of states and fulfil their obligation since the states themselves, with their judicial system, are deemed not to be in a position to hold alleged perpetrators for crimes of such a magnitude to account. In this regard, ad hoc tribunals take on the function of working towards the realisation of the right to truth since the state(s) in question have failed to do so. In addition, international criminal trials offer "reliable findings of fact and collections of evidence for use in domestic courts and other forums".[87] They can function as "starters" of the truth realisation process which is to be continued at state level or complemented through other processes.

Despite the prospect of realisation of important elements of the right to the truth through the conduct of international criminal proceedings, the avenue is not available to many victims and families who need answers. International criminal actions are relatively few in number, and since individuals are unable to initiate an action, they must simply hope that the circumstances of an action coincide with their own needs for truth. Alternatively, they need to find other ways of working toward the realisation. Notwithstanding the truth-seeking function of international criminal tribunals, their primary goal remains the determination of guilt or innocence of the defendant. The determination and nature of truth which they produce tends to be allied to that goal, but realisation cannot be guaranteed, resulting in the risk that victims may feel disappointed and disenchanted with the lack of truth realisation, primarily at the individual and narrative level.

85 International Military Tribunal, Trial of the Major War Criminals Before the International Military Tribunal 104 (1947) at 99.
86 *Prosecutor v Karadžić and Mladić* (11 July 1996) para 3.
87 Groome *supra* note 1 at 176.

References

Clark J N, *International Trials and Reconciliation: assessing the impact of the international criminal tribunal for the former Yugoslavia* (Routledge 2014).
Combs N, *Guilty Pleas In International Criminal Law : Constructing A Restorative Justice Approach* (Stanford University Press 2007).
Ellis S, 'Truth and Reconciliation Commission of South Africa Report, Volumes 1–5. Pretoria: Government Printer, October 1998' (2000) 42 Transformation 61.
Fletcher L, Weinstein H and Rowen J, 'Context, timing and the dynamics of transitional justice: A historical perspective' (2009) 31(1) Human Rights Quarterly 163.
Fletcher L and Weinstein H, 'Violence and Social Repair: Rethinking the Contribution of Justice to Reconciliation' (2002) 24 Human Rights Quarterly 573.
Gaynor F, 'Uneasy Partners – Evidence, Truth and History in International Trials' (2012) 10(5) Journal of International Criminal Justice 1257.
Groome D, 'The Right to Truth in the Fight Against Impunity' (2011) 29(1) Berkeley Journal of International Law 175.
Henckaerts J-M and Doswald-Beck L, *Customary International Humanitarian Law, Volume I: Rules* (Cambridge University Press 2006).
Herman J, *Trauma and Recovery: The aftermath of violence – from domestic abuse to political terror* (Basic Books 1997).
Hodzic R, 'Post-Karadzic Bosnia and Herzegovina: The End of the Criminal Justice Era' (4 November 2016) www.ictj.org/news/karadzic-bosnia-herzegovina-criminal-justice#.VwvL_wtXbgc.twitter accessed 14 February 2019.
International Committee of the Red Cross, 'Guiding Principles/Model Law on the Missing' (2009) available at www.icrc.org/en/document/guiding-principles-model-law-missing-model-law accessed 14 February 2019.
International Criminal Tribunal for the Former Yugoslavia, 'The Cases' available at www.icty.org/en/action/cases/ accessed 14 February 2019.
Jacobs D, '6 Quick Thoughts on the Karadzic Judgment' https://dovjacobs.com/2016/03/25/6-quick-thoughts-on-the-karadzic-judgment/ accessed 14 February 2019.
Jones B, Baumgartner E and Gabriel S, 'A Transformative Approach to Dealing with the Past' (February 2015) swiss peace.
Koskenniemi M, 'Between Impunity and Show Trials' in Frowein J and Wolfrum R (eds) *Max Planck Yearbook of United Nations Law* (Martinus Nijhoff Publishers 2002) 1.
Kostovicova D, 'The Karadzic verdict: How the trial played out and what it means for Bosnia' http://blogs.lse.ac.uk/europpblog/2016/03/24/the-karadzic-verdict-how-the-trial-played-out-and-what-it-means-for-bosnia/ accessed 14 February 2019.
May R and Weirda M, 'Evidence before the ICTY' in May R, Tolbert D and Hocking J (eds) *Essays on Procedure and Evidence: In Honour of Gabrielle Kirk McDonald* (Kluwer 2001).
Parmentier S, 'Global Justice in the Aftermath of Mass Violence. The Role of the International Criminal Court in Dealing with Political Crimes', 13th World Congress of Criminology. Reducing Crimes and Promoting Justice: Challenges to Sciences, Policy and Practice (10–15 August 2003).
Schabas W, *Unimaginable Atrocities* (Oxford University Press 2012).
Scharf M and Williams P, 'The Functions of Justice and Anti-Justice in the Peace-Building Process' (2003) 35 Case Western Reserve Journal of International Law 161.

Skinner M, Alempijevic D and Djuric-Srejic M, 'Guidelines for International Forensic Bio-archaeology Monitors of Mass Grave Exhumations' (2003) 134(2) Forensic Science International 81.

Smith E, 'Investigating Rape at the International Criminal Court: The Impact of Trauma', 2012 (2) Issues in International Criminal Justice 99.

Stepakoff S, Reynolds S, Charters S and Henry N, 'Why testify? Witnesses' Motivations for Giving Evidence in a War Crimes Tribunal in Sierra Leone' (2014) 8 International Journal of Transitional Justice 426.

Stover E, *The Witnesses. War Crimes and the Promise of Justice in The Hague* (University of Pennsylvania Press 2005).

Stover E, Balthazard M and Koenig A, 'Confronting Duch: Civil Party Participation in Case 001 at the Extraordinary Chambers in the Courts of Cambodia' (2011) 93 International Review of the Red Cross 503.

Szoke-Burke S, 'Searching for the Right to Truth: The Impact of International Human Rights Law on National Transitional Justice Policies' (2015) 33(2) Berkeley Journal of International Law 526.

Toe R, 'Bosnian Media Split Over Karadzic Verdict' Balkan Transitional Justice (26 March 2016).

Van Schaack B and Slye R C, *International Criminal Law and Its Enforcement* (Foundation Press 2007).

Wald P, 'The International Criminal Tribunal for the Former Yugoslavia Comes of Age: Some Observations on Day-To-Day Dilemmas of an International Court' (2001) 5 Journal of Law & Policy 87.

Wald P, 'Foreword: War Tales and War Trials' (2008) 106 Michigan Law Review 901.

10 The right to the truth and the International Criminal Court

Introduction

The previous chapter on international criminal trials has demonstrated that, in principle and in some aspects of practice, such trials make a contribution towards the realisation of the right to the truth, even if this has not been done *expressis verbis*. In this chapter we turn to the International Criminal Court as the permanent institution for international criminal justice. Like other statutes of international criminal institutions, the Rome Statute too is silent on the right to the truth. And yet much hope on behalf of victims is pinned on the Court's ability to realise their right to justice, truth and remedy.[1] In fact, it has been written that "[t]he primary, and perhaps most important, right of victims in the context of international criminal proceedings is their right to the truth".[2] As the following discussion will show, this hope not only hinges around victim participation[3] but also on the statutory provisions for an investigation to "establish the truth"[4] and for the Court "to request the submission of all evidence that it considers necessary for the determination of the truth".[5]

While the Rome Statute includes a number of victim-focused provisions, the victim is not a party to the action, and so is unable to directly pursue his or her right to the truth against the defendant.

1 For a discussion of victims' role before the ICC see, for example, Brianne McGonigle Leyh, *Procedural Justice? Victim Participation in International Criminal Proceedings* (Intersentia 2011); Christine Chung 'Victims' Participation at the International Criminal Court: Are Concessions of the Court Clouding the Promise' (2008) 6(3) Northwestern Journal of International Human Rights 459; Salvatore Zappalà, 'The rights of victims v the rights of the accused' (2010) 8(1) *Journal of International Criminal Justice* 137; and Mariana Pena and Gaelle Carayon, 'Is the ICC making the Most of Victim Participation' (2013) 7(3) International Journal of Transitional Justice 518.

2 Guénaël Mettraux, 'Victims' participation in international criminal law' (2010) 8(1) Journal of International Criminal Justice 75 at 77. See also *Prosecutor v Kenyatta* (20 February 2014) at 9

3 Article 68(3) of the Rome Statute provides that: "[w]here the personal interests of the victims are affected, the Court shall permit their views and concerns to be presented and considered at stages of the proceedings determined to be appropriate by the Court and in a manner which is not prejudicial to or inconsistent with the rights of the accused and a fair impartial trial." (Rome Statute of the International Criminal Court (17 July 1998))

4 Article 54(1)(a).

5 Article 69(3).

However, at the ICC, the right to the truth has been invoked to urge for an effective investigation[6] as well as victim involvement in investigations,[7] demand accurate charging,[8] argue against delays of proceedings,[9] reiterate the importance of victims to be heard[10], request access to information[11] and in relation to reparations.[12]

In the following we will thematically examine these submissions and decisions before analysing the role judges may play in advancing the right to the truth, particularly with reference to Article 69(3).

Calling for the right to the truth

The most explicit discussion of the right to the truth at the ICC came through the single judge decision by Judge Steiner in the *Katanga and Ngudjolo* case in 2008 on a set of procedural rights attached to the status of victims at the pre-trial stage.[13] In fact, a small section on victims' right to the truth is included. This decision explains how victims' core interests are affected, outlining first the empirical rationale for victims to seek judicial measures against alleged perpetrators to lie in their desire "to have a declaration of the truth by the competent body".[14] Therefore, and to achieve this authoritative declaration, victims have an interest in the accurate determination of facts, as well as the naming and identification of those deemed responsible along with a determination of their responsibility. This, Judge Steiner suggests, is the basis for the "well-established right to the truth for the victims of serious violations of human rights".[15] In support of this, she references the right to Articles 32 and 33 of the 1977 Additional Protocol I to the Geneva Conventions, jurisprudence of the human rights courts and national courts, and academic opinion suggesting the right is emerging as a customary norm.[16] Expressly, Judge Steiner includes the identification of responsible persons as a key element of victims' right to the truth.

6 *Situation in the Republic of Kenya* (3 August 2015); *Prosecutor v Bemba* (21 December 2009). This argument was also brought by an accused in *Prosecutor v Gaddafi and Al-Senussi* (31 May 2013); and the defence when asking the Prosecutor to accept errors in its evidence collection and appraisal (*Prosecutor v Ruto and Sang*, (8 May 2013).
7 *Situation in Darfur* (24 June 2008).
8 *Prosecutor v Kenyatta* (24 July 2012).
9 *Prosecutor v Ntaganda* (30 June 2015); *Prosecutor v Kenyatta* (23 May 2013).
10 *Prosecutor v Blé Goudé* (9 February 2015).
11 *Prosecutor v Gbagbo* (8 August 2012); *Prosecutor v Bemba* (21 December 2009). The defence has also argued that disclosure on behalf of the victims would be in the interest of the truth (*Prosecutor v Katanga and Ngudjolo* (10 November 2009).
12 *Prosecutor v Lubanga* (18 April 2012).
13 *Prosecutor v Katanga and Ngudjolo* (13 May 2008).
14 Ibid para 31.
15 Ibid para 32.
16 Ibid at footnote 39.

In seeking to satisfy the right to the truth as part of international criminal proceedings, victim participation is important insofar as the victims

(i) bring clarity about what indeed happened; and
(ii) close possible gaps between the factual findings resulting from the criminal proceedings and the actual truth.[17]

Further, she contends that findings regarding the accused (whether this results in an acquittal or conviction) affect the very "core interests of those granted the procedural status of victim in any case before the Court insofar as this issue is inherently linked to the satisfaction of their right to the truth".[18] For victim participation to be meaningful includes the pretrial stage of a case as well.[19] In addition, such participation, she outlines later in the decision, will also ensure societally relevant information (such as culture)[20] is revealed, which would add legitimacy to the Court, foster dissemination and advance accountability.[21]

Judge Steiner's conception of the right to the truth presupposes that individual victims ought to contribute to the fact-finding and proceedings before the ICC. The right to the truth is the link explaining victims' interest. Victims' contributions may advance the understanding of some particular circumstances and individual suffering, but also societal aspects and information relevant to a specific population. More so, the judge identifies a potential discrepancy between the legal/judicial truth emanating from criminal proceedings and the "actual truth". In her view, victims are able to make the two congruent through offering additional, complementary information. This is an admission of the inherent truth-value-limits of legal/judicial truth; it does not necessarily fulfil the meaning of the "right to the truth". Yet, the judge suggests that a function of the Court ought to work towards the realisation of the right. In other words, the right to the truth should be considered as an outcome of the Court. For the legal/judicial truth to offer the *accurate* determination of facts, as well as the naming and identification of those deemed responsible along with a determination of their responsibility, an element of victims' narratives is needed. We called this narrative truth in the previous chapters. Only then, in Judge Steiner's reading, can the right to the truth be fulfilled through ascertaining the "actual truth". Without it, legal/judicial truth risks falling short of what the right to the truth requires.

Investigations meeting the right to the truth?

Investigations conducted for criminal tribunals are typically concerned with one particular geographical area and temporal scope (albeit potentially a number of

17 Ibid para 34.
18 Ibid para 35.
19 Ibid para 157
20 Ibid para 162
21 Ibid para 163.

conflicts). At the ICC, however, a number of situations concurrently may need investigation if a situation has been referred by a state party (Article 14), initiated proprio motu by the prosecutor (Article 15) or been referred via a Security Council referral. Out of these situations, and following the initiation of an investigation (Article 53), cases may arise. In line with Article 54(1)(a), the prosecutor, "[i]n order to establish the truth, [shall] extend the investigation to cover all facts and evidence relevant to an assessment of whether there is criminal responsibility under this Statute, and, in doing so, investigation incriminating and exonerating circumstances equally".

An effective investigation

Naturally, victims have an interest in effective investigations since they will ensure that the truth is established and those responsible are tried. The question then arises, what would an effective investigation that would satisfy the requirements of the right to the truth look like? Following the collapse of the *Kenya II* cases, this question came to the fore: victims suggested that the prosecution had failed to conduct an effective investigation into the crimes committed. In a submission to the Court, the legal representative of victims argued that an effective investigation "imposes an obligation to proceed even in unconducive environments, including in the face of obstruction of justice".[22] A number of measures beyond Article 54(2) and (3) are at the prosecution's disposal. They include Article 56 on an unique investigative opportunity, Article 57(3) powers of the Pre-Trial Chamber, Article 64(6) on Trial Chamber powers and Article 69(3) powers, but also provisions to ensure the security interests of states or concerns are resolved cooperatively (Article 72(5)) and to secure cooperation (Articles 87(7) and 93(1)). In particular, Article 93(1)(i) requires states parties to comply with requests for assistance in "the provision of records and documents, including official records and documents". And Article 93(1)(g) suggests state cooperation in "the examination of places or sites, including the exhumation and examination of grave sites".[23] Failure, on behalf of the prosecutor, to effectively investigate and prosecute would constitute a breach of Article 54(1).[24]

To further flesh out what an effective investigation under Article 54(1) means, the submission resorts to international law and international human rights standards (as expressed, for example, in the Basic Principles or the Principles on the Effective Prevention and Investigation of Extra-Legal, Arbitrary and Summary

22 *Situation in the Republic of Kenya* (3 August 2015) para 5.

23 The prosecutor concluded such a memorandum of understanding with the Libyan authorities to support investigations and the exchange of information, subject to confidentiality provisions (see John Ciociari and Jesse Frabzblau, 'Hidden Files: Archival Sharing, Accountability, and the Right to the Truth' (2014) 46(1) *Columbia Human Rights Law Review* 1. Despite this, an ICC decision in December 2014 ruled on the non-compliance of Libya with request for cooperation and referred the matter to the UN Security Council (*Prosecutor v Gaddafi* (10 December 2014)).

24 *Situation in the Republic of Kenya* (3 August 2015) para 41.

Executions), suggesting an investigation has to be prompt, thorough and impartial. Jurisprudence from the European Court of Human Rights and the Inter-American Court is cited to support the view that "the right of a victim of serious crimes to timely and robust investigation and prosecution"[25] has been established.

Since obstruction to the investigation has come from the state of Kenya, a remedy is available through Article 87(7). When a state fails to comply with cooperation requests from the Court and thus prevents the Court from exercising its functions under the Rome Statute, the Court can refer the issue to the Assembly of States Parties or the Security Council (if the situation was referred by the Security Council). In any event, the submission argues, "the prosecution remains bound under article 54(1)(b) to continue to take appropriate measures in order to ensure that its investigation and prosecution are effective".[26] The Statute acknowledges challenging environments for investigations and provides for the possibility of states unwilling to assist to ensure the effective investigative duty of the prosecution is fulfilled.

Reviewing prosecutorial decisions regarding investigations

The key point made by the legal representative of victims is that victims must have standing to challenge the prosecutorial decision and to test the validity of the decision when there is doubt due to an error of procedure, an error of law or an error of fact, since victims' rights to the truth, justice and reparation are at stake. The submission states emphatically that

> [t]he framers of the Statute cannot have intended victims to be without recourse in such a situation. To the contrary, the Statute places the victims at the centre of the justice process. Victims have a right to a just process, and to be treated fairly, at all stages of the proceedings, including the investigation phase.[27]

Representations by victims under Article 15 were made, and Rule 93 stipulates that a "Chamber may seek the views for victims or their legal representatives participating pursuant to Rules 89 to 91 on any issue".[28] As a general principle, Rule 86 provides that "the needs of all victims and witnesses" should be taken into account by a Chamber or other organ of the Court when making any direction of order.[29]

25 Ibid para 49. See also chapters 6 and 7 where the authority of an investigation and the effectiveness of an investigation are discussed.

26 Ibid para 51.

27 Ibid para 89.

28 International Criminal Court, Rules of Procedure and Evidence (9 September 2002) Rule 93.

29 Rule 86.

Whilst the statute does not explicitly discuss a remedy for victims in a case where the prosecution has failed in its duty, the legal representative suggests (in the submission on the collapsed Kenya cases), that therefore a review of the decision under Articles 68 and 21 is appropriate, since there exists a lacuna in the statute. Under those circumstances, a chamber may have recourse to general principles of law derived from national law (Article 21(1)(c)) and ensure that its application and interpretation of the statute is consistent with internationally recognised human rights law (Article 21(3)). The submission goes on to give numerous examples of judicial reviews.

Alternatively, the submission argues that a review of the decision can also be made under Article 53(3)(b) which provides for review of a prosecutorial decision not to proceed if that decision is based on an investigation or prosecution not serving the interest of justice. The prosecutor, in this case, believed a prosecution would be in the interest of justice but accepted its own investigative shortcoming. The Office of the Prosecutor (OTP) made a decision not to proceed. The victim representative invites the chamber to nonetheless apply the "not in the interest of justice" category to the decision since the prosecutor has chosen not to prosecute despite a case satisfying statutory criteria for investigation and prosecution.[30]

On 5 November 2015, the request was rejected.[31] The Chamber did not agree that there was a lacuna in the statute, since Article 53 regulates a Pre-Trial Chamber's competence to review the prosecutor's exercise of her power regarding investigation and prosecutions. A "constructive interpretation"[32] of the statute through Articles 21 and 68 was dismissed. Furthermore, regarding a possibility for review under Article 53, the Chamber reiterates the prosecutorial position that "a decision not to prosecute has not been taken".[33] No notification under Rule 106 which governs a decision by the prosecutor not to prosecute has been recorded.[34] The decision is silent on what an effective investigation might mean.

This outcome is unsurprising and consistent with other ICC decisions. Review of prosecutorial decisions not to continue with an investigation has not been possible due to the fact that the prosecution has not formally closed but only suspended investigations.[35] In that way, the prosecution has essentially avoided having their prosecutorial discretions questioned or overseen. This can be viewed as detrimental to the victims interest as so clearly outlined by the legal representative statements that "[t]he Victims' rights under the Statute to truth, justice and reparation have proved wholly illusory".[36] On the other hand, if a case ends in

30 *Situation in the Republic of Kenya* (3 August 2015) para 151.
31 Ibid.
32 Ibid para 18.
33 Ibid para 25.
34 Ibid para 27.
35 *Situation in the Democratic Republic of Congo* (17 August 2007) at 5. For a discussion of Art 53 see Gilbert Bitti, 'ICC Statute Article 53' (23 June 2017) available at www.cilrap.org/cilrap-film/53-bitti accessed 14 February 2019.
36 *Situation in the Republic of Kenya* (3 August 2015) para 111.

an acquittal based on insufficient evidence, then the victims' rights, including the right to the truth would be equally compromised.

Two key issues arise for the right to the truth: first, since there has not been such a review, we do not know what an effective investigation in the context of the ICC means. Therefore, we can only speculate, in line with the legal representative, what it ought to mean. Second, it is unclear whether the effective investigation would be interpreted in light of the right to the truth. This is significant, because, as discussed in the human rights chapters of this book, the right to the truth is seen as part of the procedural limb by which the state is under the duty to undertake an effective investigation into human rights violations. At the ICC, the investigative element is carried out by the prosecutor with the authoritative declaration then made by the Court following its own independent fact-finding (if needed). According to the single judge ruling, we know that the right to the truth is a consideration for victim participation and the determination of their interests. What we do not know is whether there is a duty on the prosecutor in line with Article 54 to have regard to the right to the truth. The Statute clearly stipulate that they shall "establish the truth". Implicitly, one can infer that the right to the truth of victims, together with Rule 86, falls within this truth-seeking function, but this has not been confirmed.

Independent investigation

Investigation related decisions on behalf of the prosecutor can significantly limit the emergence of facts and, consequently, the truth as opposed to advancing it.[37] An independent, authoritative, investigation is desirable (and an aspect of the right to the truth). This was noted in a decision on the admissibility of the case against Gaddafi, where an investigation under the auspices of the ICC was initially favoured over a national investigation which would "promulgate stereotypes and will be deleterious to the rights of victims and the international community to know the truth"[38] (interestingly here, and in relation to heinous crimes, the international community becomes the right holder of the public element of the right to the truth).[39] Therefore, it is worth remembering why the conduct of an

37 Aptel suggests the Prosecutor is seeking to preserve her prosecutorial discretionary powers to the detriment of victims' interests (Cécile Aptel, 'Prosecutorial Discretion at the ICC and Victims' right to a Remedy', (2012) 10(5) Journal of International Criminal Justice 1357).

38 *Prosecutor v Gaddafi and Al-Senussi* (31 May 2013) para 95. There was also concern expressed that the accused was at risk of being tortured and killed in detention thus also depriving victims of the right to the truth (ibid., para 169).

39 In an unsigned statement by Saif al Islam Gaddafi, he also extends the right to truth to himself: 1. I want to face justice. 2. I want to do so because I believe that Libya, the victims in Libya, the internationally [sic] community and myself – all have a right to the truth, and for the truth to be made public. 3. I would have liked to have been tried in Libya by Libyan judges under Libyan law in front of the Libyan people. But what has been happening in my case cannot be called a trial. 4. The truth is only possible in a fair and impartial trial. 5. There will be no truth if I am kept locked up and silenced in a remote mountain village, with no or

independent investigation and prosecution process is so important: it is believed to be the guarantor for an authoritative investigation of both the events that led to atrocity and to the particular circumstances of suffering. Crucially, since the prosecutor is not an agent of any given state, the independence of an ICC investigation could be deemed greater than one conducted domestically. That said, the "in the interest of justice" discretion is available to the prosecutor and criticism has been voiced over the way in which the Court has accommodated states and major powers.[40] The results of an investigation, in turn, will be publicly reported, communicated and challenged during the trial phase. Only after that, a declaration by the Court is issued. Insofar as the investigation produces the evidence relied upon during the trial, it is an essential part of the Court's truth-finding exercise.

Precisely this lack of an "authoritative declaration" in the situation phase has been brought as an argument against victim participation, since "the right to truth cannot be realised at this stage, nor can it ever be realised outside of the context of a specific case".[41] Whilst that may be so, nonetheless decisions taken at the pre-trial phase significantly impact on the paths taken during proceedings. Some element of influence over and input into these investigative activities may be beneficial to bring to the Court's attention relevant information not considered by the prosecution. Such consultation of victims at the pretrial stage has been suggested.[42] Yet the only formal way for victims to influence the prosecutor's line of inquiry is through Article 15(3) if investigations are initiated by the prosecutor proprio motu[43] (as was the case in *Kenya II*). However, it has been noted that "victims are unlikely to impact on what arguably impacts them the

---

very limited possibility to speak to my lawyers in order to convey my defence. 6. There will also be no truth if witnesses are faced with possible life sentences for simply testifying in my favour, there is no security or protection for them, nor any consequences if these witnesses are threatened and killed. 7. There will certainly be no justice in the case, if the prosecution is based on evidence extracted from torture and other inadmissible evidence, or persons who are too scared to say the truth'.

40 E.g. David Bosco, *Rough Justice: The International Criminal Court's Battle to Fix the World, One Prosecution at a Time* (Oxford University Press 2014).

41 *Situation in Darfur* (3 July 2008) para 63.

42 See Pena and Carayon *supra* n 1.

43 According to Article 15(3) victims are entitled to "make representations to the Pre-Trial Chamber". In the Kenya situation, Pre-Trial Chamber II issued an order for the VPRS to "(1) identify, to the extent possible, the community leaders of the affected groups to act on behalf of those victims who may wish to make representations (collective representation); (2) receive victims' representations (collective and/or individual); (3) conduct an assessment, in accordance with paragraph 8 of this order, whether the conditions set out in Rule 85 of the Rules have been met; and (4) summarize victims' representations into one consolidated report with the original representations annexed thereto" (*Situation in the Republic of Kenya* (10 December 2009) at 9). See also *Situation in Cote D'Ivoire* (6 July 2011).These victims' representations can influence pre-trial chamber decisions regarding the gravity threshold, geographical region, time range, widespread nature, category and elements of crime, nature of conflict as well as interest of justice considerations (*Situation in the Republic of Kenya* (13 March 2010); see also Hans-Peter Kaul, 'Developments at the International Criminal Court' (2005) 99 The American Journal of International Law 370).

most – the nature and scope of the prosecutor's investigation".[44] Legal representatives have argued the same, saying that "[p]recluding Victim Participation at the Very Gateway of the Proceedings, the Situation Stage, Threatens to Deny Victims Their 'Right to Truth'".[45] If victims are not able to meaningfully participate at the investigation stage, then what follows in the proceedings may not reflect the "actual truth" of events. However, and this was stressed by the defence, the right to the truth is not synonymous with victim participation.[46] The right to the truth exists independent of victim participation, and Article 68(3) enshrines that participation is compatible with a fair and impartial trial.

One victims' group submission for a line of investigation may potentially conflict with the interest of another victim or victim group, whether that group or individual is represented at the ICC or not. Whose right to the truth is to prevail? Here we have the potential for tension in the realisation of the right to the truth aspects: the individual victim's desire for an investigative line of inquiry might not be compatible with that of others or with the public element of right to the truth (and vice versa). The prosecution might argue that it will seek to investigate in the most "representational manner", where specific crimes, including victim suffering, are representative of the pattern of abuse, or what it deems to be societally most relevant and pertinent (bearing in mind that the gravity of crimes adjudicated before the ICC automatically implies the most heinous of crimes). In other words, the prosecution could contend that precisely the right to the truth of victims motivates its decision-making. In this sense, the defence submitted that "the primary mechanism by which alleged victims can seek to facilitate the Court's search for the truth at this phase is via the interaction with the Prosecutor rather than the Pre-Trial Chamber".[47] The defence deems Article 15(2) more suitable for such a communication as opposed to Article 15(3). The latter permits the making of representations by victims to the Pre-Trial Chamber when the prosecutor investigates proprio motu. However, a victim seeking to have their right to the truth realised, quite naturally would seek any possibility available to them to further the realisation of the right. This is particularly so as alternate avenues, especially at state level, have presumably failed or been exhausted, or else the ICC would not be involved. Hence a representation under Article 15(3) seems a reasonable step permissible under the Statute.

At the ad hoc tribunals (with the exception of the ECCC), there was no formal division or challenge from within the system (in the form of victims) to the prosecutor's representative capacity of victims' interests and the international

44 Carla Ferstman, 'The Participation of Victims in International Criminal Court Proceedings. A Review of the Practices and Consideration of Options for the Future', REDRESS Report (October 2012) at 44. The 2006 framework decision on a general right to participate in the investigation was confined by an appeal chamber decision to judicial proceedings arguing that the investigation phase as a whole does not constitute a judicial proceeding (e.g. *Situation in the Democratic Republic of Congo* (19 December 2008).

45 *Situation in Darfur* (24 June 2008) section VII heading at 23.

46 *Situation in Darfur* (3 July 2008) para 60.

47 Ibid para 64.

community. Therefore, one could argue that victims' interests were naturally, and without recourse to challenges, assumed by the prosecutor during investigations.

Charges: the selection of offence and modes of offending

Allied to the investigation is also the charging strategy of the prosecution. Decisions at the Court have recognised the personal interests of victim in the pre-trial stages outcomes and the confirmation of charges since they either confirm "the charges against those allegedly responsible for perpetrating the crimes which caused the victims to suffer harm" or, in the alternative, decline "to confirm the charges against those not responsible for such crimes, so that the search for those who are criminally liable can continue".[48] Observations by victims in the case of Muthaura and Kenyatta link the realisation of the right to the truth logically to accurate charging that reflects the nature and magnitude of their suffering.[49] Only then will victims feel that the acts included in the charges matches what happened to them. In fact, the very notion of victim hinges around the prosecution theory and charges brought since they determine what can be in the interest of victims and might exclude an alternate acknowledgment of victimhood and the corresponding version of the truth.

Victim representatives have been keen to stress that the interests of the prosecution and the victims may be different and that the victims would not become a second prosecutor.[50]

In *Ruto, Kosgey and Sang*, a victim representation submission to broaden the charges under Article 61(7)(c)(ii), which allows for "[a]mending a charge because the evidence submitted appears to establish a different crime within the jurisdiction of the Court", was unsuccessful.[51] Yet, during a charges hearing, the Prosecutor stressed his office's concern for victims and the prosecution's desire to "show respect, respect for the truth, respect for the victims, and also respect for the person before the Judges".[52]

Delay of procedure and disclosure of evidence

Victim representatives have also taken recourse to the right to the truth when arguing against delays in proceedings[53] and for disclosure of evidence that would be in the interest of victims.[54] As noted, the content of the right to the truth encompasses the verification and full public disclosure of the facts associated with the crimes from which victims or their relatives suffered. It is therefore clear that

48 *Prosecutor v Abu Garda* (6 October 2009) para 5.
49 *Prosecutor v Kenyatta* (24 July 2012).
50 E.g. *Prosecutor v Katanga and Ngudjolo* (22 January 2010).
51 *Prosecutor v Ruto, Kosgey and Sang* (23 January 2012) at para 277 and 278.
52 *Prosecutor v Bemba* (12 January 2009) 65.
53 *Prosecutor v Ntaganda* (30 June 2015); *Prosecutor v Kenyatta* (23 May 2013).
54 *Prosecutor v Gbagbo* (8 August 2012); *Prosecutor v Bemba* (21 December 2009).

victims have an interest in the disclosure of relevant evidence and also the speedy conclusion of proceedings to get the authoritative declaration from the Court. Delay of proceedings may not be in victims' interest, since that

> would negatively impact on the right of the victims to know the truth about the crimes in question, to have those responsible convicted, and to receive just reparation, all within a reasonable time. For these reasons, the subject matter at issue is directly related to the interests of victims.[55]

Similarly, the victims' interests may be affected through lack of disclosure. In *Bemba*, the legal representatives argued that

> to not allow the Prosecution to disclose additional evidence has an impact on the personal interests of the victims participating in the proceedings in so far as it impacts on their right to seek the truth and justice.[56]

It was held that, as a general rule, Rule 131(2) provides participating victims and their legal representatives with the right to consult the record of the proceedings, including the index, subject to restrictions concerning confidentiality and the protection of national security information.[57] In other words, public filings are accessible to the legal representatives of victims. There may be grounds for exceptions:

> if confidential filings are of material relevance to the personal interests of participating victims, consideration shall be given to providing this information to the relevant victim or victims, so long as it will not breach other protective measures that need to remain in place.[58]

Rule 92(5) governs that victims or their legal representatives shall be notified in a timely manner of all public proceedings and filings before the Court.

Whilst the inspection of materials in the possession of the prosecution and the defence as provided for in Rules 77 and 78 relate only to the prosecution and the defence, the Chamber indicated an option available to the victim participants: upon the making of a specific request, Article 68(3) could operate to

> provide individual victims who have been granted the right to participate with any materials within the possession of the prosecution that are relevant to the personal interests of victims which the Chamber has permitted to be

55 *Prosecutor v Kenyatta* (7 June 2013) 6.
56 *Prosecutor v Bemba* (21 December 2009) para 11.
57 *Prosecutor v Lubanga* (18 January 2008) para 105.
58 Ibid para 106.

investigated during the proceedings, and which have been identified with precision by the victims in writing.[59]

The Court has also stated that the right to introduce evidence during trials before the Court is not limited to the parties, not least because the Court, pursuant to Article 69(3), has a general right (that is not dependent on the cooperation or the consent of the parties) to request the presentation of all evidence necessary for the determination of the truth.[60] This can include evidence coming from victim participants. In the interest of fairness to the accused, the interest of justice and the interest of all victims who have the right to know the truth, the defence has argued that, therefore, an obligation to disclose exonerating material in their possession should be placed on victims.[61] This obligation, it is claimed, would arise out of the right to the truth of all victims, since participating victims have not a monopoly on the right to the truth. However, neither the Statute nor the Rules of Procedure and Evidence contain disclosure obligations of this kind and the rights of the accused are safeguarded with respect to victim participation by virtue of Article 68(3).[62] No such disclosure obligation in the name of the right to the truth of all victims have been imposed.

The point is, however, the recurring question on behalf of whom the right to the truth is invoked. The argument here is that establishing the overarching truth has to be the main goal and therefore all relevant evidence, including exonerating evidence in the possession of victims, should be utilised to contribute to this one common goal. But it is not clear that, beyond the moral desirability, there is such a thing as one common goal of establishing the truth, since a number of victim groups with differing interests may exist.

Victims to be heard

As discussed in the previous chapter, narrative truth recounted by individual victims fulfils one aspect of the right to the truth. At the ICC, a unique configuration for ascertaining the truth has emerged contributing, as one victim representative said, "to the evolution of international criminal law":[63] parties to the proceedings are still the prosecution and the defence. However, victim participants have a role to play and judges have an active truth-seeking function based on Article 69(3).

The value of victims being heard has been formally acknowledged in the Rome Statute through victim participation and expressly in its jurisprudence (see the decision on procedural rights by Judge Steiner, above). The emphasis placed by victim representatives within the ICC is that victims not only have the possibility

59 Ibid para 111.
60 Ibid para 108.
61 *Prosecutor v Katanga and Ngudjolo* (10 November 2009) para 17.
62 *Prosecutor v Katanga and Ngudjolo* (16 November 2009).
63 *Prosecutor v Katanga* (16 May 2012) 36.

to tell their story but crucially to have it heard within the judicial framework,[64] so that it plays an active role within proceedings:

> the possibility to tell their stories and to share their difficult and painful experiences with the judges constitutes one of the ways whereby the victims can positively contribute to the search for the truth.[65]

This is all the more important since those victims surviving often escaped death, unlike many of their fellow victims on whose behalf too they wish to testify. However, it has also been noted that only a small minority of surviving victims actually get to recount their story to the judges, since very few enjoy the dual status of participating victims and witnesses. Instead, for the majority, the recounting of experiences is during the application for victim participation process and not before the judges. On successful application, their interaction with the Court is most likely to be through the legal representative. This, it is argued, helps them

> point out that they were victims of pain and suffering, and that their truth and their story be told so that their concerns can be brought to bear through submissions by [...] their legal representative, who in so doing enables the Court to have a clearer view of the entire case and therefore contribute to the emergence of the truth.[66]

Whilst the truth propagating rhetoric at the Court is loud and clear, the voices of individuals in terms of narrative truth, beyond that of their legal representatives, is perhaps not significantly clearer to discern. What are very noticeable are the truth-invoking submissions filed by victim representatives, defence teams and the prosecutor's office to further their interests. Yet, the participating victims called to give evidence in the *Lubanga* case cast something of a cloud in terms of advancing the truth and with it the realisation of these victims' right to the truth.[67] Their testimony was deemed to "contain internal inconsistencies

64 *Prosecutor v Blé Goudé* (9 February 2015).

65 Ibid para 12. Victims, it is reported, can go to great length to ensure they meet with their legal representative and place great hopes in the ICC. "One of the reasons the victims are participating is to vindicate their right to justice, to vindicate their right to the truth. That is a right that is noted and established in the jurisprudence of this Court. A woman that I met in my recent trip in Kenya woke up at 5.00 a.m. in the morning. She walked on foot for about 50 miles to meet me in Kisumu, Kenya in order to participate in this process. And when they took turns telling me why they came to meet me, she said she came because she felt their lot would be better now that they're engaged in the ICC." (*Prosecutor v Muthaura, Kenyatta and Ali* (21 September 2011) 61).

66 *Prosecutor v Katanga* (16 May 2012) 53–54.

67 Though the legal representative, in her closing statement, argued their statement was given to advance the truth and also at great personal risk: "By appearing before your Chamber, the three participating victims in the proceedings had only one concern, promote their right

which undermine their credibility"[68] and reliability.[69] It is perhaps worth pointing out that, in a more general sense, testimonies during international criminal proceedings may not always provide the useful and credible facts desired by the fact-finders.[70] The *Ngudjolo* judgment in its analysis discusses such unreliability of witnesses,[71] taking into account the multiple obstacles that may affect credibility of witnesses: their demeanour may be defensive, discrepancies between their account and initial statement may become apparent or their expressions appear emotionless. This perceived unreliability may have its roots in trauma and the resulting difficulties in recalling and portraying events accurately or may stem from cultural differences. Furthermore, it has been noted that the victims' views of the case "may, or may not, be conducive to the truth-finding process",[72] suggesting that victim's interests in the truth may, in fact, be better advanced through the prosecution rather than too much reliance on victim participation, and narrative truth in particular. This would resort back to the model adopted by the ad hoc international tribunals.

Reparations

Victim representatives have been keen to stress that reparations are only one, and not the key, motivating factor behind victim participation.[73] Jurisprudence at the Court links the right to truth with the right to justice and the right to reparation, since

> the personal interest of the victims flows from (i) the desire to have a declaration of truth by a competent body (right to truth); (ii) their wish to have

---

to truth and justice, a right that was recognised by the Single Judge in the Pre-Trial Chamber in the case the Prosecutor versus Katanga and Ngudjolo" (*Prosecutor v Lubanga* (25 August 2011) 78).

68 *Prosecutor v Lubanga* (14 March 2012) para 499.

69 Ibid at para 502.

70 Nancy Armour Combs, *Fact-finding Without Facts. The Uncertain Evidentiary Foundations of International Criminal Convictions* (Cambridge University Press 2010). Studies have also demonstrated the limits and inaccuracies of eyewitness testimony especially by those witnesses that have been exposed to extensive trauma. Years after the events memories can fade or be altered depending on information received post-events. Comb purports that "testimony of international witnesses often is vague, unclear and lacking in the information necessary for fact finders to make reasoned factual assessments" (ibid., at 5) and that deficient testimony during international criminal proceedings are more prevalent than in domestic cases.

71 *Prosecutor v Ngudjolo* (18 December 2012).

72 Christine Van den Wyngaert, 'Victims before International Criminal Courts: Some Views and Concerns of an ICC Trial Judge' (2012) 44 Case Western Journal of International Law 475 at 488.

73 *Prosecutor v Gbagbo* (12 March 2015) para 9:

> "In particular, the Common Legal Representative submits that besides the interest to receive reparations, which is far from being the sole motivation of the victims, the core interest of the victims in this case is to effectively exercise their rights to truth and justice under

those who victimized them identified and prosecuted (right to justice) and (iii) the right to reparation.[74]

Recognised in international law and now through the ICC also in international criminal law, reparation not only includes the state bearing responsibility but also the individual perpetrator, as he or she becomes liable for the harm caused to victims. Pursuant to Article 75, reparation may be awarded to victims with reparation including restitution, compensation and rehabilitation.[75] However, any order of the Court which seeks to assist victims in their realisation of the right to the truth must be carefully drafted and strictly aligned to the specific charges which the accused has been convicted of in order to avoid the perception that the Court is implicitly judging the responsibility of the state.[76] The way that charges narrows the specific truth value to emerge for victims, they also limit the reparations since they are contingent on the charges against and conviction of the accused. This has been clearly expressed in the *Lubanga* case:

> The standard of causation is a "but/for" relationship between the crime and the harm and, moreover, it is required that the crimes for which Mr Lubanga was convicted were the "proximate cause" of the harm for which reparations are sought.[77]

The *Lubanga* Appeal Chamber noted "that the imposition of liability for reparations on the convicted person is also consistent with the UN Basic Principles on Reparation for Victims".[78] This is significant, since Principle 22 of the Basic Principles on Satisfaction includes

> (b) Verification of the facts and full and public disclosure of the truth to the extent that such disclosure does not cause further harm or threaten the safety and interests of the victim, the victim's relatives, witnesses, or persons who have intervened to assist the victim or prevent the occurrence of further violations;
> (c) The search for the whereabouts of the disappeared, for the identities of the children abducted, and for the bodies of those killed, and assistance in the recovery, identification and reburial of the bodies in accordance with the expressed or presumed wish of the victims, or the cultural practices of the families and communities;

---

the Rome Statute, as generally recognised by international human rights law, doctrine and the constant jurisprudence of the Court."

74 *Prosecutor v Abu Garda* (25 September 2009) para 3.

75 Article 75(1) of the Rome Statute.

76 See Conor McCarthy, 'Reparations under the Rome Statute of the ICC and Reparative Justice Theory' (2009) 3(2) International Journal of Transitional Justice 250 at 264–5.

77 *Prosecutor v Lubanga* (3 March 2015) Order for Reparations (amended), para 59.

78 Ibid para 100.

(d) An official declaration or a judicial decision restoring the dignity, the reputation and the rights of the victim and of persons closely connected with the victim;
(e) Public apology, including acknowledgement of the facts and acceptance of responsibility;
(f) Judicial and administrative sanctions against persons liable for the violations;
(g) Commemorations and tributes to the victims;
(h) Inclusion of an accurate account of the violations that occurred in international human rights law and international humanitarian law training and in educational material at all levels.[79]

Aspects of the right to the truth realisation can therefore form part of reparation and remedy. Interestingly, in its submission to the Court, the prosecution too suggested that satisfaction should be taken into consideration for the reparations phase. Thus reparations, the OTP argued, could include for example, the "verification of the facts and full disclosure of the truth"[80] and the search for the disappeared and abducted, their identification but also a public apology.[81] In essence, the prosecutor argued for the continuation of investigations it seemingly left incomplete, or further investigations, to allow for the realisation of the right to the truth. This equates to an admission of the limitations arising from prosecutorial choices, pointing to "outstanding truth-finding needs" of victims. Though such a continuation of efforts is not part of the reparations order made by the Court in *Lubanga*.

This aside, the advancement of the right to the truth is linked to, if not forming part of, the Court's mandate, remit and objectives with regards to reparation. First, the dissemination of an authoritative declaration, such as a judgment, is in itself a form of "just satisfaction" as described in Principle 22(b) and (d).[82] This is why criminal trials have been identified as powerful instruments for the realisation of the right to the truth. Second, the dissemination of truth as part of training and educational material can also work towards safeguarding efforts that might prevent a repetition of past wrongs. This was argued by the victim representatives and has been confirmed by the ECCC, which held that

> the wide circulation of the court's findings may contribute to the goals of national healing and reconciliation by promoting a public and genuine

79 Basic Principles and Guidelines on the Right to a Remedy and Reparation for Victims of Gross Violations of International Human Rights Law and Serious Violations of International Humanitarian Law (21 March 2006) (hereinafter Basic Principles) Principle IX para 22.

80 Ibid at para 22(b). See *Prosecutor v Lubanga* Prosecution's Submissions on the principles and procedures to be applied in Reparations, ICC-01/04–01/06–2867 (18 March 2012) para 12.

81 Ibid para 22(b) and 22(e).

82 See also *Velásquez-Rodríguez v Honduras* (21 July 1989) para 36.

> discussion on the past grounded upon a firm basis, thereby minimising denial, distortion of facts, and partial truths.[83]

Third, commemorations and memorials explicitly acknowledge the victims and their suffering. Such measures have not only truth propagating and remembering but also reparative value. The ECCC, which can order collective and moral reparations, underscored the express moral value of memorials and their individual as well as societal benefit:

> The "moral" requirement is satisfied by the fact that memorials restore the dignity of victims, represent a public acknowledgement of the crimes committed and harm suffered by victims, and, as lasting and prominent symbols, assist in healing the wounds of victims as a collective by diffusing their effects far beyond the individuals who were admitted as Civil Parties. Additionally, memorials contribute to national reconciliation by strengthening public knowledge of past crimes, promoting a culture of peace among the current and future generations, and contributing to a global message of concord to all potential visitors.[84]

This view is noteworthy insofar as memorials are seen as unifying truth promoting vehicles, whereas experience from the Balkans tells us that they can also be perceived as one-sided, monolithic narratives underscoring division.[85] Notwithstanding this naïve interpretative caveat of the ECCC's decision, memorials may symbolise and physically/visibly stand for a particular truth and thus offer authority and acknowledgment. But such collective reparative measures risk being established based on a group stereotype as opposed to individual victim's needs. They therefore are more likely to address the public element of the right to the truth, and even that possibly only partially insofar as they speak to one segment of society. At the ICC, the benefit of commemorative reparations was expressed cautiously in relation to child-soldiers:

> Programmes that have transformative objectives, however limited, can help prevent future victimisation, and symbolic reparations, such as commemorations and tributes, may also contribute to the process of rehabilitation.[86]

Both dissemination and memorialisation efforts would require assistance from state parties and the international community, pursuant to Part 9 of the Rome

83 *Case 001 against Kaing Guek Eav alias Duch* (3 February 2012) para 708. The emphasis on seeking to ascertain a complete truth (as opposed to a partial truth) as part of a trial is also noteworthy.

84 Ibid para 683.

85 E.g. Janine Natalya Clark, *International Trials and Reconciliation: assessing the impact of the international criminal tribunal for the former Yugoslavia* (Routledge 2014).

86 *Prosecutor v Lubanga* (3 March 2015) Order for Reparations (amended) para 67(v).

Statute, to help implement such measures. This was clearly expressed in the amended *Lubanga* Reparations Order.[87] But in this, as we have seen for investigations, lies a clear limit of the ICC's (and the Trust Fund for Victims') ability to effectively advance the right to the truth. It is reliant and contingent on state cooperation.

Finally, apologies and acceptance of responsibility can advance the right to the truth realisation if they include an "acknowledgement of the facts and acceptance of responsibility".[88] As a form of reparation, the Appeal Chamber suggested that "Mr Lubanga is able to contribute to this process by way of a voluntary apology to individual victims or to groups of victims, on a public or confidential basis".[89] In contrast to Mr Lubanga, defendant Katanga, following his guilty verdict, offered an apology without a reparations order. He accepted the judgment and offered his sincere regrets to those who suffered from his actions. To the surprise and disappointment of the legal representative of victims, this resulted in the defence and prosecution discontinuing their respective appeals against the judgment.[90] The offer of an apology therefore had mixed results; the sincerity of the expression of regret was tainted by the consequence: a lack of appeal. Since the calls for appeal were halted by both prosecution and defence, victims had no standing and could not ask for the judgment to be revisited.

A curious incident involving apologies and ICC proceedings is the case of Kenyan President Uhuru Kenyatta. Following the collapse of the case in December 2014, victim representatives stated:

> The Victims have been denied both by the Government and by the Court all five of the forms of reparation described in principles 19–23 of the Basic Principles and recognized by international human rights law (namely, restitution, compensation, rehabilitation, satisfaction and guarantees of non-repetition).[91]

This submission was made against the backdrop of lack of state cooperation with ICC investigations. Yet on 26 March 2015, during his state of the nation speech, Kenyatta made the following apology:

> I stand before you today on my own behalf, that of my government and all past governments, to offer the sincere apology of the Government of the Republic of Kenya to all our compatriots for all past wrongs.[92]

87 Ibid Order for Reparations (amended) para 50 and 67(vi).
88 Basic Principles *supra* note 79 at para 22(e).
89 *Prosecutor v Lubanga* (3 March 2015) Order for Reparations (amended) para 67(viii).
90 *Prosecutor v Katanga*, Defence and Prosecution notices of Discontinuance of the Appeal (25 June 2014) and *Prosecutor v Katanga* (26 June 2014).
91 *Situation in the Republic of Kenya* (3 August 2015) para 113.
92 Parliament of Kenya: Joint Sitting of the National Assembly and the Senate (26 March 2015).

The issuing of an apology was part of the recommendations formulated by the Kenyan Truth, Justice and Reconciliation Commission,[93] and can be seen as a reparative measure on behalf of the government. Yet the apology also suggests that in Kenya a restorative justice approach as opposed to a retributive one should be adopted to the 2007–2008 post-election violence cases. The apology therefore stands "without other key measures of accountability",[94] including efforts at the ICC against Kenyatta, resulting in potential impunity. The apology is therefore of a limited value regarding the advancement of the right to the truth for victims, as it risks curtailing investigative measures towards accountability.

Since the right to the truth has reparative value, it is no surprise that, in principle, the reparations phase at the ICC holds promise for an advancement of the right to the truth. All that said, nowhere in the "Order for Reparations" in the *Lubanga* case does the Appeal Chamber mention the right to the truth, truth as a rationale for reparative measures or truthful accounts as part of reparations. The right to the truth argument does not feature *expressis verbis* in the Court's jurisprudence regarding reparations except through reference to the Basic Principles.

Can judges focus on the realisation of the right to the truth?

It may be possible that the judges take on an active role in the truth realisation. Since it was for the Court to decide the rules of evidence and procedures, safeguarding the rights of defendants whilst also determining the mode of victim participation, there may be room for discretion available to the judges in balancing a multitude of rights within the ICC's procedures. "[H]ow interventionist judges will be within that framework" has been a question posed since the beginning of the ICC's journey.[95] The predictions were that the "judicial role will be a fairly active one at the ICC, because under Article 74(5) ICCSt., the Trial Chamber is obliged to give a full reasoned statement of its findings of fact and legal conclusions".[96] Whilst no-one would deny victims the moral right and need for the truth, is there scope for the translation of the right into the Court's processes through the statutory obligations placed on judges – in particular through Article 69(3), which gives judges the authority to request evidence submissions to aid the determination of the truth?

93 E.g. Christopher Gitari Ndungú, 'Lessons to Be Learned: An Analysis of the Final Report of Kenya's Truth, Justice and Reconciliation Commission' (International Centre for Transitional Justice Report May 2014).

94 Ruben Carranza, Cristián Correa, and Elena Naughton, 'More than Words. Apologies as a Form or Reparation' (International Centre for Transitional Justice Report December 2015) at 4. It is worth noting that the Inter-American Court of Human Rights can continue its judgment even after the respondent state has accepted liability.

95 Claus Kreß, 'The Procedural Law of the International Criminal Court in Outline: Anatomy of a Unique Compromise' (2003) 1 Journal of International Criminal Justice 603 at 612.

96 Ibid.

It has already been discussed that the Pre-Trial Chamber, upon request by the referring state of the Security Council, under Article 53(3)(a) has the ability to review a decision of the prosecutor under Article 53(1) and (2) not to proceed. On its own initiative, the Pre-Trial Chamber can also review the prosecutor's decision not to proceed if the decision is based on the "interest of justice" criteria. What precisely is meant by the "interest of justice" criteria is not specified. But it is possible that prosecutorial practice decisions resting on the "interest of justice" criteria could in effect limit the truth-discovering remit in order to safeguard important justice considerations, though the judges would need to oversee this.

Under Article 56, the Pre-Trial Chamber has also a role in relation to what is called a "unique investigative opportunity", which allows the prosecutor to initiate the early taking of evidence. Similarly here, the judges have the possibility of overruling such decisions thus giving the chamber a role as an investigative body[97] in overseeing such a decision. So in principle, if, as we have seen in the previous chapter, not in practice, there is scope for the judges to influence the investigative remit of the prosecutor and her duty to establish the truth pursuant to Article 54 of the Rome Statute.

Ideally, as discussed earlier, victims should benefit from the conduct of an investigation. It is conceivable that any initial investigation will be relatively broad before it focuses on specific charges in light of available evidence. Much information uncovered by investigations might respond to the information needs of the many victims but is unlikely to feature in a final judgment or indeed in proceedings. Therefore, such material will never receive authoritative acknowledgment of victim suffering. It would be useful to contemplate a process whereby information could be disclosed to victims – to the extent that doing so would not compromise the investigation, affect the fair trial rights of the defendant or endanger other future prosecutions. Cooperation between the prosecutor and the registry would be required in this regard. No such activity is expressed in the Statute, nor does the Statute preclude it. Whether the judges could play a role in this disclosure of information exercise too is unexplored since it falls outside the scope of a chamber's remit.

Unlocking Article 69(3) for more truth-finding

Article 69(3) states, "the parties may submit evidence relevant to the case, in accordance with article 64. The Court shall have the authority to request the submission of all evidence that it considers necessary for the determination of the truth". The provision, when read independently from the first sentence, holds significant discretional power on behalf of the Court to request the submission of

97 Ibid at 608.

additional evidence which the judges may consider necessary for the determination of the truth. This was expressed clearly in *Lubanga*:

> While mindful that the Prosecutor bears the onus of proving the guilt of the accused, it is nevertheless clear that "the Court has the authority to request the submission of all evidence that it considers necessary for the determination of the truth" (article 69 (3) of the Statute). The fact that the onus lies on the Prosecutor cannot be read to exclude the statutory powers of the court, as it is the court that "must be convinced of the guilt of the accused beyond reasonable doubt" (article 66 (3) of the Statute).[98]

But, as is to be expected, the decision also qualifies the remit of the truth-finding scope to be limited in the context of the innocence or guilt of the accused. Whilst victims are not parties to the procedure, the Court has acknowledged "that victims may possess evidence that may assist the Chamber in its determination of the truth in accordance with Article 69(3) of the Statute".[99] They may therefore submit an application for the presentation of evidence in accordance with Rule 89, which parties can provide observations on before the Chamber determines whether the evidence is, in fact, relevant to the victims' personal interest, establishment of the truth and consistent with fair trial requirements.[100] Through this, it has been argued, life is given to "the 'spirit and intention' and provision relating to victim participation in trial proceedings".[101] Victims are therefore allowed to propose the submission of evidence to assist the Chamber in ascertaining the truth but it is not an "unfettered right" with victims "required to demonstrate why their interests are affected by the evidence or issue, upon which the chamber will decide, on a case-by-case basis whether or not to allow such participation".[102] Such participation is therefore subject to Article 68(3) preconditions and subject to admissibility considerations under Article 69(4).[103]

Controversially and relevant here, the provision under Article 69(3) is not *expressis verbis* limited to the matter of victim participation. But there is no settled jurisprudence beyond victim participation and the request of evidence in relation to Article 69(3). Nonetheless, Plevin envisages four scenarios in which Article 69(3) could be invoked:[104] first, the legal representatives of victims can request the presentation of additional evidence followed by a case-by-case determination on behalf of the trial chamber; second, following the successful application of a party

98 *Prosecutor v Lubanga* (11 July 2008) para 95.
99 *Prosecutor v Muthaura and Kenyatta* (3 October 2012) para 76.
100 Ibid.
101 Adrian Plevin, 'Beyond a "Victims' Right": Truth-finding Power and Procedure at the ICC' (2014) 25 Criminal Law Forum 441 at 444.
102 *Prosecutor v Lubanga* (11 July 2008) para 99.
103 For a more detailed discussion of these see Plevin *supra* note 101 and Ferstman *supra* note 44.
104 Ibid (Plevin) at 452–55.

arguing additional evidentiary materials are in the hands of the opposing party or the opposing party has access to, order such production; third, an amicus curia brief or other submissions (from a state, for example) in line with Rule 103[105] to the Court could draw the chamber's attention to the existence of important evidence that would further their understanding of the case and advance the determination of the truth; fourth, the chambers, trusting in their own assessment and knowledge of existing evidence, could suggest the production thereof in court. Such a mechanism could be similar to that of relying on Regulation 44[106] to call experts proprio motu, which the judges have made use of.[107] The use of expert witnesses called by the Chamber can be viewed as a potential avenue to avoid or contextualise reliability issues of witnesses, especially victim witnesses, and in that way advance the truth. To portray the context and background evidence surrounding the offences better, an expert witness may be a useful option to provide evidence, including, where appropriate, on the psychological and physical suffering victims have endured, from a position of neutrality.[108] Using Article 69(3) to further the truth through the production of additional evidence would serve such a purpose too.

Any such use of Article 69(3) would be limited by the need to safeguard fair trial requirements, including the need to avoid undue delay. But other provisions can be read in conjunction and as supporting a broad reading of Article 69(3),[109] such as Article 64(6)(d) on ordering "the production of evidence in addition to that already collected prior to the trial or presented during the trial by parties". Article 69(3) has been used in relation to victim participation. In *Katanga*, it was expressly said that

> [b]ecause article 64(6)(d) of the Statute specifically refers to evidence in addition to that which has been presented during the trial by the parties, it

105 International Criminal Court, Rules of Procedure and Evidence (9 September 2002) Rule 13 states:

> 1 At any stage of the proceedings, a Chamber may, if it considers it desirable for the proper determination of the case, invite or grant leave to a State, organization or person to submit, in writing or orally, any observation on any issue that the Chamber deems appropriate.
> 2 The Prosecutor and the defence shall have the opportunity to respond to the observations submitted under sub-rule 1.
> 3 A written observation submitted under sub-rule 1 shall be filed with the Registrar, who shall provide copies to the Prosecutor and the defence. The Chamber shall determine what time limits shall apply to the filing of such observations.

106 International Criminal Court, Regulations of the Court (26 May 2004) Regulation 44 (4) "[t]he Chamber may proprio motu instruct an expert."

107 E.g. in Lubanga the judges called four additional experts (*Prosecutor v Lubanga* (14 March 2012)).

108 E.g. Adrian Fulford, 'Reflections of a Trial Judge' (2011) 22 Criminal Law Forum 215. Former ICC judge Adrian Fulford sees the use of expert witnesses as a way to reduce the need to call a great number of individual witnesses (ibid at 219).

109 For a full discussion of the framework underpinning Article 69(3) see Plevin *supra* note 101.

> is clear that it is intended to give effect to the power of the Trial Chamber under the second sentence of article 69(3) of the Statute.[110]

In the same judgment, the chamber also determined that disclosure obligations, as contained in Rules 76 and 84 do not extend to participating victims.[111] That said, the chamber "retains the authority to order the production of exculpatory or mitigating evidence itself, if and when it considers that such information would be necessary for the determination of the truth"[112] in accordance with Articles 64(6)(d) and 69(3) of the Statute. This would ensure that the Trial Chamber "does not receive the evidence in a distorted manner".[113] The chamber therefore has the ability to request the disclosure of information in the hand of victims that would further their capacity to determine the truth. In other words, the chamber retains the power to determine the disclosure regime applicable to victim participants and to ensure this does not adversely affect fair trial requirements.[114] This is significant insofar as victim participants are not reliant on the prosecutor alone to provide evidence. The Article 69(3) truth-finding mechanisms can thus fill in gaps or supplement the information offered by the prosecutor.

In addition, it can be argued, that the other three avenues under Article 69(3) offering quasi-investigative powers to the judges have similar promise to advance the truth but are unexplored. Whilst inherent risks lie in such investigative measures potentially infringing the equality of arms principle, they allow the judges to focus on their truth-finding mandate implicit (that is subject to judicial reasoning) in the Rome Statute. This is not to say that such an active role would counteract investigative shortcomings of the prosecutor which have been described as "generally reactive, highly dynamic, and unpredictable".[115] Whilst it is, in principle conceivable, in practice, however, the role of the prosecutor has been described as "resembling that of an *officer of justice* rather than a partisan advocate".[116] In that sense, the Article 69(3) mechanism would allow for a strategically broad complementary way in which the truth-seeking function placed on the Court – that is prosecutor and judges – can be operationalised. This is all the more so, since the jurisprudence of the Court is seeking to ensure investigations are largely completed by the confirmation hearing stage,[117] despite the investigative duty of the

110 *Prosecutor v Katanga* (16 July 2010) para 44.

111 Ibid para 77. Interestingly, the defence, referring to the right to truth of non-participating victims and other interested parties suggest that not disclosing such information would, in turn, diminish their right to the truth (*Prosecutor v Katanga and Ngudjolo* (10 November 2009) para 14).

112 Ibid para 86.

113 Ibid para 85.

114 For a detailed discussion on how the rights of the accused should 'always' have primacy over those of victims see Zappalà *supra* note 1.

115 Alex Whiting, 'Dynamic investigative practice at the International Criminal Court' (2013) 76 Law and Contemporary Problems 163 at 163.

116 Kreß *supra* note 95 at 608.

117 *Prosecutor v Mbarushimana* (30 May 2012) para 44.

prosecutor, pursuant to Article 54(1)(a), to establish the truth extending beyond the confirmation hearing stage.[118] Only in exceptional circumstances, therefore, should postconfirmation investigations be conducted.[119]

Interestingly, in *Katanga and Ngudjolo* the judges referred to the right to the truth as a rationale for their actions in relation to charging, with the judges inserting a footnote containing the following defence submission:

> It has been held that article 69(3) gives the Court a general right that is not dependent on the cooperation or the consent of the parties to request the presentation of all evidence necessary for the determination of the truth. This is so because the Trial Chamber is viewed as a "truth-finder" invested with the difficult task of ascertaining the truth in relation to the guilt of the defendant for which it is believed that the greatest accessibility to the evidence is necessary. [...] The accurate determination of the guilt or innocence of persons prosecuted before the ICC is important, not only for the accused who has the presumption of innocence, but also for the wider audience, in particular for victim participants "insofar as this issue is inherently linked to the satisfaction of their right to the truth."[120]

This judicial summary of a defence statement would suggest that a broad reading of Article 69(3) is not only contemplated by parties (in this case the defence) but is also linked directly to the right to the truth – individually and collectively. Furthermore, it is an argument the judges refer to in order to substantiate their decision, thus expressing an implicit possibility of such a reading, if not an endorsement.

Judgment

As part of the right to the truth realisation, an authoritative declaration by a competent body is required. Pursuant to Article 74(2), the trial chamber decision "shall be based on its evaluation of the evidence and the entire proceedings. The decision shall not exceed the facts and circumstances described in the charges and any amendments to the charges". The decision has to be "in writing and shall contain a full and reasoned statement of the Trial Chambers' findings on the evidence and conclusions".[121] Article 74(2) underscores the importance of the charges delineating the remit of what a judgment can contain.

118 *Prosecutor v Lubanga* (13 October 2006) para 52.

119 *Prosecutor v Kenyatta* (26 April 2013). This approach has been criticised as unwise: "Although the prosecution cannot investigate its case forever, and the right do the defense require that it know the case that it must answer, there must be some flexibility in allowing the prosecution to continue its investigations even after confirmation in order to insure that it fulfils its obligation to uncover the truth" (Whiting *supra* note 115 at 189.

120 *Prosecutor v Katanga and Ngudjolo* (17 December 2012) footnote 21. See also *Prosecutor v Katanga and Ngudjolo* (10 November 2009) paras 10 and 11.

121 Rome Statute Article 74(5).

Within this demarcation, part of the judgment will need to spell out what has happened in order to be "a full and reasoned statement". Therein lies scope for the ICC to make a contribution to the realisation of the right to the truth. The truth-telling function of judgments, whether a guilty verdict or an acquittal, has been acknowledged.[122] Similarly, the importance of acknowledging the suffering of victims is understood. The March 2014 minority opinion of Judge Van den Wyngaert perhaps demonstrates this, in part, by stating that innocent people lost their lives and that her disagreement with the majority does not "diminish the gravity of what allegedly took place in Bogoro on 24 February 2003".[123]

Unquestionably the conviction has to be based on the beyond a reasonable doubt proof required by the Statute with Article 66(3), stating "[i]n order to convict the accused, the Court must be convinced of the guilt of the accused beyond reasonable doubt". Furthermore, a trial chamber can only convict if satisfied that the accused bears criminal responsibility beyond reasonable doubt based on the entirety of the admitted evidence.[124] However, what is set out in a judgment as a description of events on which the decision is based is of great significance to individual victims, survivor populations and the international community at large – whether it results in a conviction or not. It has been suggested that the beyond reasonable doubt requirement may not necessarily need to extend to this type of preliminary information contained in a judgment that would provide a description of what happened.[125] In other words, the "full statement" requirement under Article 74(5) could be based on a sufficient evidence standard or a balance of probabilities test as standard of proof[126] when setting out exhaustively everything, every piece of evidence that the chamber finds credible to describe what happened (but not directly relating to the defendant's guilt). At the ICC, judges are no strangers to differing standards of proof: Article 58(1), for the issuance of an arrest warrant, requires "reasonable grounds to believe that the person has committed a crime within the jurisdiction of the Court"; Article 61(7), for the confirmation of charges, demands "sufficient evidence to establish substantial grounds to believe that the person committed each of the crimes charged"; and finally, the beyond reasonable doubt requirement of Article 66(3) applies to the accused.

122 *Prosecutor v Ljubičić* (23 December 2008) at footnote 18.

123 *Prosecutor v Katanga* (7 March 2014) Minority Opinion of Judge Christine Van den Wyngaert para 6 and also para 4. Though she clearly states that she cannot, "in good conscience" say that she understood "exactly what really took place" due to the limitations of evidence available. In fact, the evidence presented, according to Judge Van den Wyngaert, does not meet the standard of proof required, thus preventing her to make a finding "beyond reasonable doubt" (ibid at 317).

124 *Prosecutor v Ntagerura at al.* (7 July 2006) at 278.

125 Fergal Gaynor, 'Uneasy Partners – Evidence, Truth and History in International Trials, (2012) 10(5) Journal of International Criminal Justice 1257.

126 For a discussion of the balance of probabilities as representing a description of a historian's approach to truth-finding, see Gaynor (ibid).

Such an approach is, perhaps, not realistic and of limited desirability as it might result in artificially divorcing the full and reasoned statement from the full evidence and risk exceeding the facts and circumstances described in the charges. But other creative methods could be found, as discussed in the previous chapter in relation to the ICTY's use of appendices to judgments, for disclosing detailed further information of value to victims. This, however, would be contingent on a conviction. The dissent by Judge Van den Wyngaert hardly offers victims the justice result they were hoping for; it merely gives them some acknowledgment of suffering, and possibly only since the majority issued a conviction. The value of this kind of acknowledgment might be greatly diminished without the sense of justice or even undermined without a conviction. In this regard, justice and truth, while distinct, very much go hand in hand.

In addition, the idea of a lowering of the standard of proof in order to enable the truth to be declared to a wide range of victims might have the negative result of lessening the authority of the Court's declaration of the truth which would undermine the full satisfaction of the right to the truth.

Finding an approach that would work towards greater victim satisfaction by providing an acknowledgment of the preliminary events that happened whilst also advancing the realisation of a right to the truth on behalf of victims by including a plausible account of circumstances into the court record is desirable. Hayner contemplates that, following the conclusion of cases pertaining to the same situation, information collected during the prosecutor's investigations is collated into summary report of findings "[t]o take advantage of this wealth of information, and to contribute to a broad public understanding of a conflict or a period of authoritarian rule".[127] These records need not contain names of suspects to avoid jeopardising national proceedings. But for many victims, waiting until such time when all trials are complete and records would become available may not present a satisfactory process. It has also been suggested that, taking into account the need to protect legitimate public interests, the Court could make information on the wider situation and conflict that is not needed for the trial but potentially of great interest to the victims available to them.[128]

Another way to enhance the truth messages from international criminal tribunals rests in effective outreach mechanisms. This is not only important to manage expectations of victims and counter politicisation by those opposing the Court, but also to convey vital information and explanations on the judgments themselves and what they contain. Making judgments more accessible as to their content through explanatory headnotes, summaries and other outreach activities need not compromise the legal substance of a judgment but can enhance the understanding of those affected.[129]

127 Priscilla Hayner, *Unspeakable Truths. Transitional Justice and the Challenge of Truth Commissions* (2nd edn, Routledge 2011) at 109

128 Nijono Mue, 'Policy Brief: Enhancing the Societal Impact of International Criminal Tribunals' (Impunity Watch, February 2015).

129 Ibid policy recommendations, point 5 at 13.

Judges and state cooperation

The realisation of the right to the truth, as discussed in the previous chapter, depends much on the cooperation of the state, especially cooperation with the investigations. In line with the principle of complementarity, the ICC was always designed to ensure states comply with the duty to prosecute and advance the right to the truth themselves. The ICC was only designed to prosecute a few cases. All the more ironic therefore is when cases such as the *Kenyatta* one collapse because of lack of cooperation. Nationally and internationally, therefore, states have the ability to obstruct prosecutions and the determination of the truth through this avenue. Beyond a finding pursuant of Article 87(7) on non-cooperation and referring the matter to the Assembly of State Parties, there is little the judges can do about a lack of cooperation.

Such limited ability to enforce cooperation and its detrimental effect on the realisation of the right to the truth has been noted by Judge Eboe-Osuji in the decision that there was insufficient evidence to continue with the *Ruto and Sang* case. This decision declared a mistrial without prejudice to future prosecutions[130] – a controversial decision in itself and a first for international criminal law.[131] In his outline of reasons, Judge Eboe-Osuji contemplates whether the "meddling" with an ongoing international criminal investigation amounts to an internationally wrongful act which under customary international law would result in the need for reparations to be made.[132] In this regard he raises a number of questions that are of great significance for the right to the truth:

> Does it or does it not amount to an internationally wrongful act for the government of a State to set out to meddle with an on-going case before an international criminal court, with the view to occasioning its abortion without proper consideration of the charges? Is it material or not that such meddling may have occurred against both a history of failure to protect the victims of the harm that is the subject matter of the judicial inquiry and/or lack of indication that the meddling State had conducted genuine investigation or prosecution? Does such manner of interference raise serious questions of denial of justice for the victims, in relation to their right to the truth (also an element of reparation in international human rights law)? But does that denial not come with it [sic] a potential denial to victims of their

130 *Prosecutor v Ruto and Sang* (5 April 2016) Reasons of Judge Eboe-Osuji, para 207.

131 See William Schabas, 'The Mistrial, An Innovation in International Criminal Law' (8 April 2016) http://humanrightsdoctorate.blogspot.co.uk/2016/04/the-mistrial-innovation-in.html and Kevin Jon Heller, 'The Ruto Trial Chamber Invents the Mistrial Without Prejudice (8 April 2016) http://opiniojuris.org/2016/04/08/the-icc-invents-the-possibility-of-a-mistrial/ accessed 14 February 2019.

132 *Prosecutor v Ruto and Sang* (5 April 2016) Reasons of Judge Eboe-Osuji, para 207. Judge Eboe-Osuji refers to the UNGA Resolution entitled Responsibility of States for Internationally Wrongful Acts (28 January 2002) quoting Article 1: "Every internationally wrongful act of a State entails the international responsibility of that State".

> entitlement to reparation from those individually responsible for the harm – as opposed to ex gratia compensation from the charitable instincts of the international community or a national government?[133]

Judge Eboe-Osuji expresses a clear concern here that the interference or lack of cooperation on behalf of a state has the potential to undermine international criminal justice and truth-seeking efforts to the detriment of the victims, since those allegedly responsible are not subjected to a criminal process impeding also any reparation measure that could follow from a conviction. What is more, the state that had failed to protect its population when the atrocities occurred is now also responsible for denying victims international criminal justice efforts (let alone domestic ones). The state not only failed in its obligation toward its citizens regarding protection, it also failed in its obligation to work towards the right to the truth post-events and actively undermined alternate truth-seeking mechanisms.

Arguments have been made that the ICC should serve as a catalyst for establishing national prosecutions and reparations systems.[134] But could the ICC go a step further and compel a meddling state to award reparations to victims?[135] In the words of Judge Eboe-Osuji and specifically in relation to Kenya,

> the further question arises whether the Rome Statute leaves no scope for this Court to require the Government to make adequate reparation to the victims of the post-election violence without further delay. It may be considered that the jurisdiction of the ICC for purposes of a reparation order ordinarily engages only in relation to individuals and not a State. But even so, does the question not arise that a State that meddles in the prosecution of a case at the ICC, in a manner that is reasonably likely to frustrate a prosecution and conviction, has by such conduct meddled itself into the jurisdiction of the ICC for purposes of reparation? In those circumstances, does the opinion of the ICJ in the Reparation Case afford judicial precedent for such an imposition on a State in the absence of explicit statutory provision?

Whilst no answers are offered to these questions, the contemplation of them, read in conjunction with the creative decision of a "mistrial without prejudice to future prosecutions" – a notion that cannot be found in the Rome Statute[136] – suggests at

133 Ibid.

134 Assembly of State Parties, RC/11, Annex V(a) Stocktaking of international criminal justice, The impact of the Rome Statute system on victims and affected communities, Final report by the focal points (Chile and Finland), Appendix III Discussion Paper 86.

135 Though this raises another issues as to whether reparations at state level would be impartial or would be administered at all due to a malfunctioning or collapsed judicial system. For a detailed discussion see Lisbeth Zegveld, 'Victims' reparations claims under international criminal courts: incompatible values?' (2010) 8(1) Journal of International Criminal Justice 79, at 92.

136 This is acknowledged but support is cited through Article 64(2) in conjunction with Article 4(1) of the Rome Statute (*Prosecutor v Ruto and Sang* (5 April 2016) para 190).

least one judge's willingness towards constructive interpretations of the Court's sources along with an awareness of how the victims, above all, are failed by the current system. Interestingly, the judge explicitly contemplates whether the ICC could find more effective ways to deal with state obstruction. He does not refer or defer to the role of human rights courts where such claims might be more appropriately brought. The matter of enforcement is not touched upon either.

What becomes evident from the decision in *Ruto and Sang* is that there is a danger that, when concerned with truth-finding more broadly, the Court's activities risk becoming side-lined and not focused on the accused. Judicial activism of this nature is likely to attract heavy criticism: "The unfairness to Ruto and Sang is evident – and simply reinforces the (too often justified) narrative that the judiciary is little more than a division of the OTP".[137] Such disparagement, whether justifiable or not, is understandable since third parties and not the accused had rendered the investigative efforts ineffective.[138]

As an aside, it would have been interesting to see what response the judges would have received in the *Kenya* cases had they invoked Article 69(3) seeking the production of evidence they believed to exist and considered to be necessary for the determination of the truth. Would it have made a difference? If creative intervention by the judges is desirable, taking an activist role permitted by the Statute during trial might be more beneficial than arguing for a reading that it does not explicitly contain.

Conclusion

Literature on the ICC has generally highlighted its "unique challenges when attempting to safeguard the disparate and often competing interests of the accused, the Prosecutor, victims, and the broader international community".[139] Much of this challenge comes from the decision to admit victims into the courtroom but it has far-reaching philosophical implications for international criminal justice:

> Once and for all it has been clarified that international criminal trials are not merely about punishing a few individuals. Rather, the purpose of

137 Heller *supra* note 131.

138 Though it takes on the form of hyperbole in statements such as these: "he [Judge Eboe-Osuji openly admits that their [Ruto and Sang's] right not to be put twice in jeopardy is less important than convincing states and third parties to stop being mean to the ICC' and 'Sorry, Mr Ruto. Sorry, Mr Sang. We might have acquitted you because you have no case to answer. But we can't, because unnamed others have not shown proper deference to these proceedings. You have to face re-trial in order to ensure that those unnamed others – and unnamed others who might be inclined to emulate them – behave better in the future" (ibid.). It should also be pointed out that the likelihood of a re-trial is extremely low not least since strong arguments can be made questioning the legality of this decision as a majority decision; it consists of three separate judgments by three judges.

139 Plevin *supra* note 101 at 442.

> international criminal justice is broader, comprising victim rehabilitation through participation and assuming a pedagogical dimension involving the affected communities.[140]

The right to the truth, to some extent, epitomises this struggle in operationalising a morally compelling principle without contradicting the Rome Statute, as was the case with the Judge Steiner decision.[141] Others have termed this effort to achieve "equitable justice for defendants, victims and international society as such" to be the "the foundation of all procedural norms of the Statute".[142]

That said, many limitations on the realisation for the right to the truth do not differ from those applicable to other international criminal institutions: the capacity of the ICC is not unlimited, and the crimes investigated and selected for prosecution will only ever comprise a small percentage of those perpetrated. The crimes in question need to meet admissibility as well as threshold requirements contained in the Statute. Investigations and prosecutions are likely to be narrow in scope, with the result that they may not work towards providing meaningful information to victims of the wider context in which crimes were perpetrated. In addition, the processes are lengthy and may not be available to victims for many years.

However, other, more specific issues for the right to the truth arise. What can be deduced from the foregoing is that at the ICC the right to the truth is unsurprisingly most advocated by the legal representatives for victims. Whilst the right to the truth has been identified as important for victims and their interests in proceedings, the submissions and jurisprudence to date demonstrate how little we know about the specificities, relevance and, above all, effect of this right for the ICC, apart from its general persuasive moral dimension.

Unlike at the ad hoc tribunals, the prosecutor is no longer the sole representative of and advocate for victims in court. The selection choices made during investigation, charging and prosecutorial strategy at the ICC are not only scrutinised by the defence but also by victim representatives. Doing so, and in taking recourse to the right to the truth, has exposed a number of ambiguities with regards to the specificities encompassed by the right to the truth. For example, what investigative standard needs to be employed to satisfy the right to the truth requirements remains unknown, since the prosecutor has avoided judicial review. Without a review it is also unclear whether the right to the truth would be a considering factor. It is possible that, without knowing the investigative standard required, victims, whether participating or not, benefit from the conduct of an investigation since such investigations may initially be broad before narrowed

140 Zappalà *supra* note 1 at 162–163.

141 One such example which many participants were aware of is the single judge decision by Judge Steiner in *Prosecutor v Katanga and Ngudjolo* (13 May 2008).

142 David Donat-Cattin, 'Article 68 Protection of the victims and witnesses and their participation in the proceedings', in Triffterer O (ed.) *Commentary on the Rome Statute of the International Criminal Court: Observers' Notes, Article by Article* (Nomos 1999) 876.

on specific charges. Such investigations may uncover information which might respond to the information needs of the many victims. However, this information is unlikely to feature in a final judgment and therefore will lack explicit authoritative acknowledgment required by the right to the truth.

Furthermore, victim groups seeking to argue for their right are in potential competition with other victims' right to have the truth investigated. The prosecutor has to already take strategic selections in relation to investigations, charging and prosecution. Such discourse on selection may take victims and their rights into account but this obligation of the prosecutor is only articulated through Article 54. The need for selectivity would remain. The selectivity is, however, more pronounced in terms of selection for and against victims, their suffering and consequently the truth to emerge, because a victim representative can point to the adverse effects of prosecutorial selectivity. Selectivity against particular victim groups becomes therefore more visible than in systems lacking of victim participation.

Through victim participation, the narrative element of the right to the truth is often shifted to the legal representative. It is therefore not clear that victims' own narratives (other than through a legal representative) are voiced or heard louder and clearer than they were at ad hoc tribunals when the prosecutor sought to introduce the suffering as part of the crimes into the court room. The right to the truth, however, seems to indicate an active involvement of the victims in the truth-finding process, which victim participation, as conceived by the ICC relying on legal representatives, may not be able to fulfil.

Finally, whilst the investigative process, the fact-finding during the trial and the final judgment all have a potential to realise aspects of the right to the truth, the reparation mandate issued in relation to *Lubanga* holds little by way of suggestions for furthering the right to the truth of victims, other than in a public, collective way, and by reference to the Basic Principles. Therefore, whilst it was possible to read the moral persuasiveness of the right to the truth into the work of other tribunals, ironically, at the ICC such a capacity seems almost curtailed by seeking to give specific effect to the right to the truth.

In this chapter we also explored Rome Statute provisions that judges could explore further to advance the right to the truth along with the difficult issue a lack of state cooperation presents. In many regards the judges may be the most effective locomotive behind truth realisation due to the Article 69(3) provision and through judicial activism and creativity – as was predicted at the start of the ICC's operation. Some judicial activism suggests that the moral condemnation that decisions of the Court are capable of projecting is being acknowledged and with it the need for more right to the truth realisation – though within the limits of fair trial requirements. There appears to be a struggle between policy goals (what is the ICC for?) and statutory permissibility. It is easy to mock the struggle for balancing these requirements as unequally favouring one constituent over the other; but this does little in pointing to constructive ways of balancing these demands. Naturally, such dichotomy and balancing of rights is nothing new. Crucially, and perhaps not often enough emphasised in debates and criticism of balancing acts, these rights share a common heritage: their link to human rights law. Based on the preceding analysis, the ICC is far from an ideal forum for victims to seek the realisation of their rights, despite victim participation, but they point to critical activity in terms of balancing human rights norms.

References

Aptel C, 'Prosecutorial Discretion at the ICC and Victims' right to a Remedy' (2012) 10(5) Journal of International Criminal Justice 1357.

Bitti G, 'ICC Statute Article 53' (23 June 2017) available at www.cilrap.org/cilrap-film/53-bitti accessed 14 February 2019.

Bosco D, R*ough Justice: The International Criminal Court's Battle to Fix the World, One Prosecution at a Time* (Oxford University Press 2014).

Carranza R, Correa C, and Naughton E, 'More than Words. Apologies as a Form or Reparation' (International Centre for Transitional Justice Report December 2015) www.ictj.org/sites/default/files/ICTJ-Report-Apologies-2015.pdf accessed 14 February 2019.

Chung C, 'Victims' Participation at the International Criminal Court: Are Concessions of the Court Clouding the Promise' (2008) 6(3) Northwestern Journal of International Human Rights 459.

Ciociari J and Frabzblau J, 'Hidden Files: Archival Sharing, Accountability, and the Right to the Truth' (2014) 46(1) *Columbia Human Rights Law Review* 1.

Clark J N, *International Trials and Reconciliation: assessing the impact of the international criminal tribunal for the former Yugoslavia* (Routledge 2014).

Combs N, *Fact-finding Without Facts. The Uncertain Evidentiary Foundations of International Criminal Convictions* (Cambridge University Press 2010).

Damaska M, 'What is the point of International Criminal Justice?' (2008) 83(1) Chicago-Kent Law Review 329.

Donat-Cattin D, 'Article 68 Protection of the victims and witnesses and their participation in the proceedings', in Triffterer O (ed.) *Commentary on the Rome Statute of the International Criminal Court: Observers' Notes, Article by Article* (Nomos 1999).

Gitari Ndungú C, 'Lessons to Be Learned: An Analysis of the Final Report of Kenya's Truth, Justice and Reconciliation Commission' (International Centre for Transitional Justice Report May 2014) www.ictj.org/sites/default/files/ICTJ-Briefing-Kenya-TJRC-2014.pdf Accessed 14 February 2019.

Ferstman C, 'The Participation of Victims in International Criminal Court Proceedings. A Review of the Practices and Consideration of Options for the Future', REDRESS Report (October 2012) available at: https://redress.org/wp-content/uploads/2017/12/121030participation_report.pdf accessed 14 February 2019.

Fulford A, 'Reflections of a Trial Judge' (2011) 22 Criminal Law Forum 215.

Gaynor F, 'Uneasy Partners – Evidence, Truth and History in International Trials' (2012) 10(5) Journal of International Criminal Justice 1257.

Hayner P, *Unspeakable Truths. Transitional Justice and the Challenge of Truth Commissions* (2nd edn, Routledge 2011).

Heller K J, 'The Ruto Trial Chamber Invents the Mistrial Without Prejudice (8 April 2016) http://opiniojuris.org/2016/04/08/the-icc-invents-the-possibility-of-a-mistrial/ accessed 14 February 2019.

Kaul H-P, 'Developments at the International Criminal Court' (2005) 99 The American Journal of International Law 370.
Kreß C, 'The Procedural Law of the International Criminal Court in Outline: Anatomy of a Unique Compromise' (2003) 1 Journal of International Criminal Justice 603.
McCarthy C, 'Reparations under the Rome Statute of the ICC and Reparative Justice Theory' (2009) 3(2) International Journal of Transitional Justice 250.
McGonigle Leyh B, *Procedural Justice? Victim Participation in International Criminal Proceedings* (Intersentia 2011).
Mettraux G, 'Victims' participation in international criminal law' (2010) 8(1) Journal of International Criminal Justice 75.
Mue N, 'Policy Brief: Enhancing the Societal Impact of International Criminal Tribunals' (Impunity Watch, February 2015) www.impunitywatch.org/docs/Policy_Brief_-_Enhancing_the_Societal_Impact_of_International_Criminal_Tribunals-1.pdf accessed 14 February 2019.
Pena M and Carayon G, 'Is the ICC making the Most of Victim Participation' (2013) 7(3) International Journal of Transitional Justice 518.
Plevin, 'Beyond a "Victims' Right": Truth-finding Power and Procedure at the ICC' (2014) 25 Criminal Law Forum 441.
Schabas W, 'The Mistrial, An Innovation in International Criminal Law' (8 April 2016) http://humanrightsdoctorate.blogspot.co.uk/2016/04/the-mistrial-innovation-in.html accessed 14 February 2019.
Van den Wyngaert C, 'Victims before International Criminal Courts: Some Views and Concerns of an ICC Trial Judge' (2012) 44 Case Western Journal of International Law 475.
Whiting A, 'Dynamic investigative practice at the International Criminal Court' (2013) 76 Law and Contemporary Problems 163.
Zappalà S, 'The rights of victims v the rights of the accused' (2010) 8(1) *Journal of International Criminal Justice* 137.
Zegveld L, 'Victims' Reparations Claims under International Criminal Courts: Incompatible Values?' (2010) 8(1) Journal of International Criminal Justice 79.

11 Conclusion

This book has explored the concept of the right to the truth in a range of institutional settings. In all of them (human rights courts, truth and reconciliation processes, and international criminal law), the idea of getting at the truth is already an important element of practice and jurisprudence, independent of any overarching right. Truth and reconciliation has the disclosure of truth as its purpose; human rights law insists on a state's duty to investigate and the courts, themselves, make findings of fact; and prosecutors and judiciary both have statute-based duties to discover the truth in the context of international criminal law. This raises the question whether talking in terms of a right to the truth in these contexts adds anything to what is already there.

Four suggestions

There are four suggestions emanating from the analysis in the preceding chapters.

Invigoration through association

First is an argument that through express association with the right to the truth, and through full adoption of its requirements, there results an impetus or vigour in the judicial responses to atrocity, often in the name of victims and society. The right to the truth is a complex body of moral responses to atrocity which is given normative institutional expression through institutions of international law. As such, it is the international standard applying in the circumstances of atrocity. At the global and international level, it has a distinctive authority. However, as the chapters of this book have demonstrated, it finds concrete judicial expression only indirectly through, for example, the idea of a state duty to investigate. This duty is not grounded directly on the human need for the truth in the context of atrocity but is just a necessary requirement if human rights are to be given adequate judicial protection as applies generally in any situation engaging human rights. The special circumstances of atrocity, of gross and systematic violations of human rights, does not get explicit recognition; nor is the law expressly founded on the distinct moral basis that explains and justifies the right to the truth. Associating the positive law in this context with the international standard of the right to the truth and grounding it on the moral arguments which underlie the right to the truth distinguishes the legal response to widespread atrocity from other human rights complaints (which need not be less pressing, but are different), gives that response a different moral basis and structures that response to ensure that the human needs are as well met as they can be. As the next section on "normative force" suggests, association of legal norms and practices with the right to the truth may also justify a renewed vigour, a greater normative force, to the legal response to atrocity. This argument can apply to international criminal courts even though they are already focused on atrocity. Prosecutors and judges may be justified in taking truth-disclosing steps if the discretions they have are consciously exercised in pursuit of the right to the truth.

Normative force

If the duty to investigate found in human rights law, for instance, is understood as an expression of the moral imperatives of the right to the truth, then, in the context of atrocity, this duty gains in normative force or weight. In the balancing of factors present in any judgment, the investigative duty gains in weight. As we saw in the human rights chapters, justifying legal rights and duties in terms of the morality and purposes of the right to the truth (reflecting the conditions which give rise to that right) can give a court legally compelling grounds for limiting legal provisions, which might otherwise inhibit an effective investigation, such as statutes of limitations, provisions as to jurisdiction both temporal and spatial, and good faith arguments, based on national security or confidentiality, against disclosure. The disclosure of the truth is close to an absolute right (and for this reason giving effect to the right via qualified human rights such as freedom of expression, is inadequate). But, as suggested in Chapter 7, this raises the danger that the moral force behind the right to the truth may corrupt the legal authority of the judgment (as in the way normal jurisdictional rules, essential to a compelling legal judgment based on the implicit consent of both parties, should have been set aside in the view of the dissenters in both *Janowiec* and *Cifuentes*). Similarly, in the context of the ICC, an over-enthusiastic interpretation of Article 69(3) risks being ultra vires. This has the potential to harm the right to the truth since the giving of an authoritative judgment consistent with the rule of law is, we have suggested, a proper component of the right.

The public aspect

The general purpose and principal focus of truth and reconciliation commissions, the investigative duty and the truth-seeking jurisdiction of prosecutor and judge in criminal trials, is on the victim. This is entirely proper, it is the point of the right to the truth, and these processes aim for the truth to emerge. But the right to the truth, in its normative institutional expression, has a second, public aspect. Emphasising the public aspect suggests it involves something more than the publicity ordinarily and presumptively attached to legal procedures (the presumption of open justice) and outweighed only by strong arguments to the contrary. It is also something more than that part of the justification of the investigative duty which is to ensure public confidence in the state's ability to protect human rights.

Rather, the public aspect of the right to the truth suggests that, in the context of atrocity, the purpose of truth-seeking is profoundly political, going to the character of a legitimate polis; and profoundly social, being a condition of a well-ordered society. Both points come together in a notion that a legitimate polis and a well-ordered society that treats all as equals is denied if the truth, in this context, is hidden. Domestic courts, prosecutors and judges are to judge themselves and are themselves judged against an implicit and normally unarticulated standard, found in international law, and normally expressed (e.g. in human rights case law) as a "democratic" society. This can be expressed in various ways. In political theory terms it might be thought that truth-telling about atrocity in this context is a condition that must be fulfilled before consent to government can reasonably be given or the fulfilment of obligations owed. It might be expressed more widely. It has been suggested in the book that the right to the truth is also an expression of a general, universal, condition of humanity. Here the "society" of the public aspect is universal mankind. If so, of course, the reference to a "democratic" society may be irrelevant. Societies may be peaceful, well-functioning and recognising the humanity of their population that are not "democratic" by a normal range of tests (universal franchise, regular free elections, etc.). They may/should still satisfy criteria of fairness and decency in their treatment of their population and this will include seeking and telling the truth.

Nuanced authoritative fact-finding and declarations

A fourth suggestion places emphasis on a nuanced authoritative reporting. The content of the right to the truth is suggested to comprise structural truth, individualised truth and narrative truth. All three forms ideally constitute part of the authoritative processes of reporting – be that by human rights courts, truth commissions or international criminal courts. Within this broad content of the right to the truth, we have also found different types of truth entering the complex discussion on what factuality or the best approximation to a truthful report would entail. Human rights courts have emphasised the public aspects of the right to the truth (see above). Truth commissions question the depth and specificity of truth required: does it encompass the naming of perpetrators and if so, what level of perpetrator? Finally, in the international criminal context, the historical truth, perhaps most akin to structural truth as a content of the right to the truth, has featured along with forensic truth, that is specific evidence produced by experts for the purposes of the trial. In addition, narrative truth in the form of testimonies by surviving victims is a core elements of trials. All three aspects are part and parcel of the court's record system and as such accessible to the individual and public. They also all flow into what is defined as legal truth – the final judgment, where fact-finding is, appropriately weighted as to its probative value, summarised leading to determinations on the innocence or guilt of the accused.

Such nuances are worth noting as part of the institutional framework designed to realise the right to the truth. Understanding the complex nature of fact-finding may assist in making the process as well as the outcome meaningful.

Not only does the right to the truth make a special contribution as indicated earlier, but it also has other significant legal ramifications to which we now turn.

In most expressions of the right to the truth, truth is linked to other rights

These marginal contributions of the right to the truth, these expressions of its specialty, are not necessarily truth-confined. The expressions of the right to the truth, whether the "moral right", the UN non-judicial institutional right, or judicial expressions through, for example, the duty to investigate or the arguments for an emphasised recognition of truth for victims in the international criminal context, all (as has been demonstrated in the book) tend to integrate truth-seeking with other rights especially to justice (i.e. the right to have a perpetrator punished and to legal/judicial protection of rights) and to reparations. These expressions of its specialty (invigoration through association with a broader, international, moral and legal drive; increased normative force; the public aspect and nuanced reporting) are all perfectly consistent with the right to the truth being a portmanteau including these other rights and obligations that are not truth focused. The right to the truth is often, if not normally, expressed in terms of the whole process of providing justice for victims: discovering and communicating the truth of what happened to individuals in context, identifying, bringing to justice and punishing perpetrators and providing appropriate reparations. The discovery and communication of the truth is necessary for and instrumental in this process but not, by itself, the only point.

The separation argument

This book has explored the independent value of truth in the atrocity context. The book, on the other hand, has explored the extent to which the discovery and publication of the truth about dreadful atrocities can be thought of as an interest of sufficient power and weight that it justifies duties imposed on others (predominantly states and, if states fail, international bodies) which are fulfilled through discovery and promulgation of the truth even if other rights or duties, prosecution and reparations in particular, cannot be discharged. As we have seen, for some commentators this is to raise an abstract distinction, a false dichotomy between truth and justice, and also one with deleterious consequences if it results in amnesty.

But the book has acknowledged the special awfulness for a relative of not knowing, such as where human rights courts have accepted that not knowing the fate of (at the least) a disappeared person can be distinct grounds for a violation of the right not to be tortured and so forth, where such a person's emotional response of rage or disgust or whatever at an improper amnesty or inadequate reparation does not cross that threshold of severity. It can be suggested, for example, that the "normative force" argument, which presumes the near to absolute right to "the truth", is best grounded on the distinct agony of ignorance; the absolute argument does not apply with such strength to other rights and duties associated with responses to atrocities. Furthermore, as Judge Mac-Gregor argued (see Chapter 3), granting the right to the truth independent status assists in clarifying and strengthening the other associated rights.

To the same effect some iterations of the right to the truth have accepted that, reasonable, well-founded and democratically endorsed arguments may justify political compromises in respect of, for instance, the degree with which perpetrators are pursued and punished. Peace may justify amnesty. The margin of appreciation allowed to states by international law in respect of action aimed at the pursuit of peace and moving forward for the next generation, is greater in respect of amnesty, which reflects the particular social and political situation in the country concerned, than for investigating and disclosing the truth – though this point may be narrower than at first articulated insofar as there is a legal consensus against amnesty for international crimes.

Right to the truth presupposes a legal process

"Right" implies an entitlement and much of this book, as much of the discourse on "the right to the truth", is a search for and exploration of the legal status of this right – its status as a rule of law directly enforceable or having strong persuasive authority as a general principle of law. An aspect of this is that to call on the right to the truth implies an acceptance of proper judicial process as a means by which the truth can be disclosed. The best truth we can achieve, given the human condition, is the result of a process (the proper application of scientific method or moral reasoning from first principles, etc.) and in the case of the right to the truth in the context of atrocity, it is found in the results of impartial investigation and "due process" which characterise legality. In the context of the right to the truth, these include the impartial application of rules of evidence, presumptions of responsibility and the reasonable allocation of burdens of proof, but also proper recognition of the rights of others including alleged perpetrators. The right to the truth requires an "authoritative" account and authority is rooted in the procedures of legality. Invoking the right to the truth assumes, with Hannah Arendt, that truth from legal procedure is possible. Her ideal of "certain public institutions, established and supported by the powers that be, in which, contrary to all political rules, truth and truthfulness have always constituted the highest criterion of speech and endeavor"[1] and that "among these we find notably the judiciary"[2] is taken seriously in the right to the truth. The right to the truth

1 Hannah Arendt, 'Truth and Politics' *The New Yorker* (25 February 1967) https://idanlandau.files.wordpress.com/2014/12/arendt-truth-and-politics.pdf accessed 14 February 2019 at 310.

2 Ibid.

presumes that there is a point and virtue in the notion of a good faith, impartial attempt to get at the truth and the result is authoritative, legitimate and truthful. And, following Arendt's assessment, "it can hardly be denied that, at least in constitutionally ruled countries the political realm has recognized, even in the event of conflict, that it has a stake in the existence of men and institutions over which it has no power".[3]

Ideal conceptions of judicial procedure are qualified by practice, there is a "politics of the judiciary" and political, legal and constitutional context can impose limits of what can be done. The exposure of the truth may be limited by entirely proper disagreements on matters within legality such as the scope of the "living instrument" doctrine (as in *Janowiec*) or the demands of "reasonable doubt" (as in Judge Van den Wyngaert's dissent in *Prosecutor v Katanga*). But what is possible is the identification of failures of fair process. These include judicial corruption, cronyism, individual acts of bad faith, failing to take into account relevant matters, constitutional and institutional failures to ensure judicial independence, failing to balance state with individual interests and so on.

But does this legal process satisfy victims?

The question then arises: is this assumption that truth emerges from a proper procedure embodying good faith, impartiality and due process enough to satisfy victims – given that it is the interests of victims that is the purpose and moral drive behind the right to the truth?

It is clearly a legalistic/juristic approach to getting at the truth, to related functions such as punishment and to performing the full range of other functions associated with transition. Truth and reconciliation commissions are less procedurally constrained, but they too are limited (on issues such as the naming of suspects or the granting of amnesties) by laws, juridical issues and practices. As has been emphasised in this book, especially in the chapters on human rights, the right to the truth indicates a series of state functions (investigation, prosecution, etc.) all of which involve a degree of state action independent of victims' wills. The idea of a victim's "right" is to some extent used metaphorically, or is improperly so called, since the victim-subject cannot control it in respect of issues such as prosecutorial discretion, judicial decisions as to truth-seeking or rules on admissibility of evidence; the state should initiate investigations, a requirement seen as an expression of a victim's interests which, in principle, the victim cannot voluntarily forgo.

There may be an element of alienation or disengagement from the process for victims. Although, certainly in the ICC and truth and reconciliation procedures, but much less in the human rights context, significant steps are taken for not just the protection but also the involvement of victims. Whilst much is claimed in their name, they are not at the centre of the procedure itself despite their interests being central to its context and purpose.

3 Ibid.

Truth as a meaningful outcome

Furthermore, the account that is given through a process that is satisfactory in meeting the judicial criteria of independence and integrity may nevertheless be, from the victim's point of view, incomplete, partial or arrested. It may be rejected as being based on misunderstanding or otherwise untrue. For victims it may fail to convince. Victims have no reason, necessarily, to be satisfied with whatever comes from a fair procedure. The right to the truth suggests substantive truth. And something more – which may be expressed as a meaningful (for victims) outcome to engagement with the process. A particular point, and example, is that with the exception of truth and reconciliation, the juridical procedures we have been discussing in this book, do not give a major opportunity for "narrative truth" – the opportunity for victims to tell their story in their own words and without being undermined by cross-examination.

Studies have been conducted into the reasons and motivations of victims participating in international criminal justice mechanisms, and a useful comparison may be drawn from this to other perspectives, such as those of human rights and truth and reconciliation. For victims of gross violations and international crimes engaging in a judicial process may be motivated by seeking to achieve a sense of justice. This essentially comprises a psychological state in which they feel that adequate amends have been made for the wrong committed. A sense of justice is understood as the point at which their experience(s) of abuse are no longer seen by them as unfinished business, but instead, they are able to look and move forward. Some empirical studies have been conducted to ascertain what it is that survivors seek to achieve by virtue of their engagement with justice mechanisms. A review of the findings suggests that victims have a range of reasons for participation which by themselves or collectively may produce an outcome which for the victim has a point; for them it is meaningful. These may include to tell their stories, to contribute to public knowledge and accountability, to publicly denounce the wrongs that were committed against them and others, to bear witness on behalf of those who did not survive, and to receive reparations, public acknowledgment or apologies. They may wish to confront the accused, to find out the truth about what happened to their loved ones, to contribute to peace goals or to help prevent the perpetration of further abuse. Many risk their own personal safety to tell their stories, or those of victims who did not survive.[4]

A number of the truth-realisation aims such as "telling their story" or "contributing to public knowledge" can be important for the individual and for the benefit of society. They are by no means congruent with the direct aims of the juridical processes by which the right to the truth is given effect.

The aim of testifying is both altruistic and self-serving. Furthermore, we can see that the motivating factors straddle the categories of truth-telling, justice and

4 For a full discussion of the justice needs of victims before the ICC see Ellie Smith, "The World would start turning again": identifying and measuring victims' restorative justice needs at the International Criminal Court (2016) Bournemouth University, Doctorate Thesis.

reparations but may also work towards non-recurrence ("preventing the perpetration of further abuse"). This implies a more general interest than one confined to the individual's own experience – there is strong interest in going beyond the mere "conglomerate of facts" towards a meaningful truth and justification. If these accounts are correct, then "meaningful" participation for victims is partially public – letting the world know, protecting society from future abuse, and so on. It also suggests that although, as has been discussed in this book, there are discrete interests in knowing the truth, victims themselves might find the separation of truth-finding and disclosure from other outcomes such as justice and reparations unconvincing, as something complex and artificial. Despite this, separating the right to the truth from other rights may work for the purpose of clarifying victims' rights and offering avenues for claiming a right. Whilst truth may have primacy over justice as an immediate need, the right to the truth may very swiftly carry other important right claims, such as justice and reparation, implicitly with it. And engagement with justice mechanisms may be diminished for not wanting public scrutiny, risk loss of privacy or security.

But does this satisfy *sub specie humanitatis*?

The right to the truth is given effect, we suggest, largely through a range of juridical processes which, in a sense, victims must accept as the main avenue open to them. The juridical processes serve the interests of victims but also, as discussed in Chapter 4 and earlier in this chapter, have a socio-political aspect – the truth is to be made public and thereby will improve society. Furthermore, as suggested earlier, it seems that victims also are likely to find meaning through participation insofar as these juridical processes represent or are the basis for something broader.

Victims' interests and the complex mesh of their reasons for participation in the procedures giving effect to the right to the truth, coincide with the view that the concept of the right to the truth expresses wider public and moral concerns. Public, at least, in the sense of pertaining to the state and society involved and its transition and recovery. Moral in the sense of invoking the universal position of humanity, and the duty to discover, disclose, condemn and rebuild.

Pablo de Greiff, in relation to fact-finding, suggests that this may no longer be

> about the clarification of cases, the fate of individual victims, and perhaps, when allowed and possible, the identifies of those responsible for these violations – as fact-finding was initially understood. Rather, "fact-finding" became an effort to understand comprehensively root causes, circumstances, factors, context, and motives of countrywide situations of violence. This, not unlike historical accounts, is much more than a mere collection of facts.[5]

5 Pablo de Greiff, '"Truth without Facts": On the Erosion of the Fact-Finding Function of Truth Commissions' in Alston P and Knuckey S (eds), The Transformation of Human Rights Fact-Finding (Oxford 2016) 281–302. De Greiff is Special Rapporteur on the promotion of truth, justice, reparation and guarantees of non-recurrence.

This pursuit of a wider, more contextual, meaning is of course still focused on the particularities of the society involved in the atrocities; but it also opens out the possibility for judgment against more universal criteria.

> Reality is different from, and more than, the totality of facts and events, which, anyhow, is unascertainable. Who says what is – λεγει τα εοντα – always tells a story, and in this story the particular facts lose their contingency and acquire some humanly comprehensible meaning.[6]

To make the inhuman "humanly comprehensible" invokes a language of limited hope and the possibilities, if only for subsequent generations or those who were not direct victims, of transition towards a world in which all are treated as equals. In a moral sense, this is "meaningful".

Clearly, though, if the right to the truth is to have this deeper moral foundation, a contradiction or at least a difficulty emerges. The wider the scope of the judgments to be made, the more the authoritative "sayer of what is" must characterise the bigger picture of history, culture, constitutional structures and so on, necessary to understand as well as to record, then the less is this an appropriate and, for a divided population, convincing activity for a juridical body to perform.[7] A possible answer may lie in the twin-track approach implied by the European Court of Human Rights in *Tagayeva v Russia*.[8] where particular rights (to life, to physical integrity) are protected by a victim focused criminal investigation where fuller and wider truth-needs can be satisfied by a range of other enquiries, such as parliamentary investigations.

Separation and meaning

On this view the "separation thesis" is qualified. The individual victim's rights to know are necessarily linked to other rights, or, at least, it is fruitless to distinguish them to practical effect. But the broader examination, going to the range of factors through which victims may revive their agency and find the experience of participation "meaningful" (indicated above), are all matters in which the events, their context, the attribution of responsibilities, are descriptive and analytical activities predicated on the need for truth, no matter what else.

Role of the law

But the danger remains: the more the outcome is "meaningful" in de Greiff's sense the less focused becomes any legal "right" to the truth and the less imperative its requirements. This returns us to the legal status of the right to the truth: are

6 Arendt *supra* note 1 at 311.

7 For example, Williams considers the difficulties of using "public law" in the UK to deal with claims of systemic, not just individual, abuse by British forces in Iraq (Andrew Williams, 'The Iraq abuse allegations and the limits of UK Law' (2018) Jul Public Law 461).

8 Discussed in Chapter 7.

victims better served by (1) seeking to conceptualise the right to the truth as a stand-alone right so that it is a directly enforceable legal right limited to the satisfaction of descriptive and analytical needs only; or (2) the "conservative" position which is subsuming the descriptive and analytical (i.e. truth alone) needs under other established human rights and accepting that truth is inescapably bound in with rights to justice, judicial protection and reparation; or (3) keeping the right as a background moral right articulated as part of the four transitional justice rights (truth, justice, reparation and non-repetition) to give it moral, persuasive weight since there are so many seamless overlaps with other rights as well as individual and societal components.

Considering our analysis in the previous chapters, the answer is not clear cut, not least because option (1), conceptualising it as a hard right ('I/we have the right to the truth and I/we will claim it'), may still be hypothetical for some to the extent that the right does not feature *expressis verbis* in the statutes of human rights courts nor at criminal tribunals. Truth commissions on the other hand may be set up with the goal of fulfilling a right to truth. Insofar as it might be seen as satisfying victim entitlements, it could undermine the drive to ban amnesty for the most egregious crimes despite the contribution thereby to peace. It may be too narrow since the immediate interest of "alleviating suffering by knowing the truth", at least in the institutions we have examined here, may only partially be realisable and is, in any event, contingent on state actions. And it is only the human rights courts that can authoritatively demand its realisation through the investigative duty. Option (2) has the problem that the discussion on subsuming the right is only an explicit one at the human rights courts. In other places victims have no standing beyond their participation rights in the international criminal realm; truth commissions operate in a different manner. It appears that option (3) mirrors closely the current status quo: the right to the truth is an aspirational goal with increasing recognition, linked persuasively with other rights in the sense of providing jurisprudentially sound justifications for developing and refining positive legal rights in directions that help to satisfy victim and public interests in knowing what happened. The various adjudication mechanisms may (or may not) take it into account in different ways which emphasise the individual or societal component, depending on what is at issue.

Option 3, no doubt, provides victims, NGOs and others the grounding for persuasive arguments for a comprehensive redress of past gross human rights abuses since it allows for a multitude of background rights to be invoked *at once*. It is not confined to the human rights courts and provides reasons for persuading criminal judges to, for instance, give greater effect to their truth-seeking role and persuading states to establish other truth-seeking mechanisms. But it lacks legal certainty (all the more so if the point is to obtain some more "meaningful" engagement in seeking the elimination of atrocity) and so nothing in the right to the truth, no matter how conceived, should undermine (e.g. by requiring more than can be given) the positive right to an effective investigation (option 2), which is grounded on jurisprudentially credible developments of express rights in respect of which victims have locus standi. On this positive law, the wider desiderata of the right to the truth can be furthered. Conceptualising the right to the truth as a stand-alone right in international law, along the lines of option (1), establishes a clear benchmark and obligation on states to give effect to it: the state must fulfil its duties to the individual and the collective. This will then mean that if human rights courts or truth commissions make a recommendation to this effect, they can do so with strong authority and greater clarity. But it will also enable especially criminal courts to be able to say with authority and clarity when and why they feel that the right to the truth has to be taken into account or not, particularly within the discussions on victim participation and judicial remit, precisely because it will clarify the political aspect of the right from the individual one and settle matters of standing.

Concluding remarks

Over the past ten chapters, we dissected the right to the truth in a number of ways: we have considered the truth needs that arise for individuals and society following gross human rights violations to appreciate what is at stake when it comes to not knowing what happened or having truth threatened by lies or inaction. We traced the origins of the right in the transitional justice discourse and through its emerging formulation within international law. We have argued for an interest-based conception of the right of individuals and explored the difference between collective and individual aspects of the right. In so doing, we explored the possibilities for a conceptualisation of the right as distinct from justice, reparations and guarantees of non-recurrence.

We touched upon the difficulties in properly defining truth as a realisable right without too great an entanglement in philosophical debates, instead seeking to analyse it within the parameters of procedures, standards and rules. Truth-finding is contingent on investigating and testifying but the way in which investigations, bearing witnesses and making authoritative declarations occur, are different depending on institutions. We considered the human rights courts, truth commission and international criminal trials to appraise in what ways they can satisfy the right to the truth definition.

It is important to grasp the complexities of what the right to the truth is seeking to achieve. And much of what truth-finding unearths is intertwined with seeking justice, reparations and guarantees of non-recurrence, and remains in the transitional justice framework. Realisation of the right to the truth is primarily a matter of political will, stability and resources in investigating individual cases of human rights violations and communicating them. It depends on the extent to which the state (and its organs) is willing and capable of realising the right to the truth.

It is apt to end on the state because, for all the reasoning on the right to the truth there is no escaping that the judicial inquiries capable of fulfilling victims and society's needs will have to come through state level judicial inquiries. Of course, serious fact-finding missions by NGOs and expert commissions may also make authoritative findings of facts but, unlike the state, lack the power to compel disclosure.

Naturally, and assuming states may be reluctant to do so, this does reiterate the need for the international institutions to find ways to oblige states to realise the right and to advance the prospects of right realisation. Furthermore, there is an important reason to stipulate certain aspects of a truth-realisation (as the IACtHR does) and to pronounce on aspects of the truth at international level: to delegate all truth-finding powers to the state would give states too great a power-monopoly on truth. This in turn would increase the risk of states misappropriating it for their own legitimisation.

In light of this and our analysis, truth-realisation might only ever partially be fulfilled at the international judicial level but it offers a most important balance of power and authority to ensure veracity, validity and safeguarding of fact as well as their reporting. The more precise, clear and differentiated the right to the truth in its expression, whether as a background right with moral gravitas or a fully-fledged stand-alone right as we have considered, if it serves the purpose of compelling states to take it fully and properly into account, it has achieved an important goal. The right to the truth may be one way of seeking to contain the "contingency of all factual reality. Since everything that has actually happened in the realm of human affairs could just as well have been otherwise, the possibilities for lying are boundless".[9] This boundlessness must be kept in check.

References

Arendt H, *The Origins of Totalitarianism* (Penguin Classics 2017)

Arendt H, 'Truth and Politics' *The New Yorker* (25 February 1967) https://idanlandau.files.wordpress.com/2014/12/arendt-truth-and-politics.pdf (accessed 14 February 2019)

de Greiff P, '"Truth without Facts": On the Erosion of the Fact-Finding Function of Truth Commissions' in Alston P and Knuckey S (eds), The Transformation of Human Rights Fact-Finding (Oxford 2016)

Smith E, "The World would start turning again": identifying and measuring victims' restorative justice needs at the International Criminal Court (2016) Bournemouth University, Doctorate Thesis.

Williams A, 'The Iraq abuse allegations and the limits of UK Law' (2018) July Public Law 461

9 Hannah Arendt, *The Origins of Totalitarianism* (Penguin Classics 2017) at 308.

Index

For Product Safety Concerns and Information please contact our EU representative GPSR@taylorandfrancis.com
Taylor & Francis Verlag GmbH, Kaufingerstraße 24, 80331 München, Germany

www.ingramcontent.com/pod-product-compliance
Ingram Content Group UK Ltd.
Pitfield, Milton Keynes, MK11 3LW, UK
UKHW020014200926
475702UK00014B/1880
9780367726867